MICHELIN GUIDE

NEW YORK CITY

2019

THE MICHELIN GUIDE'S COMMITMENTS

Whether they are in Japan, the USA, China or Europe, our inspectors apply the same criteria to judge the quality of each and every establishment that they visit. The MICHELIN guide commands a **worldwide reputation** thanks to the commitments we make to our readers—and we reiterate these below:

Our inspectors make **anonymous visits** to restaurants to gauge the quality of cuisine offered to the everyday customer. They pay their own bill and make no indication of their presence. These visits are supplemented by comprehensive monitoring of information—our readers' comments are one valuable source, and are always taken into consideration.

Our choice of establishments is a completely **independent** one, made for the benefit of our readers alone. Decisions are discussed by inspectors and editor, with the most important considered at the global level. Inclusion in the Guide is always free of charge.

The Guide offers a **selection** of the best restaurants in each category of comfort and price. A recommendation in the Guide is an honor in itself, and defines the establishment among the "best of the best."

All practical information, the classifications, and awards are revised and updated every year to ensure the most **reliable information** possible.

The standards and criteria for the classifications are the same in all countries covered by the MICHELIN guides. Our system is used worldwide and easy to apply when selecting a restaurant.

As part of Michelin's ongoing commitment to improving **travel and mobility**, we do everything possible to make vacations and eating out a pleasure.

THE MICHELIN GUIDE'S SYMBOLS

Michelin inspectors are experts at finding the best restaurants and invite you to explore the diversity of the gastronomic universe. As well as evaluating a restaurant's cooking, we also consider its décor, the service and the ambience - in other words, the all-round culinary experience.

Two keywords help you make your choice more quickly: red for the type of cuisine, gold for the atmosphere.

Italian • Elegant

FACILITIES & SERVICES

	Notable wine list
	Notable cocktail list
	Notable beer list
	Notable sake list
	Wheelchair accessible
	Outdoor dining
	Private dining room
	Breakfast
	Brunch
	Dim sum
	Valet parking
	Cash only

AVERAGE PRICES

	Under $25
$$	$25 to $50
$$$	$50 to $75
$$$$	Over $75

THE MICHELIN DISTINCTIONS FOR GOOD CUISINE

STARS

Our famous one ✿, two ✿✿ and three ✿✿✿ stars identify establishments serving the highest quality cuisine – taking into account the quality of ingredients, the mastery of techniques and flavors, the levels of creativity and, of course, consistency.

✿✿✿ Exceptional cuisine, worth a special journey

✿✿ Excellent cuisine, worth a detour

✿ High quality cooking, worth a stop

BIB GOURMAND

Inspectors' favorites for good value.

MICHELIN PLATE

Good cooking.
Fresh ingredients, capably prepared:
simply a good meal.

DEAR READER,

It's been an exciting year for the entire team at the MICHELIN guides in North America, and it is with great pride that we present you with our 2019 edition to New York City. Over the past year our inspectors have extended their reach to include a variety of establishments and multiplied their anonymous visits to restaurants in our selection in order to accurately reflect the rich culinary diversity this great city has to offer.

As part of the Guide's highly confidential and meticulous evaluation process, our inspectors have methodically eaten their way through the entire city with a mission to marshal the finest in each category for your enjoyment. While they are expertly trained professionals in the food industry, the Guides remain consumer-driven and provide comprehensive choices to accommodate your every comfort, taste, and budget. By dining and drinking as "everyday" customers, they are able to experience and evaluate the same level of service and cuisine as any other guest. This past year has seen some unique advancements in New York City's dining scene. Some of these can be found in each neighborhood introduction, complete with photography depicting our favored choices.

Our company's founders, Édouard and André Michelin, published the first MICHELIN guide in 1900, to provide motorists with useful information about where they could service and repair their cars as well as find a good quality meal. In 1926, the star-rating system was introduced, whereby outstanding establishments are awarded for excellence in cuisine. Over the decades we have made many new enhancements to the Guide, and the local team here in New York City eagerly carries on these traditions.

As we take consumer feedback seriously, please feel free to contact us at: michelin.guides@michelin.com. You may also follow our Inspectors on Twitter (@MichelinGuideNY) and Instagram (@michelininspectors) as they chow their way around town. We thank you for your patronage and truly hope that the MICHELIN guide will remain your preferred reference to New York City's restaurants.

CONTENTS

INDEXES

MANHATTAN

CHELSEA

DIVERSITY IN DINING

Chelsea is a charming residential neighborhood combining modern high-rises and sleek lofts with classic townhouses and retail stores aplenty. To that end, this neighborhood is a shopper's paradise, offering everything from computer marts and high fashion boutiques, to emporiums like **Chelsea Market**—the city's culinary epicenter. And let's not forget the art: these once-dilapidated warehouses and abandoned lofts are currently home to over 200 prominent galleries, as well as the artists who contribute to them. Naturally, it is a burgeoning cultural scene; and to feed its well-educated, art-enthusiast residents and out-of-towners on pilgrimage, Chelsea teems with cafeterias. Those old-world Puerto Rican luncheonettes that used to dot Ninth Avenue have now given way to mega-hip temples of fusion cooking—where diners are accommodated in stylish digs and the cocktail menu packs a potent punch.

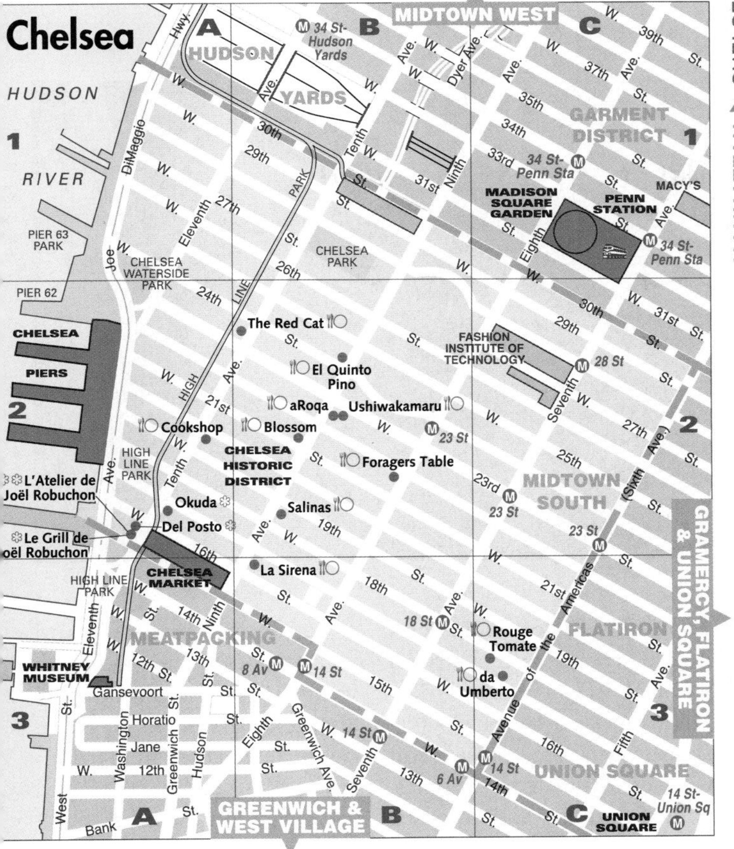

Carousers party until last call at such high-energy hangouts as **1 OAK**, launched by Greenmarket-obsessed chef, Alex Guarnaschelli's Butter Group. Patrons of this hot spot may then jump ship to the likes of **Marquee**, while others remain loyal to such late-night stalwarts as **Robert's Steakhouse at Scores New York**. Nestled inside the infamous Penthouse Executive Club, it's really all about the "meat" here, where suits seem far more interested in the likes of char-grilled steaks on their plates than the ladies on their laps.

Located above Manhattan's mean streets and atop an elevated freight railroad, The High Line is a lengthy public space with a large presence in Chelsea. Populated by yuppies, young families and tourists, and punctuated by acres of indigenous greenery as well as surprisingly stunning views of the Hudson River, this city-center oasis also offers unique respites for refreshment. For instance, **Bubby's High Line** is perpetually packed for its impressive repertoire of food and drink. Envision a number of young locals ordering off a kid's menu, or late-night revelers devouring a "midnight brunch" and you will begin to understand what this neighborhood is all about. Too rushed to dwell over dessert? Their retail store also sells pastries and ice cream sandwiches to-go, after which a shot of single-origin drip espresso at **Blue Bottle Coffee Café** is not just fitting, but obligatory. As history would have it, the last functional freight train that passed through The High Line had cars filled with meat. Ergo, it seems only natural that **La Sonrisa Empanadas** proffers pastry pockets stuffed with ropa vieja, pulled pork and other eats to ease the summer heat. Nearby, **Terroir at The Porch** is a seasonal (summer-only) open-air, full-service café with small plates, wine and beer to boot.

In 1997, the 1898 Nabisco factory reopened as **Chelsea Market**, a fabled culinary bazaar whose brick-lined walkways are cramped with stores selling everything—from lemons to lingerie. Carb-addicts begin their circuitous excursion here, at **Amy's Bread**, where artisan-crafted loaves are as precious as crown jewels. Then they might linger at **Bar Suzette** for their range of fluffy crêpes. Meanwhile, the calorie-counters collect at **Beyond Sushi** for healthy renditions of this Japanese staple, wrapped here in black rice and topped with tofu. Seal such stellar bites with a cooling kiss from **L'Arte del Gelato**. Sound like bliss? It is.

From Asian signatures to everyday Italian, **Buon Italia** will not only help stock your pantry for a night in with nonna, but also sate those inevitable hunger pangs while you're at it—a stand up front even sells cooked foods and sandwiches to crowds on the run. Other welcome members to this epicurean community include **Dickson's Farmstand Meats** for the likes of house-made pâté; **Sarabeth's** or **Fat Witch Bakery** for holiday goodies; and **Creamline** for comfort food classics. Keep trekking northward before closing the (evening) deal at **La Piscine** (located on the rooftop of Hôtel Americano) with a snack of any kind along with a sip (or several) of vino!

AROQA

Indian • Chic

MAP: B2

With its selection of creative shared plates, aRoqa ensures that reasonably priced, contemporary Indian food is now easier to find. Inside, the aura is more romantic than family-friendly, courtesy of the talented team behind other successes like Bhatti Grill and Moti Mahal Delux.

Embellished menu descriptions seem to promise the world, but deliver dishes that are familiar and Indian at heart, finished with creative flair. Thoroughly enjoyable starters include spiced mushroom duxelles wrapped with crispy shredded phyllo and creamy goat cheese. Don't forget to also sample the khade tamatar ka murgh, served as bone-in chicken drumsticks in a rich, sweet and spicy tomato-butter curry that practically begs to be sopped up by a toasty onion seed-flecked naan.

206 Ninth Ave. (bet. 22nd & 23rd Sts.)
23 St (Eighth Ave.)
(646) 678-5471 — **WEB:** www.aroqanyc.com
Lunch Sun Dinner nightly **PRICE:** $$

BLOSSOM

Vegan • Intimate

MAP: B2

Unpretentious and welcoming, this is a vegan favorite with spot-on spicing and delicious surprises. The cream-colored interior is dim with dark velvet curtains and votive candles reflected in round mirrors. A thematically appropriate "living wall" resides in one corner of the space. The vibe may seem moody come evening, but the staff is always warm and affable.

A black-eyed pea cake composed with crushed potatoes is pan-fried to render a golden breadcrumb exterior; while Moroccan tagine bobbing with chickpeas, a host of vegetables including carrots, turnips and zucchini, and topped with crispy tofu strips is all heart and soul. Come dessert, try the hand-churned cashew ice cream or a lemony cheesecake with a mixed berry reduction and coconut-cookie crust.

187 Ninth Ave. (bet. 21st & 22nd Sts.)
23 St (Eighth Ave.)
(212) 627-1144 — **WEB:** www.blossomnyc.com
Lunch & dinner daily **PRICE:** $$

COOKSHOP

American • Neighborhood

MAP: A2

It's a delight just to enter this beautiful neighborhood mainstay, with its airy, impeccably clean and sunlight-flooded dining room. The plant-filled space is furnished with ethically sourced American oak tables as well as a wall of banquettes; and the bar is perfect for solo dining. And all this charm awaits you even before you sink your teeth into Cookshop's ultra-delicious food.

Chef de Cuisine Andrew Corrigan's contemporary, product-driven, and Mediterranean-inspired menu focuses on local sourcing, and includes dishes like ricotta gnudi with brown butter-apple sauce; grain salad with sesame, pomegranate and poached egg; or grilled bigeye tuna with dried fig anchoiade. Breakfast is served during the week, while weekends offer a full brunch menu.

156 Tenth Ave. (at 20th St.)
23 St (Eighth Ave.)
(212) 924-4440 — **WEB:** www.cookshopny.com
Lunch & dinner daily

PRICE: $$

DA UMBERTO

Italian • Osteria

MAP: C3

There is a finely tuned harmony to dining at such classic New York restaurants as this one. The Italian menu is familiar and unpretentious, the kitchen is adept and ingredients are superb. But, what truly sets it apart is an ability to serve exactly what you crave without seeming trite or predictable. Even the look is a perfectly conjured mix of warm neutrals, with a sleek yet informal Northern Italian style and impeccably timed servers.

Start with the traditional antipasto and then proceed to one of the daily specials like veal Milanese or a lavish dish of garganelli with mushrooms and black truffles. When the dessert cart rolls around, expect an array of excellent house-made sweets like pristine berries under whisked-to-order zabaglione.

107 W. 17th St. (bet. Sixth & Seventh Aves.)
18 St
(212) 989-0303 — **WEB:** www.daumbertonyc.com
Lunch Mon - Fri Dinner Mon - Sat

PRICE: $$$

DEL POSTO ✿

Italian • Luxury

MAP: A2

Dishes from Executive Chef Melissa Rodriguez at the uniquely opulent and fashionable Del Posto are gorgeously crafted, but in truth, it is her playful interpretation of Italian cuisine that makes this kitchen creative. Of course, with neighbors like the High Line, Whitney Museum and Chelsea Market, not only is its location most desirable, but there is a distinct sense of luxury here as evidenced by their beautifully dressed tables, polished marble and silk-draped windows.

Balconies sit above the striking bar with live piano music pouring through the room. Despite the formality, there is a warm buzz among diners as the impressive suited staff attends to them. The menu highlights canapés and top-notch classics like vitello tonnato, but indulge in such updated creations as a warm fennel and radicchio salad tossed with balsamic and raisins. Next-level pastas like farfalle with roasted beets and smoked ricotta reflect influences from up north. Then, gnocchi studded with halibut and finished with caviar is an all-round delight, as is the highly enjoyable chocolate budino with coconut sorbet.

A worthy exception to the all-Italian wine list is a superb offering of some 300 champagnes.

---

85 Tenth Ave. (at 16th St.)

14 St - 8 Av

(212) 497-8090 — **WEB:** www.delposto.com

Lunch Mon - Fri Dinner nightly

PRICE: $$$$

EL QUINTO PINO

Spanish • Tapas bar

MAP: B2

This convivial tapas spot, compliments of Chef/co-owners Alex Raij and Eder Montero, is small but oh-so-warm and friendly. A bustling bar greets you upon entry; behind that lies a sweet little dining space with large windows, mismatched chairs and a huge woven mural. Service is engaging and attentive. The food may hit the table swiftly, but nonetheless, the multiple courses are very well paced.

This kitchen has a talent for frying to perfection, but the highlight of the menu is arguably their lineup of warm, crusty bocadillos (sandwiches). The menu offers a full range of Spanish tapas that includes regional touches from areas like Andalusia, Asturias or Menorca—and clever creations like garlic shrimp with ginger and jalapeño or delicious shrimp po' boy.

401 W. 24th St. (bet. Ninth & Tenth Aves.)
23 St (Eighth Ave.)
(212) 206-6900 — **WEB:** www.elquintopinonyc.com
Lunch Sat - Sun Dinner nightly **PRICE: $$**

FORAGERS TABLE

Contemporary • Chic

MAP: B2

This restaurant-and-market is an offshoot of an independent grocer in DUMBO, though its kitchen philosophy seems to have arrived via California. The dining room radiates functionality through large and unencumbered windows as well as basic hardwood tables. It's staffed and patronized by the sort of local-loving sycophants who consider it an honor to dine here—and it actually is.

The kitchen team will impress you with their skilled cooking featuring local produce from the market's own farm in Columbia County. Heirloom tomatoes are whirled into a lush gazpacho; artisanal dried pasta produced in Brooklyn from organic grain is deliciously dressed; and roasted chicken with Hudson Valley corn polenta is comfort food extraordinaire.

300 W. 22nd St. (at Eighth Ave.)
23 St (Eighth Ave.)
(212) 243-8888 — **WEB:** www.foragersmarket.com
Lunch Sat - Sun Dinner Mon - Sat **PRICE: $$**

LA SIRENA

Italian • Chic

MAP: B3

If you want a stylish alfresco dinner in Chelsea, this is your spot. La Sirena calls the gorgeous plaza of the Maritime Hotel home. Anchored by a pretty lounge, where the custom mosaic-tiled floor endures a nightly stampede of stilettos, and a bar with sunlight glinting off its counter, other design highlights include a wall of glass overlooking the vast patio. Overall, the space offers both a more casual vibe as well as an upscale dining room complete with leather furnishings and smart service.

The Italian menu turned out of this adept kitchen is enjoyable to say the least. Homemade pastas are good: try the ravioli all'Amatriciana, featuring a plate of these round parcels filled with guanciale and enhanced by a spring onion-flecked butter sauce.

88 Ninth Ave. (bet. 16th & 17th Sts.)
14 St - 8 Av
(212) 977-6096 — **WEB:** www.lasirena-nyc.com
Lunch Sat - Sun Dinner nightly **PRICE:** $$$

THE RED CAT

American • Intimate

MAP: B2

If crowds indicate quality (and downtown they often do) then this clear favorite is still going strong, even after 20-some years. Loyal customers as diverse as the city itself flood this long bar and richly colored room for lunch, dinner or just for a finely mixed cocktail and snack. Flowers give the space a touch of luxury; Moorish lanterns add warmth.

The pleasures here are the straightforward items, which arrive courtesy of Chef/owner Jimmy Bradley. Begin with umami-rich and visually stunning roasted broccoli, finished with slivered almonds and parmesan shavings, before moving on to a crisped tranche of salmon crowned with peekytoe crab in saffron aïoli. Finish in style with a perfectly composed pistachio semifreddo draped with dark chocolate sauce.

227 Tenth Ave. (bet. 23rd & 24th Sts.)
23 St (Eighth Ave.)
(212) 242-1122 — **WEB:** www.theredcat.com
Lunch & dinner daily **PRICE:** $$

L'ATELIER DE JOËL ROBUCHON ❀❀

French • Luxury

MAP: A2

The late, beloved and globally acclaimed chef, Joël Robuchon, returned his L'Atelier to the Big Apple, having traded in a former East Side luxury hotel for this fashionable downtown address. The hip locale is the cherry on top for his fan base, who know just what to expect: excellent cuisine, steep prices and the best pommes purée your palate has ever been privy to.

This sleek and sultry space dons an ultra-modern design that features the signature red-and-black color scheme, as well as a pristine open kitchen. Centered around a glossy cherry wood counter, the dining room draws inspiration from those convivial sushi and tapas bars; it also offers an up close and personal view of the cooks in action. As expected, the iconic cuisine is every bit as luxurious as one might imagine. Lavish ingredients like foie gras, truffle and caviar aren't just accents here, but stellar components of many plates. The carte may feel intimidatingly long at times, but the prix-fixe is an easy way to sample sea bass with a fennel broth and sea urchin; or spiced Long Island duck with young turnip and rhubarb confit.

The breads are baked by the in-house boulanger, so save room for these gorgeous crumbs.

---

85 Tenth Ave. (at 15th St.)

14 St - 8 Ave

(212) 488-8885 — **WEB:** www.joelrobuchonusa.com

Dinner Mon - Sat **PRICE: $$$$**

LE GRILL DE JOËL ROBUCHON

French • Chic

MAP: A2

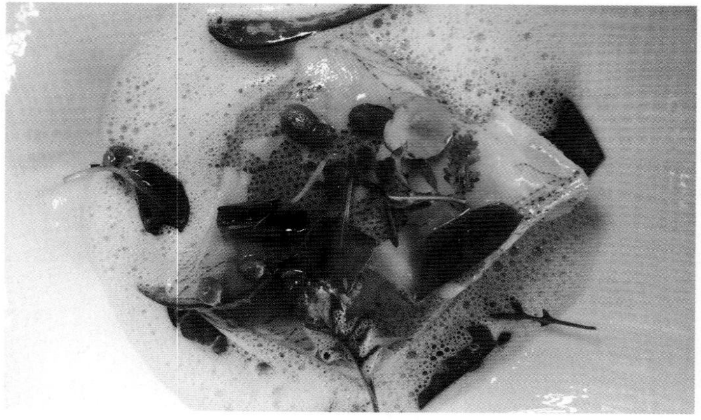

As the relatively relaxed counterpoint to L'Atelier from dearly departed chef Joël Robuchon, whose culinary legacy lives on in all its quality, Le Grill serves comparably excellent, contemporary and more approachable French food. While both dining rooms share the same address, a glass wall of wine separates them. Le Grill still feels cavernous, with burgundy leather couches, a long bar and black tables that all work together to enhance the sense of comfort here. Soft lighting and exposed brick warm the oversized space. Luxe touches include the sparkling crystal and gleaming rosewood paneling. Service is friendly but maintains the strict professionalism that befits any Robuchon restaurant.

The cuisine here serves as a constant reminder that you are in the hands of a world-class kitchen. Begin with a salad that is elevated beyond any other, featuring herbs dressed in a lush vinaigrette and set over thick slices of parmesan-topped artichoke hearts. Gently cooked salmon then follows; served in a pool of saffron foam and draped with a translucent sheet of pasta, it makes for an arresting show. Desserts are always a technical yet beautiful display of edible art; while beverages—from cocktails and wine to coffee—are nothing less than enticing.

---

85 Tenth Ave. (at 15th St.)

14 St - 8 Av

(212) 488-8885 — **WEB:** www.joelrobuchonusa.com

Dinner nightly

PRICE: $$$$

OKUDA ✿

Japanese • Minimalist

MAP: A2

The flurry of Japanese exports laying down roots in NYC takes a high-end turn with the arrival of Okuda, courtesy of Chef/owner Toru Okuda. Fresh on the heels of launching successful branches in Tokyo and Paris, he turns to Executive Chef Mitsuhiro Endo to carry out his vision of refinement, elegance and seasonality here in Chelsea.

In the realm of traditional kaiseki cuisine, this kitchen pays tribute to the seasons down to the detail, offering a style so nuanced you'll want to note each element to fully appreciate the chef's every sensibility. Meticulous handiwork, delicate knife cuts and ingredient sourcing (from Japan and more local environs) all come together to produce an enchanting experience.

Hidden in plain sight, the small, sleek space feels private, with a seven-seat, chef-facing counter that requires reservations. The food is truly the star though, commencing with buttery sheets of barely cooked Wagyu shabu-shabu style, paired with luscious Maine uni as well as yuba in dashi. Then silver-skinned sea perch may follow with a chewy mochi ball. At the end, miso-glazed mackerel is elevated with creamy potato, crisp lotus root spiced with togarashi and pickled turnip.

---

458 W. 17th St. (bet. Ninth & Tenth Aves.)

14 St - 8 Av

(212) 924-0017 — **WEB:** www.okuda.nyc

Dinner Wed - Sun

PRICE: $$$$

ROUGE TOMATE

Contemporary • Chic

MAP: C3

Sited in a converted carriage house (and previous home to the Gracie family of Gracie Mansion), Rouge Tomate is sleek and inviting, with brick and reclaimed wood (some of it salvaged from Hurricane Sandy debris) intermingling to create a sort of urbane farmhouse mien. The staff may verge on casual, but they are as amicable as ever.

The raison d'être here is S.P.E. (Sanitas Per Escam) or "health through food." Picture ethically raised meats, seasonal produce, and minimal dairy accompanied by mocktails, fresh juices and biodynamic wines. Sold? Dinner may even unveil surprises like roasted, free-range chicken served over barley with roasted squash, Treviso and miso-caramel sauce; or wild Alaskan halibut with sugar snap peas and delicious pickled leeks.

126 W. 18th St. (bet. Sixth & Seventh Aves.)
18 St
(646) 395-3978 — **WEB:** www.rougetomatechelsea.com
Lunch Mon - Fri Dinner Mon - Sat **PRICE: $$$**

SALINAS

Spanish • Rustic

MAP: B2

What's not to love here? Even if the lip-smacking tapas menu didn't draw customers in droves, a sexy décor dressed with oodles of fresh roses and the warm glow of candlelight would do the trick. A slender hallway opens up into a narrow dining hall featuring dark walls; tufted velvet banquettes; and a backyard dining area topped by a retractable roof.

The Spanish cuisine, skillfully rendered by chef and San Sebastian native, Luis Bollo, arrives as intricate tapas or hearty large plates, depending on your appetite. Tuck into arroz brut a la plancha, a tender, griddled cake of short grain brown rice, studded with savory merguez, peas and raisins; or baked fideuà sauced with squid ink and topped with shaved sepia, garlicky aïoli and watercress sprouts.

136 Ninth Ave. (bet. 18th & 19th Sts.)
18 St
(212) 776-1990 — **WEB:** www.salinasnyc.com
Dinner nightly **PRICE: $$$**

USHIWAKAMARU

Japanese • Simple

MAP: B2

Ushiwakamaru is a good fit for Chelsea because it can offer different dining experiences to different people. You can pop in after work and sit at a table for some good value à la carte dishes like shrimp tempura, black cod in miso or clam soup; or you can make it an occasion by booking at the counter for the market-price omakase and the personal attention of one of the chefs. Choose the latter and your nigiri will be served piece by piece, which is preferable to having a selection brought to you on a plate if you're seated at a table.

Sashimi with sake is one of the great food pairings and they flaunt a good list, available by the glass, carafe or bottle. The place is also run with care and sincerity and offers a calm sanctuary from the world outside.

362 W. 23rd St. (bet. Eighth & Ninth Aves.)
23rd St (Eighth Ave.)
(917) 639-3940 — **WEB:** www.ushiwakamarunewyork.com
Dinner Mon - Sat **PRICE: $$$$**

Remember, stars are awarded for cuisine only! Elements such as service and décor are not a factor.

CHINATOWN & LITTLE ITALY

As different as chow mein and chicken cacciatore, these two neighborhoods are nonetheless neighbors and remain as thick as thieves. In recent years however, their borders have become increasingly blurred, with Chinatown gulping up most of Little Italy. It is said that New York cradles the maximum number of Chinese immigrants in the country, and settlers from Hong Kong and mainland China each brought with them their own distinct regional cuisines.

EAT THE STREETS

Chowing in Chinatown can be delectable and delightfully affordable. Elbow your way through these cramped streets to uncover a flurry of markets, bubble tea cafés, bakeries and much, much more. Freshly steamed pouches of chicken, seafood and pork are all the rage at **Vanessa's Dumpling House**, a neighborhood fixture with a long counter and even longer queue of hungry visitors. There is lots more deliciousness to be had in this locale—from freshly pulled noodles; ducking into a parlor for a scoop of black sesame ice cream; or even breezing past a market window with crocodile meat on display—claws included! **New Kam Man** is a bustling bazaar offering everything from woks to wontons; while Vietnamese mecca, **Tan Tin-Hung**,

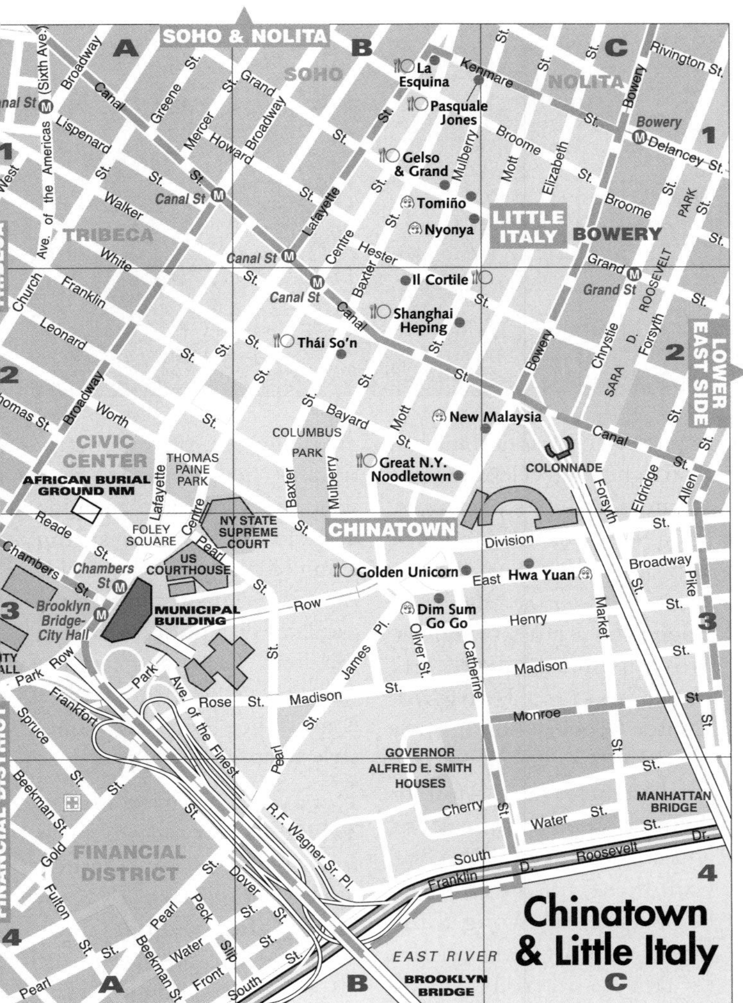

is a mini but "super" market proffering the best selection of authentic ingredients in town—red perilla, rau ram and culantro are ready for your home kitchen. Over on Mulberry Street, **Asia Market Corp.** is a sight for sore eyes as shelves spill over with Malaysian, Indonesian and Thai specialties. The space is tight, but the variety of

imported goods is nothing less than right. Find celebrity chefs at these Asian storefronts, haggling over flipping fish and quality produce, before sneaking under the Manhattan Bridge for a crusty bánh mì. Moving on to chilies and curry pastes, **Bangkok Center Grocery** boasts every ingredient necessary for a Thai-themed feast—not to mention their publications and friendly owner! Fans of Cantonese cuisine join the line outside **Big Wong King**, where comfort food classics (congee and roast duck anyone?) are as outstanding as the setting is ordinary. **Amazing 66** is a brightly lit, bi-level darling with two dining rooms. Here dishes arrive almost as swiftly as the crowds go in and out, making it a spot where taste and efficiency are of superlative quality. Then comes dim sum, which is a longtime tradition and name of the game at **Jing Fong**. Make your way inside this bi-level bijou and take the escalator up a floor to arrive at this loud, flashy and fragrant mainstay, where the service is gruff but the Hong Kong-style treats are very tasty.

For a more snug vibe, head to **Tai Pan Bakery**, also popular for its pastries. The exquisitely light sponge cake at **Kam Hing Coffee Shop** has made it a worthy competitor in the "Best bakeries around town" contest; or stop by **Golden Fung Wong** for lesser-known, but equally delicious bean paste-stuffed hopia. Klezmer meets Cantonese at the **Egg Rolls and Egg Creams Festival**, an annual summer street celebration honoring the neighboring Chinese and Jewish communities of Chinatown and the Lower East Side. Every year during Chinese New Year, partygoers pack these streets, with dragons dancing down the avenues accompanied by costumed revelers and firecrackers.

LITTLE ITALY

The Little Italy of Scorsese's gritty *Mean Streets* is slowly vanishing into what may now be more aptly called "Micro Italy." The onetime stronghold of a large Italian-American population has dwindled today to a mere corridor—Mulberry Street between Canal and Broome streets. However, rest assured that the spirit of its origins still pulses in century-old markets, cramped delis, gelato shops and mom-and-pop trattorias. Seasoned palates love **Piemonte Ravioli** for their homemade sauces, as well as dried and fresh pastas—available in all shapes with a variety of fillings. **Alleva Dairy** (known for its ricotta) is the oldest Italian cheese store in the country; while **Di Palo's Fine Foods** boasts more of the same (cheeses) alongside imported salumi. Primo for pastries and espresso, fans never forget to frequent **Ferrara Bakery and Cafe** on Grand Street. Of course, during the warmer months, Mulberry Street becomes a veritable pedestrian zone with one big alfresco party—the **Feast of San Gennaro** is particularly raucous. While these days you can certainly get better Italian food elsewhere in the city, tourists and old-timers still gather here to treasure and bathe in the nostalgia of this nabe.

DIM SUM GO GO

Chinese • Neighborhood

MAP: B3

This wildly popular joint is still packed to the gills most days, and for good reason: the Cantonese fare and dim sum served here is as good as the food you'll find in those super-authentic places in far-flung Queens. Even better, they take reservations—and dim sum orders are taken by the staff, thereby ensuring that the food stays fresh. However, guests should avoid shared tables during the weekend rush as service can verge on chaotic.

If the price seems a bit higher than its competitors, you'll find it's worth it for dishes like sweet shrimp, rolled in rice paper and laced with dark soy sauce. Plump snow pea leaf dumplings are spiked with vibrant ginger and garlic and may be tailed by rich duck dumplings or an irresistibly flaky roast pork pie.

5 East Broadway (at Chatham Sq.)
Canal St (Lafayette St.)
(212) 732-0797 — **WEB:** N/A
Lunch & dinner daily

PRICE: $$

GELSO & GRAND

Italian • Rustic

MAP: B1

It takes considerable skill to make design look so easy. This corner restaurant may tick all the zeitgeist boxes by sporting an ersatz-industrial look, complete with exposed brick, neat light fixtures and metal chairs, but it's one that's tempered by huge windows that let the sun pour in. Equally bright service keeps the atmosphere light and even the name is clever—"Gelso" being Italian for Mulberry, the cross street with Grand.

The kitchen, too, is a cut above the norm. The homemade pastas are standouts, from brown butter gnocchi with braised lamb to lighter, if equally filling, choices like ricotta and spinach agnolotti. The wood-fired oven is used to good effect, especially with the pizzas, and flavors are as generous as the portions themselves.

186 Grand St. (at Mulberry St.)
Spring St
(212) 226-1600 — **WEB:** www.gelsoandgrand.com
Lunch & dinner daily

PRICE: $$

GOLDEN UNICORN

Chinese • Family

MAP: B3

This age-old dim sum parlor, spread over many floors in an office building, is one of the few Cantonese spots that actually has the space and volume to necessitate its parade of steaming carts brimming with treats. While Golden Unicorn's system is very efficient and part of the spectacle, arrive early to nab a seat by the kitchen for better variety and hotter items.

A helpful brigade of suited men and women roam the space to offer the likes of exquisitely soft roast pork buns, or congee with preserved egg and shredded pork. Buzzing with locals and visitors, it is also a favorite among families who appreciate the kid-friendly scene as much as the delectable, steamed pea shoot and shrimp dumplings, pork siu mai and rice rolls stuffed with shrimp.

18 East Broadway (at Catherine St.)
Canal St (Lafayette St.)
(212) 941-0911 — **WEB:** www.goldenunicornrestaurant.com
Lunch & dinner daily

PRICE: $$

GREAT N.Y. NOODLETOWN

Chinese • Simple

MAP: B2

When heading to Great N.Y. Noodletown, invite plenty of dining companions to share those heaping plates of roasted meats and rice and noodle soups served at this bargain favorite. Locals stream in until the 4:00 A.M. closing bell for their great Cantonese dishes—food is clearly the focus here, over the brusque service and unfussy atmosphere. Guests' gazes quickly pass over the imitation wooden chairs to rest on the crispy skin of suckling pig and ducks hanging in the window.

These dishes are huge, so forgo the rice and opt instead for deliciously chewy noodles and barbecue meats. Incredible shrimp wontons, for instance, are delicate and thin; and the complex homemade e-fu noodles demonstrate technique and quality to a standout level that is rarely rivaled.

28 Bowery (at Bayard St.)
Canal St (Lafayette St.)
(212) 349-0923 — **WEB:** N/A
Lunch & dinner daily

PRICE: ⊕

HWA YUAN

Chinese • Elegant

MAP: C3

After a 30 year hiatus, Hwa Yuan has reopened to give locals what is quite literally a taste of history. The famed cold noodle recipe dates back to 1968 and is as delicious as ever. Owned and operated by the same family since day one, today the restaurant is striving to regain its status as the neighborhood's focal point. The tri-level space evokes Chinatown's heyday, with gracious service and polished surroundings befit for a glamorous evening out. If Shorty himself is around, ask about the good old days and he might even break out the old photographs.

Stick to the menu's familiar Sichuan dishes for a successful meal. Highlights include the "must-try" dry sautéed tangy beef and crispy chicken, served as a half chicken with crispy, golden-lacquered skin.

42 E. Broadway (bet. Catherine & Market Sts.)
East Broadway
(212) 966-6002 – **WEB:** www.hwayuannyc.com
Lunch & dinner daily **PRICE: $$**

IL CORTILE

Italian • Romantic

MAP: B2

Beyond this quaint and charming façade lies one of Little Italy's famed mainstays, ever-popular with dreamy-eyed dates seeking the stuff of Billy Joel lyrics. The expansive space does indeed suggest a nostalgic romance, with its series of Mediterranean-themed rooms, though the most celebrated is the pleasant garden atrium (il cortile is Italian for courtyard), with a glass-paneled ceiling and abundant greenery.

A skilled line of cooks presents a wide array of familiar starters and entrées, from eggplant rollatini to chicken Francese; as well as a range of pastas, such as spaghettini puttanesca or risotto con funghi. Several decades of sharing family recipes and bringing men to one bent knee continues to earn Il Cortile a longtime following.

125 Mulberry St. (bet. Canal & Hester Sts.)
Canal St (Lafayette St.)
(212) 226-6060 – **WEB:** www.ilcortile.com
Lunch & dinner daily **PRICE: $$**

LA ESQUINA

Mexican • Trendy

MAP: B1

When La Esquina opened it was a breath of fresh air, offering enjoyable cuisine that stood tall among the paltry selection of Manhattan Mexican. Thankfully, the city's south-of-the-border dining scene has evolved since then. However, this idol remains a fun and worthy option. More playground than restaurant, the multi-faceted setting takes up an iconic downtown corner and draws a hip crowd to its grab-and-go taqueria, 30-seat café and subterranean dining room-cum-bar. The spirit here is alive and kicking, with classic renditions of tortilla soup; mole negro enchiladas filled with excellently seasoned chicken; as well as carne asada starring black Angus sirloin with mojo de ajo.

A baby sib in Brooklyn continues to thrive thanks to its retro vibe.

114 Kenmare St. (bet. Cleveland Pl. & Lafayette St.)
Spring St (Lafayette St.)
(646) 613-7100 — **WEB:** www.esquinanyc.com
Lunch & dinner daily

PRICE: $$

NEW MALAYSIA

Malaysian • Simple

MAP: C2

Mad for Malaysian? Head to this lively dive, sequestered in a Chinatown arcade. Proffering some of the best Malaysian treats in town, including all the classics, this address sees a deluge of regulars who pour in for a massive offering of exceptional dishes. Round tables cram a room furnished with little more than a service counter. Still, the aromas wafting from flaky roti canai and Melaka crispy coconut shrimp keep you focused on the food.

Capturing the essence of this region are brusque servers who speedily deliver abundant and authentic bowls of spicy-sour asam laksa fragrant with lemongrass; kang-kung belacan, greens with dried shrimp and chili; and nasi lemak, the national treasure starring coconut rice, chicken curry and dried anchovies.

46-48 Bowery (bet. Bayard & Canal Sts.)
Canal St (Lafayette St.)
(212) 964-0284 — **WEB:** N/A
Lunch & dinner daily

PRICE:

NYONYA

Malaysian • Simple

MAP: B1

Nyonya flaunts a comfy setting composed of brick walls and basic wood tables, but really, everyone's here for their outstanding Malaysian food. Speedy servers steer diners through the varied menu—and perhaps even away from such delicacies as prawn mee, an exceptionally spiced and sour shrimp broth with noodles, pork, vegetables and bean sprouts floating in its goodness.

Asians and other locals know to stick to such faithful and deeply satisfying dishes as nasi lemak, which is a delightful combo of coconut rice, pickled veggies, crispy anchovies, curried chicken and hard-boiled egg. Mee siam spotlights noodles stir-fried with tofu and shrimp in a chili sauce that puts all others to shame, while coconut batter-fried jumbo prawns are nothing short of—omg—wow!

199 Grand St. (bet. Mott & Mulberry Sts.)
Canal St (Lafayette St.)
(212) 334-3669 — **WEB:** www.ilovenyonya.com
Lunch & dinner daily

PRICE:

PASQUALE JONES

Italian • Fashionable

MAP: B1

This stylish Italian charmer is a neighborhood restaurant fit for the modern age. Expect blistered Neapolitan-style pizzas straight from the wood oven; excellent handmade pastas; and vegetable-focused small plates.

The space is snug, so try to nab reservations ahead—a challenging feat given its popularity. For a thoroughly 21st century bit of hospitality, request a text message when a counter seat opens. Plump diver scallops arrive seared to golden, sporting crisp fennel slivers, crushed hazelnut and juicy mandarin orange, while al dente rigatoni is tossed in a ricotta sauce dotted with pork sausage. For dessert, the seasonal option may feature lime curd topped with mascarpone ice cream, smoky meringue and hazelnut cookie crumble.

187 Mulberry St. (at Kenmare St.)
Bowery
N/A — **WEB:** www.pasqualejones.com
Lunch Tue - Sun Dinner nightly

PRICE: $$

SHANGHAI HEPING

Chinese • Simple

MAP: B2

When faced with the long, no-frills menu, there should read a caution sign to not miss out on the crab and pork soup dumplings. The plump, juicy filling and flavorful broth held in each delicate wrapper with soy-ginger seasoning explains the afternoon crowd lunching out of takeout boxes at the entrance.

Large bamboo steamer baskets line most tables, and the seared pan-fried pork dumplings are not to miss either. Cold appetizers also shine, like dark soy- and sugar-cooked bamboo shoots with wheat gluten, or thinly sliced stir-fried eel with chives. There are larger, steaming hot plates to choose from like Shanghai rice cakes with beef. The "Eight Jewel Rice" dessert matches a mound of sticky rice with red bean paste, dates and golden raisin "jewels."

104 Mott St. (bet. Canal & Hester Sts.)
Canal St (Lafayette St.)
(212) 925-1118 — **WEB:** shanghaihepingnyc.com
Lunch & dinner daily

PRICE: $$

THÁI SO´N

Vietnamese • Simple

MAP: B2

Thái So´n is by far the best of the bunch in this Vietnamese quarter of Chinatown. It's neither massive nor fancy, but it's bright, clean and perpetually in business. One peek at the specials on the walls (maybe golden-fried squid strewn with sea salt) will have you begging for a seat in the crammed room.

Speedy servers scoot between groups of City Hall suits and Asian locals as they order the likes of cha gio, pork spring rolls with nuoc cham; or goi cuon, fantastic summer rolls filled with poached shrimp and vermicelli. Naturally, pho choices are abundant, but the real star of the show is pho tai—where raw beef shavings are cooked to tender perfection when combined with a scalding hot, savory broth replete with herbs, sprouts and chewy noodles.

89 Baxter St. (bet. Bayard & Canal Sts.)
Canal St (Lafayette St.)
(212) 732-2822 — **WEB:** N/A
Lunch & dinner daily

PRICE:

TOMIÑO

Spanish • Chic

MAP: B1

Tomiño Taberna Galega is a treasure trove of delicious tapas from Northwestern Spain, located here on the border of Little Italy and Chinatown. To call it a tavern may be a misnomer, as the dining room is attractively decorated with handsome wood tables, ocean-blue banquettes and a skylight overhead. Head to the roomy bar for a more typical perch from which to enjoy the great Spanish art of small-plate dining.

The kitchen may offer some of the usual favorites, but the real emphasis is on Galician regional specialties. Start with croquetas, their golden shells rough and crumbly over a creamy béchamel filling studded with jamón or shellfish. Then move on to a crock of caldo Gallego—intensely flavored pork stew with collard greens and white beans.

192 Grand St. (bet. Mott & Mulberry Sts.)

Spring St (Lafayette St.)

(212) 933-4763 – **WEB:** www.tominonyc.com

Lunch & dinner daily **PRICE:** $$

Look for our symbol spotlighting restaurants with a serious cocktail list.

FERRARA
EST. 1892

EAST VILLAGE

Long regarded as the capital of cool, the East Village was once a shadier incarnation of Tompkins Square Park and second home to squatters and rioters. However, the neighborhood today is safer, cleaner and far more habitable. And while cheap walk-ups filled with struggling artists or aspiring models may be a thing of the past, the area's marked renovation hasn't led to any sort of dip in self-expression or creativity. In fact, reflecting its independent and outspoken spirit for which this neighborhood is known, the East Village flaunts a distinct personality and vibrant dining landscape.

CHEAP EATS

Budget-friendly bites abound in these parts of town. Family-run **Veselka**, located in the heart of this 'hood has been serving traditional Ukrainian specialties for over 60 years, and is a particularly fitting homage to the area's former Eastern European population. After a night of bar-hopping or other mischief, grab a restorative bite of salt and fat at **Crif Dogs**, where deep-fried hot dogs are

doled out until 4:00 A.M (every Friday and Saturday). Along these streets, also discover a number of food-related endeavors that are the product of laser-focused culinary inspiration. **Bánh mi zòn** for instance is a smash-hit for crackling-skinned Vietnamese pork sandwiches. **Superiority Burger** is a hot spot loved for its lip-smacking vegan take on the classic burger; while **Luke's Lobster** has expanded into an international network presenting rolls stuffed with crustaceans straight from Maine. For ramen, Japanese-import **Ippudo** churns out steaming bowlfuls to its boisterous patrons. A new kind of noodle is trending in New York, this time from southwestern China. "Mixian" rice noodle shops are popping up everywhere, but the recommended spot to savor them is **Little Tong Noodle Shop**, run by a former fine dining vet. Meanwhile, **Brodo** (the brainchild of Hearth Chef/owner Marco Canora) is a trendsetting "window" that dispenses comforting cups of broths, such as the Hearth broth, Organic Chicken and Gingered Grass-fed beef. Others may join the constant queue of students looking for a crusty slice of white from **Artichoke Basille's Pizza** on 14th Street. Of course, while on the topic of cravings of all stripes, the sensory assault around St. Mark's Place offers

an immersion in Asian flavors that is delightfully kitschy and completely worthwhile. If that doesn't have you salivating, duck into **Boka** for spicy Korean fried chicken. Others simply follow the scent of takoyaki frying and sizzling okonomiyaki at **Otafuku**. Hungry hordes know to look for the red paper lanterns that hang outside haunts like **Yakitori Taisho**; while taste buds are always satiated at divey izakayas such as **Village Yokocho**. And yet, among this area's sultry sake dens, none rivals the outrageous offering at subterranean favorite—**Decibel**—constantly packed for its delicious eats and urban beats.

A SWEET SIDE

Badass 'tudes and savory dishes aside, the East Village also has a very sweet side. **Moishe's Bake Shop** is a Kosher delight where challah, rugelach and marble sponge cake have been on the menu since 1978. In operation since 1894, **Veniero's Pasticceria & Caffé** brings yet another taste of the Old World to these newly minted locals. This Italian idol draws long lines, especially around holiday time, for baked goods. And, don't forget to make these sweets just a bit more beautiful with a shipment

of flowers from Fleurs Bella. There can never be a dearth of caffeine in the city, and chic-geeks love **Hi-Collar**—a nifty, Japanese-esque coffee house decked with a brass counter and back wall accented by rice paper screens. Stay late and you may even be served some sake. Celebrity chef David Chang's dessert darling **Momofuku Milk Bar** also rents space here and serves clever variations on dessert. Birthday cake truffles and "Compost" cookies have sweet teeth swooning (and returning). **Big Gay Ice Cream** may have started life as a modest truck on the move, but is now established as a top-seller for signatures like the Dorothy—a swirl of vanilla, dulce de leche and crushed Nilla wafers.

CRAFT COCKTAILS

The craft cocktail movement has taken firm root in this "village" of trend, where many subtly (and even undisclosed) locations offer an epicurean approach to mixology. **Death & Co.** is a dimly lit, hot-as-hell spot that is packed to the gills, but when in need of a more intimate scene, make your way to the wooden phone booth inside **Crif Dogs** to access **PDT** (Please Don't Tell). Here, Benton's Old-Fashioned composed from bacon-smoked Bourbon may just be every cocktail critic's dream come true. Cached behind a wall in a Japanese restaurant, **Angel's Share's** snazzy bartenders shake and stir for a civilized crowd; just as polished **Pouring Ribbons**, devoted to vintage chartreuse, continues to be praised in this nabe as a sanctuary of sorts for those in-the-know.

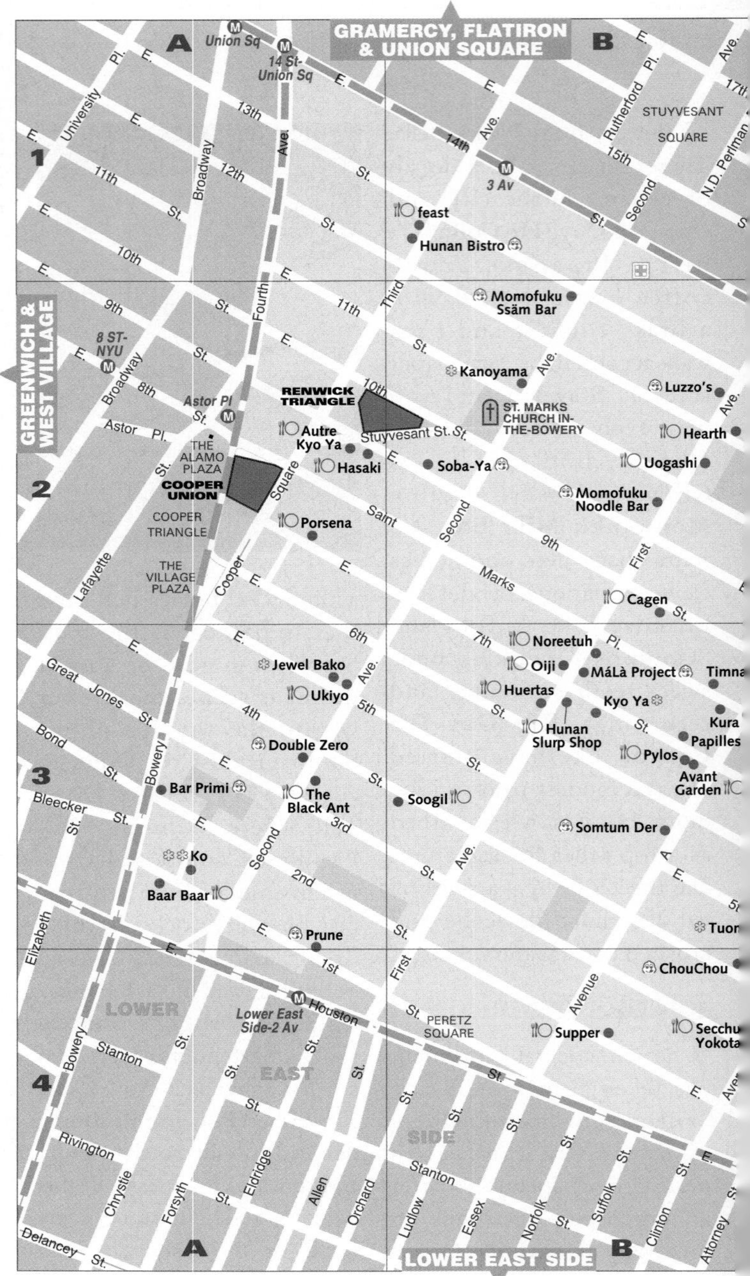
GRAMERCY, FLATIRON & UNION SQUARE
GREENWICH & WEST VILLAGE
LOWER EAST SIDE
feast
Hunan Bistro
Momofuku Ssäm Bar
Kanoyama
Luzzo's
Hearth
Uogashi
RENWICK TRIANGLE
ST. MARKS CHURCH IN-THE-BOWERY
Autre Kyo Ya
Hasaki
Soba-Ya
Momofuku Noodle Bar
COOPER UNION
THE ALAMO PLAZA
COOPER TRIANGLE
THE VILLAGE PLAZA
Porsena
Cagen
Noreetuh
Oiji
MáLà Project
Timna
Jewel Bako
Ukiyo
Huertas
Kyo Ya
Kura
Hunan Slurp Shop
Papilles
Double Zero
Pylos
Avant Garden
Bar Primi
The Black Ant
Soogil
Somtum Der
Ko
Baar Baar
Tuome
Prune
ChouChou
PERETZ SQUARE
Supper
Secchu Yokota
Union Sq
14 St-Union Sq
3 Av
8 ST-NYU
Astor Pl
Lower East Side-2 Av
STUYVESANT SQUARE
LOWER EAST SIDE
A
B
1
2
3
4

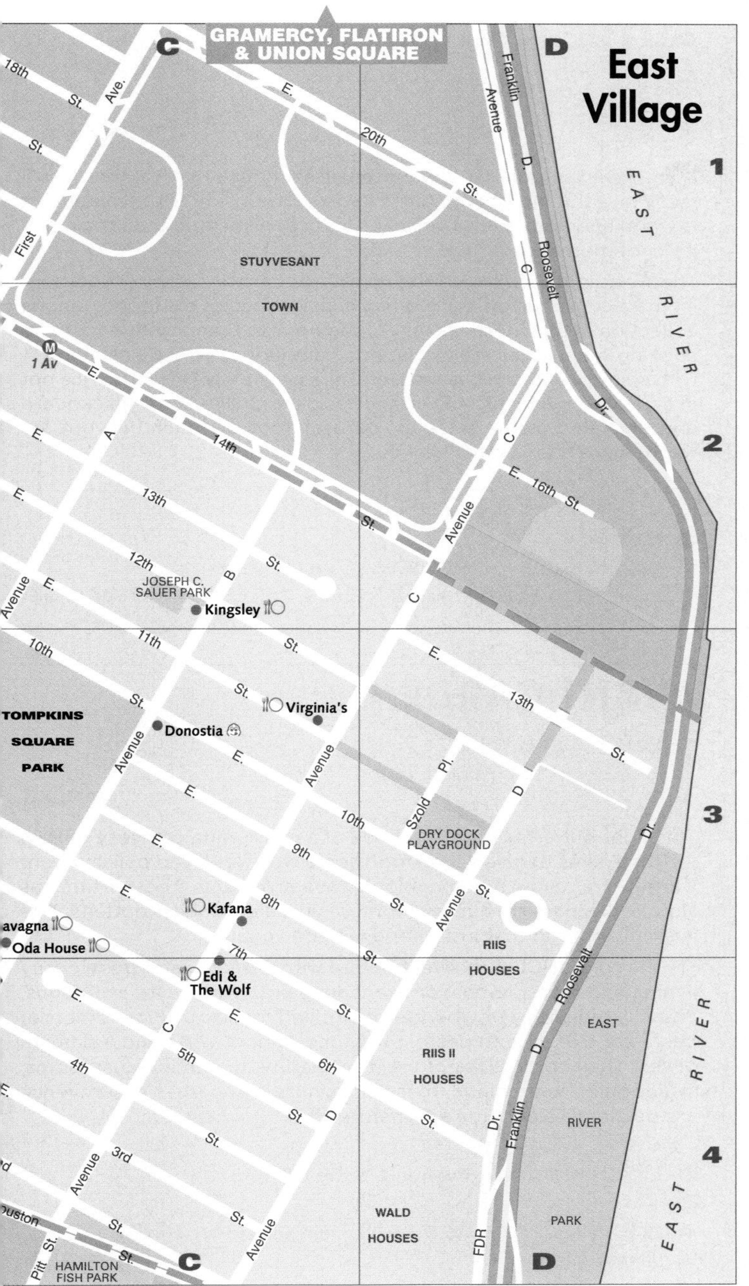
East Village
GRAMERCY, FLATIRON & UNION SQUARE
C
D
1
2
3
4
STUYVESANT
TOWN
1 Av
TOMPKINS
SQUARE
PARK
JOSEPH C.
SAUER PARK
Kingsley
Virginia's
Donostia
Kafana
Oda House
Edi &
The Wolf
DRY DOCK
PLAYGROUND
RIIS
HOUSES
RIIS II
HOUSES
WALD
HOUSES
EAST
RIVER
PARK
EAST RIVER
HAMILTON
FISH PARK
First Ave.
E. 20th St.
E. 18th St.
E. 14th St.
E. 16th St.
E. 13th St.
E. 12th St.
E. 11th St.
E. 10th St.
E. 9th St.
E. 8th St.
E. 7th St.
E. 6th St.
E. 5th St.
E. 4th St.
E. 3rd St.
Houston St.
Pitt St.
Avenue A
Avenue B
Avenue C
Avenue D
Szold Pl.
Franklin D. Roosevelt Dr.
FDR Dr.

AUTRE KYO YA

Fusion • Rustic

MAP: A2

If you love the popular Japanese kaiseki house Kyo Ya, then you'll really love this hip sibling, Autre Kyo Ya. The inside of the restaurant is warm and homey, and while it's less sophisticated than the elder, it's a lot more fun.

The space is lined with cozy banquettes, a bar and plenty of nooks for intimate conversation. But the real highlight here is the food, a unique collection of Japanese dishes amped up with French influences and cooking techniques—think pâté de campagne; a crispy cauliflower with spicy peanut sauce; and Berkshire pork belly kamadaki rice pot in a garlic-ginger sauce. Even the specials, chalked on a blackboard and delivered to the table for perusal, tout a French flair but are worth more than a quick glance.

10 Stuyvesant St. (bet. Third Ave. & 9th St.)
Astor Pl
(212) 598-0454 – **WEB:** www.autrekyoya.com
Lunch Sat - Sun Dinner Tue - Sun **PRICE:** **$$**

AVANT GARDEN

Vegan • Cozy

MAP: B3

This tight but artsy little jewel box of a restaurant, courtesy of Ravi DeRossi, aims to give vegan food some well-deserved polish. Avant Garden's dynamic menu couldn't have arrived at a better time, as New York diners are hungry for more upscale meatless options. This is excellent food that just happens to be vegan.

Try the cold, salt-baked sweet potato with puréed watercress, crispy jicama and Meyer lemon; or avocado, paired with white asparagus, crunchy radishes, strawberries and grilled garlicky ramps. Sheets of pasta are tossed with pesto, tomatoes, haricot verts and Kalamata olives. Their thick slices of toast topped with cremini mushrooms, sweet onion marmalade, toasted walnuts and herbes de Provence are destined to become a signature item.

130 E. 7th St. (bet. Avenue A & First Ave.)
1 Av
(646) 922-7948 – **WEB:** www.avantgardennyc.com
Dinner nightly **PRICE:** **$$$**

BAAR BAAR

Indian • Chic

MAP: A3

This delightful restaurant delivers contemporary Indian cuisine that brings a refined touch to familiar South Asian flavors. All thanks are due to Chef Sujan Sarkar, who landed in NY fresh from his success in San Francisco. Baar Baar may bill itself as a gastropub, but dining is the focus here. In fact, its vast, inventive menu is filled with such delicious condiments, as if to prove that no detail is too small for this kitchen. Try a plate of paneer chili, where slices of cheese and a spiced tomato achar are wrapped inside crisp kataifi shreds and served with ginger chutney. Other highlights include lamb keema or Brussel sprouts foogath.

The large, industrial space can feel cold, but warm, jeweled tones and even warmer service make up the difference.

13 E. 1st St. (bet. Bowery & Second Ave.)
2 Av
(212) 228-1200 – **WEB:** www.baarbaarnyc.com
Lunch Sunday Dinner nightly

PRICE: $$$

BAR PRIMI

Italian • Osteria

MAP: A3

Chef Sal Lamboglia and Chef/owner Andrew Carmellini clearly know what they wanted to do in this kitchen: make excellent Italian (and Italian-American) food with a delicious twist here and surprise ingredient there. The result is a restaurant we would all want to have just around the corner. Great wine, a friendly service team and two floors of comfortable seating make it easy for guests to pile in, night after night.

Start with meatballs, a far cry from the generic kind, stuffed with Fontina and braised until tender in a chunky tomato sugo. Pasta here rivals Italy, especially the spaghetti with small, briny clams and spicy 'njuda crumbles topped with breadcrumbs and parsley. Daily specials are also a delight, as is the simply delicious hazelnut gelato.

325 Bowery (at 2nd St.)
Bleecker St
(212) 220-9100 – **WEB:** www.barprimi.com
Lunch & dinner daily

PRICE: $$

THE BLACK ANT

Mexican • Contemporary décor

MAP: A3

Bringing a dose of Mexico City chic to the area, this restaurant takes its name from the ancient Mesoamerican fable of an ant and incorporates that imagery throughout the setting. Black-and-white checkerboard flooring, wall tiles bearing the insect's motif, and a cool giant ant mural reinforce the theme. The menu is an unrestricted look at this nation's cuisine. It is only fitting that specialties here include the Climbing Ant cocktail with tequila, Aperol and mole bitters; guacamole seasoned with crushed ant salt; and grasshopper-crusted shrimp tacos. Bug-free creations are just as appealing, as in tacos with fried cod cheek and cabbage-mango slaw.

For a more traditional but moodier experience, stop by sister restaurant Ofrenda in the West Village.

60 Second Ave. (bet. 3rd & 4th Sts.)
2 Av
(212) 598-0300 – **WEB:** www.theblackantnyc.com
Lunch Sat - Sun Dinner nightly **PRICE:** **$$**

CAGEN

Japanese • Minimalist

MAP: B2

Unless you're only interested in gazing into your date's eyes, you'll want to sit at Cagen's sleek elm counter rather than a table—that way, you'll get to witness the skill and dexterity on display firsthand. Chef Toshio Tomita spent an age at the legendary Nobu, and his alma mater's influence is obvious here.

There may be only one omakase option to choose from, but rest easy as it includes the chef's legendary sashimi and nigiri (employing seasonal and unique fish from Japan) as well as his outstanding homemade soba noodles. Speaking of which, be sure to mix the sobayu (the water in which the noodles were originally cooked) with the tsuyu dipping sauce for a flavorsome sip at the end. Satisfying, and, as the word "cagen" implies—"just right."

414 E. 9th St. (bet. Avenue A & First Ave.)
Astor Pl
(212) 358-8800 – **WEB:** www.cagenrestaurant.com
Dinner Tue - Sun **PRICE:** **$$$$**

CHOUCHOU

Moroccan • Rustic

MAP: B4

There are two schools of thought when it comes to menu design: one is the encyclopedic, all-inclusive tome and then there is ChouChou.

This East Village hangout, complete with romantic hanging lanterns, is best described as hyper-focused. In fact, the tightly edited menu is divided into just two categories: tagines and couscous. Choose from six couscous preparations ranging from lamb and chicken to lobster, while four tagines tempt from their iconic conical vessels. Once decided, an array of tangy salads and sides arrive. Lifted tableside, the delightful fragrance contained within these tagines immediately seduces, as the silky lamb and spiced couscous delight in all their classic Mediterranean goodness. Moroccan pastries end meals on a sweet note.

215 E. 4th St. (bet. Avenues A & B)
1 Av
(646) 869-1423 — **WEB:** www.chouchounyc.com
Dinner Tue - Sun

PRICE: $$

DONOSTIA

Spanish • Tapas bar

MAP: C3

You'll want to bring friends and graze your way through these Basque delights oh-so-slowly. Offering traditional tapas and pintxos, the menu at Donostia features small plates like delicate, cold water-brined boquerónes, drizzled with grapeseed oil and vinegar; or tender razor clams, laced with white bean purée, piment d'Espelette and lemon zest. The traditional tortilla with thinly sliced potatoes and mayonnaise is yet another big hit.

The minute you walk through the door, the dining room feels abuzz with excitement. A narrow row of tables tucked under the antique map of "Donostia" welcomes groups. Lone diners can snag a small perch facing Tompkins Square Park for people-watching, while others may head to the back to see dishes being plated as they eat.

155 Avenue B (bet. 9th & 10th Sts.)
1 Av
(646) 256-9773 — **WEB:** www.donostianyc.com
Dinner nightly

PRICE: $$

DOUBLE ZERO

Vegan • Contemporary décor

MAP: A3

There are wine bars and then there is this amazing concept from plant-based food guru, Matthew Kenney. But let's just dwell on this space for a moment. Outfitted with tall, communal tables, backlit wine shelves and artwork, the scene inside is sexy and urbane.

With his unique vision behind Double Zero, the chef contends he is "crafting the future of food." There is no dairy or meat here; and by the taste of things, no one is missing it either. A long, tantalizing lineup of low-gluten pizza and "not pizza" dominate the menu, along with occasional specials like wickedly good sweet potato cavatelli. A vegan cheese plate might feature creamy truffled cashew or almond ricotta. All chased down with exquisite organic wine? Food nirvana, indeed.

65 Second Ave. (bet 3rd & 4th Sts.)
Bleecker St
(212) 777-1608 — **WEB:** www.matthewkenneycuisine.com
Lunch Sat - Sun Dinner nightly

PRICE: **$$**

EDI & THE WOLF

Austrian • Rustic

MAP: C4

This is as much an Austrian heuriger (wine tavern) that one can find in New York. While the menu has some modern and creative elements, the décor is comprised of wood planks and thick coils of rope for an attractively barn-like feel. That cozy and disheveled character makes you forget where you are—same goes for the superb list of German and Austrian wines. On warm days, head to the equally pleasing and tiny back patio.

Most everyone knows to go for the schnitzel, served with potato salad, cucumbers and lingonberries. Still, you won't go wrong with a host of rustic small plates like crisped Brussels sprouts tossed in pork ragout with scallions and pickled mustard seeds, or perhaps roasted beets with pickled walnuts, walnut milk and dill.

102 Avenue C (bet. 6th & 7th Sts.)
1 Av
(212) 598-1040 — **WEB:** www.ediandthewolf.com
Lunch Sat - Sun Dinner nightly

PRICE: **$$**

FEAST

Contemporary • Cozy

MAP: B1

This straightforward but promisingly named East Village stalwart is a rustic and textbook amalgam of wood, brick and tiles. And the kitchen consistently offers several prix-fixe menus, served family-style. These might be based on specials from the farmer's market or even include a nose-to-tail meal of lamb, including merguez stew, as well as lasagna layering shank, broccoli rabe and goat cheese. If you're not up for a whole feast, dine à la carte on meaty, ocean-fresh oysters capped by cocktail sauce aspic; or a nouveau take on incredibly tender chicken and "dumplings," flaunting liver-stuffed pan-fried gnocchi and wisps of crisped skin.

End with the awe-inspiring Valrhona chocolate pudding—leaving a single dark chocolate cookie crumb behind is impossible.

102 Third Ave. (bet. 12th & 13th Sts.)
3 Av
(212) 529-8880 — **WEB:** www.eatfeastnyc.com
Lunch Sat - Sun Dinner nightly **PRICE:** $$

HASAKI

Japanese • Minimalist

MAP: A2

Since the mid-eighties, this local darling has been doing solid business thanks to its elevated ingredients, skilled kitchen and excellent value. For around $20, the soba lunch set will warm the heart of any frugal fan of Japanese cuisine. This feast unveils a bowl of green tea noodles in hot, crystal-clear dashi stocked with wilted water spinach and fish cake, accompanied by lean tuna chirashi, yellowtail and kanpyo. The ten-don, a jumbo shrimp tempura served over rice, is just as enticing. The à la carte offerings draw crowds seeking seasonal fish sourced from Japan as well as a host of tasty cooked preparations.

Diners who make their way into this minimalist dining room may choose to sit at one of their many wood tables or sizable counter.

210 E. 9th St. (bet. Second & Third Aves.)
Astor Pl
(212) 473-3327 — **WEB:** www.hasakinyc.com
Lunch Fri - Sun Dinner Tue - Sun **PRICE:** $$

HEARTH

Italian • Neighborhood

MAP: B2

Duck your head into this beloved old guard, its loyal patrons buzzing about as happy as ever, to get a sense of what the fuss is all about. This kitchen is still all about delicious Italian, yes, but now the ingredients are more carefully sourced, on the healthy side and with a deep commitment to GMO-free grains, less butter and no processed oils.

Chef Marco Canora's focus on vegetables, grains and brodi is a winning combo; make sure to begin with their warm whole-grain bread with creamy lardo. Then Sorana beans are braised to perfection with garlic and mackerel "bottarga;" while cured egg yolk and chervil tops carrot and beet tartare. Meat lovers take heart—Hearth's excellent maccheroni pork ragù, "variety burger," and meatballs are still available.

403 E. 12th St. (at First Ave.)
1 Av
(646) 602-1300 — **WEB:** www.restauranthearth.com
Lunch Sat - Sun Dinner nightly **PRICE:** $$$

HUERTAS

Spanish • Cozy

MAP: B3

Huertas is lovely—even lovelier than you might expect for its gritty location. The casual space is deep, with a long bar pouring cider or sherry, dedicated counter where a host of cured meats including jamón is sliced, and larger tables in the back.

The Basque-leaning menu showcases pintxos like stuffed and batter-fried squash blossoms, duck croquetas and skewers of white anchovies with olives and pickled peppers. The selection of conservas promises the type of fare that only the Spanish can do, as in zamburiñas in a complex tomato sauce with lemon, herbs and bread topped with a heavy drizzle of mayo. A handful of larger platos round out the menu with dishes like deep-fried porgy with toasted garlic, pickled chilies and manzanilla olives.

107 First Ave. (bet. 6th & 7th Sts.)
Astor Pl
(212) 228-4490 — **WEB:** www.huertasnyc.com
Lunch Sat - Sun Dinner nightly **PRICE:** $$$

HUNAN BISTRO

Chinese • Simple

MAP: B1

Delicious, lip-scorching and hearty Hunan food makes its way to the East Village and everyone's just a little bit happier for it. Nestled into a narrow space with dark wood paneling, industrial lighting and large planters, Hunan Bistro offers swift, but helpful service—and an all-together welcoming dining space for exploring this intriguing cuisine.

Dinner might kick off with such typical specialties as sour string beans sautéed with minced pork, chilies and toothsome konjac noodles. Next up: pork belly braised in their signature soy- rice wine- and star anise-broth, best eaten with greens and some soft, white rice. Finally, fish fillets dusted with cumin and set in a warm oil infused with toasted sesame hints at the raw firepower that is Hunan heat.

96 Third Ave. (bet. 12th & 13th Sts.)
3 Av
(212) 388-9855 — **WEB:** www.hunanbistrony.com
Lunch & dinner daily

PRICE: $$

HUNAN SLURP SHOP

Chinese • Contemporary décor

MAP: B3

When you consider the fact that the owner is an artist-turned-chef, it's no revelation that this long and slender East Village incomer is so beautifully conceived. Its décor boasts a modern aesthetic, cleverly incorporating the use of raw materials like exposed bulbs and wooden slats. That fused with a bit of great taste makes this one of the most sleek and affable spots downtown.

Suitably baptized, this "slurp shop" is a noteworthy destination for noodles—specifically mifen—which originally hail from Southwest China. Heartier appetites though will find much to savor in skewered cumin beef; or smoked pork and tofu slivers sautéed with garlic and scallions. Everyone should get the house-made salted chili oil to add a dose of flavor and spice.

112 First Ave. (bet. 6th & 7th Sts.)
1 Av
(646) 585-9585 — **WEB:** www.hunanslurp.com
Lunch & dinner Tue - Sun

PRICE: $$

JEWEL BAKO ✿

Japanese • Fashionable

MAP: A3

Only a discreetly marked door and tiny glass windows signal the entrance to this beloved sushi bijou. Once inside, you'll find a deeply elegant scene highlighting sloped bamboo slats that frame a row of beautifully plated, close-knit tables. There's a gorgeous blonde wood sushi bar in the back, while gentle jazz music plays in the background. The overall effect is very appealing and particularly serene. Service is excellent and begins at the door, with the reserved host carefully attending to your belongings. The waiters have an eagle eye for detail, managing to be so unobtrusive that you're able to enjoy intimate conversation.

You can choose from multiple options—pick from a wide variety of fish à la carte or leave it up to the talented chef by going with the fixed-price omakase. Either way, you're in for a culinary treat. The quality and seriousness of the kitchen remains excellent with each passing year, turning out exquisite dishes like seasonal lobster sashimi laced with ponzu—its head and innards later presented in a savory miso soup. The sashimi that follows is equally astounding, from the slicing technique to the fish quality, much of it seasonal and flown in directly from Japan.

---

239 E. 5th St. (bet. Second & Third Aves.)

Astor Pl

(212) 979-1012 — **WEB:** www.jewelbakosushi.com

Dinner Mon - Sat

PRICE: $$$

KAFANA

Eastern European • Simple

MAP: C3

If the Eastern European intelligentsia needed somewhere to plan a revolution or maybe just talk politics, they would meet here. Walls papered with Cyrillic newspapers set a deliciously covert scene, yet overall, the effect is inviting.

The menu highlights Serbian fare that is hard to find in Manhattan. That said, some specialties will seem familiar, like zeljanica, a buttery wedge of classic phyllo pie folded with chopped spinach, garlic, herbs and feta. Unique dishes feature dried prunes stuffed with crumbly cheese, rolled in chicken liver and bacon. Also try gently dredged and fried spearing fish, piled on butcher paper with urnebes dip. _evapi are the catchall for sausages from the same area and here they highlight finely ground pork with herbs.

116 Avenue C (bet. 7th & 8th Sts.)
1 Av
(212) 353-8000 — **WEB:** www.kafananyc.com
Lunch Sat - Sun Dinner nightly

PRICE: $$

KINGSLEY

Contemporary • Chic

MAP: C2

The crowds are clamoring for a table at this East Village charmer, and for good reason: Kingsley's splurge-worthy cuisine is sophisticated, surprising and delicious. And the cozy space makes for a rare oasis amid the neighborhood's raucous dining scene.

Featuring an interesting juxtaposition of flavors and textures while being reminiscent of classic fare, dinner here might begin with a ridiculously fresh summer bean salad starring cranberries, rattlesnake and Romano beans paired with bacon marmalade, crème fraîche and sautéed spicy greens. Razor clams, grilled ramps, fiddlehead ferns and earthy-sweet snails present a medley of interesting spring flavors, while hearty appetites will appreciate the Gloucester Spot pork with a swipe of creamy polenta.

190 Avenue B (bet. 11th & 12th Sts.)
1 Av
(212) 674-4500 — **WEB:** www.kingsleynyc.com
Lunch Sat - Sun Dinner Tue - Sun

PRICE: $$$

KANOYAMA ✿

Japanese • Rustic

MAP: B2

The spotlight shines here on the seriously talented Chef Nobuyuki Shikanai who commands the rear room's attention as he performs his magic before the few coveted seats along his omakase counter. Beyond this, the space has a row of tables where you might observe a group indulging in a tuna rib that appears large enough to have come from a cow: first sliced raw, then cooked to enjoy this incredible fish both ways.

Unlike the monastic atmosphere often found elsewhere, the mood here is celebratory and upbeat. The service team is swift and friendly even as they work in the shadow of their master.

Kanoyama's omakase is really the only way to experience Chef Shikanai's artistry. It's also profoundly personal, as he displays each morsel with cupped hands, to be taken with your fingers. Pieces are precisely crafted yet delicate and very beautiful in that traditional Edomae style. Overall, the meal is a progression from light and firm fish to vivid and buttery salmon and toro with exciting stops along the way, including cherry trout hakozushi (box-pressed) or jackfish with grains of Icelandic sea salt and a drizzle of lemon. Finish with an extraordinary block of cake-like tamago.

---

175 Second Ave. (at 11th St.)

3 Av

(212) 777-5266 — **WEB:** www.kanoyama.com

Dinner nightly

PRICE: $$$

KO

Contemporary • Trendy

MAP: A3

It's still salutary to make reservations for this dining room, where a handsome three-sided counter wrapped around the open kitchen entitles guests to a front row seat and an evening of culinary distinction. Each element just works so well here: from the judicious lighting that makes everything feel more sensual, to the music (never too intrusive but far from anodyne) and the delightful servers who appear ninja-style from nowhere to be at your side when you need something.

Completed dishes are handed over by the chefs, who may have perfected the bad boy/girl looks of the modern urban cook, but speak with unalloyed pride when they describe what you're about to eat. Flavors are refined yet assured, innovative yet expertly balanced, as in the buttery dry-aged Elysian Fields lamb basted in a fish liver and anchovy sauce. Tarte Tatin is brilliantly reworked with mandarin oranges and goat's milk Gouda shavings to offset the bitterness of the rinds.

The Ko Bar isn't just a pass-through on the way to the main arena; it's a complementary, yet entirely new way to experience Ko. It's also an about-face to the dining room's multi-course tasting menu, where you can pop in and order à la carte.

---

8 Extra Pl. (at 1st St.)

2 Av

(212) 500-0831 — **WEB:** www.momofuku.com

Lunch Fri - Sun Dinner Tue - Sat — **PRICE: $$$$**

KURA

Japanese • Minimalist

MAP: B3

From first glance, Kura is everything that a personal, well-run and very authentic Japanese restaurant should be. Inside, the master dons a traditional samue and greets each guest who approaches the L-shaped counter, as he begins to prepare the next course. Also find a few tables in the front of the room where groups manage to squeeze in.

The menu offers four different levels of omakase, beginning with the likes of braised fava beans; a whole stuffed squid brushed with a sweet-salty reduction; as well as rice topped with nori and ikura. Settle in to the ten-piece nigiri, presented as an array of hyper-seasonal fish dabbed with soy, gently torched or wrapped in cured cherry leaf. Finish with a familiar and delicious cube of chilled tamago and miso soup.

130 St. Marks Pl. (bet. Avenue A & First Ave.)
Astor Pl
(212) 228-1010 — **WEB:** N/A
Dinner Mon - Sat

PRICE: $$$$

LAVAGNA

Italian • Osteria

MAP: C3

The little menu at this neighborhood fixture proves that quality trumps size. Lavagna's kitchen is snug, but still manages to make ample use of a wood-burning oven to bake everything from delicate pizzette to whole roasted fish. Pastas are always a treat, while other tasty options can include pan-fried smoked scamorza paired with a roasted red pepper-topped crostini, juicy rack of lamb or a slice of spot-on crostata filled with seasonal fruit and dressed with caramel sauce.

Framed mirrors, a pressed-tin ceiling and candlelight produce a mood that is almost as warm as the genuinely gracious service, which ensures that regulars receive the royal treatment. That said, everyone who steps through these doors will feel welcome and well taken care of.

545 E. 5th St. (bet. Avenues A & B)
2 Av
(212) 979-1005 — **WEB:** www.lavagnanyc.com
Lunch Sat - Sun Dinner nightly

PRICE: $$

KYO YA ✿

Japanese • Intimate

MAP: B3

Tucked away down a discreet flight of steps in an unremarkable East Village building, it's easy to cruise right past Kyo Ya. But what a shame it would be to miss this brilliant jewel. If the mostly Japanese crowd doesn't tell you you're onto something special, the relentless charm and hospitality of the staff will win you over completely.

This is a cozy and intimate room with lots of polished wood and displays of lovely ceramics. A row of counter seats cuts down the middle of the space, along with a smattering of small tables. A six-seat counter at the back is reserved for those having the kaiseki menu.

Kyo Ya's dishes are delicate, exquisite and perfectly balanced. And as if that isn't enough, most of them use authentic, imported ingredients, which are not commonly found in domestic kitchens. The kaiseki, for example, might unveil a chewy kuruma-fu served in a winter melon soup bobbing with spicy pink peppercorns, mizuna and kinira ohitashi. Finally, the oshokuji course—presented in an earthenware pot full of earthy burdock root- and mushroom-steamed rice—is served with umami-rich miso pickled turnips, citrus pickled cabbage and grilled unagi for a true highlight.

---

94 E. 7th St. (bet. First Ave. & Avenue A)

Astor Pl

(212) 982-4140 – **WEB:** N/A

Dinner Wed - Sun

PRICE: $$$

LUZZO'S

Pizza • Neighborhood

MAP: B2

Ovest Pizzoteca, Da Mikele, Luzzo's and Luzzo's BK: you can't throw a stone without hitting one of the talented Michele Iuliano's restaurants these days, and for good reason. Nestled in the East Village, this original outpost of Luzzo's boasts a colorful exterior, treasured, century-old coal-burning oven that pushes out not only ace pizzas, but also Neapolitan classics like frusta, la quadrata and pizza fritta. The term pizzeria just doesn't do this lovely spot justice.

And judging by the patient crowds lined up outside, the neighborhood knows a good thing when they see it. Once inside, guests are treated to a charming interior of exposed brick, mismatched chairs and kitschy knickknacks. Soft Italian music plays beneath the happy hum of friends and family chatting.

211-13 First Ave. (bet. 12th & 13th Sts.)
1 Av
(212) 473-7447 — **WEB:** www.luzzosgroup.com
Lunch & dinner daily **PRICE: $$**

MÁLÀ PROJECT

Chinese • Trendy

MAP: B3

Add this delicious venture to the growing list of Chinese restaurants that are finally giving Manhattanites a chance to feast on spice levels once reserved for the outer boroughs. Inside MáLà Project's two rooms, find seating that includes a long, group-friendly communal table tucked into a nook, exposed brick walls, beautiful floors and big green leafy plants.

Dinner could go in any number of delicious directions, but a MáLà dry pot is really the best way to go. Diners are given a choice of ingredients—meat, poultry, seafood, vegetables, rice—and then asked for their desired degree of spiciness. A pot of lamb, bok choy, wood ear mushrooms, shrimp balls and chicken gizzards make their way into a wok with a fragrant "secret sauce" and complex spice oil.

122 First Ave. (bet. 7th St. & St. Marks Pl.)
1 Av
(212) 353-8880 — **WEB:** www.malaproject.nyc
Lunch & dinner daily **PRICE: $$**

MOMOFUKU NOODLE BAR

Asian • Minimalist

MAP: B2

This elder member of David Chang's culinary empire is hipper and hotter than ever. A honey-toned temple of updated comfort food, decked with wood counters and a sparkling open kitchen, the service here may be brisk. But rest assured, as the menu is gutsy and molded with Asian street food in mind.

Those steamed buns have amassed a gargantuan following thanks to decadent fillings like moist pork loin kissed with Hollandaise and chives. Additionally, that bowl of springy noodles doused in a spicy ginger-scallion sauce is just one instance of the crew's signature work. Korean fried chicken with seasonal greens is fit for a king; while more modest items, including desserts like candy apple truffle, are beautifully crafted and rightfully elevated to global fame.

171 First Ave. (bet. 10th & 11th Sts.)
1 Av
(212) 777-7773 — **WEB:** www.momofuku.com
Lunch & dinner daily

PRICE: $$

MOMOFUKU SSÄM BAR

Contemporary • Trendy

MAP: B2

Ssäm Bar is still very much a David Chang operation, but the chef in this kitchen is Singapore native and Ko alum, Max Ng. Under his realm, the menu is infused with all the spice and funk of genuine Southeast Asian cooking, and never holds back from delivering bold flavors and heat levels that can leave timid palates a bit, well, intimidated. It's the kind of memorable food that patrons crave and return for again and again.

Dive into a fluke crudo with shaved kimchi ice, before indulging in the spicy shell-on shrimp—crisp, garlicky, buttery and better than the best shrimp chip in town. While most hone in on the Southeast Asian specials, always keep room for sweets like pandan-flavored coconut-custard pie topped with lightly salted whipped coconut cream.

207 Second Ave. (at 13th St.)
3 Av
(212) 254-3500 — **WEB:** www.momofuku.com
Lunch & dinner daily

PRICE: $$

NOREETUH

Fusion • Cozy

MAP: B3

For a taste of something different, make a beeline to this unique Hawaiian-flavored spot. Headed by a trio of Per Se veterans, Noreetuh features an intimate setting of two slender dining rooms adorned with hexagonal mirrors and shelving units used to store bottles from the impressive wine list.

The kitchen turns out contemporary and sophisticated interpretations of Hawaiian cuisine. Classics like the humble musubi is elevated with the likes of pork jowl and beef tongue, while the parmesan cheese-topped Kalua pork cavatelli's richness is balanced by perfect portions of pickled cabbage. Imported ingredients such as shrimp from Kauai and the famous King's Hawaiian sweet bread are sure to invoke nostalgia among the expats.

Brunch is very popular.

128 First Ave. (bet. 7th St. & St. Marks Pl.)
Astor Pl
(646) 892-3050 — **WEB:** www.noreetuh.com
Lunch Sat - Sun Dinner Tue - Sun

PRICE: $$

ODA HOUSE

Central Asian • Simple

MAP: C3

For a taste of something different, the inviting Oda House serves up intriguing specialties from Georgia. The vibe is simple and rustic with pumpkin-stained walls, exposed brick and wood furnishings. Of course, this nation's proximity to Azerbaijan, Turkey and Armenia results in a vibrant and diverse cuisine.

A liberal use of spices, kebabs, khinkali (oversized meat-and-cheese dumplings), and khachapuri typify the kitchen's preparations. But, more classic dishes may reveal satsivi, or boiled chicken, served cool in a warmly spiced and seasoned walnut sauce, accompanied by gomi (hominy grits in a mini cauldron studded with rich and stretchy cheese).

Balance out this hearty feast with a bright garden salad perfectly dressed with green ajika sauce.

76 Avenue B (at 5th St.)
2 Av
(212) 353-3838 — **WEB:** www.odahouse.com
Lunch Fri - Sun Dinner nightly

PRICE: $$

OIJI

Korean • Minimalist

MAP: B3

Oiji's modern take on Korean dining is a reminder that this food is so much more than barbecue. Devoid of smoky tabletops, the dining room is small and attractive, with an open kitchen offering sneak peeks at the talented chefs as they prepare a cuisine rooted in culinary tradition, but with creative and refined touches.

Signature dishes do not disappoint, so try the wonderfully original pine-smoked mackerel, balancing the rich fish with citrus-soy sauce. Jang jo rim pairs soy-braised beef shank with radish kimchi, trumpet mushrooms and a soy egg atop buttered rice. Manila clams, squid and shrimp in a hot broth hit with minced black truffle is particularly enticing—crispy rice cakes on top soften up to become a sponge for its aromatic flavors.

119 First Ave. (bet. 7th St & St. Marks Pl.)
Astor Pl
(646) 767-9050 – **WEB:** www.oijinyc.com
Dinner nightly

PRICE: $$

PAPILLES

French • Contemporary décor

MAP: B3

Don't let the small space fool you. The elegant, contemporary dishes gliding on to tables at Papilles are going to knock your socks off. Four young owners comprise the team behind this hot spot, but their combined experience in the industry comes together to form culinary magic.

Chef/co-owner Andréa Calstier's dishes features stylish plating and careful cooking. If that's not enough, he also has a true knack for combining clear and complementary flavors. Dinner might begin with citrus-cured, sushi-grade mackerel, touched with heat and paired with an avocado-wasabi crèmeux, yuzu-crème fraîche and radish. Black Angus beef is then seared to perfection, before being served with anchovy-tarragon butter, beef jus and charred broccolini for an enriching plate.

127 E. 7th St. (bet. Avenue A & First Ave.)
Astor Pl
(646) 850-5345 – **WEB:** www.papillesrestaurant.com
Lunch Sat - Sun Dinner Tue - Sun

PRICE: $$$

PORSENA 

Italian • Trattoria

MAP: A2

It's a neighborhood darling, but make no mistake, Porsena is also a solid destination. Sarah Jenkins' menu reflects the chef/owner's passion for Italian cuisine, a fact further proven by her cookbooks on display out front.

Pasta is undoubtedly the star of the show, but guests would do well to also consider their endlessly creative appetizer menu or after-dinner drinks list. Speaking of the former, homemade orecchiette di grano arso is paired with artichokes, garlic and parmigiano for a decadent feast, while ravenous appetites can be seen relishing a perfectly charred skirt steak set over smashed fingerling potatoes and finished with a red wine reduction. Reservations are highly recommended as the space is small and stays packed for good reason.

21 E. 7th St. (bet. Second Ave. & Taras Shevchenko Pl.)
Astor Pl
(212) 228-4923 — **WEB:** www.porsena.com
Dinner nightly

PRICE: $$

PRUNE

Contemporary • Cozy

MAP: A3

This beloved neighborhood bistro won locals' hearts many moons ago, but Chef/owner/writer Gabrielle Hamilton's evolving talents keep them loyal. The tiny space packs a big punch—both for its sweet décor, which is surprisingly comfy to linger in, and for the kitchen's adventurous food. From greeting to check, Prune delivers the whole package—and consistently at that. Chef Hamilton's dishes are soulful and unpretentious. Savor tender stewed tripe Lyonnaise in a luxurious broth with carrots, celery and bay leaf; or perfectly poached chicken in a deliciously fatty and restorative stock with ham and oxtail. Guests can also watch the excitement unfold in the open kitchen while nursing a drink.

Nightly specials, listed on the chalkboard, are always worth perusing.

54 E. 1st St. (bet. First & Second Aves.)
2 Av
(212) 677-6221 — **WEB:** www.prunerestaurant.com
Lunch Sat - Sun Dinner nightly

PRICE: $$

PYLOS

Greek • Mediterranean décor

MAP: B3

Restaurateur Christos Valtzoglou has found the winning formula with this longstanding hideaway in the vibrant East Village. Pylos continues to sparkle as brightly as the Aegean Sea on a summer day. And, taking its name from the Greek translation of "made from clay," this contemporary taverna also features a ceiling canopy of suspended terra-cotta pots, dressing up a room with rustic whitewashed walls and lapis-blue insets.

Pale-green stemware and stark white crockery are used to serve Greek wines and a menu of rustic home-style cooking. Gigantes are baked in honey-scented tomato-dill sauce; grilled marinated octopus is drizzled with balsamic reduction; and aginares moussaka is a creamy vegetarian take on the classic, made here with artichokes.

128 E. 7th St. (bet. First Ave. & Avenue A)
Astor Pl
(212) 473-0220 — **WEB:** www.pylosrestaurant.com
Lunch Wed - Sun Dinner nightly **PRICE:** $$

SECCHU YOKOTA

Japanese • Intimate

MAP: B4

This bijou flies under the radar somewhat, and that's just the way their loyal fan base likes it. Those who understand the fine art of tempura know how pristine the quality is here, where diners are treated to a mouthwatering omakase featuring succulent red shrimp, Japanese eggplant, and meaty king crab. You probably won't need it, but a choice of lemon, wasabi salt and charcoal salt is provided as enhancements.

The man to thank for these treats is Chef Yokota, who takes his craft (and business) seriously, putting his clients first. Dining here is an intimate and deeply personal experience that highlights ingredients sourced mostly from Japan. As a bonus, his tempura is typically bookended by unique dishes that display his French culinary training.

199 E. 3rd St. (bet. Avenues A & B)
Essex St
(212) 777-1124 — **WEB:** www.secchuyokota.com
Dinner Mon - Sat **PRICE:** $$$$

SOBA-YA

Japanese • Neighborhood

MAP: B2

There are a ton of Japanese restaurants that line this stretch of the East Village, so why Soba-Ya? Why not Soba-Ya, its ultra-dedicated patrons would argue, for the buckwheat soba as well as the hearty udon on tap here are consistently off-the-charts good. Co-owner and mini-mogul, Bon Yagi, favors authenticity over flash in his establishments. And here he employs that traditional aesthetic to sweet perfection—along with a graceful, but simply appointed dining space; and quiet, well-timed service.

A meal might begin with uni and grated mountain yam, kissed with wasabi and crispy, toasted nori. Then, transition to a seasonal noodle dish like warm soba mingled with plump, pickled oysters, mountain yam, cilantro and tempura root vegetables.

229 E. 9th St. (bet. Second & Third Aves.)
Astor Pl
(212) 533-6966 — **WEB:** www.sobaya-nyc.com
Lunch & dinner daily **PRICE:**

SOMTUM DER

Thai • Simple

MAP: B3

Tucked along the fringes of Alphabet City, a little taste of authentic Isaan Thai awaits. Originally based out of Bangkok, the New York outpost of Somtum Der offers a cozy little enclave for the East Village set, stylishly accented with bright pops of red and a welcome glimpse of the kitchen's somtum station. There, you'll spy large glass jars of peanuts, dried red chilies and spices—the contents of which are ground by mortar and pestle to produce what some claim is the city's best green papaya salad.

Order big here, for the portions aren't massive and the food is so terrific you'll inevitably want more. The kitchen is happy to kick things up a notch, spice-wise, but you'll need to request the hotter end of the spectrum for greater authenticity.

85 Avenue A (bet. 5th & 6th Sts.)
2 Av
(212) 260-8570 — **WEB:** www.somtumder.com
Lunch & dinner daily **PRICE:** $$

SOOGIL

Korean • Minimalist

MAP: B3

Chef Soogil Lim earned his chops at the illustrious Daniel and humble Hanjan, so it should come as no surprise that this eponymous restaurant is peppered with references to fine dining. Having said that, this place is decidedly casual, with a neighborhood kind of vibe, comfortable setting and kitchen spotlighting modern Korean cooking.

Sharing is the way to go here, where the menu is categorized by Garden, Sea and Land with a handful of options in each. Hungry diners could easily order the entire menu especially if accompanied by friends, but make sure to hone in on such delights as the crispy sweet potato beignets, crisped pork belly and the perfectly seasoned Spanish mackerel—all of which show off creativity, skill and ingredient quality.

108 E. 4th St. (bet. First & Second Aves.)
2 Av
(646) 838-5524 — **WEB:** www.soogil.com
Lunch Sat - Sun Dinner nightly **PRICE:** $$

SUPPER

Italian • Neighborhood

MAP: B4

A meal at Supper promises the kind of fuss-free Italian cooking that true-blue New Yorkers keep in regular rotation. This competent kitchen succeeds in delivering comfort and consistency in spades (as well as to your door), but bring a stash of cash as settling up with credit cards isn't an option.

The open kitchen with its leaping flames is theatrical to say the least, but it's not all about show here. Twirl your fork into delicious pastas like spaghetti pomodoro, featuring a long-simmered sauce with chunky bits. Simply dressed spaghetti al limone is light and delicious, while daily specials include a breaded chicken cutlet with roasted potatoes. Mashed potatoes are fluffy and addictive, not unlike the inventive and enjoyable tiramisu.

156 E. 2nd St. (bet. Avenues A & B)
2 Av
(212) 477-7600 — **WEB:** www.supperrestaurant.com
Lunch Sat - Sun Dinner nightly **PRICE:** $$

TIMNA

Middle Eastern • Rustic

MAP: B3

Diners may end up arguing about which of Timna's appetizing and complex Middle Eastern dishes is the most memorable, but almost everything whipped up by Chef Nir Mesika will have you buzzing. Tucked below street level, this deep and narrow space features plenty of exposed brick, as well as a welcoming bar located up front.

Start with the addictive kubaneh, a Yemenite brioche-and-challah hybrid served with crushed tomato sauce, butter-thick yogurt and jalapeño salsa. For a refreshing treat, dive in to the Chinatown salad—glass noodles tossed with a pesto of fragrant herbs, palm sugar and fish sauce, then topped with crispy tempura green beans. Finish the evening with a yuzu tart featuring piña colada-panna cotta and sweet strawberry coulis.

109 St. Marks Pl. (bet. First Ave. & Avenue A)
Astor Pl
(646) 964-5181 — **WEB:** www.timna.nyc
Lunch Sat - Sun Dinner Tue - Sat **PRICE:** $$

UKIYO

Contemporary • Intimate

MAP: A3

Chef Marco Prins has taken over the dining room next to Jewel Bako (formerly the home of Degustation) and put together a menu that combines his personal story with his culinary experience—from Brooklyn Fare to Spain's acclaimed Martín Berasategui. This diminutive space is hardly enough to contain his talent, but the up close and personal vibe feels very downtown and tuned in.

Razor clams prepared with Indonesian-inspired accents speak to Chef Prins' Dutch heritage. Also a testament to his remarkable abilities are the pristinely prepared fish items. The five-course tasting menu is a great value, unveiling a beautifully composed striped bass with tom kha-inspired coconut sauce; and fried fish skins for an inspired and crunchy garnish.

239 E. 5th St. (bet. Second & Third Aves.)
Astor Pl
(212) 979-1012 — **WEB:** www.ukiyo-nyc.com
Dinner Tue - Sat **PRICE:** $$$

TUOME ✿

Fusion • Intimate

MAP: B3

Classically trained Chef Thomas Chen, who cut his teeth at some of New York City's finest kitchens before venturing out on his own, is the man to thank for the fabulous Tuome. The Asian-inspired menu is truly exciting, for Chen is a master at weaving together a surprising roster of delicious ingredients to craft a uniquely layered dish.

Tucked into a quiet street in Alphabet City, this cozy space is decked out with exposed brick walls behind the backlit bar, flower arrangements, and two large wooden-framed bay windows lined with plush purple seating. Service here, not unlike the room, is casual, unfussy and deeply knowledgeable.

Don't miss the crowd-pleasing but totally exquisite chicken liver, matched with maple syrup, toasted milk bread, pepitas and crispy chicken skin. Other noteworthy plates may include a pristine fluke crudo dressed in a coconut vinaigrette and paired with micro watercress as well as juicy little cubes of watermelon; or delectably tender octopus with textbook pommes aligot. A dessert of deep-fried buns arrives as a trio of Chinese "beignets" filled with delicious apple jam and accompanied by a scoop of creamy vanilla ice cream laced with red bean paste.

---

536 E. 5th St. (bet. Avenues A & B)
2 Av
(646) 833-7811 – **WEB:** www.tuomenyc.com
Dinner Mon - Sat

PRICE: $$

UOGASHI

Japanese • Neighborhood

MAP: B2

Uogashi is named for the first fish market in Japan, which was the precursor to Tsukiji and literally means "fish market." The décor is quite simple, featuring an expansive L-shaped bar, standard ceramics and imitation paper lanterns on the walls.

Expensive omakase counters may be taking over New York City, but this kitchen combats that trend by serving top-quality fish at affordable, everyday prices. Whether you order à la carte or go for one of the Edomae-style omakase menus, expect nothing but pristine quality from the skillfully crafted dishes. Cooked options, like the light and delicate chawanmushi, are just as well prepared. Refined palates also know to inquire about their seasonal specials—such treats are normally reserved for higher-end sushi-yas.

188 First Ave. (bet. 11th & 12th Sts.)
1 Av
(212) 253-0626 — **WEB:** www.uogashiny.com
Dinner Tue - Sun

PRICE: $$$

VIRGINIA'S

Contemporary • Chic

MAP: C3

Perfectly East Village in scale, this intimate and ambitious bistro named after Owner Reed Adelson's mother is composed of two slender rooms. These are unified by butterscotch-colored banquettes and whitewashed brick walls hung with vintage menus. Fine stemware and items presented on wooden boards lend an upscale manner to the experience.

The kitchen takes risks while building upon a steady foundation of timeless classics. A crostino of fava bean tapenade and shredded squash is a wonderful seasonal treat—best paired with an icy glass of rosé. Dry-aged and perfectly seasoned duck with maitake mushrooms and cherries is sauced with a vibrant pea pureé, while baby carrots arranged with a taste of sumac and feta offer a light but bright finish.

647 E. 11 St. (bet. Avenues B & C)
1 Av
(212) 658-0182 — **WEB:** www.virginiasnyc.com
Lunch Sat Dinner Tue - Sat

PRICE: $$

COFFEE

FINANCIAL DISTRICT

New York City's Financial District is home to some of the world's largest companies. Previously cramped with suits of all stripes, this buzzing business center is becoming increasingly residential thanks to office buildings being converted into condos and a sprouting culinary scene. Every day like clockwork, Wall Street warriors head to such venerable stalwarts as **Delmonico's** for their signature Angus boneless ribeye. If that's too heavy on the heart (or expense account), change course to **Industry Kitchen**, the lunch spot boasting a waterfront view and authentic wood-fired pizzas.

NOSTALGIC NIGHTS

At sundown, bring a picnic basket and catch the Shearwater for a memorable sail around Manhattan. Alternatively, step aboard **Honorable William Wall**, the floating clubhouse of the Manhattan

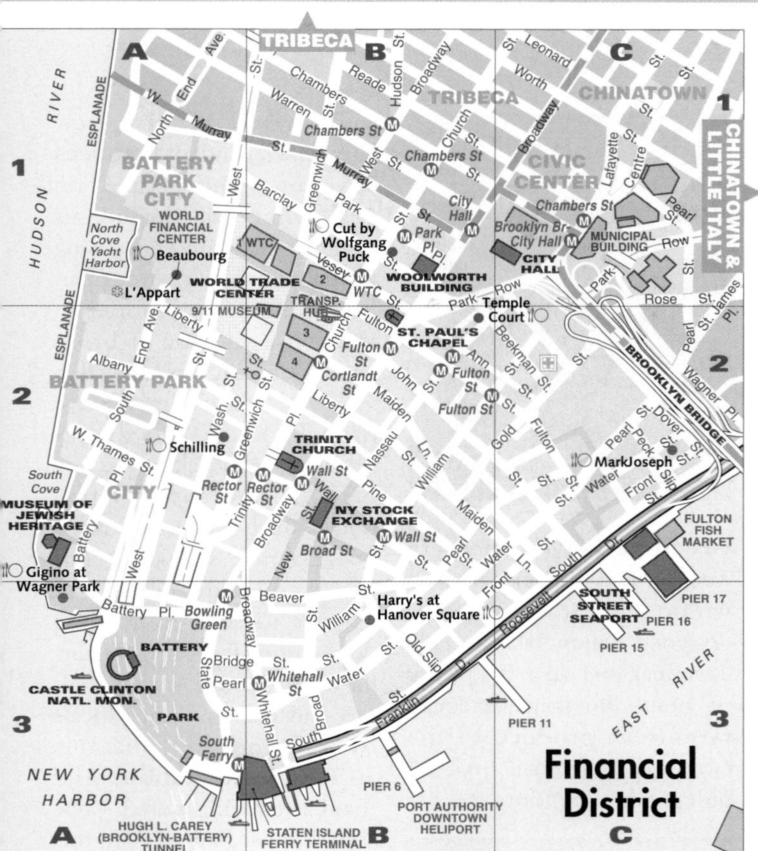

Yacht Club, anchored in the New York harbor from May through October every year. Not only does this stunning platform let you get up, close and personal with Lady Liberty herself, but it also proffers a stellar view of the evening sailboat races. Of course, don't forget to have a drink while you're at it! Every year as summer approaches, weekend trips to Governor's Island—a lush parkland featuring playing fields and hills—are not just popular but make for a wonderful escape among families and friends alike. Recuperated public markets also point to the residential boom in this neighborhood. Case in point: the burgeoning **Staten Island Ferry Whitehall Terminal**

Greenmarket (open every Tuesday and Friday) is housed within the large and well-designed Staten Island Ferry Terminal, and deserves plenty of praise for sourcing local, farm-fresh produce to the community from a host of independent vendors.

BARS & BEVVIES GALORE

During the weekdays, restaurants downtown seem to go into buzzing mode with finance wizzes drowning their worries in martinis, and reviewing portfolios over burgers and beer. One of the neighborhood's largest tourist draws, **South Street Seaport**, is flanked by a collage of fantastic eateries and convivial, family-friendly bars. The legendary **Fraunces Tavern** is a fine specimen on Pearl Street that includes a restaurant and museum paying homage to early American history. While they proffer an impressive selection of brews and cocktails, crowds also gather here for comprehensive brunch, lunch and dinner specials. Every self-respecting New Yorker loves happy hour, which is almost always buzzing here with 130 craft beers and ciders to boot. Thanks to such flourishing destinations, buttoned-up suits have learned to loosen their ties and chill out with locals over the creative libations at **The Dead Rabbit**. And thanks to being voted "The World's Best Bar" in 2016 this delightful watering hole has been drawing city slickers to Water Street as much for the specialty cocktails as for their well-conceived setting and small plates. If the ground floor's sawdust proves too rustic for your taste, head up to **The Parlor** for a whiff of elegance. While here, take a moment to relish some of their homemade punch before perusing the cocktail menu—a work of art in and of itself. Then chase down its American bar menu with that classic drink of choice (beer, of course) at South Street's **Watermark Bar**. Speaking of bars, revelers may also lounge in style at the **Living Room Bar + Terrace**, accommodated in the sleek **W Hotel,** and accoutered with lofty windows set above specially designed seats that afford unobstructed views of the glimmering skyline. By cooking up classic plates in conjunction with a litany of enticing martinis, this spot remains a coveted summer venue for concerts, corporate events and other such occasions.

BITES ON-THE-GO

Jamaican food sensation **Veronica's Kitchen** carries on the food-cart craze in the FiDi with its spectrum of flavorful Caribbean classics. Locals never seem to tire of the food here, and return on the regular for smoky and deliciously tender jerk chicken. Similarly, carb lovers rejoice at **Adrienne's Pizzabar**'s brick oven pies and other Italian delights, after which **Financier Patisserie** is a dream for tantalizing sweets. Top these off with a steaming cuppa' joe at one of the many vendors nearby and heave a satisfied sigh. Even food-focused events like the **Stone**

Street Oyster Festival play to this area's strengths—what better way to lift your spirits and celebrate the local Blue Point harvest in September than by slurping up oysters, outdoors on narrow, sinuous and charming Stone Street? Located in the shadows of the monumental and glitzy World Trade Center is **Hudson Eats**—a substantial food court complete with a notable lineup of nibbles and sips. If visions of a prime beef short rib stroganoff come to mind, you have arrived in the right place. The **Eataly** brand continues to mushroom with a downtown location at 4 World Trade Center; and **Osteria della Pace**, the emporium's pretty dining room nestled in its own corner, offers a welcome respite from shopping and sightseeing. Finally, custom pastries, coffee and cake from **Le District** (in Brookfield Place) deliver much decadence to the local palate by way of unique fillings, frostings and flavors. Even chocolate lovers are welcome here to gorge on truffles, nougats, toffee and biscuits.

BEAUBOURG

French • Brasserie

MAP: A1

Talk about a room with a view. As part of the French market, Le District, Beaubourg sits on the banks of the Hudson, facing a wide promenade and a beautiful row of yachts. Diners linger over crisp French wine and excellent cheeses, soaking in the scene. It's a picture postcard in the making, but this brasserie is more than just a pretty face.

Start with phenomenal house-made charcuterie—from the velvety foie gras to the dense terrines and creamy pâté de campagne, everything is luscious. The wonderful steak tartare, dressed with anchovy, briny capers and a tiny, quivering quail egg, arrives with crispy pommes gaufrettes; and entrées like perfectly roasted chicken and delicate Dover sole in lemon butter make for a refined and elegant finish.

225 Liberty St. (at West St.)
World Trade Center
(212) 981-8588 — **WEB:** www.ledistrict.com/beaubourg
Lunch & dinner daily **PRICE:** $$$

CUT BY WOLFGANG PUCK

Steakhouse • Contemporary décor

MAP: B1

Wolfgang Puck shot to fame after opening LA's Spago in 1982, and it wasn't long before he reached megabrand status. CUT by Wolfgang Puck is by far his most expansive venture, with six outposts spanning the globe. This Manhattan locale is tucked at the base of the swanky downtown Four Seasons Hotel, and sports a fittingly elegant look with deep magenta chairs, floor-to-ceiling marigold draperies and lovely artwork from the chef's private collection.

Kick things off with Puck's signature tuna tartare studded with ginger, avocado and shallots, then brought to elegant new heights with wasabi aïoli, more avocado and togarashi crisps. Wagyu arrives charred to caramelized perfection, sporting a gorgeous rosy medium-rare center and graced by béarnaise.

99 Church St. (bet. Barclay St. & Park Pl.)
Chambers St (Church St.)
(646) 880-1995 — **WEB:** www.wolfgangpuck.com
Lunch & dinner daily **PRICE:** $$$$

GIGINO AT WAGNER PARK

Italian • Mediterranean décor

MAP: A3

To find food this tasty in a rather touristy neck of the woods is a welcome surprise. A setting that boasts views of the Statue of Liberty, Ellis Island and Hudson River is unique enough that they could probably get away with less than this very good Italian-ish food.

In warmer months, the best seats are out on the patio amid blinking harbor lights and a gorgeous vista. A tastefully subdued dining room and unpretentious service make it a pleasant place to while away an evening.

This is a kitchen that cuts no corners, especially in the superb potato gnocchi coated in a silky tomato ragù with braised meatballs. Melanzane alla Sorrentina features layers of mozzarella, basil, chunky tomato sauce and thick slices of fried eggplant.

20 Battery Pl. (in Wagner Park)
Bowling Green
(212) 528-2228 – **WEB:** www.gigino-wagnerpark.com
Lunch & dinner daily **PRICE:** $$

HARRY'S AT HANOVER SQUARE

Steakhouse • Chic

MAP: B3

You can't shake a stick in the Financial District without hitting a steakhouse, so it takes a lot to turn heads in these parts. Harry's, however, stands apart from the pack in the best way possible—by offering prime cuts of meat (aged in-house), and then cooking them to unadorned excellence. A vast, well-executed menu showcasing seafood and more, as well as a revamped cocktail program only up their status.

Located on the ground floor of the historic Hanover Bank building, the stunning and entirely redone interior now features original artwork and booths cloaked in leather. The front bar flaunts a more casual vibe and is ideal for a quick bite with friends, while the stylish dining room complete with a wine vault and art installation necessitates lingering.

1 Hanover Sq. (at Stone St.)
Wall St (William St.)
(212) 785-9200 – **WEB:** www.harrysnyc.com
Lunch & dinner Mon - Sat **PRICE:** $$$$

L'APPART 

French • Intimate

MAP: A1

Secreted within the sprawling food hall of Le District, L'Appart is not so much a dining room as a crown jewel. Designed to resemble a Parisian apartment—hence its name—a meal here feels like attending a dinner party, albeit one with potentially 28 guests. You will be handed a drink as soon as you enter and are thereafter introduced to affable chef, Nicolas Abello.

Comprised of everything that its surrounding boulangerie, fromagerie, poissoinnerie and boucherie can offer, it's clear that this kitchen is intent on pushing the traditional barriers of classic French cuisine. The staff is genuinely warm and quite keen to please.

From then on, things settle down into a more recognizable format. The set menu kicks off with artistic little canapés that warm up your taste buds. Imagine lobster tartare with dashi gelée or a parmesan-and Chantilly-filled round of pâte à choux. Then it's on to the lineup of dishes, made using all manner of modern technique, like the foie gras torchon with candied chestnut purée, or Colorado lamb enhanced by a bold mojo-seasoned sauce. These flavors may be unapologetically rich but are always on point—not unlike the creamy jasmine rice pudding kissed with pear sorbet.

---

225 Liberty St. (at West St.)

World Trade Center

(212) 981-8577 — **WEB:** www.lappartnyc.com

Dinner Tue - Sat

PRICE: $$$$

MARKJOSEPH

Steakhouse • Contemporary décor

MAP: C2

Well positioned on a historic and touristy stretch to attract diners from near and far, MarkJoseph is more approachable than the clubby competition, but rest assured that these steaks are treated with the utmost care. The dining room looks rather masculine, flaunting chairs with plush fabric and dark brown pinstripes.

This is the kind of place where the namesake salad does away with lettuce, leaving a refreshing combo of poached shrimp, porky bits of lardons, string beans and beefsteak tomatoes. Meticulously chosen, aged and cooked steak, often served sizzling on platters for two or more, is what distinguishes this dedicated and skilled kitchen. Most meals here may be bookended by seafood platters and unapologetically decadent desserts.

261 Water St. (bet. Peck Slip & Dover St.)
Fulton St
(212) 277-0020 — **WEB:** www.markjosephsteakhouse.com
Lunch Mon - Fri Dinner nightly **PRICE: $$$**

SCHILLING

Austrian • Rustic

MAP: A2

Thanks to reclaimed wood, vintage lighting and a garage door façade, Chef Eduard Frauneder's sweet little spot has been cleverly designed to not look too designed. It's a good choice for a date, the choice of area notwithstanding; and the communal table in the middle, used mostly for walk-ins, adds to its affability.

It's an Austrian restaurant but an Austrian who likes to head south for the holidays, so along with the perennial Viennese classics are others inspired by the sunnier climes of the Med. For every spätzle there's homemade orecchiette; for every Wiener schnitzel, roasted branzino; and you can even trade your apple strudel for panna cotta. The kitchen has an assured yet light touch and judicious pricing means you'll still have some schillings left.

109 Washington St. (bet. Carlisle & Rector Sts.)
Rector St
(212) 406-1200 — **WEB:** www.schillingnyc.com
Lunch Mon - Fri Dinner nightly **PRICE: $$$**

TEMPLE COURT

French • Vintage

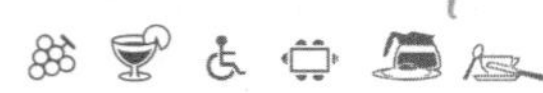

MAP: B2

Tucked inside the Financial District's Beekman Hotel, which marries old-school glamour with modern indulgences, Temple Court is a stunning spot long on charm with a cozy atmosphere. The luxe dining room finds its match in ceiling-high stained glass windows, but the Bar Room is worthy of an early arrival (or extended departure) simply for the chance to ogle the impressive nine-level atrium.

This culinary and architectural feat hails from the Colicchio restaurant family, and Chef Carlos Benedicto composes French-inspired dishes with Mediterranean twists. Think of beef bourguignon with dry-aged sirloin and braised short ribs, or ricotta agnolotti with peas, ramps, spring garlic and earthy morel mushrooms.

Lunch is a particulary good value.

5 Beekman St. (bet. Nassau St. & Theater Alley)
Park Place
(212) 658-1848 — **WEB:** www.templecourtnyc.com
Lunch & dinner daily **PRICE:** $$$$

The symbol indicates a private dining room option.

GRAMERCY, FLATIRON & UNION SQUARE

Anchored around the residents-only Gramercy Park, this neighborhood of the same name is steeped in history, classic beauty and tranquility. Even among thoroughbred New Yorkers, most of whom haven't set foot on its private paths, the park's extreme exclusivity is the stuff of legend—because outside of the residents whose homes face the square, Gramercy Park Hotel guests are among the few permitted entrance.

Bounded by touristy Union Square and the fashionably edgy Flatiron District, Gramercy is a quiet enclave that boasts of beautiful brownstones, effortlessly chic cafés, artisanal restaurants and haute hotels. Channel your inner Dowager Countess of Grantham as you nibble on dainty finger sandwiches at the super-chic **Lady Mendl's Tea Salon**, a Victorian-style parlor tucked inside the Inn at Irving Place. Stroll a few blocks only to discover assorted pleasures at Maury Rubin's **The City Bakery**, a popular haunt for fresh-baked pastries and—in true New York City style—pretzel croissants. Old-timers love the warm chocolate babka from **Breads Bakery** and

Mediterranean delights from **Lamazou**. For those who like a bit of spice, trek a few blocks north to **Curry Hill**, where restaurants focused on the greasy takeout formula reside alongside such choice ingredient paradises as **Foods of India**. After combing its aromatic shelves, head on over to nearby **Kalustyan's**, an equally celebrated spice emporium showcasing exceptional products like orange blossom water and some thirty-plus varieties of dried whole chilies. Moving across the pond to Italy, **Todaro Brothers** is a modest grocer proffering an array of gourmet cheeses, imported goodies and deli items since 1917. From humble eats and heavenly American treats to great Gallician bites, **Hill & Bay**, **Moonstruck East**, as well as **Vino Tapa** are all key to this local culinary scene.

FLATIRON DISTRICT

Named after one of the city's most notable buildings, the Flatiron District is a commercial center-turned-residential mecca. Engulfed with trendy clothing boutiques and chic eateries, the area today is a colorful explosion of culture and shopping. A few blocks to the west is Madison Square Park with its own unique history and welcoming vibe. Ergo, it is only fitting that visitors here are greeted by the original outpost of burger flagship, **Shake Shack**, serving its signature fast food from an ivy-covered kiosk. While burgers and Chicago-style dogs are all the rage, it is their house-made custard that has patrons fixated and checking the online "custard calendar" weekly for favored flavors. Tourists looking to trend it up should hang with the cool

kids at the Ace Hotel who take their sip from **Stumptown Coffee Roasters** to savor in the hipster-reigning lobby. The equally nifty NoMad Hotel is home to Gotham's first **sweetgreen** and socialites watching their waistline along with "Silicon Alley" staffers can't get enough of their cold-pressed juices, salads and frozen yogurt. A long way from clean tastes, barbecue addicts remain committed to the **Big Apple Barbecue Block Party** held every June. This weekend-long fiesta features celebrity pit masters showing off their "smoke" skills to hungry aficionados. Another frequented spectacle is **Eataly NYC Flatiron**. Originally founded in 2007 in Turin (Italy) by Oscar Farinetti, it was the first outpost in Manhattan. This *molto* glam marketplace incorporates everything Italiano under one roof, including a dining hall with delicious eats, regional specialties and aromatic food stalls.

UNION SQUARE

Nearby Union Square is a formidable historic landmark characterized by a park with tiered plazas that host political protests and rallies. Today it may be best known for its **Greenmarket**—held on Mondays, Wednesdays, Fridays and Saturdays—heaving with a spectrum of seasonal produce. Beyond the market, find some fine wine to complement your farm-to-table meal from **Union Square Wines & Spirits**, or even **Italian Wine Merchants**. Further evidence of this piazza's reputation as a culinary center is the flourishing presence of **Whole Foods** and the city's very first **Trader Joe's** —both of which are set within just blocks of each other.

YOU DESERVE TO WAKE UP HAPPY
jcpenney

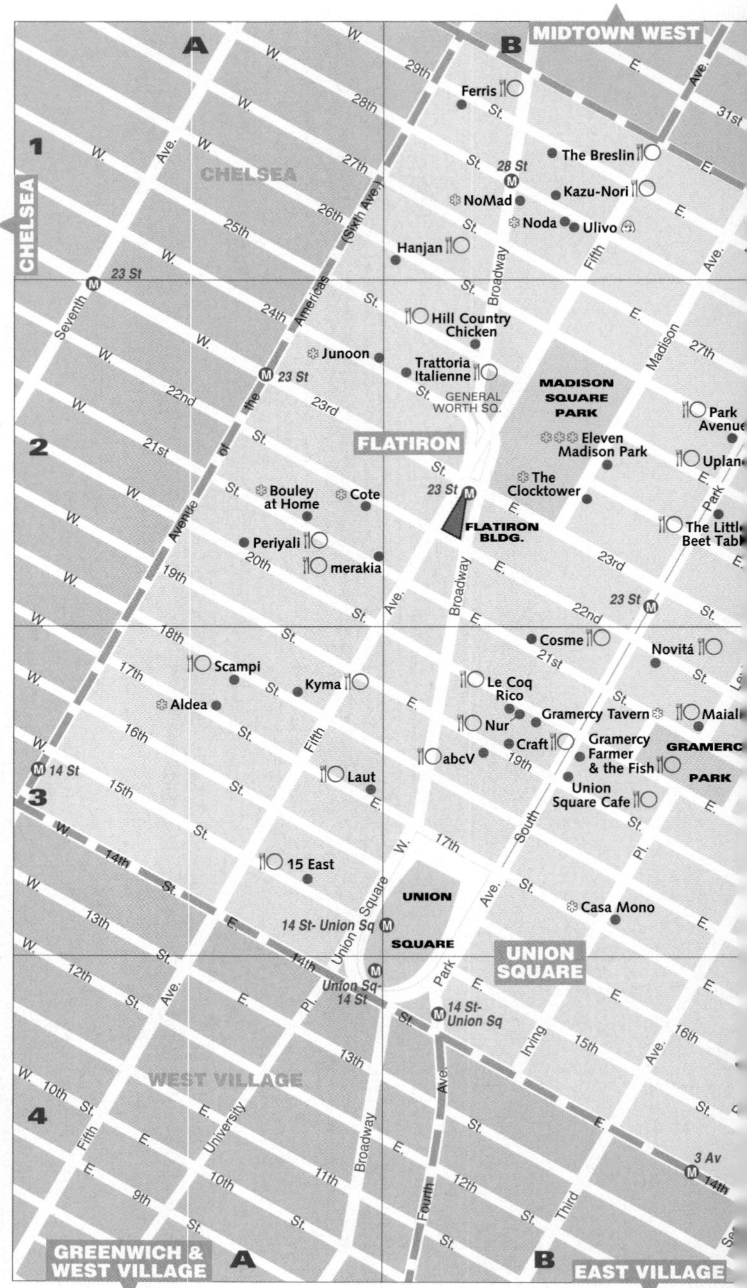
MIDTOWN WEST
CHELSEA
FLATIRON
MADISON SQUARE PARK
GENERAL WORTH SQ.
FLATIRON BLDG.
UNION SQUARE
GRAMERCY PARK
WEST VILLAGE
GREENWICH & WEST VILLAGE
EAST VILLAGE
Ferris
The Breslin
Kazu-Nori
NoMad
Noda
Ulivo
Hanjan
Hill Country Chicken
Junoon
Trattoria Italienne
Eleven Madison Park
The Clocktower
Park Avenue
Bouley at Home
Cote
Periyali
merakia
Cosme
Novitá
Scampi
Kyma
Aldea
Le Coq Rico
Gramercy Tavern
Nur
Craft
abcV
Gramercy Farmer & the Fish
Laut
Union Square Cafe
15 East
Casa Mono
28 St
23 St
14 St
14 St- Union Sq
Union Sq- 14 St
3 Av
Broadway
Fifth Ave.
Madison
Avenue of the Americas (Sixth Ave.)
Seventh Ave.
Park Ave. South
Irving Pl.
University Pl.
Union Square W.
Fourth Ave.
Third Ave.

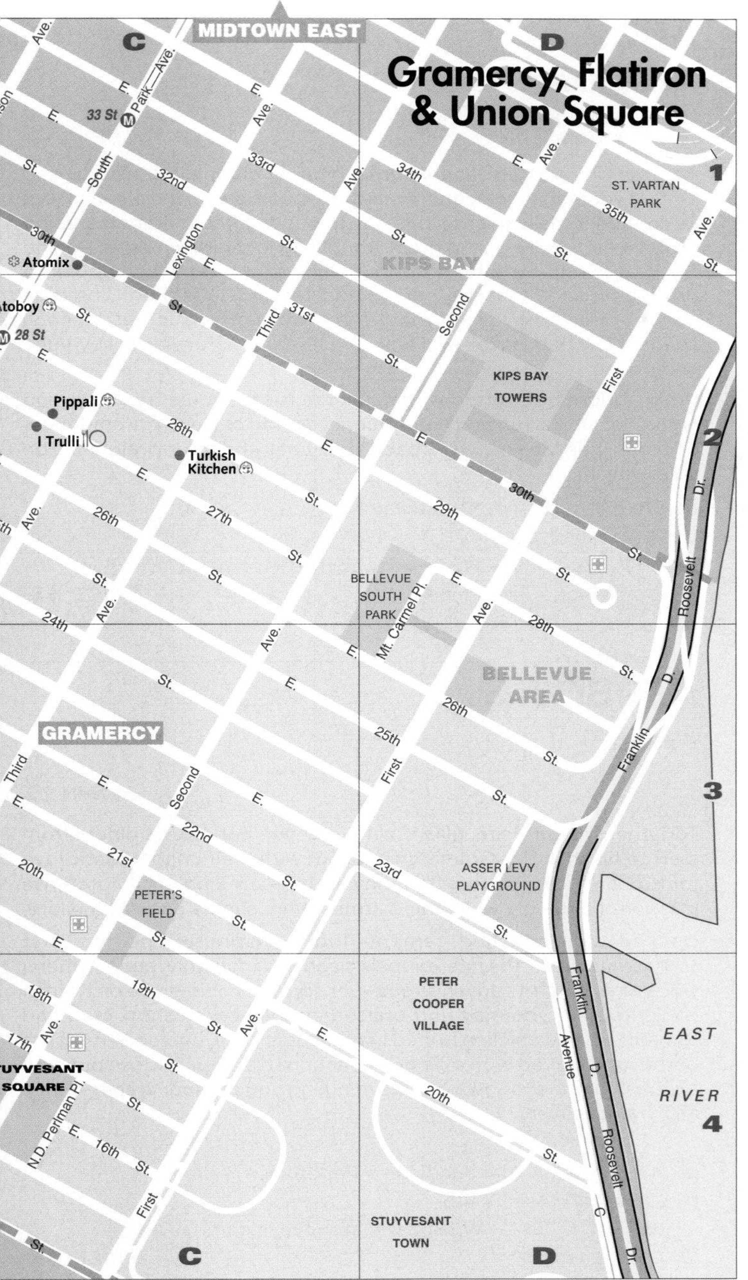
MIDTOWN EAST
Gramercy, Flatiron & Union Square
C
D
1
2
3
4
33 St
28 St
Atomix
Pippali
I Trulli
Turkish Kitchen
KIPS BAY
KIPS BAY TOWERS
ST. VARTAN PARK
BELLEVUE SOUTH PARK
BELLEVUE AREA
GRAMERCY
PETER'S FIELD
ASSER LEVY PLAYGROUND
PETER COOPER VILLAGE
STUYVESANT TOWN
EAST RIVER
Mt. Carmel Pl.
N.D. Perlman Pl.
Franklin D. Roosevelt Dr.
Franklin D. Roosevelt Dr.
Avenue
Lexington
Park Ave. South
Third Ave.
Second Ave.
First Ave.
E. 34th St.
E. 35th St.
E. 33rd St.
E. 32nd St.
E. 31st St.
E. 30th St.
E. 29th St.
E. 28th St.
E. 27th St.
E. 26th St.
E. 25th St.
E. 24th St.
E. 23rd St.
E. 22nd St.
E. 21st St.
E. 20th St.
E. 19th St.
E. 18th St.
E. 17th St.
E. 16th St.

ABCV

Vegetarian • Design

MAP: B3

Another offspring in Jean-Georges Vongerichten's ABC family, and his first vegetarian restaurant, may have been long in the planning but its confidence is writ large: this isn't about vegetables impersonating protein—it's about giving them star billing in their own right. Behind the glass wall, his kitchen uses plenty of modern techniques to produce dishes that are perky, colorful and satisfying. The best options are those of international provenance, such as spinach spaghetti with broccoli and kale; and creamy tofu with crispy yuba and ponzu.

White, bright but dotted with color, the room shouts freshness and vigor; the vibe is fun and hearteningly devoid of New Age smugness or pious worthiness. Just check your coat and your prejudices on your way in.

38 E. 19th St. (bet. Broadway & Park Ave. South)

14 St - Union Sq

(212) 475-5829 — **WEB:** www.abchome.com/eat/abcv

Lunch Mon - Fri Dinner nightly **PRICE:** $$

ATOBOY

Korean • Trendy

MAP: C2

Together with his wife, Ellia, Chef Junghyun Park wows diners from start to finish at this Gramercy hot spot with their unapologetic love for Korean food. The fact that they eschew any kind of city pretense in favor of a deeply welcoming atmosphere simply adds to the lure.

Decked with polished cement floors, distinctive posters and communal tables, the interior feels clean and industrial, and the menu woos diners with its adventurous—yet approachable—take on Korean cooking. Here you may find braised eggplant with snow crab and tomato; or fried chicken brined in pineapple juice, coated in tempura batter, and served with a ginger-peanut butter sauce. Close out with a refreshing sujeonggwa granité mingling yogurt, sour cream, honey and walnut slivers.

43 E. 28th St. (bet. Madison & Park Aves.)

28 St (Park Ave. South)

(646) 476-7217 — **WEB:** www.atoboynyc.com

Dinner nightly **PRICE:** $$

ALDEA ❀

Mediterranean • Contemporary décor

MAP: A3

With a name that means "village" in Portuguese, Aldea strives to recreate a sunny, coastal clime via those bleached wood accents and blue seats scattered throughout its narrow space. The first-floor open kitchen adds a sense of liveliness to the room, while the second floor is quieter and more intimate for a date. Both fill with stylish couples and groups who appear to delight in a petisco or two before beginning their meals.

This menu is best enjoyed as a four- or seven-course prix-fixe grounded in the tastes and traditions of Portugal as well as the Iberian peninsula. However, Chef George Mendes continues to find inspiration from afar, as evident in dishes integrating the flavors of shiso, kombu and Meyer lemon.

Every item tastes bright and good, as it appears beautiful yet sensible and never fussy on your plate. The outstanding sauce of lemon, garlic and pimentón that bathes the shrimp alhinho is an example of the flawless balance that this talented kitchen is able to strike time and again. Still, the most clever plate of the night may just be the duck breast, cooked a la plancha and coupled with quince, pear and shaved black truffle for a bit of earthiness and whole lot of luxury.

---

31 W. 17th St. (bet. Fifth & Sixth Aves.)

14 St - 6 Av

(212) 675-7223 — **WEB:** www.aldearestaurant.com

Dinner Tue - Sat **PRICE:** $$$$

ATOMIX

Korean • Design

MAP: C1

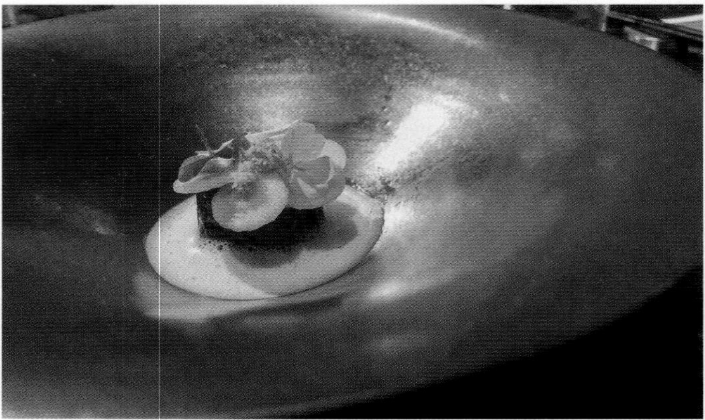

Chef Junghyun Park's latest Gramercy offering is upscale, sophisticated, beautifully designed and capable of elevating Korean dining to a new level. Guests are first welcomed into the restrained lounge for tasty canapés, before moving on to a seat at the luxurious counter. Everything manages to be high-end but also cool and youthful.

The night's meal is communicated to the diner via custom-designed cards that explain each course and underline key ingredients and techniques. Look out for their house-pressed oils, Korean soy sauce and rice polished in-house. Banchan are reconceived with contemporary twists, as in the outstanding oyster poached in kimchi juice, or a little box presenting whelk, mushrooms and braised tofu. Binchotan grilling plays a definitive role during parts of the meal, and that technique reaches its apex in the whole Spanish turbot—which is grilled, then braised in dried seafood stock, presented to diners, and finally returned to the kitchen to plate its supremely tender and flaky morsels.

Skill and talent carries through to dessert, culminating in a rice pudding cooked with heavy cream and drizzled with intense green honey infused with pickled spruce tips.

---

104 E. 30th St. (bet. Park & Lexington Aves.)

28 St (Park)

N/A — **WEB:** www.atomixnyc.com

Dinner Tue - Sat

PRICE: $$$$

BOULEY AT HOME

Contemporary • Design

MAP: A2

Fans of the acclaimed chef will instantly recognize the unmistakable trademark marking the entrance to Bouley at Home—a progressive and ingenious concept from the chef extraordinaire himself—David Bouley. His multi-dimensional and highly refined "home" is no small feat, showcasing a foyer scented with apple-lined walls and dining room with display kitchens as well as a cooking school. As they say, go big or go home.

The polished main room may be brightly lit, and at times, noisy, but a seat at one of the three counters will put you eye-to-eye with the team in action. The chefs are the servers here, and there's ample communication about the cuisine. If you're intrigued by a dish, you can even learn how to make it in the on-site kitchen.

As for the cuisine itself, Chef Bouley has always managed to integrate his philosophy of nutrition and healing into his food, and here he does it again with great ease. Dinner might begin with a soothing porcini mushroom flan topped with Alaskan Dungeness crab. Then move on to eggplant terrine tucked with a purée of red bell peppers, before closing out over Long Island duck breast set over polenta and paired with pruneaux d'Agen-studded wild rice.

---

31 W. 21st St. (bet. Fifth & Sixth Aves.)
23 St (Broadway)
(212) 255-5828 — **WEB:** www.davidbouley.com
Lunch & dinner Tue - Sat

PRICE: $$$

THE BRESLIN

Gastropub • Pub

MAP: B1

This sleek English taproom in the Ace Hotel has been painstakingly crafted to replicate the décor of a proper British pub, complete with dark leather banquettes, distressed wood floors and bits of flea market-chic striving to imply timelessness. It remains as popular today as it was upon opening. Service is either wonderfully attentive or totally uneven.

Menu attractions include the winter citrus salad of cool, juicy segments doused in olive oil with sprinkles of dry mint—it all comes together to taste like a trip to the Mediterranean. The Scotch egg is, of course, its own New York classic: deep-fried with a runny yolk encased in sausage, then halved and served with cornichons and chili ketchup. As you might expect, the fries here are also a big hit.

16 W. 29th St. (bet. Broadway & Fifth Ave.)
28 St (Broadway)
(212) 679-1939 – **WEB:** www.thebreslin.com
Lunch & dinner daily

PRICE: $$$

COSME

Mexican • Contemporary décor

MAP: B3

Donning a hip and urbane demeanor, Chef Enrique Olvera's Cosme is a cherished destination. This contemporary space features a sleek and handsome bar up front that pours a litany of stirring cocktails. Then add in the roomy dining tables and soft lighting to its playful Mexican food, and you have quite a winning formula.

One glance at the menu will also tell you why this kitchen headed by Daniela Soto-Innes is so beloved. Duck enmoladas draped with mole rojo and crowned by crème fraîche is the very picture of temptation; while a tostada with creamy avocado, uni and bone marrow salsa is, fittingly, a big hit. This cooking is clever, and, at times, surprisingly delicate. Even desserts like churros with Mexican hot chocolate offer serious bursts of flavor.

35 E. 21st St. (bet. Broadway & Park Ave. South)
23 St (Park Ave. South)
(212) 913-9659 – **WEB:** www.cosmenyc.com
Lunch & dinner daily

PRICE: $$$$

CASA MONO ✿

Spanish • Tapas bar

MAP: B3

There's something reassuring about a kitchen that gets in whole beasts and does its own butchery— you just know it understands the essence of what good cooking is all about and that their creations will be borne out of a love of food, not balance sheets.

Here at the small, but perfectly formed Casa Mono, dishes are designed for sharing but are big enough to do so, and there are none of those one-bite-and-it's-gone plates that blight so many places these days. Nor do they arrive in a stampede at your table. Instead, they are sent out in a sensible and well-paced order for the benefit of the diner rather than the convenience of the kitchen. Having said that, with so many appealing items on the menu, it's very easy to over-order.

The kitchen is nominally influenced by the Costa Brava, but rest assured that its reach is far greater than that and the tapas are far more sophisticated than they pretend to be. Creamy scrambled eggs with uni is a must; caramelized scallops come with a well-balanced green curry; confit goat will make you question why you don't see more of it on other menus; and the spiced lamb sausages really pack a flavor punch. This is food to cure what ails you.

---

52 Irving Pl. (at 17th St.)

14 St - Union Sq

(212) 253-2773 – **WEB:** www.casamononyc.com

Lunch & dinner daily

PRICE: $$$

THE CLOCKTOWER ✿

Contemporary • Elegant

MAP: B2

Nothing shouts "Brit" like a billiards room and there's one to be enjoyed at this swanky dining den of the Edition hotel—a collaboration between restaurateur Stephen Starr and British chef Jason Atherton.

The restaurant shares the same decorative style as sibling Berners Tavern, which is housed inside the London Edition, with high ceilings, handsome wood-paneling and every inch of wall space covered with framed pictures of the good and great. But whereas the London elder is one huge room, this handsome retreat comes divided into three manageable sections, all attended to by a cadre of affable and attentive service staff.

There's a subtle and contemporary British accent to the menu too. Their version of fish and chips takes the national dish to a whole new level, with sweet English peas and triple-cooked chips, while a chutney made from plum and shallots is served with tender roasted Long Island duck and woodsy chanterelles. However, there are other European influences at play, so you may start with a decadent crab and uni risotto, or perfectly done quail and pigeon pie. Make sure to end this feast by sharing a plump, bronzed apple tarte Tatin for two coupled with vanilla ice cream.

---

5 Madison Ave. (bet. 23rd & 24th Sts.)

23 St (Park Ave. South)

(212) 413-4300 — **WEB:** www.theclocktowernyc.com

Lunch & dinner daily **PRICE: $$$**

COTE 

Korean • Fashionable

MAP: A2

This Korean steakhouse is a high-minded tribute to owner Simon Kim's home country, and its renowned love for great beef. Make your way past a long, dark hallway to arrive at this well-designed, slate-colored room with such elegant touches as brass accents and crystal glasses. However, those still in doubt of the restaurant's forte should head downstairs to the glass-enclosed aging room filled with hanging slabs of luscious meat.

Begin with banchan that are categorically untraditional, but nonetheless divine. Then dive into crisp Korean "bacon," which is even better than it sounds, served as little shards of jerky-like sweet and smoky pork belly topped with pickled jalapeño. A pedestrian-sounding kimchi stew is elevated with sophisticated anchovy consommé, potatoes and zucchini; and the marbling on their aged ribeye, cut into cubes for tabletop searing, looks like something Michelangelo may have sculpted. Match this with grilled mushrooms and galbi for a true feast. Come summertime, pair those sizzling steaks with cold noodles—bi-bim somyun—mingled with white radishes in a mild chili paste.

After hours, locals may carve a slot at their impressive bar for more cocktails and fun.

---

16 W. 22nd St. (bet. Fifth & Sixth Aves.)
23 St (Broadway)
(212) 401-7986 — **WEB:** www.cotenyc.com
Dinner Mon - Sat

PRICE: $$$

CRAFT ℗

American • Design

MAP: B3

It's been years since Tom Colicchio first opened Craft to great acclaim, but the easy charms of the celebrity chef and TV personality's downtown institution haven't waned a bit. The room is still busy most nights of the week with stylish patrons who appreciate the triple threat of cozy décor, elegant food and a crackerjack service team.

As the name suggests, guests «craft» a meal from seasonal, perfectly executed dishes that may feature pristine ingredients. Dinner might kick off with a cured slice of crudo, served with shaved fennel, radish and microgreens in a Meyer lemon dressing. Don't leave without trying one of the chef's legendary pastas, like a gorgeous tangle of capellini with lemon zest, grated cheese, ramps and Calabrian chilies.

43 E. 19th St. (bet. Broadway & Park Ave. South)
14 St - Union Sq
(212) 780-0880 — **WEB:** www.craftrestaurantsinc.com
Lunch Mon - Fri Dinner nightly **PRICE:** $$$$

FERRIS ℗

American • Contemporary décor

MAP: B1

There may be nothing special about its location, but make your way past the Made hotel lobby and into its basement to arrive at the snug and deeply hospitable Ferris. The vibe here is rousing—with a bar overlooking an open kitchen and a chill staff who is on top of their game. Always. So, kick back and look forward to some creative laissez "fare." Lobster toast sprinkled with black sesame seeds, kombu and freeze-dried roe is an absolute study in luscious savors, while soft stracciatella with crispy rice, endive and broccolini is the essence of deliciously contrasting flavors.

Is this today's version of nouvelle cuisine? Perhaps—especially considering such ingenious desserts as frozen yogurt topped with waka momo peaches, yuzu-olive oil and a whit of salt.

44 W. 29th St. (bet. Broadway & Sixth Ave.)
28 St. (Broadway)
(212) 213-4420 — **WEB:** www.ferrisnyc.com
Dinner nightly **PRICE:** $$$

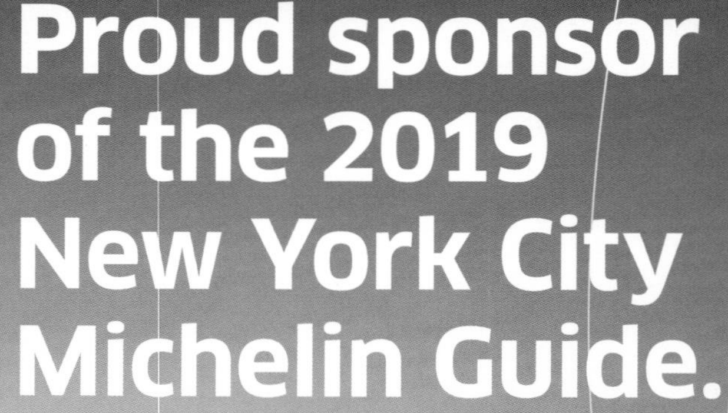

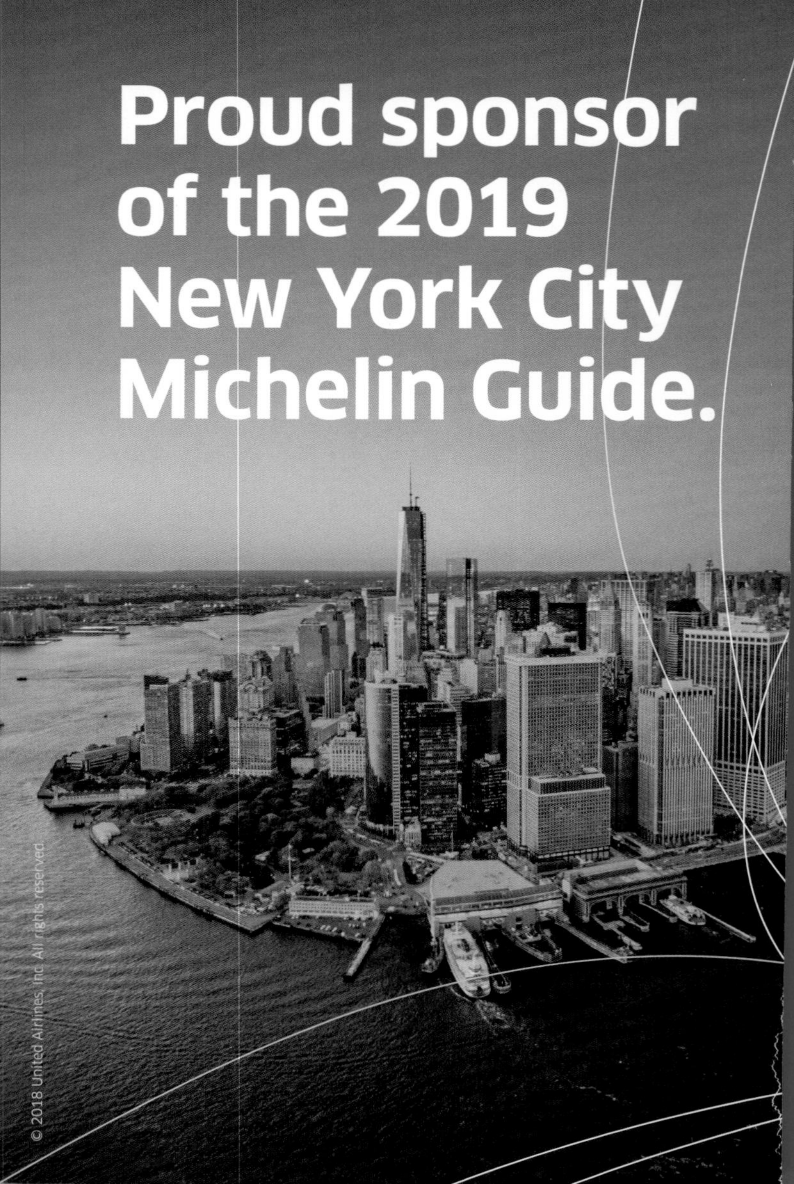
Proud sponsor of the 2019 New York City Michelin Guide.
© 2018 United Airlines, Inc. All rights reserved.

ELEVEN MADISON PARK ✿✿✿

Contemporary • Design

MAP: B2

This freshly minted dining room displays the virtues of symmetry, with not so much as a chair pushed out of its proper place. Everything is custom made, from the staff's Todd Snyder suits to the handblown water vases. Other significant changes include a paring down of crowds—they now cater to a smaller audience. This is all evidence of Chef Daniel Humm's masterful precision that extends through the cuisine as it artfully unfolds before each guest.

In place of a menu, servers offer a brief description of the night's meal, along with a few selections that you are invited to make. Courses are so well conceived that they often seem as continuations of the same dish. Revel over flaky brioche with scallop gelée-crowned butter, before moving on to the purest tasting of scallop slivers set over uni in an ice-cold shell. This kitchen's signature way with delicate presentations reaches a peak in a tin of caviar served with smoked ham custard, Hollandaise sabayon and mini English muffins.

Specialties arrive by trolley, perhaps bearing a shaved truffle-topped flatbread brushed with aged-cheddar sauce, which when removed goes on to reveal stuffed wild mushrooms in an intense broth. Want more? We all do.

---

11 Madison Ave. (at 24th St.)

23 St (Park Ave. South)

(212) 889-0905 – **WEB:** www.elevenmadisonpark.com

Lunch Fri - Sun Dinner nightly **PRICE: $$$$**

15 EAST

Japanese • Elegant

MAP: A3

A Japanese restaurant divided in two: you can perch at the counter and watch the sushi chefs in action, or you can go next door and sit at a table in a slickly run, narrow room decked out in earthy tones. Either way, you'll be well looked after by an attentive team.

The menu is also divided—between sushi and sashimi from the bar, and hot dishes from the kitchen. Regulars, however, relish the highly enjoyable omakase that features everything from octopus, ikura and tuna, to creamy shrimp and lightly roasted grunt fish. Hot dishes range from the traditional to the more innovative and adapted, but steer clear of tempura and go straight for the soba. Made in house, these springy noodles swim in a warm, wasabi-infused dashi loaded with mushrooms and cilantro.

15 E. 15th St. (bet. Fifth Ave. & Union Sq. West)
14 St - Union Sq
(212) 647-0015 — **WEB:** www.15eastrestaurant.com
Lunch & dinner Mon - Sat **PRICE:** $$$

GRAMERCY FARMER & THE FISH

American • Contemporary décor

MAP: B3

The kitchen is always seasonal and dishes incomparably fresh since most of the produce comes from its own farm and seafood from the owner's company.

Yet loving care and creativity abound in cooking that has its own Mid-Atlantic meets New England slant, resulting in creations like a lobster roll enhanced with bone marrow. This is the kind of place to indulge in a daily array of raw seafood, butter-poached king crab or one of their extraordinary shellfish towers. The menu goes on to offer refined all-American preparations of chicken, pork and farm-fresh vegetables. Desserts may bear humble names but are deliciously elevated, like the "s'mores" made with graham cracker cookie crumbles, dark chocolate ice cream and caramel meringue.

245 Park Ave. South (bet. 19th & 20th Sts.)
23 St (Park Ave. South)
(646) 998-5991 — **WEB:** www.farmerandthefish.com
Lunch & dinner daily **PRICE:** $$$

GRAMERCY TAVERN

Contemporary • Fashionable

MAP: B3

In a roll-call of New York's most beloved restaurants of the last couple of decades, Gramercy Tavern would be high on many people's list. It is one of those places that manage the rare trick of being so confident in its abilities that it can be all things to all people. You'll probably leave happy whether you've come on a date or are here to impress the in-laws; whether you're closing a deal or simply lubricating the thought processes behind a deal.

The "Tavern" side is the prized spot for lunch, especially if there are only two of you and you can sit at the bar—it doesn't take bookings so get here early and join in the grown-up "I'm not really queuing, I'm just standing here" queue outside. The "Dining Room" is for those who like a little more pomp with their pappardelle, and really comes into its own in the evening.

The cooking is the perfect match for the warm and woody surroundings: this is creative American food sure of its footing and unthreatening in its vocabulary. The main component, be it the sea bass or pork loin, is allowed to shine and there is a refreshing lack of over-elaboration on the plate that demonstrates the confidence and dexterity of this kitchen.

---

42 E. 20th St. (bet. Broadway & Park Ave. South)

23 St (Park Ave. South)

(212) 477-0777 — **WEB:** www.gramercytavern.com

Lunch & dinner daily **PRICE: $$$$**

HANJAN

Korean • Tavern

MAP: B1

This contemporary take on Korean cuisine continues to thrive and is cherished among locals and visitors alike. A convivial crowd gathers along a cluster of tables in the petite space, where ivory-hued ceramic pieces are set against grey walls.

Small plates arranged as "traditional" and "modern" highlight quality ingredients and stimulating presentations. The signature house-made tofu is unmissable: these chilled scoops of soybean curd are a toasty shade of brown, sprinkled with slivered green onion, sesame seeds and accompanied by soy sauce and perilla vinaigrette. Lunch is an equally enticing affair, featuring a handful of starters, mains like bibimbap, as well as popular noodle dishes—perhaps mixing pork belly and vegetables doused in black bean sauce.

36 W. 26th St. (bet. Broadway & Sixth Ave.)
28 St (Broadway)
(212) 206-7226 — **WEB:** www.hanjan26.com
Lunch Mon - Fri Dinner Mon - Sat **PRICE:** $$

HILL COUNTRY CHICKEN

American • Simple

MAP: B2

Gussied up in a happy palette of sunny yellow and sky blue, this 100-seat homage to deep-fried down-home country cooking serves exemplary fried chicken offered in two varieties. The "classic" sports a seasoned, golden-brown skin; "Mama El's" is skinless and cracker-crusted. Both are available by the piece or as part of whimsically named meals, like the "white meat solo coop."

Step up to the counter and feast your eyes on cast-iron skillets of chicken, as well as sides like creamy mashed potatoes, pimento macaroni and cheese, or grilled corn salad with red peppers and green onion. And then there's pie. More than 12 assortments, baked in-house and available by the slice, whole or blended into a milkshake for a drinkable take on "à la mode."

1123 Broadway (at 25th St.)
23 St (Broadway)
(212) 257-6446 — **WEB:** www.hillcountrychicken.com
Lunch & dinner daily **PRICE:**

I TRULLI

Italian • Contemporary décor

MAP: C2

Although it's merely steps away from perpetually-buzzing Park Avenue South, find yourself checking the street signs to confirm that you're still in Manhattan as you enter this Italian gem. Beloved I Trulli showcases a polished-as-ever design, featuring blue walls, a gleaming marble bar, and tables covered with thick linen. The multi-seasonal walled garden is also bound to leave you smitten.

This family-run restaurant has a long history of doling out elevated comfort food. Following suit, look for Mamma Dora who has her own perch in the dining room and can be found happily making the likes of orecchiette with rabbit ragù among other delicious pastas. Few things are as reliable as her handmade creations, which may put to shame other versions in town.

124 E. 27th St. (bet. Lexington Ave. & Park Ave. South)
28 St (Park Ave. South)
(212) 481-7372 — **WEB:** www.itrulli.com
Lunch Mon - Fri Dinner nightly

PRICE: $$$

KAZU-NORI

Japanese • Minimalist

MAP: B1

After the enormous success of Sugarfish and its spin-offs, LA's sushi pioneer Chef Kazunori Nozawa has arrived in New York City. The concept couldn't be simpler: a sleek bar surrounds two chefs who do nothing but craft hand rolls to order. Each place is set with small plates of ginger and wasabi. Sashimi is available as are other rolls and orders to go, but most everyone comes here for those thoughtfully composed hand rolls filled with soft rice and delicate fish. Highlights also include the hamachi roll with minced scallions, toro and scallops and accompanied by kewpie mayo. Overall, prices here are a bargain, even though "luxury" ingredients like lobster and blue crab don't always deliver.

The best way to avoid the endless line? Go solo.

15 W. 28th St. (bet. Fifth & Sixth Aves.)
28 St (Broadway)
(347) 594-5940 — **WEB:** www.kazunorisushi.com
Lunch & dinner daily

PRICE:

JUNOON ✿

Indian • Elegant

MAP: A2

Inventive cooking, attention to detail and a striking décor set Junoon apart from its upscale Indian brethren. Step through those handsome ebony wood doors, and you'll arrive inside this welcoming space adorned with treasures from the subcontinent. The large bar up front delivers sophistication and fun. By day, lunch is served in the airy (Patiala) room; service is top-notch at all times.

Dinner guests are treated to the more theatrical room, walking through an ancient wooden arch and carved panels, seemingly afloat in a reflecting pool. This leads to an amber-tinted dining arena where tables are luxuriously spaced, and the vibe is exotic and transporting.

The talented kitchen is particularly adept at bringing out contrasting flavors and textures in myriad dishes, including tandoori octopus. Sliced and plated with a black garlic- and squid ink-aïoli, it flaunts that essential, deep sense of umami. Ghost chili murgh tikka reaches epic heights of char and flavor when coupled with an excellent cashew nut purée and pickled cabbage to temper its heat, while sweet and tender pork ribs arrive under a glass cloche swirling with smoke and steeped in an enticingly spiced vindaloo.

---

27 W. 24th St. (bet. Fifth & Sixth Aves.)

23 St (Sixth Ave.)

(212) 490-2100 – **WEB:** www.junoonnyc.com

Lunch & dinner daily

PRICE: $$$$

KYMA

Greek • Elegant

MAP: A3

As its name in Greek suggests, this stunner is making "waves" in town by way of Roslyn, New York. The bi-level space transports diners to the Ionian Sea but it's not just beauty that bewitches here. All Hellenic meals begin with a panoply of spreads, so using a warm pita scoop up the pikilia trio with feta, hummus and taramasalata. Calamari stuffed with four cheeses and served over a Nafpaktos tomato sauce is a winner. Not far behind, find that phyllo-wrapped spanakopita delight with spinach and cheese. The menu also lists a series of fresh-caught fish ready for "your pleasure." Carnivores though will also get their fill by way of the short rib youvetsi.

Ekmek kataifi featuring shredded phyllo and semolina custard is a fine way to end this Greek feast.

5 W. 18th St. (bet. 5th & 6th Aves.)
23rd St
(212) 268-5555 – **WEB:** www.kymarestaurants.com
Dinner nightly **PRICE:** $$$

LAUT

Asian • Simple

MAP: A3

At once cheerful and authentic, this Southeast Asian restaurant offers diners a pleasant place to sit and talk for a while. Likewise, it remains true to its downtown spirit, set in a space that features dim lighting and exposed brick adorned with chalk drawings of orchids and water lilies.

The personable staff keeps things rolling along on a timely basis. Portions are generous and the pricing is exceptionally wallet friendly, especially when ordering the lunch specials. Popular menu choices include the nasi lemak, a classic dish of chicken, sambal shrimp, pickled veggies and a chili anchovy peanut paste atop a mound of fluffy coconut rice. Another sure thing is the roti canai, a crispy Indian-style pancake with a rich curry dipping sauce.

15 E. 17th St. (bet. Broadway & Fifth Ave.)
14 St - Union Sq
(212) 206-8989 – **WEB:** www.lautnyc.com
Lunch & dinner daily **PRICE:** $$

LE COQ RICO

French • Elegant

MAP: B3

Chicken takes the spotlight at Le Coq Rico, but these birds go well beyond the basic. Tucked into a gleaming interior at the base of a Beaux-Arts building, the restaurant offers two distinct dining areas—the main room with its stylized décor of whitewashed brick and white oak floors, as well as a glossy counter overlooking the open kitchen.

There is a list of chicken breeds to choose from including Plymouth Rock, New Hampshire and Rohan Farm Duck. The menu offers plenty to mull over—imagine eggs, soups and salads of sautéed guinea fowl and artichokes à la Barigoule. Finally, mains like chicken fricassée sided by rice pilaf or Maine lobster served with shellfish jus are just as delightful as a dessert of vanilla-raspberry vacherin.

30 E. 20th St. (bet. Broadway & Park Ave. South)
23 St (Park Ave South)
(212) 267-7426 — **WEB:** www.lecoqriconyc.com
Lunch & dinner daily **PRICE:** $$$

THE LITTLE BEET TABLE

American • Contemporary décor

MAP: B2

A healthy, wholesome, gluten-free, "vegetable forward" menu may sound as appealing as dining with that overly earnest, mildly pious relative you know you should see more often, but in truth there is something irredeemably cute about this more formal offshoot of fast-casual Little Beet.

The menu is divided into four sections—small plates, salads, vegetables and mains—but the sizes of dishes vary considerably so it's best to use price as a guide and assemble your own feast. Highlights include crispy pearl rice with shishito peppers and, of course, anything with beets—especially good here when partnered with caramelized fennel. There is actually more meat on the menu that you might expect—the organic herb-roasted chicken is well worth ordering.

333 Park Ave. South (bet. 24th & 25th Sts.)
23 St (Park Ave South)
(212) 466-3330 — **WEB:** www.thelittlebeettable.com
Lunch & dinner daily **PRICE:** $$

MAIALINO

Italian • Contemporary décor

MAP: B3

Housed inside the legendary Gramercy Park Hotel, Danny Meyer's Maialino is one of the sexiest trattorias of late—buzzing day to night with New Yorkers and visitors alike in all their trendy glory. Reservations are always a good idea here, though you can always try for a seat at the charming bar, with its tasty little salumi and bread stations.

The menu is deliciously simple and hearty: well-sourced food rendered to sweet satisfaction. A starter of tender fried artichokes is paired with lemon aïoli, and al dente bucatini all'Amatriciana arrives with well-rendered pork bits, guanciale, tomato sauce and pecorino. Of course, the Berkshire pork chop, served with tender, braised turnips and a sweet-and-sour plum mostarda, remains a perpetual highlight.

2 Lexington Ave. (at 21st St.)
23 St (Park Ave South)
(212) 777-2410 – **WEB:** www.maialinonyc.com
Lunch & dinner daily

PRICE: $$

MERAKIA

Mediterranean • Design

MAP: A2

The full name of this delightful retreat is "Merakia Greek Mountain Thief Spithouse Steak," but the moniker isn't the only memorable thing about it. To start with, the ample space is quite the looker, featuring a glinting open kitchen, cushy steel-blue velvet booths and massive arches overhead.

Of course, then there's the equally impressive cooking—don't miss the "spit + sigs" (labeled "dancing with the lamb"), which is a spectacular plate of off-the-spit lamb. Other signatures may include a starter of ripe tomatoes paired with cool little triangles of feta, tailed by tender and slow-cooked octopus. Grilled lamb chops from the "American Meat" section, coupled with roasted lemon potatoes, will transport you to the Med and back, minus the jet lag.

5 W. 21st St. (bet. Fifth & Sixth Aves.)
23 St (Broadway)
(212) 380-1950 – **WEB:** www.merakia.com
Lunch & dinner daily

PRICE: $$$

NODA

Japanese • Luxury

MAP: B1

This is one of the most impressive sushi-yas to open in New York City in recent years, but you'll have to look hard to find it. There is no signage at Noda, so keep an eye peeled for the dark-suited man out front. He'll usher you in from the street to a gorgeous, clandestine lounge, where you might want to pause for a taste from their extensive Japanese whisky selection.

From there, it's on to that exquisite counter. Located in a former speakeasy and gambling parlor, this space skips the neutral blonde wood tones that embody the typical sushi aesthetic, in favor of a lush, bohemian vibe. Think: cobalt-blue and dusty rose velvet furnishings, stained glass windows, as well as pearl inlaid cocktail tables. The impressive curved wooden counter offers eight plush seats; and old-timey American tunes play overhead.

Trained at the esteemed Sushi Iwa in Tokyo, Chef Shigeyuki Tsunoda's nigiri procession is guaranteed to surmount to the very peak. But before that heavenly parade even begins, guests tuck into the likes of chilled, creamy egg custard topped with Hokkaido uni and Osetra caviar; or meltingly tender Nagasaki sea perch in a savory sake broth, bobbing with spring vegetables.

---

6 W. 28th St. (bet. Broadway & Fifth Ave.)

28 St (Broadway)

(212) 481-2432 — **WEB:** www.noda.nyc

Dinner Mon - Sat

PRICE: $$$$

NOMAD

Contemporary • Chic

MAP: B1

Battle past the gathering crowds and you'll find yourself in the seductive surroundings of a restored Beaux-Arts building that hosts the NoMad hotel. One reason for its continued popularity is that Daniel Humm and Will Guidara, of Eleven Madison Park, run its restaurant.

In contrast to their illustrious flagship, the cooking here is less intricate and more approachable, but still undertaken with considerable skill. Attempting "variations" of Brussels sprouts would be quite a reach for many a chef, yet here demonstrates a kitchen's ability to turn the ordinary into the sublime. While whole-roasted chicken with black truffle and foie gras is their specialty, the cooking of all meats is done extremely well, as seen in succulent suckling pig, served with chicory and pears. Accompanying it all is a terrific wine list strong on riesling and pinot noir.

To be in the heart of the action, ask for a table in the glass-ceilinged Atrium, even though it can be something of a thoroughfare for those going to and from the bar, which it adjoins. The Parlour, true to the word's original meaning, is the better choice for diners who want their conversations to involve less bellowing and more privacy.

1170 Broadway (at 28th St.)

28 St (Broadway)

(212) 796-1500 – **WEB:** www.thenomadhotel.com

Lunch & dinner daily **PRICE: $$$$**

NOVITÁ

Italian • Contemporary décor

MAP: B3

Enjoyable and quietly elegant, Novitá boasts a genuine Italian sensibility both in setting and service. The small size and low ceilings foster a surprisingly serene ambience that is all but disappearing in the city. Prices are not cheap, but the quality is high. The cooking does not necessarily break new ground, but is nonetheless good. Rather than explore the costlier dishes that perhaps feature Kobe beef or black truffles, it's best to stick to the tried-and-true favorites.

Start with a superb combination of pan-fried shiitake caps filled with shrimp and scallions. Then, move on to tiny orecchiette mingled with just the right amount of slow-cooked and fiery lamb ragù, broccoli rabe and grated cheese. The espresso-soaked tiramisu is a perfect pick-me-up.

102 E. 22nd St. (bet. Lexington Ave. & Park Ave. South)
23 St (Park Ave South)
(212) 677-2222 — **WEB:** www.novitanyc.com
Lunch Mon - Fri Dinner nightly **PRICE: $$$**

NUR

Middle Eastern • Rustic

MAP: B3

Tel Aviv's Meir Adoni has made a big splash with this culturally adroit restaurant. Its appetite-whetting cuisine is nuanced, with plenty of influences from the Middle East and Northern Africa. The menu spotlights recognizable dishes, but there are a number of unfamiliar newcomers that are a must.

Start with fantastic breads, like the kubaneh with its toasty brown exterior and buttery, feathery interior. Palestinian hand-cut beef tartare is given a regional slant with sliced jalapeño and thick, tart yogurt and tahini. The Damascus qatayef are Syrian pancakes, almost like empanadas, filled with spiced lamb and nicely paired with an Aryan chaser, a light and refreshing Turkish yogurt drink. Even desserts, like that grapefruit Campari tart, are rave-worthy.

34 E. 20th St. (bet. Broadway & Park Ave. South)
23 St (Park Ave South)
(212) 505-3420 — **WEB:** www.nurnyc.com
Dinner nightly **PRICE: $$$**

PARK AVENUE

Contemporary • Elegant

MAP: B2

For some, walking into a restaurant one knows well is as comforting as a warm embrace; others may feel there's a thin line between familiarity and monotony. The USP of Michael Stillman's Flatiron establishment is that the decorators and designers change the look of the place four times a year to match the seasons, which is no mean feat considering the vastness of this restaurant.

The kitchen sticks to its part of the bargain by also adhering closely to the seasons. Dishes are generally light and easy to eat and the cooks know not to crowd a plate. There are salads aplenty but the best options are those, like the fish dishes, which come with a little dash of Mediterranean color— whatever the weather outside.

360 Park Ave. South (at 26th St.)
28 St (Park Ave. South)
(212) 951-7111 — **WEB:** www.parkavenyc.com
Lunch & dinner daily

PRICE: $$$

PERIYALI

Greek • Mediterranean décor

MAP: A2

Relaxing and stylish for grown-ups, Periyali serves the kind of straightforward Greek cooking that remains blissfully unconcerned with trends. Think grilled octopus is boring? Think again, when presented with charcoal-grilled morsels, marinated for two days in red wine and finished with olive oil and parsley sauce. Salmon may not be native to Greece, but it gets its due respect here, wrapped with herbs and baked in phyllo, served alongside stewed okra. A puréed dish of fava kremidaki showcases a terrific blend of textures, colors and flavors that is the heart and soul of this rustic kitchen.

The dining room echoes the culinary theme with a suspended wall of shimmering decorative fish, abundant flower arrangements, and a back room flooded with natural light.

35 W. 20th St. (bet. Fifth & Sixth Aves.)
23 St (Sixth Ave.)
(212) 463-7890 — **WEB:** www.periyali.com
Lunch Mon - Fri Dinner nightly

PRICE: $$$

PIPPALI

Indian • Simple

MAP: C2

Pippali offers a pleasing study on the myriad regional cuisines of India with an array of sensational curries, seafood dishes and so much more. On-point service makes it a dream destination for date night or dinner with friends, and a muted color scheme in the sleek dining room provides an ideal backdrop for the kitchen's rout of boldly seasoned dishes.

Standards are done right, but focus on their specialties for a unique perspective: melagu chemeen is a must—black pepper-rubbed Chilean sea bass simmered in a coconut-rich red chili curry; while Bombay dabeli unveils soft buns slathered with spicy mashed potatoes and crispy sev. Presentations are careful and unfussy, as found in baingan ka salan replete with peanut, sesame and of course, more spice.

129 E. 27th St. (bet. Lexington Ave. & Park Ave. South)
28 St (Park Ave. South)
(212) 689-1999 — **WEB:** www.pippalinyc.com
Lunch & dinner daily **PRICE:** $$

SCAMPI

Italian • Contemporary décor

MAP: A3

Wander past Scampi and you're likely to stop in your tracks, if only to take in the view of its stunning interior. Lofty windows afford fantastic views into this modern lair, decked out with pretty furnishings, striking lights and abundant greenery.

Chef PJ Calapa pays homage to his Southern Italian roots on this menu. Seafood is a staple, starring sweet and briny razor clams tossed with olive oil, as well as chopped Manila clams finished with a salty kick from prosciutto. While tuna acquapazza offers a peppy take on tartare with chili oil and jalapeños, this kitchen truly shines during pasta time. Despite a rustic lean, there is clear skill in Chef Calapa's curly edged ribbons of mafaldini with shrimp scampi, or spaghetti with n'duja, squid and mint.

30 W. 18th St. (bet. 5th & 6th Aves.)
18th St (Broadway)
(212) 888-2171 — **WEB:** www.scampinyc.com
Lunch Mon - Fri Dinner Mon - Sat **PRICE:** $$$

TRATTORIA ITALIENNE

Mediterranean • Contemporary décor

MAP: B2

Two Italians in one: the front room is the more animated and relaxed, with a counter bar and a menu of snacks and sharing plates; in the larger and somewhat rustically decorated dining room at the back you'll find more ambitious cooking and a team of enthusiastic servers.

Here Chef/co-owner Jared Sippel's menu is divided into: Stuzzichini; Per la Tavola; Pasta; Secondi and Contorni. The influences are pan-Italian with the occasional foray over the border into France. Start by sharing some of their freshly sliced Prosciutto di San Daniele. Follow this up with homemade pastas, like pappardelle with snail ragout, which are a welcome departure from the usual. Mains like rabbit with apricot and speck show that this kitchen knows its way around an animal.

19 W. 24th St. (bet. Broadway & Sixth Ave.)
23 St (Sixth Ave.)
(212) 600-5139 — **WEB:** www.italiennenyc.com
Dinner Mon - Sat

PRICE: $$$$

TURKISH KITCHEN

Turkish • Contemporary décor

MAP: C2

Turkish Kitchen showcases all the classics but excels in the preparation of grilled meats. Indulge in yogurtlu karisik, a dish of moist and smoky char-grilled lamb, chicken and spicy kebabs on a cooling bed of garlic-scented yogurt and pita bread. Pillowy beef dumplings also wade in a pool of that signature sauce topped with paprika-infused oil as well as a dusting of sumac, oregano and mint. A wide selection of Turkish wines makes a fine accompaniment to a hearty meal.

Dangling globe light fixtures give the entrance to this cavernous, multi-level restaurant with floor-to-ceiling windows a modern glow. Tables are topped with pristine white cloths and set between black and white striped chairs; cherry-red walls lend a pop of color.

386 Third Ave. (bet. 27th & 28th Sts.)
28 St (Park Ave. South)
(212) 679-6633 — **WEB:** www.turkishkitchen.com
Lunch Sun - Fri Dinner nightly

PRICE: $$

ULIVO

Italian • Trattoria

MAP: B1

One bite makes it clear that this kitchen boasts a skilled chef who knows how to deliver the best of authentic Italian food. Of course, this should come as no surprise as Chef and co-owner Emanuel Concas is the man who heads this kitchen.

Start with a platter of fritture featuring fried zucchini and octopus. Then move on to delicacies that prove the chef's Sardinian origins, like bottarga di muggine di Cabras, liberally shaved over house-made pici. Schiaffoni con salsa di granseola piccante (spicy braised stone crab sauce) is yet another delight that may be tailed by seadas—a unique Sardinian treat—featuring a fritter filled with pecorino and topped with honey. Stop to appreciate the olive oil at the heart of this cooking and pick up a bottle or two to go.

4 W. 28th St. (bet. Broadway & Fifth Ave.)
28 St (Broadway)
(212) 684-8000 – **WEB:** www.ulivonyc.com
Lunch & dinner daily **PRICE:** $$

UNION SQUARE CAFE

American • Fashionable

MAP: B3

An integral part of Manhattan's culinary scene, Union Square Cafe is big, bi-level and beautiful. The bar is perpetually abuzz with achingly trendy types, but with such a versatile and approachable menu boasting something for even the most picky eater, who can really complain?

Nobody does relaxed elegance like Danny Meyer, and this «café» is no exception. Service is exemplary whether you're a local or Broadway star, and diners love the kitchen's upmarket takes on crowd faves—everything from the hearty burger to a silky and savory cauliflower sformato that is surrounded by tender, flavorful romanesco (brassica). And with an option like the triple-layer chocolate cake with locally roasted espresso ganache on the carte, you'd be crazy to skip dessert.

101 E. 19th St. (at Park Ave. South)
23 St (Park Ave South)
(212) 243-4020 – **WEB:** www.unionsquarecafe.com
Lunch & dinner daily **PRICE:** $$$$

UPLAND

Mediterranean • Trendy

MAP: B2

The stars must have aligned to bring Chef Justin Smillie, restaurateur Stephen Starr and design firm Roman and Williams together to form this bright spot along Park Avenue South. Everything seems to click at Upland—the design is urbane and cozy, with vintage floors as well as glowing jars of preserved lemons and backlit wine bottles lining the walls. Earthy and bountiful, it's the ideal backdrop for Smillie's Mediterranean-influenced dishes. A meal from this kitchen might reveal sprouted fava-bean falafel paired with a tahini- garlic- and cashew-sauce; or estrella, star-shaped tubular pasta with chicken livers and herbs. Yuzu soufflé with calamansi curd makes for a crowning finish.

Traveling to Miami? A South Beach outpost has crowds swooning.

345 Park Ave. South (at 26th St.)
28 St (Park Ave South)
(212) 686-1006 — **WEB:** www.uplandnyc.com
Lunch & dinner daily

PRICE: $$$

Share the journey with us!
@MichelinGuideNY
@MichelinInspectors

GREENWICH & WEST VILLAGE

Once occupied by struggling artists, poets and edgy bohemia, Greenwich Village today continues to thrive as one of New York City's most artsy hubs. With Washington Square Park and NYU at its core, this area's typically named (not numbered) streets wear an intellectual spirit as seen in its many cafés, shops, indie theaters and music venues.

ASSORTED PLEASURES

Mamoun's has been feeding students for decades with some of the best falafel in town. Locals however have been known to experience similar gratification at **Taïm**, which features updated renditions of this fried delight. Tail these savory bites with one of their smoothies or opt for a cup of fair trade coffee at **Kopi Kopi,** known for its Indonesian flair. For those looking to lunch on the run, **Good Stock** is a popular take-out soup and chili spot; while **Urban Vegan Kitchen** brings you flavorful food and interesting wines in a casual yet cozy setting. Also captivating the culinary elite are those delicate, very satisfying

rice- and lentil-flour crêpes served with character and flair at food truck sensation, **N.Y. Dosas**, but for crêpes in their original, faithful form along with other excellent French items, stop by **Patisserie Claude**, before unearthing a slice of Italy by way of old-time bakeries and butchers also settled here. **Faicco's Pork Store** and **Ottomanelli & Sons Meat Market** have been tendering their meats for over 100 years now. Take home a round of parsley and cheese sausage or tray of arancini—even though the staff insist that one must be eaten warm, before leaving their store. Setting aside the dusty floors and minimal décor, **Florence Prime Meat Market** in operation for over 70 years, is every gourmand's go-to haunt for Christmas goose, Newport steak and much, much more. And really, what goes best with meat? Cheese, of course, with **Murray's Cheese Shop** initiating hungry neophytes into the art and understanding of their countless varieties. Completing Italy's culinary terrain in Greenwich Village is **Raffetto's**, whose fresh,

handmade pastas never cease to please. From here, hop countries to arrive in London via **A Salt & Battery**, where fish and chips are crafted from the finest ingredients and served with a range of first-rate sides. Think: curry sauce, Heinz baked beans and mushy peas. Of course, no Village jaunt is complete without pizza, with some of the finest to be found coal-fired and crisp, only by the pie, at **John's of Bleecker Street**. **Joe's** is another gem dishing up thin-crust selections that promise to leave you with a lifetime addiction. Close the carb feast with a uniquely textured scoop from **Cones**, available in surprisingly tasty flavor combinations...including watermelon!

WEST VILLAGE

Located along the Hudson River and extending all the way down to Hudson Square, the West Village is predominately residential, marked by angular streets, quaint boutiques and chic eateries. Once known as "Little Bohemia," numerous old-fashioned but resilient food spots continue to thrive here and offer a taste of old New York. For a nearly royal treat, stop by **Tea & Sympathy** for high tea, followed by a full Sunday supper of roast beef and Yorkshire pudding. **Dominique Ansel Kitchen** serves up delectable pastries topped with an abundance of French flair; and over on Commerce Street, fans are swooning over **Milk &**

Cookies' unapologetically sinful goodies. These are reputedly as sensational as the breakfast and burgers always on offer at **Elephant & Castle**. The influential **James Beard Foundation** is also situated steps away, in a historic 12th Street townhouse that was once home to the illustrious food writer. If in need of more sweet and savory eats, **Mah-Ze-Dahr** is a beautiful little bakery from Pakistani-American baker, Umber Ahmad. This stylish café sells her famous choux puffs and brioche donuts among other excellent treats. Manhattan's love for brunch is a time-tested affair that continues to thrive in this far west stretch. Find evidence of this at **La Bonbonniere**, a pleasing diner whose brazen and notable creations are excelled only by their absurdly cheap prices. Pack a basket of egg specialties and enjoy a picnic among the urban vista of roller skaters and runners at Hudson River Park. While strolling back across bustling Bleecker, let the overpowering aromas of butter and sugar lead you to the original **Magnolia Bakery**. Proffering over 128 treats, this official sweet spot is a darling among tourists and date-night duos. **Li-Lac** is one of the city's oldest chocolatiers dispensing the best chocolate-covered pretzels in town—take your pick between dark and milk! Beyond bakeries, the bar scene in this area is always abuzz. Night owls pound through pints at the **Rusty Knot**, while relishing

cheap meals and fantastic live beats. Equally expert mixologists can be found pouring "long drinks and fancy cocktails" at **Employees Only**; just as bartenders reach inventive heights at **Little Branch**—where an encyclopedic understanding of the craft ensures dizzying results. At the foot of Christopher Street and atop the waterfront, **Pier 45** is a lovely destination for icy cold drinks, hot dogs and sunbathing.

MEPA

Everyone from fashionistas, curious locals and stiletto-clad socialites make the pilgrimage further north to the notoriously trendy Meatpacking District. Once home to slaughterhouses, prostitution services and drug dens, today MePa is packed with moneyed locals and savvy tourists looking to get their snack, sip and groove on. Thanks to the huge success of the High Line—an abandoned 1934 elevated railway that is now a 19-block-long park—these once-desolate streets currently cradle some of Big Apple's coolest retreats and hottest nightclubs. As if in defiance of these cautious times, luxury hotels, "starchitect" high-rises and festive bistros have risen—and these modish minions cannot imagine living elsewhere. But in the midst of all this glitz, find **Upholstery Store**, a precious find (read: repurposed furniture store) also serving stirring cocktails. Of course, **The Standard** hotel is the area's social mecca with beer and bratwursts running the show every summer at **The Biergarten**. Come fall, hipsters soak up the scene at **Kaffeeklatsch**, a pop-up shop preparing hot beverages for freezing skaters doing the rounds at Standard Plaza; while foodies flock to **Valbella** for Northern Italian cooking. Finally, obfuscated by this haute hotel, **Hector's Café** is a modest, welcoming holdout that continues to feed the few remaining meatpackers here—usually all day, everyday.

A STANDARD TO WHICH
AND THE HONEST CAN REPAIR
IS IN THE HAND OF GOD

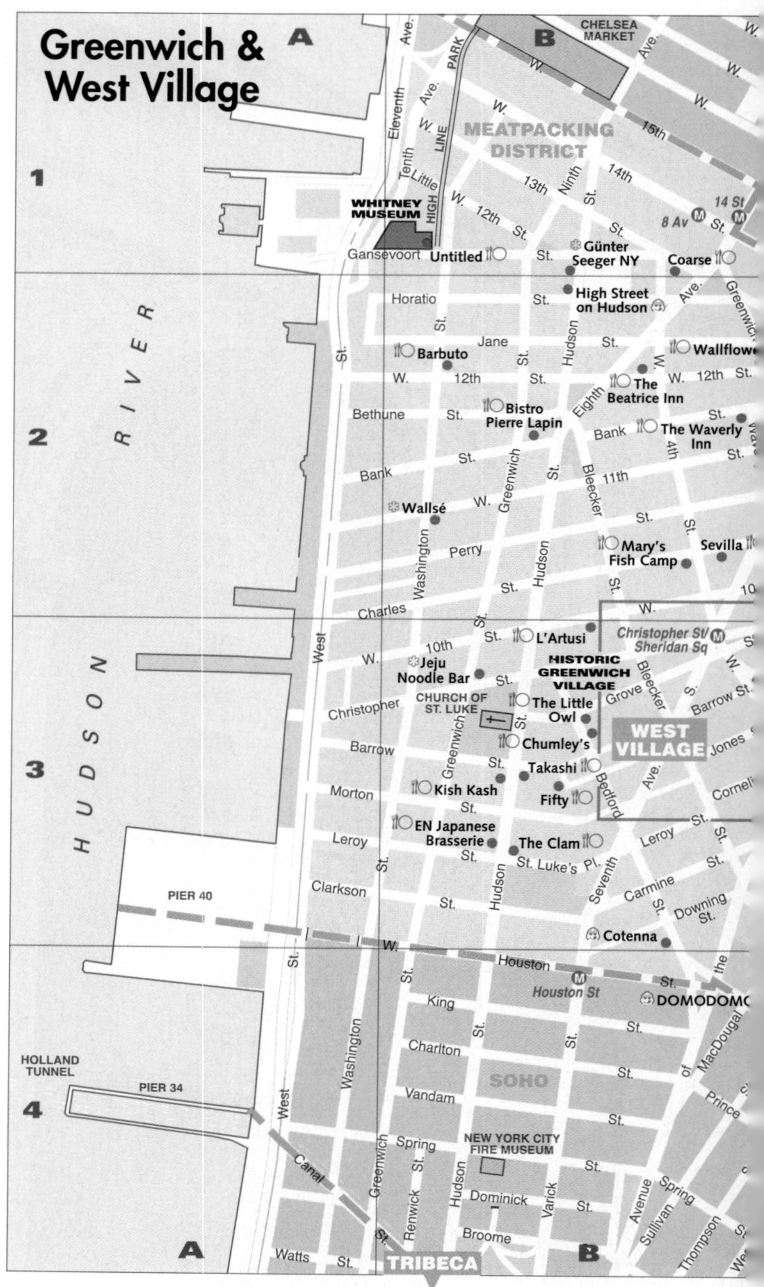

Greenwich & West Village
A
B
1
2
3
4
HUDSON RIVER
CHELSEA MARKET
MEATPACKING DISTRICT
HIGH LINE PARK
WHITNEY MUSEUM
Untitled
Günter Seeger NY
Coarse
High Street on Hudson
Barbuto
Wallflower
The Beatrice Inn
Bistro Pierre Lapin
The Waverly Inn
Wallsé
Mary's Fish Camp
Sevilla
Christopher St/Sheridan Sq
L'Artusi
Jeju Noodle Bar
HISTORIC GREENWICH VILLAGE
CHURCH OF ST. LUKE
The Little Owl
Chumley's
WEST VILLAGE
Takashi
Kish Kash
Fifty
EN Japanese Brasserie
The Clam
Cotenna
Houston St
DOMODOMO
SOHO
NEW YORK CITY FIRE MUSEUM
HOLLAND TUNNEL
PIER 40
PIER 34
TRIBECA
14 St
8 Av
Gansevoort St.
Horatio St.
Jane St.
W. 12th St.
Bethune St.
Bank St.
W. 11th St.
Perry St.
Charles St.
W. 10th St.
Christopher St.
Barrow St.
Morton St.
Leroy St.
Clarkson St.
W. Houston St.
King St.
Charlton St.
Vandam St.
Spring St.
Dominick St.
Broome St.
Watts St.
Canal St.
West St.
Washington St.
Greenwich St.
Hudson St.
Bleecker St.
Eighth Ave.
Seventh Ave.
Bedford St.
Grove St.
Jones St.
Cornelia St.
Carmine St.
Downing St.
St. Luke's Pl.
Varick St.
Renwick St.
Sullivan St.
Thompson St.
Avenue of the Americas
MacDougal St.
Prince St.
Eleventh Ave.
Tenth Ave.
Ninth Ave.
Little W. 12th St.
W. 13th St.
W. 14th St.
W. 15th St.
W. 4th St.
Greenwich Ave.

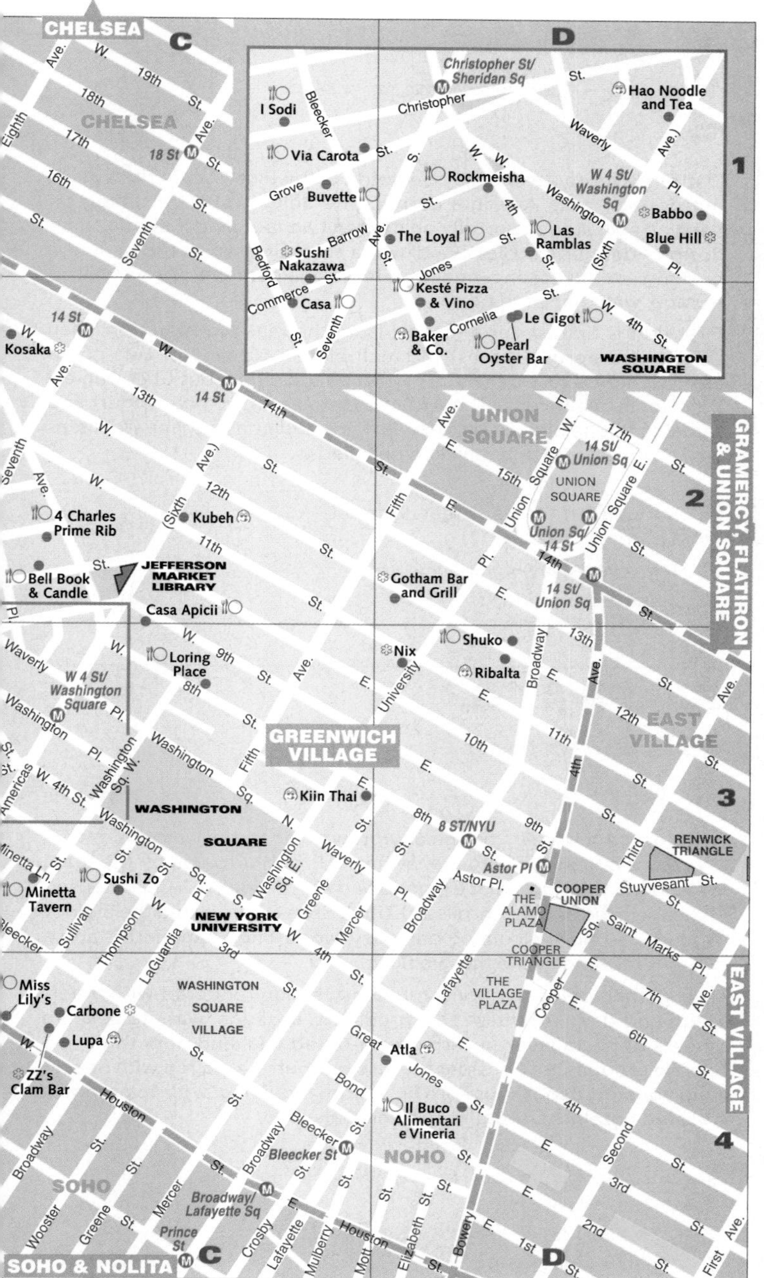
CHELSEA
C
D
1
2
3
4
Christopher St/ Sheridan Sq
I Sodi
Via Carota
Buvette
Sushi Nakazawa
Casa
Rockmeisha
The Loyal
Las Ramblas
Kesté Pizza & Vino
Baker & Co.
Le Gigot
Pearl Oyster Bar
Hao Noodle and Tea
W 4 St/ Washington Sq
Babbo
Blue Hill
WASHINGTON SQUARE
18 St
14 St
Kosaka
4 Charles Prime Rib
Kubeh
Bell Book & Candle
JEFFERSON MARKET LIBRARY
Casa Apicii
Loring Place
Gotham Bar and Grill
UNION SQUARE
14 St/ Union Sq
Union Sq/ 14 St
Shuko
Ribalta
Nix
GREENWICH VILLAGE
EAST VILLAGE
GRAMERCY, FLATIRON & UNION SQUARE
Kiin Thai
8 ST/NYU
Astor Pl
COOPER UNION
RENWICK TRIANGLE
THE ALAMO PLAZA
COOPER TRIANGLE
THE VILLAGE PLAZA
Sushi Zo
Minetta Tavern
NEW YORK UNIVERSITY
WASHINGTON SQUARE VILLAGE
Miss Lily's
Carbone
Lupa
ZZ's Clam Bar
Atla
Il Buco Alimentari e Vineria
Bleecker St
NOHO
SOHO
Broadway/ Lafayette Sq
Prince St
SOHO & NOLITA

ATLA

Mexican • Contemporary décor

MAP: D4

Flatiron favorite Cosme may be doted on by diners and critics alike, but nobody puts Atla in a corner. The delightful little sibling on Lafayette St. stands proudly on its own two feet, and if the dazzling design—defined by black-and-white tiles, tiny wood tables and a bustling, worldly scene—makes it feel like a contemporary Mexican terrace, well that's the point.

First things first: order a mezcal from the massive selection, then settle in to peruse the list of small plates. A party of two could easily sample every delicious morsel on the menu, but Chef Daniela Soto-Innes really rocks the Arctic char tostada; quinoa, yogurt and tomatoes done pico de gallo-style; farro and quail egg meatballs; as well as the spectacular chicken enchiladas.

372 Lafayette St. (at Great Jones St.)
Astor Pl
N/A – **WEB:** www.atlanyc.com
Lunch & dinner daily

PRICE: $$

BAKER & CO.

Italian • Rustic

MAP: D2

With only a few years on the downtown circuit, this chic charmer is already a bonafide Village sweetheart. Brought to you by the team behind the wildly popular Emporio and Aurora, Baker & Co. is housed in the beloved and much-missed Zito & Sons Bakery—and the interior features a long, welcoming bar, cozy, wood-lined banquettes and a vibrant red-and-white mosaic floor.

The kitchen doles out honest, unfussy Italian rendered with a deft hand and deep attention to ingredients. Lasagna, with its delicate sheets of pasta layered with cream-tinted veal and pork ragù, is a classic production. Consider the luscious burrata, paired with pencil-thin roasted asparagus, or the tender branzino with asparagus, toasted hazelnuts, arugula and chili flakes.

259 Bleecker St. (bet. Cornelia & Jones Sts.)
W 4 St - Wash Sq
(212) 255-1234 – **WEB:** www.bakernco.com
Lunch & dinner daily

PRICE: $$

BABBO ✿

Italian • Osteria

MAP: D1

While a restaurant can rarely be all things to all people, it should certainly adapt to the various needs and moods of its customers. Come for lunch at Babbo, for example, and there'll be Stan Getz playing gently in the background to accompany the quiet clinking of cutlery and the soft murmur of conversation. Turn up for dinner with friends and Led Zeppelin or Tom Petty will be the soundtrack to the far more excitable vibe.

This stalwart has been a Village favorite for over two decades. The reason for its longevity is pretty apparent as soon as you walk in: the place just feels right, everything they do they have practiced and every need you have and every request you make will be accommodated. It's also a decidedly handsome space, with the first-floor room adorned with fresh flowers and a staircase leading to a bright, raised second level.

The menu offers a comprehensive selection of regional Italian dishes with some contemporary liberties (think fennel-dusted sweetbreads with sweet and sour onions and duck bacon). The homemade pasta dishes are a strength and the kitchen can show a remarkably light touch when required, especially with certain classic desserts like panna cotta.

- 110 Waverly Pl. (bet. MacDougal St. & Sixth Ave.)
- W 4 St - Wash Sq
- (212) 777-0303 – **WEB:** www.babbonyc.com
- Lunch Tue - Sat Dinner nightly

PRICE: $$$$

BARBUTO

Italian • Neighborhood

MAP: B2

Jonathan Waxman's West Village stalwart occupies a former garage whose doors can be flung open in the summer to bring the outside in. On colder days, the wood-burning oven in the open kitchen provides a focal point in what is a fairly utilitarian space, but one with an appealingly laid-back feel, which is helped along by confident service and a plethora of regulars.

The kitchen offers something for everyone, with many of the dishes big enough to share. Pasta mains come with a languid muscularity while, for many, the roast chicken is a must. There are unexpected surprises: those who shudder at the mere existence of kale will find that—with the addition of pecorino, breadcrumbs and anchovies—it can be transformed into something quite sublime.

775 Washington St. (at 12th St.)
14 St - 8 Av
(212) 924-9700 — **WEB:** www.barbutonyc.com
Lunch & dinner daily

PRICE: $$

THE BEATRICE INN

Steakhouse • Fashionable

MAP: B2

Its glitzy and glamorous history makes this one of those restaurants about which everyone has an opinion—regardless of whether they've been here or not. The celebrity cavalcade may have now moved on, but that appealing sense of speakeasy secrecy remains, with its low ceiling and even lower lighting adding to the sense of intimacy and intrigue.

Chef/co-owner Angie Mar has produced a classic chophouse menu, where meat is king. There are plenty of dishes for sharing, whether that's the dry-aged rack of lamb or the applewood-smoked rabbit, but even standard dishes designed for one are on the hefty size. Flavors are big and bold but the richness of the meat is balanced by a judicious use of herbs and fruits. That said, make sure you come hungry.

285 W. 12th St. (bet. W. 4th St. & Eighth Ave.)
14 St (Seventh Ave.)
(212) 675-2808 — **WEB:** www.thebeatriceinn.com
Dinner Tue - Sun

PRICE: $$$$

BELL BOOK & CANDLE

American • Tavern

MAP: C2

Funky, relaxed and locally minded, the idea behind this farm-to-table style of dining might seem overdone if the cooking here wasn't so good. Enter carefully down a steep set of stairs to find low ceilings, large canvas artwork and comfortable seating that lets you settle in and ponder just how very local the lettuce can be (answer: the rooftop).

In fact, much of the produce here was harvested from their aeroponic rooftop garden, while the rest is sourced from local purveyors. From start to finish, the American fare is consistently pleasing. Highlights include crispy fried P.E.I. oysters with jalapeño-buttermilk dressing, thick and juicy grilled sausage with house pickles and flatbread and gooey chocolate brownies with pistachio ice cream.

141 W. 10th St. (bet. Greenwich Ave. & Waverly Pl.)
14 St (Seventh Ave.)
(212) 414-2355 — **WEB:** www.bbandcnyc.com
Lunch Sun Dinner nightly

PRICE: $$$

BISTRO PIERRE LAPIN

French • Neighborhood

MAP: B2

Chef Harold Moore left a hole in the local dining scene when he closed his beloved Commerce, but devoted fans will thrill to his latest venture. The cooking here is still on point, and if that's not enough of a draw, this cozy, open-all-day bistro offers so much more than your basic steak frites. In fact, its diverse menu is filled with the classics (like delicious fricassée de champignons), market-driven vegetables and fresh pastas. Of course, every meal kicks off with a generous plate of garnishes for their excellent house baguette: think house-made butter, savory country pâté, as well as a crowd-pleasing parmesan-and-black truffle spread.

The whole experience here is utterly charming—from the friendly service to the vintage, flea market-inspired space.

99 Bank St. (bet. Hudson & Greenwich Sts.)
14 St - 8 Av
(212) 858-6600 — **WEB:** www.pierresnyc.com
Lunch Sun Dinner nightly

PRICE: $$$

BLUE HILL 

American • Elegant

MAP: D1

Knowing when to leave something alone, whether you're a painter, singer or cook, requires confidence in your material and your own ability. Here at Blue Hill, Dan Barber's kitchen displays its utter trust in the products at hand not only by not interfering with them too much but also giving them space in which their natural flavors can shine. Think Frank Sinatra, but with sweet corn and tomatoes.

This intimate, sophisticated space is as popular as ever and the team clearly shares the chef's passion and pride. The "farm to fork" mantra may be something of a cliché today, but this chef demonstrates that the startlingly obvious equation of great seasonal ingredients equals great food remains the cornerstone of every serious restaurant. A majority of ingredients come from Stone Barns Center in Westchester County and the eponymous farm in Massachusetts.

Diners decide between a six-course "Farmer's Feast" tasting or a four-course "Daily Menu." Dishes are described in refreshingly terse terms to reflect the relative simplicity of what's on the plate, whether that's this morning's farm egg with seasonal vegetable pistou or Montauk black bass with dill purée. This is food that tastes and feels good.

---

75 Washington Pl. (bet. Sixth Ave. & Washington Sq. Park)

W 4 St - Wash Sq

(212) 539-1776 — **WEB:** www.bluehillfarm.com

Dinner nightly

PRICE: $$$$

BUVETTE

French • Bistro

MAP: C1

Charming and proudly French, this self-proclaimed gastrothèque serves delicious Gallic plates to a notably svelte set. While carb addicts can barely fit into these wee seats, it's worth the squeeze for Chef Jody Williams' famously rustic cooking. Inside, everything comes alive with jazz and chatter. Instagrammable dishes take their cue from French classics and may feature crusty olive oil-drizzled country bread slathered with fluffy scrambled eggs, salty prosciutto and nutty parmesan. Then await croissants—fresh, buttery and flaky—served with sweet fruit preserves for a typically French and very decadent treat.

If not up the block at her other spot or in Paris or Tokyo, you may even find the chef herself holding meetings over a potent, frothy and flawless cappuccino.

42 Grove St. (bet. Bedford & Bleecker Sts.)
Christopher St - Sheridan Sq
(212) 255-3590 — **WEB:** www.ilovebuvette.com
Lunch & dinner daily

PRICE: $$

CASA

Brazilian • Simple

MAP: C2

Somehow, this warm little Brazilian café has been hiding in plain sight for over two decades. The white room's clean décor, votive candles and jazz music keep it homey yet fashionable enough for the sophisticated downtown locals who regularly seem to populate it.

Come here on a wintery night for a downright perfect bowl of canja di galinha, starring a rustic and flavor-packed chicken soup with string beans, leeks and rice. Alternatively, go for a bowl of tantalizingly spiced feijoada and find the accoutrements as delicious as the main dish itself—you can expect an array of creamy black beans, tangy orange segments, crunchy farofa (fried cassava), garlicky spinach and diabolically hot preserved red peppers. Desserts are appealing and very well priced.

72 Bedford St. (at Commerce St.)
Christopher St - Sheridan Sq
(212) 366-9410 — **WEB:** www.casarestaurant.com
Lunch Sat - Sun Dinner nightly

PRICE: $$$

CARBONE

Italian • Vintage

MAP: C4

With nostalgia at the forefront, Carbone is plain gorgeous. While this big, bold and beautiful ode to Italian-Americana comes alive at night under the low lights, lunch is equally admired among brash bankers with big appetites and their Valentino-donning divas. That same sense of history pervades the entire space, which highlights plush banquettes, impressive ceramics and glittering chandeliers. Was the striking tiled-floor inspired by a certain restaurant scene in The Godfather? Indeed.

Mid-century classics are what this menu is all about, but exalted ingredients, skill and presentations will excite even the most cynical savant. Stylish servers—who work the floor with a little flirt and lot of flair—remain in character while presenting top antipasti like crusty garlic bread, soppressata and fresh, particularly divine olive oil-dunked mozzarella. Spaghetti alla gricia may be simple but dazzles just the same, and chicken scarpariello in a garlicky crumb coating dolls up traditional red-sauce cooking with a chunky stew-like sauce with peppers and mushrooms.

Though the prices here are jaw-dropping, all is forgiven after one bite of the drool-worthy, six-layer blackout cake.

---

181 Thompson St. (bet. Bleecker & Houston Sts.)

Houston St

(212) 254-3000 — **WEB:** www.carbonenewyork.com

Lunch Mon - Fri Dinner nightly **PRICE: $$$$**

CASA APICII

Italian • Contemporary décor

MAP: C2

If in the mood for cocktails, head to the second floor of this townhouse, where Bar Fortuna entices with a categorically stirring selection. Then dinner waits at Casa Apicii—run by the who's who of NY dining, with resumes that include Daniel and Lincoln Ristorante.

The main room is loud, but let's just call it "lively" since everyone here seems to be enjoying it. An alabaster fireplace, starburst chandeliers and leather seats fashion an ambience so welcoming that it almost lets you forget about the errors in service. The "mozzarella menu" is a statement of their dedication to both their house-made and imported cheeses. Other highlights include freshly made strozzapreti in an exceptionally rich tomato-based sauce of octopus, pancetta and bone marrow.

62 W. 9th St. (bet. Fifth & Sixth Aves.)
Christopher St - Sheridan Sq
(212) 353-8400 — **WEB:** www.casaapicii.com
Dinner Tue - Sat

PRICE: $$$$

CHUMLEY'S

Gastropub • Historic

MAP: B3

There's little resembling the Chumley's of old, save the name, door and framed book jackets of writers who apparently found their muse in a glass here. This famed watering hole, which had to shutter temporarily a decade ago after a chimney collapse, has risen from the proverbial ashes as a serious contender. Leather banquettes, French-oak tables and patterned wallpaper are long on looks, but rest assured, as it's all about the (really good) food here.

Dishes sound familiar—steak tartare and lobster rolls—but there's nothing ho-hum about this menu, which bears a French twist (bouillabaisse, we see you). Savory apple tart is a well-executed and creative starter, but it's the dry-aged burger topped with bone marrow that remains a much-ordered treasure.

86 Bedford St. (bet Barrow & Grove Sts.)
Christopher St - Sheridan Sq
(212) 675-2081 — **WEB:** chumleysnewyork.com
Dinner Mon - Sat

PRICE: $$$$

THE CLAM

Seafood • Cozy

MAP: B3

If you're going to name your place after a single item of food, you need to have mastered its cooking. Fortunately, Chef/co-owner Mike Price knows exactly how to get the best out of these versatile little tidbits of delight—whether they're grilled in their shells with buttered crumbs or atop a pizza. It's even worth ordering the clam dip here while you decide which other clam items to order.

Don't fall into the trap of thinking, however, that this sweet little corner bistro is in any way gimmicky or one dimensional. In truth, there are plenty of equally appealing, non-clam-specific seafood dishes that also hit the spot, like roast halibut with gem lettuce or grilled scallops with anchovy aïoli. But lovers of the bivalve mollusk will love The Clam.

420 Hudson St. (at Leroy St.)
Houston St
(212) 242-7420 — **WEB:** www.theclamnyc.com
Lunch & dinner daily **PRICE:** $$

COARSE

Contemporary • Chic

MAP: B1

Art and food collide at this charming West Village restaurant courtesy of the talented duo, Vincent Chirico and Marco Arnold, whose food is teeming with depth, flavor and ingenuity. These chefs showcase their formidable culinary talent alongside the incredible artwork of Amon Focus and Noëmi Manser.

Diners can choose from areas labeled Raw, Garden, Sea, or Land—or just leave it up to the chef, who hand-delivers each plate from the semi-open kitchen into the fun, artsy room. Seafood is a particular strength here, so a night in their capable hands might unveil wildly fresh Long Island fluke with Fuji apple, coriander and fennel. Also try luscious hamachi, artistically plated with avocado, Fresno chili and a cool, clear ginger-kissed consommé.

306 W. 13th St. (bet. Eighth Ave. & W. 4th St.)
14 St - 8 Av
(646) 896-1404 — **WEB:** www.coarsenyc.com
Dinner Tue - Sat **PRICE:** $$$

COTENNA

Italian • Cozy

MAP: B3

The elusive sign, the secretive feel, the tiny space, the keenly priced menu with a plate for every palate—yes, this is the sort of place we'd all like up our sleeve when friends want a recommendation in the Village. It's warm, welcoming and cozy and you'll be reluctant to venture back out into the real world afterwards.

The jewels are in the cicchetti section, like tender porchetta on crostini; grilled sardines with pine nuts, onions and bags of flavor; as well as deliciously sweet dates stuffed with gorgonzola and wrapped in speck. The pasta dishes aren't lacking in oomph either; wild boar pappardelle and garganelli osso buco both pack a punch. The only challenge will be finding enough space on your little table for all the food you'll order.

21 Bedford St. (bet. Downing & Houston Sts.)
Houston St
(646) 861-0175 – **WEB:** N/A
Lunch & dinner daily

PRICE: $$

DOMODOMO

Japanese • Contemporary décor

MAP: B4

Situated just below street level, DOMODOMO is sleek and lovely, with carefully constructed wood furnishings and a long, smooth blonde wood counter. The buzz at the bar is magnetizing, and service is stellar with each sitting, as diners are presented with a small bowl of water and cleansing hand towel.

Sushi is plentiful in New York, of course, but this kitchen ups the ante of their hand rolls with top-notch nori, rice and fish. Some combinations are familiar while others are quirky and inspired. It's not just about sushi here, though. Two crunchy, sweet chili sauce-glazed shrimp rest atop crisp Korean pear and peppery arugula dressed in a yuzu vinaigrette for a citrusy bite; while udon satisfies with its classically seasoned broth and tender noodles.

138 W. Houston St. (bet. MacDougal & Sullivan Sts.)
Houston St
(646) 707-0301 – **WEB:** www.domodomonyc.com
Dinner nightly

PRICE: $$

EN JAPANESE BRASSERIE

Japanese • Design

MAP: B3

EN doesn't pander to the spicy tuna-loving set, but effectively pays homage to highly seasonal Japanese cooking. In such simple and delicate food, flawless execution is a must so don't hesitate to ask for a recommendation.

Also on offer are three, exceptionally priced kaiseki menus. The informed staff is happy to offer their opinion on items, be it chilled soba with a warm dipping sauce; aburi Tasmanian sea trout in an enticingly flavored pool of garlic and soy sauce; or iwashi rice coupled with crunchy sunomono and floating in a briny bonito broth. Sweet corn kernels are enrobed in nori for a delightful bit of bite.

Lofty ceilings, large windows and a glass wall lined with shelves of sake attract a young, professional and fashionable crowd.

435 Hudson St. (at Leroy St.)
Houston St
(212) 647-9196 — **WEB:** www.enjb.com
Lunch & dinner daily **PRICE:** $$$

FIFTY

American • Contemporary décor

MAP: B3

Fifty is a formidable address that has not lost a beat in keeping one of the neighborhood's most beloved dining rooms as alive and popular as ever. Even the location conjures up feelings of nostalgia—catty-corner from the Cherry Lane Theater along an iconic West Village alleyway. From inside the long, narrow room, furnished with comfortable banquettes and bistro tables, large windows frame the quaint little street.

The menu may be New American at heart, but Latin notes ensure that the delicious cooking continues to surprise. The chef's vision is clear in a crudo featuring pristine scallops with uni, coconut milk, shiso and more. Complex flavors abound in goat ribs braised with tomatoes, and set atop farro porridge, avocado and plantains.

50 Commerce St. (bet. Barrow & Bedford Sts.)
Christopher St - Sheridan Sq
(212) 524-4104 — **WEB:** www.fiftyrestaurantnyc.com
Lunch Sat - Sun Dinner nightly **PRICE:** $$$

4 CHARLES PRIME RIB

Steakhouse • Intimate

MAP: C2

Brendan Sodikoff's lovely destination makes the case that New York should be home to more Chicago influencers. This may be a meat-centric spot named for its street address, but the intimate size and modest exterior make it feel like a charming hideaway. The mood of the staff is warm and welcoming.

Some dishes may break with tradition but offer tasty results, like spaghetti carbonara twirled with pecorino and smoky guanciale set beneath a silky fried egg. Others are firmly footed classics, like a phenomenal bone-in Porterhouse for two, served alongside truffle potatoes, creamed spinach and a whole head of roasted garlic. Bookend your meal with wonderful cocktails and desserts—perhaps a dense wedge of Valrhona dark chocolate pie in an Oreo-cookie crust.

4 Charles St. (bet. Greenwich Ave. & Waverly Pl.)
Christopher St - Sheridan Sq
(212) 561-5992 — **WEB:** www.nycprimerib.com
Dinner nightly

PRICE: $$$$

HAO NOODLE AND TEA

Chinese • Contemporary décor

MAP: D1

The full name, Hao Noodle and Tea by Madam Zhu's Kitchen, was directly imported from China—as was the regional menu offering dishes not often seen on American tables. The artsy, young and vibrant ambience draws as many people in for authentic cooking as it does for afternoon tea.

Be forewarned that the food may not all fit on your tiny table, but the accommodating kitchen is sure to plan your meal accordingly, with well-timed courses arriving and disappearing in synchronicity. Sichuan chili oil makes its creeping, tingling presence known in a wonderfully chewy presentation of spicy bean curd. Chunks of sole are expertly prepared with a crisp exterior coated in a savory soy glaze. Superb taste and "Instagrammable" beauty is clear in each dish.

401 Sixth Ave. (bet. Greenwich Ave. & Waverly Pl.)
Christopher St - Sheridan Sq
(212) 633-8900 — **WEB:** www.haonoodle.com
Lunch & dinner daily

PRICE: $$

GOTHAM BAR AND GRILL

American • Elegant

MAP: D2

"Reliability" may be not be the sexiest adjective with which to describe a restaurant but that is exactly what you can expect from Gotham Bar and Grill. Whether you're hosting family, entertaining clients or just out with friends, this is a restaurant where you know you don't have to worry about it matching up to your hopes and expectations.

The large, warmly lit room comes with just the right amount of glamour to add to any sense of occasion and is helmed by a personable team who makes every diner feel like they're in safe hands. This is also the type of establishment that exudes New York from its every pore—and is ideal for those for whom eating out is a visceral pleasure, rather than something to be photographed, posted and blogged.

The cooking walks a pleasing line between comforting and creative and never feels faddish or contrived. In a refreshing break from current mores, dishes are more about flavor than presentation—and their size bears witness to the largesse of the kitchen. The sweet corn tortellini with mascarpone may sound extravagant, but is in fact effortlessly easy to eat; and the peanut butter sundae balances sweetness and saltiness in a joyful concoction of creaminess.

---

12 E. 12th St. (bet. Fifth Ave. & University Pl.)

14 St - Union Sq

(212) 620-4020 — **WEB:** www.gothambarandgrill.com

Lunch Mon - Fri Dinner nightly **PRICE: $$$$**

GÜNTER SEEGER NY

Contemporary • Elegant

MAP: B1

Named for its deeply creative, German-born chef, Günter Seeger is an original. Even the space has a uniquely personal feel, as if we are all dining in Chef Seeger's home. The main room is charming, relaxing and very elegant, starring white brick walls hung with modern art, mauve ceiling pendants and an open kitchen. Meals are perfectly timed and each dish is served with care, thanks to a staff of true professionals. This is an idyllic retreat for a romantic dinner. Gentlemen, don't forget to don your jackets here.

The kitchen's refined compositions are arranged so beautifully that guests are sure to appreciate the artistry of food rendered with finesse. Asian-inspired scallops arrive gently cooked, then topped with shaved radish, bok choy and a tableside pour of dashi. A breast and leg of hibachi-grilled squab is lovely on its own, but here it rests on a thin sheet of dried dates, before being crowned by an arresting sight of purple and saffron-hued cauliflower. The tasting menus may change with the seasons but always present completely inventive items.

Desserts stand out with the likes of matcha choux pastry filled with dark chocolate sorbet, or a wildflower honey parfait.

---

641 Hudson St. (bet. Gansevoort & Horatio Sts.)
14 St - 8 Av
(646) 657-0045 — **WEB:** www.gunterseegerny.com
Dinner Mon - Sat

PRICE: $$$$

HIGH STREET ON HUDSON

American • Chic

MAP: B2

Fresh off the success of their wildly popular Philadelphia restaurant, High Street on Market, Chef Eli Kulp opened up this lovely little spot, just steps south of MePa to well-deserved acclaim. Breakfast, lunch and dinner are available, with a focus on grains, sandwiches and wickedly good homemade breads.

This airy and entertaining corner space is welcoming, with an open kitchen and a small side counter to view the action within. Find delicious refinement in the roasted, deeply caramelized carrots "à la Mendez" arranged artfully around a brick-red mole. Perfect ribbons of mafaldine are then tossed with smoked mussels and a sauce composed of celery, garlic and pickled jalapeños. Cool things down over a honey custard topped with shards of honeycomb candy.

637 Hudson St. (at Horatio St.)
14 St - 8 Av
(917) 388-3944 — **WEB:** www.highstreetonhudson.com
Lunch & dinner daily

PRICE: $$

IL BUCO ALIMENTARI E VINERIA

Italian • Trattoria

MAP: D4

This is the kind of cooking and scene that makes us all wish we were Italian. Start with a stroll through the alimentari (located up front) to grab some pickled beans and serious cheeses. Then, head towards the rustic dining area in the back, which oozes warmth and comfort. Note the meticulously conceived copper roof, open kitchen and other decorative accents that set a picturesque backdrop for a delicious meal. The food here is authoritative and tasty, with a nice representation of Italian cooking from breakfast through dinner. The porchetta panino is timeless, amazing and vies to be the finest around. Skillfully crafted pasta includes textbook-perfect bucatini cacio e pepe. Finish with an affogato, topping a scoop of vanilla gelato with hot espresso.

53 Great Jones St. (bet. Bowery & Lafayette St.)
Bleecker St
(212) 837-2622 — **WEB:** www.ilbucovineria.com
Lunch & dinner daily

PRICE: $$$

I SODI

Italian • Intimate

MAP: C1

Manhattan has classic Italian and new Italian, but not many thoughtful Italian restaurants. Tuscany native Rita Sodi is out to change that with this ristorante. She consciously selected every aspect of the design, including the linen napkins to the thick, striated glass windows that hide the modern space from the marauding groups of youngsters on Christopher Street.

Inside this oasis, Negronis prep palates for al dente rigatoni and hearty, meat-focused dishes like the coniglio in porchetta. This exceptional rabbit preparation combines bacon-wrapped loin with a sweet wine- rosemary- and garlic-sauce. The herbal quality of such savoriness brings out the almost austere nature of the lean rabbit, showing how truly intuitive and innovative Italian cooking can be.

- 105 Christopher St. (bet. Bleecker & Hudson Sts.)
- Christopher St - Sheridan Sq
- (212) 414-5774 — **WEB:** www.isodinyc.com
- Dinner nightly

PRICE: $$

KESTÉ PIZZA & VINO

Pizza • Neighborhood

MAP: D2

Mamma mia! New York's love affair with Kesté shows no sign of stopping. This kitchen begins with a puffy, blistered crust that's perfectly salty and tangy, then tops it with ingredients like roasted butternut squash purée, smoked mozzarella and basil. And while its ingredients seem to have taken a small hit in recent years, that crust is still on point.

Co-owner Roberto Caporuscio presides over the American chapter of Associazione Pizzaiuoli Napoletani, and his daughter, Giorgia, oversees the in-house pizza making operations. Diners can choose from more than 22 pizzas (including a few gluten-free options), a roster of calzoni and nightly pie specials. The restaurant is teeny-tiny, but diners are encouraged to linger, in true Italian hospitality.

- 271 Bleecker St. (bet. Cornelia & Jones Sts.)
- W 4 St - Wash Sq
- (212) 243-1500 — **WEB:** www.kestepizzeria.com
- Lunch & dinner daily

PRICE: ◎◎

JEJU NOODLE BAR ✿

Korean • Contemporary décor

MAP: B3

Named after the South Korean island that's renowned for its high quality pork, this corner "bar" aims to take that nation's comfort food and elevate it to sophisticated heights. As envisioned by Chef/owner Douglas Kim, the kitchen specializes in ramyun—not ramen.

The dining space mixes old West Village charm with tidy minimalism for a casual, hip and convivial hangout. Pick your perch at one of the generously spaced tables, or (preferably) at the engaging counter where you can watch each dish come together. If that doesn't have your taste buds tingling, the kitchen's concise number of unique items at a steal of a price will hit the spot. Persian cucumber kimchi with a spicy plum dressing, shiso and sesame seeds is a culinary delight, while the mouthwatering aroma of pork bone broth that precedes the arrival of gochu ramyun brimming with curly noodles, bean sprouts and pickled cabbage is a veritable thesis on ace ingredients.

Pyunche salad mingling sushi-grade amberjack dabbed with chimichurri and crunchy vegetables is a simple yet delicious wonder. Not far behind is the surprising toro ssam bap highlighting the eponymous fatty fish with scrambled egg, tobiko and toasted seaweed.

---

679 Greenwich St. (at Christopher St.)

Christopher St - Sheridan Sq

(646) 666-0947 — **WEB:** www.jejunoodlebar.com

Lunch Sat - Sun Dinner Tue - Sun **PRICE: $$**

KIIN THAI

Thai • Family

MAP: C3

Smack in the middle of NYU turf and on a street choking with fast-casual eateries, Kiin Thai cuts an impressive figure design-wise, with its lofty ceilings and light-filled interior. While value-driven lunch specials might on occasion affect quality, the kitchen continues to push out precise renditions of Central and Northern Thai dishes.

Khao soi is a gorgeous orange-hued curry with chewy noodles, tender braised chicken, hard-boiled egg and the requisite condiments needed to amp the dish up to an incendiary level. Other faves include fish hor mok—a custardy curry with striped sea bass, coconut milk, and duck eggs—topped with herbs and Makrut lime; or the excellent hor nueng gai with chicken, Thai eggplant and rice, delicately steamed in a banana leaf.

36 E. 8th St. (bet. Greene St. & University Pl.)
8 St - NYU
(212) 529-2363 — **WEB:** www.kiinthaieatery.com
Lunch & dinner daily

PRICE: $$

KISH KASH

Moroccan • Simple

MAP: B3

After runaway hits like Balaboosta and the successful fast-casual mini-chain Taïm, Chef/owner Einat Admony is back with Kish Kash—her take on North African cuisine of the Jewish diaspora. Located along the western end of Hudson Street, an area teeming with local eateries and shops, the interior is minimalist and tidy, featuring pale wood tables and colorful, Moorish tiled walls.

The restaurant employs Admony's fast-casual format and though the menu is limited, the quality of food is superb. Everything is crafted with fresh ingredients and spices, but make no mistake, it is their hand-rolled, light, divine and melt-in-your-mouth couscous served with a number of different stewed and saucy meats, fish and vegetables that is the real reason why you're here.

455 Hudson St. (bet. Barrow & Morton Sts.)
Christopher St
(646) 609-5298 — **WEB:** www.kishkashnyc.com
Lunch & dinner daily

PRICE:

KOSAKA ✿

Japanese • Contemporary décor

♿ **MAP:** C2

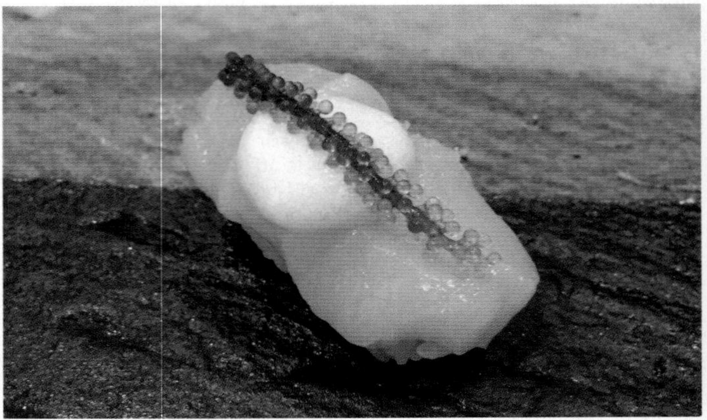

Lauded chef Yoshihiko Kousaka is in control of this superb sushiya along with partners Key Kim and Mihyun Han to offer a stellar omakase in an elegant setting. The room is sleek, modern and flaunts a handsome Japanese sensibility—there is a counter for 12, along with three small tables, as well as a relaxed but deeply attentive staff to help enhance the experience. Soft piano music plays in the background, and the crowd is energetic and warm.

Chef Kousaka often prepares each item of the omakase himself, methodically working pieces of fish into something transcendent, and explaining them in full for the bright-eyed patrons.

The impressive 15-piece version can be tailored somewhat as diners can opt for sushi only or sushi with sashimi, as well as such luxe supplemental items as uni, toro, king crab and ankimo (monkfish liver). Here, fish is minimally embellished, relying instead on original sourcing and the chef's impeccable technique. For instance, a night's parade churned out of this kitchen may include everything from red snapper, Japanese sea bass and silky shrimp, to wild winter yellowtail, firefly squid with sweet miso and tosazu jelly, as well as mackerel with ginger and scallion.

---

220 W. 13th St. (bet. Greenwich & Seventh Aves.)
14 St (Seventh Ave.)
(212) 727-1709 — **WEB:** www.kosakanyc.com
Dinner Tue - Sat **PRICE: $$$$**

KUBEH

Middle Eastern • Chic

MAP: C2

Chef/owner Melanie Shurka traveled to Israel to learn the art of making kubeh (dumplings) from the immigrant women of Kurdish, Iranian and Syrian descent. Taste the results of her education in this lovely respite, which showcases fresh, wholesome food, including a heartfelt rendition of its namesake dish. Though hand-rolled kubeh may be prevalent in the Middle East, they can be hard to find here. Don't miss the Syrian lamb version, filled with richly spiced meat served in a hamusta broth with chard and zucchini. Round out your meal with tahini-drizzled roasted eggplant, although the baklava will make it a challenge to truly call it quits.

The cuisine may be ancient, but the setting is clean and contemporary, with old-world heirlooms decorating the walls.

464 Sixth Ave. (at 11th St.)
14 St - 6 Av
(646) 448-6688 — **WEB:** www.eatkubeh.com
Lunch & dinner daily

PRICE: $$

L'ARTUSI

Italian • Contemporary décor

MAP: B3

This polished, airy West Village charmer is a magnet for beautiful people. Or maybe it's just that everyone looks gorgeous in L'Artusi's romantically lit room, divvied up into three dining options and a quiet mezzanine, alongside its more traditional dining area. A semi-open kitchen, polished and gleaming with stainless steel, pushes out wickedly good Italian dishes like tender potato gnocchi in a rabbit cacciatore, laced with garlic, sweet tomato, rosemary and sage; or perfectly charred octopus paired with creamy potatoes, spiked with chilies, olives and savory pancetta.

Polish that off with a drink from their generous list of aperitivi or fantastic selection of wines by the glass, and you'll be feeling quite beautiful yourself by dinner's end.

228 W. 10th St. (bet. Bleecker & Hudson Sts.)
Christopher St - Sheridan Sq
(212) 255-5757 — **WEB:** www.lartusi.com
Lunch Sun Dinner nightly

PRICE: $$

LAS RAMBLAS

Spanish • Tapas bar

MAP: D1

Sandwiched among a throng of attention-seeking storefronts, mighty little Las Ramblas is easy to spot—just look for the crowd of happy, munching faces. The scene spills out onto the sidewalk when the weather allows.

Named for Barcelona's historic commercial thoroughfare, Las Ramblas is a tapas treat. A copper-plated bar and collection of tiny tables provide a perch for snacking on an array of earnestly prepared items. Check out the wall-mounted blackboard for especiales. Bring friends (it's that kind of place) to fully explore the menu, which serves up delights such as succulent head-on prawns roasted in a terra-cotta dish and sauced with cava vinegar, ginger and basil; or béchamel creamed spinach topped by a molten cap of Mahón cheese.

170 W. 4th St. (bet. Cornelia & Jones Sts.)
Christopher St - Sheridan Sq
(646) 415-7924 — **WEB:** www.lasramblasnyc.com
Lunch Sat - Sun Dinner nightly **PRICE:**

LE GIGOT

French • Bistro

MAP: D2

At first glance, Le Gigot transports guests to an inviting little family-owned bistro—the kind you'd only find in La Ville-Lumière. The service exceeds expectations with uncharacteristic warmth that brings a welcoming vibe to the nostalgic dining room.

Tasty renditions of classic bistro fare dominate the menu, so expect the cooking to be familiar and pleasing. The petit bouillabaisse begins as a saffron fish broth with a red-peppery North African accent to elevate the traditional fish and seafood dish. Their cassoulet is a beloved Toulousaine version with duck confit, bacon, cannellini beans, herbs and luscious pork. Finally, brioche pudding conjures all that is simple and good in a dessert, with crème anglaise, berries and whipped cream.

18 Cornelia St. (bet. Bleecker & W. 4th Sts.)
W 4 St - Wash Sq
(212) 627-3737 — **WEB:** www.legigotrestaurant.com
Lunch & dinner Tue - Sun **PRICE: $$$**

THE LITTLE OWL

American • Neighborhood

MAP: B3

Straddling a picturesque corner of the West Village, with a name that could charm the pants off the grizzliest city diner, The Little Owl has a lot going for it. Light pours in from the windows and bright flowers dot the quaint room, while thoughtful service staff ushers you through your meal.

This seasonal menu hits it out of the park, weaving top-notch ingredients into comforting, homey creations like gravy meatball sliders, a signature dish. An Italian wedding soup is sourced from local urban gardens and loaded with tender polpettine; while a beautifully seared halibut arrives with fluffy chive-mashed potatoes and a drizzle of lemon crème fraîche. The heady scent from the chocolate soufflé cake will have others wondering what smells so good.

90 Bedford St. (at Grove St.)
Christopher St - Sheridan Sq
(212) 741-4695 — **WEB:** www.thelittleowlnyc.com
Lunch & dinner daily

PRICE: $$

LORING PLACE

American • Contemporary décor

MAP: C3

Named after the Bronx street that his father grew up on, Loring Place is where Chef Dan Kluger serves up delicious, stylistic and locally sourced Californian cuisine to a downtown crowd. And yet, none of this comes as a surprise as the chef has showcased his talents for years and been the recipient of much acclaim in the city. Following this, his cooking here is unique and spirited, starting with caramelized cauliflower served with chilies and Meyer lemon jam. Leeks arrive cool and tender, dressed with sherry vinaigrette, set over yogurt and finished with pear slices. Then duck breast is prepared with rare skill and finesse.

The generously sized room is uncluttered and mid-century chic, with bright orange window frames and boldly striped banquettes.

21 W. 8th St. (bet. MacDougal St. & Fifth Ave.)
8 St - NYU
(212) 388-1831 — **WEB:** www.loringplacenyc.com
Lunch & dinner daily

PRICE: $$$

THE LOYAL

American • Chic

MAP: D1

The Loyal may be destined to become your new favorite American brasserie. This thoughtfully designed space is classy, comfortable and full of interesting art and tidbits; when full, the room's energy is palpable.

The menu is expansive, so there is bound to be something for everyone. Chef John Fraser does not strive to reinvent the wheel, but serves beautifully made, upscale renditions of American items. Try crisp, cool radishes served over smoked trout gribiche with pearls of trout roe. Then sample house-made pici tossed in a creamy and umami-rich mushroom carbonara with bits of delicious guanciale. Classic desserts make it impossible to go wrong, whether you opt for the crowd-pleasing ice cream sundae or baked Alaska with Bourbon caramel.

289 Bleecker St. (at Seventh Ave.)
Christopher St - Sheridan Sq
(212) 488-5800 — **WEB:** www.loyalrestaurant.com
Lunch Sat - Sun Dinner nightly **PRICE:** $$$

LUPA

Italian • Trattoria

MAP: C4

Is there anything more lovely than a lazy weekend lunch at Lupa? You'd be hard-pressed to convince the regulars otherwise, as they flock in droves day and night to this Thompson Street treasure for its amicable service, interesting wines and otherworldly pasta.

Everything on the menu is so lovingly sourced: witness a warm spinach and pancetta salad tossing a perfect mix of vibrant greens with smoky bacon; or a starter of plump, marinated sardines laced with oil, coarse salt and served over diced cucumber and celery. But the real highlight of this show remains the pasta, which may reveal decadent bavette cacio e pepe, a classic dish from Lazio. It's nothing short of sweet satisfaction, dotted with sharp pecorino and freshly ground black pepper.

170 Thompson St. (bet. Bleecker & Houston Sts.)
W 4 St - Wash Sq
(212) 982-5089 — **WEB:** www.luparestaurant.com
Lunch & dinner daily **PRICE:** $$

MARY'S FISH CAMP

Seafood • Neighborhood

MAP: B2

This West Village seafood shack is much more than just a destination for lobster rolls. Located on an irresistibly cute corner and outfitted with large windows, Mary's Fish Camp tempts with creative daily specials. Scrawled on a chalkboard, these may include raw offerings and nostalgic desserts like hot fudge sundaes. Crowds pack into the stainless steel counter and fans spin lazily overhead.

The summery space offers lots of choice, but the lobster roll should not be overlooked. A toasted bun is overflowing with hunks of tender, sweet meat dressed in the perfect proportion of mayonnaise and lemon juice, with a mountain of shoestring fries on the side. Begin the meal with spicy Key West conch chowder and end with a slice of Americana—banana cream pie.

64 Charles St. (at W. 4th St.)
Christopher St - Sheridan Sq
(646) 486-2185 — **WEB:** www.marysfishcamp.com
Lunch daily Dinner Mon - Sat

PRICE: $$

MINETTA TAVERN

Gastropub • Vintage

MAP: C3

While this circa 1937 watering hole has been restored, nothing here changes and that is its beauty. It is the quintessential New York City tavern and is still decked out with dark wood, checkerboard tiled floors, red banquettes and those caricature-lined walls. Like the throwback ambience, this menu reveres tradition and reads classic gastropub with dishes such as grilled oysters with pancetta in a Fresno chili butter; and Long Island duck breast finished with a classic Bigarade sauce. Pommes aligot, whipped into submission and loaded with garlic, butter and cheddar curds, is a crowd-pleaser, not unlike the bittersweet chocolate soufflé.

The legendary burger is perhaps too-much-talked-about, though it manages to lure the crowds just the same.

113 MacDougal St. (at Minetta Ln.)
W 4 St - Wash Sq
(212) 475-3850 — **WEB:** www.minettatavernny.com
Lunch Wed - Sun Dinner nightly

PRICE: $$$

MISS LILY'S

Jamaican • Simple

MAP: C4

Authentic Jamaican flavors and thumping reggae go hand-in-hand amid Miss Lily's bright orange booths, retro artifacts and Formica-topped tables. Wide-open windows overlooking buzzy Houston Street merely add to the allure. A well-stocked bar and bins filled with produce set the mood for enjoyable classics brought to you at the hands of glam servers.

Start with jerk chicken that is insanely moist yet nearly black with intense spices, served with a Scotch bonnet sauce that will have your mouth tingling for hours. Then cool down with Melvin's "body good" salad tossing kale, radish, celery and apples in a citrus-ginger vinaigrette. From the Jamaican Sampler—think curry goat, oxtail stew and callaloo—to a boozy rum cake, this Caribbean queen reigns supreme.

132 W. Houston St. (at Sullivan St.)
Houston St
(646) 588-5375 – **WEB:** www.misslilys.com
Lunch & dinner daily **PRICE:** $$

PEARL OYSTER BAR

Seafood • Neighborhood

MAP: D2

It's not hard to find a lobster roll in this city, and for that we can thank Rebecca Charles. This seafood institution—inspired by Charles' childhood summers spent in Maine—has been stuffing sweet lobster meat into split-top rolls since 1997. The two-room setting offers a choice: counter seating or table service. Wood furnishings and white walls are low-key; beachy memorabilia perks up the space.

Start the meal by slurping your way through a classic chilled shellfish platter before tucking into that signature lobster roll, served alongside a tower of shoestring fries. The kitchen shines in daily specials, too, such as the grilled lobster served with corn pudding or pan-roasted wild bass. A hot fudge sundae is an appropriately nostalgic finish.

18 Cornelia St. (bet. Bleecker & W. 4th Sts.)
W 4 St - Wash Sq
(212) 691-8211 – **WEB:** www.pearloysterbar.com
Lunch & dinner Mon - Sat **PRICE:** $$

NIX ✿

Vegetarian • Contemporary décor

MAP: D3

The words "fun," "sensual" and "vegetarian" aren't always found in the same sentence, but this vegetable-centric restaurant shows what can happen if preconceptions and piousness are left at the front door. This isn't about abstaining from anything—it's about savoring.

The first clue is the cocktails—not many such restaurants put this sort of thought and effort into their list. At lunch there are even "modestly alcoholic" choices like the very perky plum with Lillet Blanc. At this point you should be nibbling on something from their "first order" part of the menu, such as polenta fries or tandoor bread. The main section is divided between "lighter" and "bolder" dishes, complete with an asterisk highlighting those that can be made vegan. Chef owner John Fraser (of recently shuttered Dovetail, where vegetables starred in his Monday meatless menus) uses influences from around the world to bring out the flavors of his market produce—like hoisin sauce and Thai chili to liven up the shiitake mushrooms, or nori breadcrumbs for the seaweed Caesar.

Bright, healthy, fresh, perky and clean: more words that apply here—to the look of the room, the food and indeed most of the customers.

---

72 University Pl. (bet. 10th & 11th Sts.)

14 St - Union Sq

(212) 498-9393 — **WEB:** www.nixny.com

Lunch & dinner daily

PRICE: $$$

RIBALTA

Italian • Pizzeria

MAP: D3

It all starts with the dough. That said, Ribalta's mother version apparently started nearly a century ago and has been kept alive to feed the masses since. Today, it rises for 72 hours before being baked into a crust that is so light and digestible that you might be tempted to go for a second, very authentic Margherita, topped with that perfect balance of tomato sauce, mozzarella, olive oil and basil. Pasta dishes are just as strong, so sample a duo of wonderfully tender gnocchi, thickly dressed in pesto or an excellent penne rigate con ragù Napolitano loaded with ground pork and beef.

The food may be substantial, but the space feels like La Grande Mela thanks to red leather banquettes, creatively tiled white walls and planks suspended from the lofty ceiling.

48 E. 12th St. (bet. Broadway & University Pl.)
14 St - Union Sq
(212) 777-7781 — **WEB:** www.ribaltapizzarestaurant.com
Lunch & dinner daily **PRICE:** $$

ROCKMEISHA

Japanese • Simple

MAP: D1

Tightly packed bar-height tables fill this tiny izakaya-style restaurant, which is reminiscent of a quirky canteen with a menu designed for fun. The young crowd sips Sapporo or sake against a soundtrack of old-school rock; and the décor, not far behind, ranges from vinyl records to a framed beer ad featuring Japanese women in bathing suits. The space is cramped yet enjoyable, the atmosphere lively and loose.

An appropriately moist leek omelet shows the kitchen's deft execution of simple dishes. Meaty, deep-fried chicken wings coated in a nose-tingling vinegar-based buffalo sauce are an optimal drinking accompaniment, as is a bowl of chashu ramen with pork bone broth, delicate noodles, pork belly, pickled ginger and a generous sprinkling of sesame seeds.

11 Barrow St. (bet. Seventh Ave. South & W. 4th St.)
Christopher St - Sheridan Sq
(212) 675-7775 — **WEB:** N/A
Dinner Tue - Sun **PRICE:**

SEVILLA

Spanish • Rustic

MAP: B2

Yellowed menus that haven't changed in decades make this old-school Spanish stalwart seem like a relic. Still, no one comes here to be surprised. Rather, they are plowing through their favorite renditions of paella, ranging from vegetable to seafood with chicken and chorizo. The paella Valenciana also adds clams, mussels and lobster claws. Prices are low, portions are large and lively crowds are always happy.

Dishes are made to order, so if that arroz con pollo takes 30 minutes to get to your table, know that it will be worthy of the wait. It arrives as a massive amount of saffron-tinged rice and tender bone-in chicken dotted with green onions, pepper strips, chorizo, peas and lots of garlic. Come dessert, you cannot go wrong with the flan.

62 Charles St. (at W. 4th St.)
Christopher St - Sheridan Sq
(212) 929-3189 — **WEB:** www.sevillarestaurantandbar.com
Lunch & dinner daily **PRICE:** $$

SHUKO

Japanese • Trendy

MAP: D3

There are many reasons why this counter is always full. Shuko is cool, fun and there is no need to take out a loan for dinner. For approximately $150, expect a thoroughly impressive sushi omakase that stands out from the crowd. This should be no surprise, as both of the chefs—Nick Kim and Jimmy Lau—have backgrounds that include extensive work with Masa Takayama and his American empire of high-end sushi counters.

The procession may begin with a bit of hamachi accompanied by slivered myoga and tempura crumbs before moving on to an array of nigiri crafted before your eyes. Then indulge in lean tuna, supremely tender dorado seabream with pickled plum and much, much more. Close with an ace handroll combining shiso and umeboshi wrapped in a slice of lotus root.

47 E. 12th St. (bet. Broadway & University Pl.)
14 St - Union Sq
(212) 228-6088 — **WEB:** www.shukonyc.com
Dinner nightly **PRICE:** $$$$

SUSHI NAKAZAWA

Japanese • Contemporary décor

MAP: C2

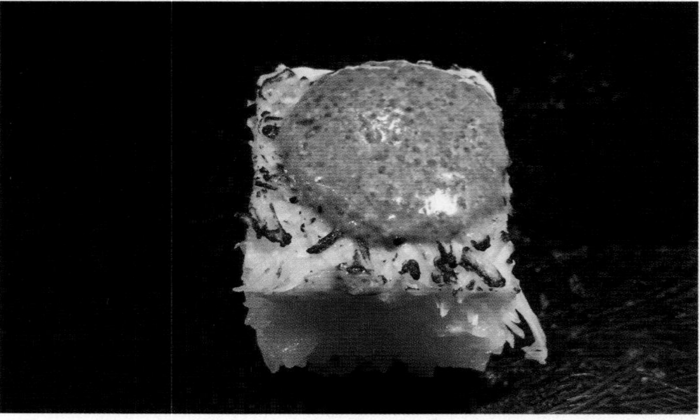

For a truly memorable sushi adventure, head to this sleek and contemporary ten-seat counter—be forewarned though that dining in the back room does not guarantee the same experience. Chef Daisuke Nakazawa's reputation is formidable, which works as a contrast to the jovial banter between the itamae from behind the counter. This simply elucidates the fact that this is a team who loves their craft and is happy to perform for their guests—perhaps using a live wriggling prawn for a bit of a spectacle.

Discover flavorful and fatty cuts of fish available here at a more palatable price point compared to many of the city's other notable sushi counters. Chef Nakazawa's signature style combines supremely tender fish with perfectly seasoned rice, a spark of wasabi and judicious brush of nikiri for consistently excellent results.

One night, for instance, may feature a spectrum of sushi from Hokkaido cherry salmon to live Massachusetts sea scallop with citrus and salt. Then move on to outstanding uni, and finally, a handroll of fatty tuna chopped so fine that it almost seems emulsified. Keep in mind that these chefs are always happy to adjust sizing based on each diner's liking.

---

23 Commerce St. (bet. Bedford St. & Seventh Ave. South)
Christopher St - Sheridan Sq
(212) 924-2212 – **WEB:** www.sushinakazawa.com
Lunch & dinner daily

PRICE: $$$$

SUSHI ZO

Japanese • Minimalist

MAP: C3

The petite space is serene and showcases a particularly pleasing mix of blonde wood and exposed brick, decorated with little more than birch branches.

Begin with a plump Kumamoto oyster with slightly sweet ponzu sauce and lime zest in the company of sashimi. Their nigiri—with bright flavors and skilled torch work—is sure to be the highlight of your meal thanks to halibut with lemon and sea salt, belt fish with wasabi, and shima aji with yuzu juice. Each slice of fish drapes off the delicate shari, but the application of sauces can be heavy handed at times. Generous proportions belie Zo's origins as a sushi-ya unafraid to flout tradition. Finish with a blue crab handroll, richly satisfying red miso soup and a scoop of hojicha ice cream.

88 W. 3rd St. (bet. Sullivan & Thompson Sts.)
W 4 St - Wash Sq
(646) 405-4826 — **WEB:** www.sushizo.us
Dinner Tue - Sat

PRICE: $$$$

TAKASHI

Japanese • Cozy

MAP: B3

The late, beloved Chef Takashi Inoue honored his Korean ancestry and Osaka upbringing with a delicious array of yakiniku favorites at this cozy space. Tremendous care, planning and sourcing of specialty cuts went into the menu design before the restaurant opened its doors to acclaim. Inside, find high-tech grills gracing the tables and cutesy wall cartoons that depict beefy cuts, offal and innards.

The carte is exotic to say the least (testicargot, anyone?), filled with meats and surprises like tripe or even namagimo—raw liver with sesame oil and roasted rock salt. The kitchen's yakiniku (table-grilling) specialties are presented to you to cook at your own pace and may include items like shio-tan (tongue) marinated in soy, apples and orange marmalade.

456 Hudson St. (bet. Barrow & Morton Sts.)
Christopher St - Sheridan Sq
(212) 414-2929 — **WEB:** www.takashinyc.com
Dinner nightly

PRICE: $$

UNTITLED

American • Design

MAP: B1

Who can outshine a world-renowned museum like the Whitney? Danny Meyer can—especially when his trendy restaurant, Untitled, is housed on site. Located by the entry to the popular High Line, the stunning, modern restaurant is a work of art in itself, with lovely floor-to-ceiling windows, sleek red chairs and a beautiful semi-open kitchen.

Talented Chef Suzanne Cupps oversees the operations here, and the results are anything but ordinary. Witness this vegetable-focused carte reveal the likes of marinated mussels with fava, yellow eye beans and edible flowers; or stradette tossed with broccoli rabe pesto, French beans and mushrooms. Then throw caution to the wind and close out with a triple-layer peanut butter and blueberry crunch cake.

99 Gansevoort St. (at Washington St.)
14 St - 8 Av
(212) 570-3670 — **WEB:** www.untitledatthewhitney.com
Lunch & dinner Wed - Mon **PRICE: $$**

VIA CAROTA

Italian • Trattoria

MAP: C1

Occasionally, predictability can be a beautiful thing, especially when it comes to rave-worthy Italian cooking. Via Carota is not so much robotically perfect as it is pleasing—in fact it's the kind of place where dishes can (and should) be piled on. Italian style and artistry combine in this homey space that features bare wood farm tables, sideboards and whitewashed brick. A no-reservations policy means long waits that are actually worth it, so join those lines.

Diners may start nibbling on deep-fried olives that are plump, piping-hot and stuffed with pork sausage. Then, a luscious (and unmissable) risotto cacio e pepe arrives loaded with pecorino and fresh pepper. For dessert, the simple-sounding flourless chocolate cake is downright excellent.

51 Grove St. (bet. Bleecker St. & Seventh Ave. South)
Christopher St - Sheridan Sq
(212) 255-1962 — **WEB:** www.viacarota.com
Lunch & dinner daily **PRICE: $$**

WALLFLOWER

French • Intimate

MAP: B2

Tucked away from the bustle of Greenwich Street is this particularly charming "wallflower." It may be billed as a cocktail lounge, but the food is well-made and the vibe, full of heart. Divided into two, the tiny jewel box is decked out with gold pressed-tin ceilings, a marble bar and bright orange seating. Filled with a host of carefully composed dishes, the menu is a true deal in this neighborhood, especially with choices from the raw bar and charcuterie.

Hearty appetites should try the country pâté or rabbit terrine, both classically prepared and perfectly seasoned. Beef short ribs are big on comfort, garnished with bacon, mushrooms and just the right drop of brawny sauce. The coffee-chocolate pot de crème is a deliciously intense dessert.

235 W. 12th St. (bet. Greenwich Ave. & W. 4th St.)
14 St (Seventh Ave.)
(646) 682-9842 – **WEB:** www.wallflowernyc.com
Dinner nightly

PRICE: $$

THE WAVERLY INN

American • Fashionable

MAP: B2

Even a good chunk of years into its charmed existence, it's still the case that one feels very lucky to score a table at Graydon Carter's Waverly Inn—though it's not for the privilege of mixing with the A-List crowd so much as the absolutely outstanding food. Of course, the beautifully renovated 1844 townhouse plays a part too. It spent many of its interim years as a tavern, and its red leather booths, ornate fireplaces and lovely, ivy-covered atrium retain a certain sexy, speakeasy appeal.

Everything on the menu is truly sublime: a silky foie gras torchon arrives with bright, juicy melon and pine nut brittle; while creamy Dover sole is delicately browned in butter, then coated in a decadent Hollandaise and served with bright green haricots verts.

16 Bank St. (at Waverly Pl.)
14 St - 8 Av
(917) 828-1154 – **WEB:** www.waverlynyc.com
Lunch Sat - Sun Dinner nightly

PRICE: $$$$

WALLSÉ 

Austrian • Contemporary décor

MAP: B2

With their roll call of "fashionable" ingredients garnered from all corners of the globe, restaurant menus can sometimes look as though they've been put together by a promiscuous explorer rather than an inquisitive chef. But, not all of us always want loquat with our lunch or dashi with our dinner—sometimes we need something that evokes a sense of place and history and Wallsé provides just that.

Those, however, who think Austrian food is all Wiener schnitzel and apple strudel should think again, because this cuisine is itself made up of a host of influences, stretching from Italy all the way to the Balkans. Chef Kurt Gutenbrunner and his kitchen also demonstrate how cuisines can evolve to respect contemporary tastes without compromising their integrity. So whilst there are plenty of classics on offer at all times, including quark spaetzle with succulent, tender rabbit, there are also lighter dishes like cod with squash and chanterelles.

This two-roomed restaurant exudes a sense of romance, so if you're here on a date go full-on Viennese when it comes to dessert by sharing a Sachertorte. The vivid modern canvasses are also a welcome change from the anodyne art found in so many places.

---

344 W. 11th St. (at Washington St.)
Christopher St - Sheridan Sq
(212) 352-2300 — **WEB:** www.kurtgutenbrunner.com
Dinner Mon - Sat

PRICE: $$$$

ZZ'S CLAM BAR ✿

Seafood • Luxury

MAP: C4

If you forget about your bank statement, don't arrive faint with hunger and leave your cynicism at the door—you'll love ZZ's Clam Bar. With just four marble tables and a small counter, this is as intimate as it gets. But you first have to navigate the bouncer at the door who'll only allow admittance with a reservation. This at least ensures that, when you're inside this bijou spot, the door doesn't swing open every minute.

Once in, you're handed a cocktail list—these are, without doubt, some of the best in town and fully justify the lofty prices. The short seafood menu comes with a couple of choices under headings like "crudo," "seared" and "ceviche." Before you do anything else, order the trout roe on toast—it's a beautiful thing and will linger long in the memory.

This is not the place for everyone. Some won't see past some of the more pretentious elements and affectations and the prices can be eye-watering—the Chianina beef carpaccio comes in at over $100. However, judicious ordering before you plunge into the cocktails, like having clams instead of caviar, can at least keep your final bill from escalating too wildly. It also helps that the place is run with considerable charm, patience and care.

---

169 Thompson St. (bet. Bleecker & Houston Sts.)

Spring St (Sixth Ave.)

(212) 254-3000 – **WEB:** www.zzsclambar.com

Dinner Tue - Sat

PRICE: $$$$

HARLEM, MORNINGSIDE & WASHINGTON HEIGHTS

This upper Manhattan pocket is best known for its 1920s jazz clubs that put musicians like Charlie Parker and Miles Davis on the map. Home to Columbia University, this capital of African-American, Hispanic and Caribbean culture lives up to its world-renowned reputation as an incubator of artistic and academic greats. Having officially cast off the age-old stigma of urban blight, these streets are now scattered with terrific soul food joints and authentic African markets that make Harlem a vibrant and enormously desirable destination.

MORNINGSIDE HEIGHTS

Considered an extension of the Upper West Side, park-lined Morningside Heights is frequented for its big and bold breakfasts. Inexpensive eateries are set between quaint brownstones and commercial buildings. When they're not darting to and from classes, resident scholars and ivy-leaguers from Columbia University can be found lounging at the **Hungarian Pastry Shop** with a sweet treat and cup of tea. Special occasions may call for an evening gathering at **Lee Lee's Baked Goods**. Rather

than be misled by its plain-Jane façade, prepare yourself for gratification here by way of their rugelach, allegedly the most delicious and decadent version in town. When spring approaches, stroll out on to the terrace and enjoy an apricot-filled treat in the breeze.

WEST HARLEM

Further north lies Harlem, a sanctuary for the soul and stomach. Fifth Avenue divides this region into two very unique sections: West Harlem, a hub for African-American culture; and East Harlem, a pulsating Spanish district also referred to as "El Barrio." Beloved for its sass and edge, West Harlem is constantly making way for booming gentrification and socio-cultural evolution. One of its most visible borders is **Fairway**, a Tri-State gourmet staple that draws shoppers from all walks of life. Pick up one of their goodies to-go or simply savor them while sifting through the extensive literary collection over at the historic Schomburg Center for Research in Black Culture. When the sun sets over the Hudson River, locals and savvy tourists may be found slipping into **Patisserie des Ambassades**, where the modern, chic décor does much to lure—for breakfast, lunch and dinner. Not only do the aromas from fresh-baked croissants, éclairs au chocolat and cream-filled beignets waft down the block, they also ensure long lines at all times. Every August, **Harlem Week** brings the community together for art, music and food. Join the fun and take in some of the most soulful tunes in town. Both east and west of Central Harlem, food has always factored heavily into everyday routine, and the choices are as diverse as the neighborhood itself. From Mexican and Caribbean, to West African cuisine, there are rich culinary delights to be had. For instance, **Lolo's Seafood Shack** cooks up Caribbean-infused steampots and serves them out of a counter; while **Manna's** on Frederick Douglass Boulevard attracts diners to its soul food steam table, where church groups rub shoulders and share stories with backpackers. Fried food junkies fantasize over Chef

Charles Gabriel's acclaimed buffet and amazing fried chicken at **Charles' Country Pan Fried Chicken**, but for an evening at home, comb the shelves at **Harlem Shambles**, a true-blue butcher shop specializing in quality cuts of meat and poultry that are sure to enhance every meal.

EAST HARLEM

Over in East Harlem, Spanish food enthusiasts and culture pundits never miss a trip to **Amor Cubano** for home-style faves. If smoked and piggy lechón served with a side of sultry, live Cuban beats isn't your idea of a good time, there's always that counter of Caribbean eats at **Sisters**. Not pressed for time? Choose to scope the tempting taco truck and taqueria scene along "Little Mexico" on East 116th Street—otherwise known as the nucleus of New York City's Mexican communities.

Almost like a vestige of the Italian population that was once dominant in this district, **Rao's** remains a culinary landmark. Operated from a poky basement and patronized by bigwigs like President Donald Trump or Nicole Kidman, it is one of the city's most difficult tables to secure. The original benefactors have exclusive rights to a seat here and hand off reservations like rent-controlled apartments. But, rest easy as there is

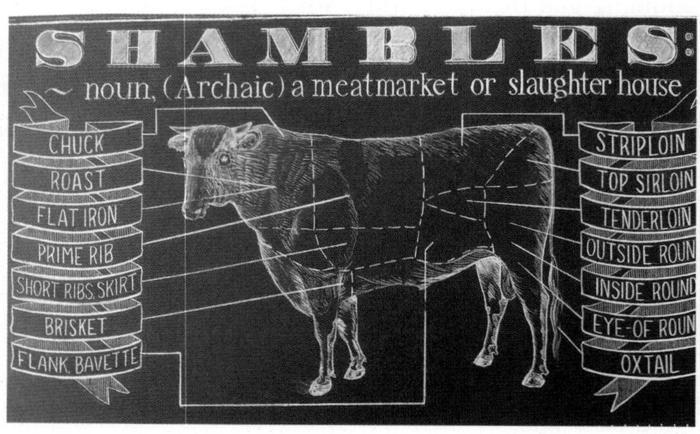

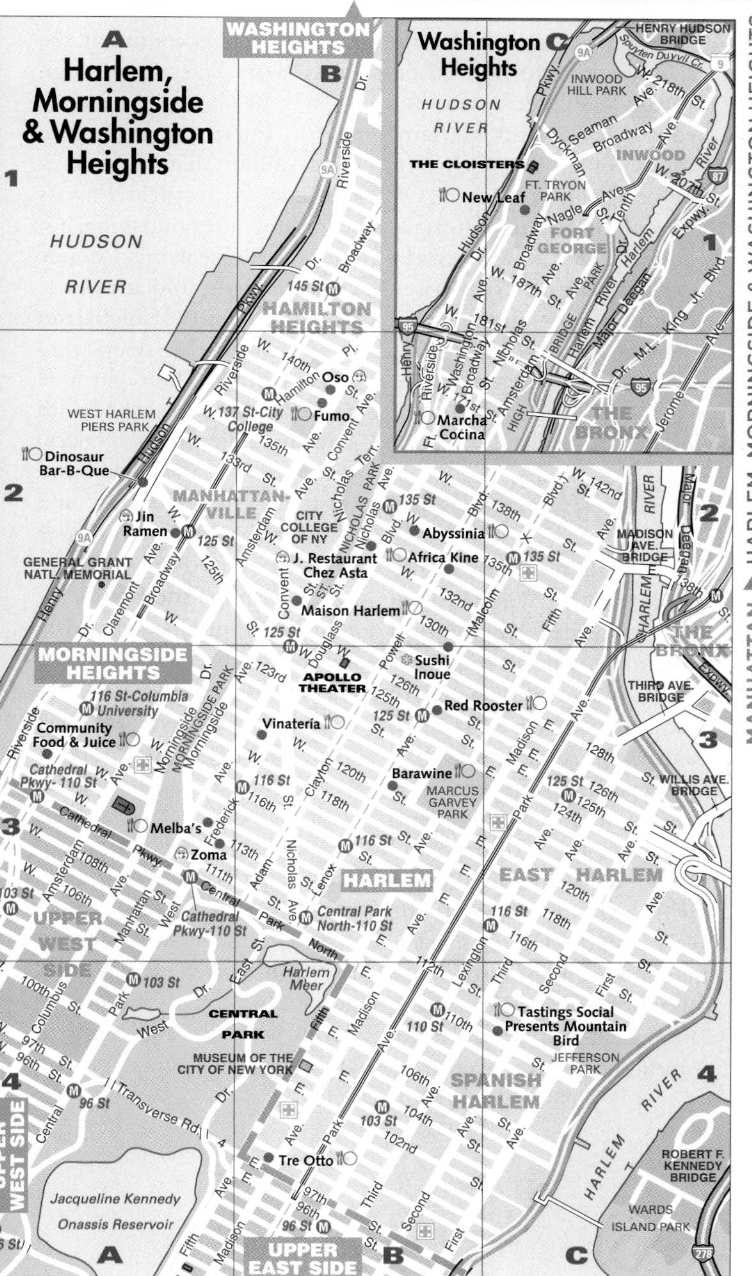
Harlem, Morningside & Washington Heights
Washington Heights
WASHINGTON HEIGHTS
HUDSON RIVER
HAMILTON HEIGHTS
MANHATTANVILLE
MORNINGSIDE HEIGHTS
HARLEM
EAST HARLEM
SPANISH HARLEM
UPPER WEST SIDE
UPPER EAST SIDE
THE BRONX
INWOOD
FORT GEORGE
INWOOD HILL PARK
FT. TRYON PARK
THE CLOISTERS
HENRY HUDSON BRIDGE
New Leaf
Marcha Cocina
WEST HARLEM PIERS PARK
Dinosaur Bar-B-Que
Jin Ramen
GENERAL GRANT NATL. MEMORIAL
CITY COLLEGE OF NY
J. Restaurant Chez Asta
Maison Harlem
Oso
Fumo
Abyssinia
Africa Kine
Sushi Inoue
APOLLO THEATER
Red Rooster
Vinateria
Barawine
MARCUS GARVEY PARK
Community Food & Juice
Melba's
Zoma
MADISON AVE. BRIDGE
THIRD AVE. BRIDGE
WILLIS AVE. BRIDGE
CENTRAL PARK
Harlem Meer
MUSEUM OF THE CITY OF NEW YORK
Tastings Social Presents Mountain Bird
JEFFERSON PARK
Tre Otto
Jacqueline Kennedy Onassis Reservoir
ROBERT F. KENNEDY BRIDGE
WARDS ISLAND PARK
HARLEM RIVER
145 St
137 St-City College
125 St
135 St
116 St-Columbia University
Cathedral Pkwy-110 St
116 St
103 St
96 St
Central Park North-110 St
110 St

additional, equally enticing Italian cooking to be enjoyed at **Patsy's Pizzeria**, another stronghold in East Harlem, famous for its hot coal oven (and occasionally its pizza). Of course **Hot Bread Kitchen**, a tenant of **La Marqueta marketplace**, continues to flourish for their global selection at both breakfast and lunch, and is reputed to be quite the holy haven among carb addicts.

WASHINGTON HEIGHTS

Set along the northern reaches of Uptown, Washington Heights offers ample food choices along its steep streets. From Venezuelan food truck sensation **Patacon Pisao**, to restaurants like **Malecon** preparing authentic morir soñando, mangu and mofongo, this colorful and lively neighborhood keeps dishing it out. In fact, the Tony award-winning musical *In The Heights* is a tribute to this ebullient district, where Dominican and Puerto Rican communities have taken root. Late-nighters never tire of the Latin beats blasting through the air here, after which a visit to Puerto Rican piragua carts selling shaved ice in a rainbow of tropical flavors seems not only nourishing, but necessary. Locals also queue up around the block outside **Elsa La Reina del Chicharrón** for their crunchy, deep-fried chicharrónes. Their parched palates may be quenched with jugos naturales (natural juices) made from cane sugar and fresh fruit for a healthy and filling treat. Hungry hordes can also be found ducking into **La Rosa Fine Foods** for a crowning meal starring fish, meat and vegetables. And if craving some sweet after this abundant savory feast, drop in at **Carrot Top Pastries** as they entice passersby with their assorted cookies, cakes and deliciously moist potato pies. Finally, first-rate fish markets and butcher shops also dot these hilly blocks, and less than ten bucks will get you a plate of traditional pernil with rice and beans at any number of diners nearby.

MARCUS GARVEY
PARK

ABYSSINIA

Ethiopian • Simple

MAP: B2

Abyssinia's expansion couldn't be better timed, for the local Ethiopian population surrounding its Harlem location has grown by leaps and bounds in recent years. Expanded digs mean no one leaves hungry, including the gluten-intolerant diners lining up for the injera—a spongy, sourdough risen flatbread that performs the task of cutlery, and is also ideal for sopping up all the great flavors from this authentic kitchen.

The dining room is spacious and flooded with natural light; the staff gracious; and the décor simple and functional. This is essentially light, healthy and spicy cooking, and the best way to experience it is to come with a group and order a slew of entrées to sample. Whatever you do, save room for the delicious slow-cooked beef awaze tibs.

268 W. 135th St. (bet. Adam Clayton Powell Jr. & Frederick Douglass Blvds.)
135 St (St. Nicholas Ave.)
(212) 281-2673 — **WEB:** www.harlemethiopianfood.com
Lunch & dinner daily **PRICE:** $$

AFRICA KINE

Senegalese • Simple

MAP: B2

Following the closure of the original location a few years ago, fans of Senegalese cuisine are happy to see the return of this West Harlem café run by a pair of Dakar natives. A giant fork and spoon hanging on the wall are whimsical decorative accents in a room of pale yellow hues and faux marble-topped tables, where placemats double as menus displaying Africa Kine's myriad offerings.

Keep it simple with grilled fish or meat sided by a salad, or opt for more succulent items such as peanut butter-enriched lamb mafe or suppa kandja (lamb and fish simmered in an okra and golden palm oil sauce). Note that some dishes are only available on certain nights, and although lunch is a more limited affair, Senegal's national treasure, thiebou djeun, is always on offer.

2267 Seventh Ave. (bet. 133rd & 134th Sts.)
135 St (Lenox Ave.)
(212) 666-9400 — **WEB:** www.africakine.com
Lunch & dinner daily **PRICE:** $$

BARAWINE

Contemporary • Bistro

MAP: B3

Amid the leafy, brownstone-lined Mount Morris Park Historic District, Barawine is an inviting dining room overseen by Fabrice Warin (formerly the sommelier at Orsay). This eye-catching space entices Lenox Avenue passersby to step in, sip and sup, either perched at the bar area's communal table or seated in the quieter, more intimate back dining room. Whitewashed walls attractively double as wine storage throughout.

The crowd-pleasing menu defies classification and embraces many influences. Quinoa salad with tofu and seaweed will please the disciplined, while mac and cheese loaded with béchamel, Gruyère and diced ham calls out to more indulgent palates. Pan-seared branzino with aromatic herbs and a drizzle of balsamic is a treat for all.

200 Lenox Ave. (at 120th St.)
116 St (Lenox Ave.)
(646) 756-4154 — **WEB:** www.barawine.com
Lunch Sat - Sun Dinner nightly

PRICE: $$

COMMUNITY FOOD & JUICE

American • Neighborhood

MAP: A3

As part of Columbia University's sprawl, this address is a godsend for students, faculty and locals from morning to night. Although it's spacious with plenty of outdoor options, the popular spot doesn't accept reservations—and has the lines to prove it. Executive Chef/partner Neil Kleinberg (also of downtown fave Clinton St. Baking Company) turns out joyful fare, and the weekday blueberry pancake special is just one reason why this place gets so much love.

For lunch, a kale salad with artichoke hearts, pickled carrots and crispy chickpeas is anything but rote. Come dinnertime, the fish or steak of the day might reveal pan-seared mahi mahi with roasted cauliflower and black truffle beurre blanc, or grilled strip steak brushed with teriyaki.

2893 Broadway (bet. 112th & 113th Sts.)
Cathedral Pkwy/110 St (Broadway)
(212) 665-2800 — **WEB:** www.communityrestaurant.com
Lunch & dinner daily

PRICE: $$

DINOSAUR BAR-B-QUE

Barbecue • Family

MAP: A2

Huge, loud and perpetually packed, this way west Harlem barbecue hall draws crowds from near and far. The bar area is rollicking, and for that reason kept separate from the dining quarters. There, wood beams and slats, swirling ceiling fans and oxblood leather booths fashion a comfortable—and quieter—setting.

The scent of wood smoke wafting through the red brick structure (which coincidentally once served as a meatpacking warehouse) only heightens the diners' carnivorous cravings. Minimize decision making and order the Extreme Sampler: a heaping feast of apple cider-brined smoked chicken, dry-rubbed slow-smoked pork ribs and lean Creekstone Farms brisket. Add on a creative side or two—perhaps the barbecue fried rice studded with bits of pulled pork?

700 W. 125th St. (at Twelfth Ave.)
125 St (Broadway)
(212) 694-1777 — **WEB:** www.dinosaurbarbque.com
Lunch & dinner daily **PRICE: $$**

FUMO

Italian • Trattoria

MAP: B2

The setting at Fumo is undeniably chic, with bright white walls, light wood tables and dark leather furnishings. A wood-fired pizza oven is in the back, while the front offers sidewalk seating under a protective awning. Attractive shelving lined with canned tomatoes frames the bar area and dining room.

The menu offers Italian favorites, executed with a deft hand and solid ingredients. Pizzas are 12-inches and come rosso or bianco, topped with the likes of vodka sauce, wild mushrooms or charred vegetables. Excellent pastas, like the penne Caprese, are tossed with tomato sauce, fresh basil and creamy mozzarella. A neatly deboned, beautifully seasoned branzino arrives subtly flavored with fresh herbs and alongside wilted spinach as well as a lemon wedge.

1600 Amsterdam Ave. (at 139th St.)
137 St - City College
(646) 692-6675 — **WEB:** www.fumorestaurant.com
Lunch & dinner daily **PRICE: $$**

JIN RAMEN

Japanese • Simple

MAP: A2

All you really need to know is that this is hands-down the best ramen above 59th Street. Sure, decorative elements are simple, and it hardly matters that this gem is hidden behind the 125th Street station's brick escalator. What comes from the kitchen however deserves kudos. The menu is concise but full of classics like pan-fried gyoza served with an addictive sesame seed-flecked dipping sauce. Shio, shoyu and miso ramen are all delightful, but the tonkatsu ramen is a special treat. This piping-hot, almost creamy, mouthcoating distillation of pork bones is deliciously rich and stocked with fragrant chasu, pickled bamboo shoots, slivered green onion and a soft-boiled egg.

For added fun, visit Kissaten Jin—an offshot serving homestyle bites and soba made by a master.

3183 Broadway (bet. 125th St. & Tiemann Pl.)
125 St (Broadway)
(646) 559-2862 – **WEB:** www.jinramen.com
Lunch & dinner daily **PRICE:**

J. RESTAURANT CHEZ ASTA

Senegalese • Simple

MAP: B2

Impressive in its authenticity, this Senegalese café is a rare bird in a neighborhood of vibrant dining choices. Meals here are exquisitely prepared and brim with unique flavors and scents, resulting in a truly transporting experience.

Spotless and comfy, the dining room offers a clutch of wood tables sturdy enough to support the heaping portions of chicken yassa or lemon-marinated chicken cooked with onions; as well as souloukhou, fish and vegetables in a peanut sauce. For a true taste of the country's flavors, go with the thiebou djeun, a one pot wonder of broken rice infused with tomato and Scotch bonnet pepper. It's cooked with fish, cabbage, okra and cassava, and speckled with xóoñ (those crusty, toothsome bits scraped from the bottom of the pan).

2479 Frederick Douglass Blvd. (bet. 132nd & 133rd Sts.)
135 St (Frederick Douglass Blvd.)
(212) 862-3663 – **WEB:** N/A
Lunch & dinner daily **PRICE:**

MAISON HARLEM

French • Bistro

MAP: B2

A steady stream of locals, phone-toting tourists and City College academics filling these well-worn wooden tables proves that this bistro has little trouble attracting a crowd. Floor-to-ceiling windows, dark red banquettes and quirky touches like vintage Gallic posters or football jerseys tacked to the walls lend a whiff of whimsy.

Maison Harlem's menu plays around with culinary traditions, with results that may include a classic rendition of coq au vin with smoky lardons, browned button mushrooms and fresh noodles to garnish the wine-braised chicken pieces. Sticking to tradition, ratatouille is a sunny bowlful of diced and stewed summer vegetables. The tarte Tatin layers thick but spoon-tender caramelized apple wedges over outrageously buttery pastry.

341 St. Nicholas Ave. (at 127th St.)
125 St (St. Nicholas Ave.)
(212) 222-9224 – **WEB:** www.maisonharlem.com
Lunch & dinner daily

PRICE: $$

MARCHA COCINA

Latin American • Colorful

MAP: B2

Located a few blocks from the United Palace is the easygoing and warm Marcha Cocina. Outfitted with a long bar, high tables and convivial crowd, this sea-blue oasis feels like the ideal Caribbean refuge. Sure, the music is loud, but with service so down-to-earth and food that impresses beyond what its casual vibe might suggest, who's really complaining?

The menu is broad and affordable, which makes a perfect excuse to sample widely. Staples from tortilla Española to gambas al ajillo are delicious executions of classic tapas. Luscious ribbons of Spanish ham are on display in the hongos e higos coca, a chewy flatbread also topped with mushrooms, figs and buttery almonds. It would be blasphemy to skip the dates wrapped in bacon or the thick-cut yucca fries.

4055 Broadway (at 171st St.)
168 St
(212) 928-8272 – **WEB:** www.marchacocinanyc.com
Lunch Fri – Sun Dinner nightly

PRICE: $$

MELBA'S

Southern • Neighborhood

MAP: A3

With its colorful spirit and lineup of Southern classics, this comfortable spot—as charming and lovely as its namesake owner, born-and-bred Harlemite Melba Wilson—is a perfect reflection of the neighborhood's flavor, culture and past. It's a place to gather and relax over good food and drinks, from Auntie B's mini-burgers slathered with a smoky sweet sauce to a golden-brown and berry-licious fruit cobbler that's nothing short of heaven on a plate.

Equally enticing is the Southern fried chicken—darkly bronzed, sweet and salty when paired with Melba's iconic eggnog waffles.

Expect other surprises like spring rolls stuffed with black-eyed peas, collards and cheddar cheese, as well as a healthy-minded grilled vegetable Napoleon with buffalo mozzarella.

300 W. 114th St. (at Frederick Douglass Blvd.)
116 St (Frederick Douglass Blvd.)
(212) 864-7777 — **WEB:** www.melbasrestaurant.com
Lunch Sat - Sun Dinner nightly **PRICE:** $$

NEW LEAF

American • Historic

MAP: C1

Talk about wowing your dinner date. Located in a 1930's slate and fieldstone cottage tucked away in Upper Manhattan's Fort Tryon Park, New Leaf Café was opened as part of the New York Restoration Project. With its stone walls and arched windows, the interior is just lovely. And lunch out on the flagstone terrace is downright stunning—offering unparalleled views of the dramatic Palisades and (if you squint a bit) the George Washington Bridge.

Delicious and modern American food is the name of the game at this kitchen. The menu touches on some usual crowd favorites (think juicy burgers and soft beignets) along with trendy, veggie-based items like avocado smeared on toasted crostini; a bowl of greens and grains; and a falafel burger.

1 Margaret Corbin Dr. (in Fort Tryon Park)
190 St
(212) 568-5323 — **WEB:** www.newleafrestaurant.com
Lunch daily Dinner Tue - Sun **PRICE:** $$

OSO 

Mexican • Simple

MAP: B2

This charming little Mexican restaurant, whose name means "bear" in Spanish, sits opposite the City College of New York. The space is dressed in wood tables, warm lighting and a Dia de los Muertos mural gracing a corner. One black-tiled dining counter is lined with vintage white metal stools, while another small bar faces the tidy open kitchen where the cooks hand-make tortillas at a steady clip.

The cuisine of Mexico City inspires Oso's menu with a concise, impressive offering of dishes like braised octopus tostada with mandarin salsa, guava- and chipotle-glazed ribs, as well as authentic tacos and antojitos. Come summer, don't miss the wonderful radish salad, served warm with fresh cilantro, serrano peppers, anchovies and tomato vinaigrette.

1618 Amsterdam Ave. (bet. 139th & 140th Sts.)
137 St - City College
(646) 858-3139 – **WEB:** www.osoharlem.com
Lunch & dinner daily **PRICE:** $$

RED ROOSTER

American • Brasserie

MAP: B3

For all his achievements, the name Marcus Samuelsson will be forever associated with Red Rooster. This Harlem landmark still draws a crowd for its most comforting of comfort food that celebrates the neighborhood in which it resides. There may now be a branch in London, but this one's the real McCoy and is run with genuine warmth and no little pizazz. And with Ginny's Supper Club downstairs, its heart is always beating.

There is just one thing you need to bring—your appetite. Shrimp & grits, chicken & waffles, mac & greens: when a dish has an ampersand it will probably be big enough to share. If you're teetering on the edge of wanton over-indulgence and need one final push, then finish with the doughnuts, which come filled with sweet potato cream.

310 Lenox Ave. (bet. 125 & 126th Sts.)
125 St (Lenox Ave.)
(212) 792-9001 – **WEB:** www.redroosterharlem.com
Lunch & dinner daily **PRICE:** $$$

SUSHI INOUE ✿

Japanese • Cozy

MAP: B3

For truly outstanding sushi, head to the heart of Harlem, where Chef Shinichi Inoue—formerly of Sushi Azabu—presides over this discreet and unexpected addition to the neighborhood.

Inside the small establishment, bamboo blinds obscuring the scene outside, combined with hushed and genuine hospitality produce a sense of calm and refinement. The Nagasaki-born chef works behind a display of sparkling fillets and a dark counter arranged with 14 washi placemats and sets of lacquered chopsticks. It is here that a concise list of omakase options is prepared increasing in price with the additions of tempura, sashimi and an uni tasting.

Chef Inoue personally looks after every detail of the meal—from the blended soy sauce to the house miso recipe. Pickled ginger placed on your tray ushers in the expertly crafted nigiri, and while the grated wasabi root that sparks most pieces can be a bit aggressive at times, the procession is delightful. Highlights include a bite of buttery shima aji from Kyushu island; shiro ika dressed with salt and sudachi; soy-marinated tuna with mustard and toasted sesame seeds; and fatty tuna from Boston—one of the rare pieces not from Japanese waters.

---

381 Lenox Ave. (at 129th St.)

125 St (Lenox Ave.)

(646) 766-0555 — **WEB:** www.sushiinoue.com

Dinner Tue - Sun

PRICE: $$$$

TASTINGS SOCIAL PRESENTS MOUNTAIN BIRD

Contemporary • Neighborhood

MAP: C4

The inspiration for Chef Kenichi Tajima and wife Keiko's popular venture no doubt sprang from the popularity of their initial and well-loved incarnation of Mountain Bird. It's clear they were missed, as this hot spot in collaboration with the events organization Tastings Social, stays hopping most nights.

This area has wanted for serious food for a while, and Mountain Bird brings it with style—the dining space, tucked into the ground floor of a red rowhouse, is intimate with a small bar and a smattering of wood tables. As the name implies, the menu bears a whimsical devotion to poultry, featuring dishes like hand-cut ostrich tartare; black truffle chicken wings and duck leg-and-turkey sausage cassoulet; along with a nightly seafood and vegetarian option.

251 E. 110th St. (bet. Second & Third Aves.)

110 St (Lexington Ave.)

(212) 744-4422 — **WEB:** www.tastingsnyc.com

Lunch Sat - Sun Dinner Tue - Sun **PRICE:** $$

TRE OTTO

Italian • Trattoria

MAP: B4

East Harlem's favorite neighborhood Italian has triumphantly returned following a move next door. Thanks to proprietors Louis and Lauren Cangiano, the popular surrounds—complete with cheery red walls, exposed brick and penny-tile floors—are as cozy and welcoming as ever.

Tre Otto's mouthwatering menu boasts home-style dishes made from recipes gathered over time. Antipasti include a luscious salad of shaved fennel and orange segments crowned by tender grilled octopus drizzled with zesty salmoriglio sauce. Freshly made trenette pasta is twirled with pesto Trapanese, a divinely rich combination of tomatoes, almonds, garlic and basil; while the flavors of pizza, topped with red onions, capers and tuna, call Sicily's sparkling coastline to mind.

1410 Madison Ave. (bet. 97th & 98th Sts.)

96 St (Lexington Ave.)

(212) 860-8880 — **WEB:** www.treotto.com

Lunch & dinner daily **PRICE:** $$

VINATERÍA

Italian • Contemporary décor

MAP: B3

Adding to Harlem and its hidden charms is Vinatería, an uptown darling brimming with wines to accompany each sublime bite. Not only is it cozy, but the attractive slate-toned room etched in chalk with scenes of decanters and menu specials will augment your appetite.

The semi-open kitchen in the back unveils such treasures as house-cured sardines with fiery piquillo peppers and crunchy croutons; or a salad of earthy golden and red beets mingled with yogurt, oranges, arugula, crunchy pistachios and tossed with a lemon vinaigrette. Herbs plucked from their copper planters may be featured in an impeccably grilled rosemary-marinated pork blade served with rich mashed potatoes; or desserts like citrus-glazed rosemary panna cotta bathed in chamomile grappa.

2211 Frederick Douglass Blvd. (at 119th St.)
116 St (Frederick Douglass Blvd.)
(212) 662-8462 — **WEB:** www.vinaterianyc.com
Lunch Sat - Sun Dinner nightly

PRICE: $$

ZOMA

Ethiopian • Contemporary décor

MAP: A3

Smart, cool, modern and always welcoming, Zoma may well be this city's most serious Ethiopian restaurant. The crowded bar emits a golden light from below to showcase its premium spirits, and the ambient dining room is filled with locals from this thriving community.

Attention to detail is clear from the steaming-hot towel for cleaning your hands to the carefully folded injera used for scooping up their chopped salads, chunky stews and saucy vegetables. Unusual starters might include green lentils with a cold and crunchy mix of onions, jalapeños, ginger, white pepper and mustard seeds. The doro wat—a chicken dish of the Amhara people—is a traditional stew with a berbere sauce of sun-dried hot peppers and ground spices.

2084 Frederick Douglass Blvd. (at 113th St.)
116 St (Frederick Douglass Blvd.)
(212) 662-0620 — **WEB:** www.zomanyc.com
Lunch Sat - Sun Dinner nightly

PRICE:

LOWER EAST SIDE

The Lower East Side is one of New York City's most energetic, stylish and fast-evolving neighborhoods. Bragging a plethora of shopping, eating and nightlife, this high-energy hub proudly retains the personality of its first wave of hard-working immigrants. But, thanks to a steady stream of artists and entrepreneurs over the last few decades, as well as a solid real estate uprising, this area faces constant transformation, with an influx of high-rises breaking through its trendy boutiques and galleries. And despite such renovation, some nooks remain straight-up dodgy as if in defiance of such rapid development; while others feel downright Village-like, in stature and spirit.

AROUND THE WORLD

Visit the Lower East Side Tenement Museum for a glimpse of the past before

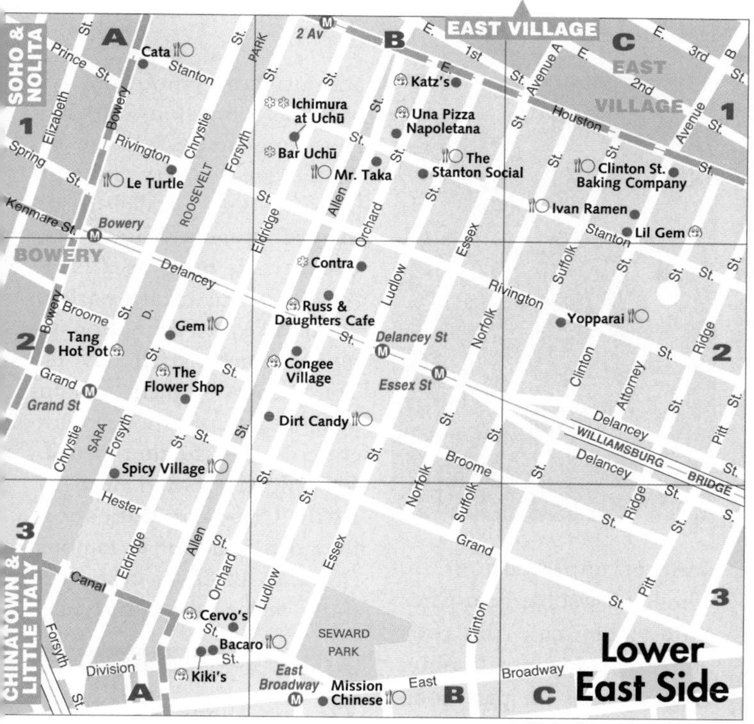

trekking its enticing, ethnically diverse streets. Then for a taste of yore, traipse into **Russ & Daughters**, which flaunts appetizing tidbits including smoked, cured fish to go with hearty bagels. This nosher's paradise was instituted in 1914, but continues to be mobbed even today, especially during the holidays when that "ultimate salmon and caviar" package is nothing short of—you guessed it—ultimate! Also inhabiting these streets are German, Italian and Chinese residents, whose opposite cultures have triggered a host of deliciously varied eats and treats. Meanwhile, an afternoon spent at **Gaia Italian Cafè** breezing through magazines and biting into delicious dolci or perfect biscotti will take you back to Rome on a dime. This toasty spot may be mini in size, but cooks up flavors that are mighty fine. **Tiny's Giant Sandwich Shop** is yet

another unpretentious but wholly irresistible gem where sandwiches rule the roost and are slung at all times. Ground zero for partygoers, punk rockers and scholars, this Rivington Street paragon is a rare find, highlighting fresh ingredients and creative presentations. Speaking of such spirited scenes, **New Beer Distributors** is a warehouse-y beer shop in operation since 1968. Housing numerous bottles and cans from the globe over, craft beer aficionados will adore perusing its metal racks for unique varietals. Then, if sweet is what you need, **Economy Candy** is a flourishing emporium of old-time confections. Moving from one timeless haven to another are two very different takes on one nostalgic treat. **Morgenstern's Finest Ice Cream** bills itself as a New American ice cream parlor, while **Ice & Vice** boasts highly experimental flavors. Try a scoop of their "opium den" or pint of smoked dark chocolate as further proof. Cake-fiends should head to **Little Cupcake Bakeshop** for a dense slice of its famous Brooklyn blackout cake or a fluffy wedge of coconut cake.

ETHNIC FUN

By the 1950s, the ethnic mosaic that defined this district intensified with a surge of new settlers, but this time they were mainly from Puerto Rico and the Dominican Republic. These communities continue to dot the culinary landscape today, so foodies come to savor such favorites as mofongo and pernil. Dominican specialties and creamy café con leche at **El Castillo de Jagua** keep the party pumping from dawn till dusk, while sugar junkies find their fix at **Tache Artisan**

Chocolate—launched by pastry chef, Aditi Malhotra. Sample their tequila-infused dark chocolate ganache, which may last just a moment in your mouth, but promises to leave a lifelong impression. Rivington Street is a perfect hybrid of the old world and new order. During the day, the mood here is chill with locals who like to linger at cozy coffee houses. Come sunset, these blocks start to fill with raucous carousers looking to land upon a sceney restaurant or popular party haunt. Further south, Grand Street is home to well-manicured residential complexes scattered amid shops and catering to a cadre of deep-rooted residents. While here, carb-addicts should be afraid, very afraid, of **Kossar's Bialys** flooded with bagels, babkas and bialys. Then there's **Doughnut Plant** proffering items crafted from age-old recipes. But to replicate that classic deli experience at home, pick up pickles to-go from **The Pickle Guys**—settled on Grand Street and stocked with barrel-upon-barrel of these briny treats.

Fire escape-fronted Orchard Street is venerated as the original nucleus of this nabe.

Once dominated by the garment trade with stores selling fabrics and notions, today it tells a different tale with sleek eateries and trendy boutiques flaunting handmade jewelry or designer skateboards. Even tailors remain a cult favorite here, offering cheap, while-you-wait service. At lunch, you may even find them along with hungry locals chowing down on mojo beef paratha tacos at Indian fusion hot spot, **Goa Taco**. Concurrently, **Dimes** (the café that exudes Cali-cool on Canal St.) is a reliable source for three square meals. Of course, it's packed to the gills during peak hours, so shoppers may cool their heels at **il laboratorio del gelato** on Ludlow.

ESSEX STREET MARKET

Every self-respecting food lover makes the pilgrimage to **Essex Street Market**, a treasure trove of gourmet food. Frequented for its top produce merchants, butchers, bakers and fishmongers all housed under one roof, this public bazaar expounds on their expertise by way of cooking demonstrations and wine tastings. Burned-out browsers however may rest their feet and calm a craving at **Essex** or even **Shopsin's General Store** known for an encyclopedic carte (and cranky owner). Finally, everything from okonomiyaki (at **Osaka Grub**); rice balls (at **Arancini Bros**); and cheese (at **Saxelby Cheesemongers**) make this emporium an enticing destination for gastronomes and curious palates alike.

BACARO

Italian • Vintage

MAP: A3

Heavy iron candelabras, crumbling stone walls and communal wooden tables lend a sultry vibe to this underground labyrinth, named for a Venetian bacaro (or counter for casual grazing of snacks and wine). The first floor's marble-topped bar beckons for small bites and a glass of wine, while nooks beneath those low stone ceilings in the downstairs dining room call for a romantic evening over candlelight.

Crafted by Frank DeCarlo, the same chef/owner of Peasant in Nolita, Bacaro's menu focuses on Northern Italian cuisine with an eye toward polenta and seafood. Insalata di granchio, fresh crab set atop a delicately fried polenta cake, is triumphant. For dessert, the velvety flourless chocolate cake topped with dried apricots, is as decadent as the setting.

136 Division St. (bet. Ludlow & Orchard Sts.)
East Broadway
(212) 941-5060 — **WEB:** www.bacaronyc.com
Dinner Tue - Sun

PRICE: $$

CATA

Spanish • Rustic

MAP: A1

Blue plaid and jean-clad waiters set the casual tone for Cata, a downtown-cool restaurant with a long bar and glass case displaying the day's seafood. Distressed mirrors, vaulted ceilings and iron accents fill the dark, cavernous space with a certain broody, old-world vibe. Long communal tables are ideal for groups lingering over small plates and an extensive list of gin-based cocktails.

Nibbling should be the strategy here, starting with whole deviled eggs stuffed with tangy-sweet gribiche beneath a single fried oyster. Crispy bite-sized bombas filled with potato, Manchego and serrano sit in a nice, mildly spicy tomato sauce. And caramelized torrija with sorbet is likely to be one of the most enjoyable versions of French toast that you've ever had.

245 Bowery (at Stanton St.)
2 Av
(212) 505-2282 — **WEB:** www.catarestaurant.com
Dinner nightly

PRICE: $$

BAR UCHŪ ✿

Japanese • Design

MAP: B1

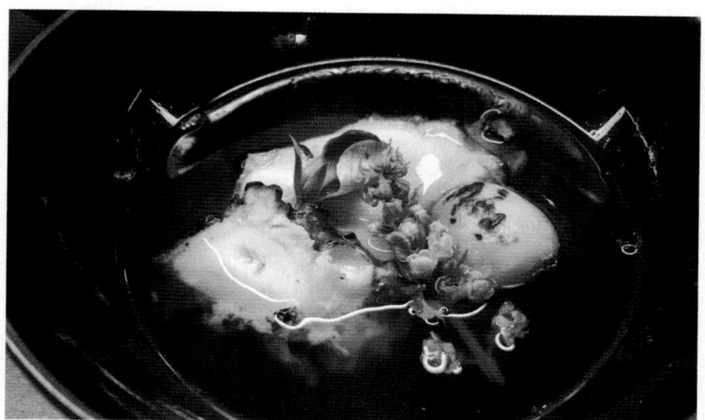

As with all the best addresses, you'll need an actual one to arrive at Bar Uchū, because their sign is so discreet you could easily walk past. Once inside, find yourself being guided gently by a member of staff to your seat at the L-shaped counter where you'll be then greeted with that most heartening of questions: "Do you drink alcohol?" Yes, this is a bar counter, not a kitchen counter—so instead of having a gaggle of diligent chefs beavering away in front of you, you'll be faced with what for some is the far more appealing sight of seductively illuminated bottles of Japanese whisky and cut-glass tumblers.

As soon as you've been served the house cocktail of the day, the kaiseki-style meal commences.

This cuisine is nominally Japanese but Chef Sam Clonts' cooking is unfettered by tradition and puts all his experience reaped at the illustrious Chef's Table at Brooklyn Fare to good use. The most striking element here is that these dishes are burnished with a roll-call of exceptionally luxurious ingredients, as might be evidenced by the golden Osetra caviar in the temaki, or the A5 Miyazaki rib-eye couched in the Hokkaido milk bread. The kitchen's largesse will leave a lasting impression.

---

217 Eldridge St. (bet. Rivington & Stanton Sts.)

2 Av

(212) 203-7634 – **WEB:** www.uchu.nyc

Dinner Tue - Sat

PRICE: $$$$

CERVO'S

Seafood • Cozy

MAP: A3

Darling and diminutive, Cervo's is perfect for date night. The dining room's canary-yellow booths, mosaic tiles and wood paneling will give you all those cozy feels.

The menu is heavy on seafood, so if plump mussels and tender scallops don't whet your appetite, this isn't the place for you. The kitchen's Spanish and Portuguese influences are evident in dishes such as black bean stew loaded with shell-on shrimp. Then mussels escabeche with beans will have you breaking off pieces of bread to sop up every drop of that olive oil-drizzled goodness. Keep the bread close when tucking in to beef tartare with clams—another dish that is bound to sate your date. The all-Spanish wine list boasts affordability while the by-the-glass selection is full of surprises.

43 Canal St. (bet. Ludlow & Orchard Sts.)
East Broadway
(212) 226-2545 — **WEB:** www.cervosnyc.com
Lunch Sun Dinner nightly

PRICE: $$

CLINTON ST. BAKING COMPANY

American • Simple

MAP: C1

What started as a bakery is now a brunch-focused legend—one that draws a perpetual crowd waiting for ample rewards. A little bit country and a little bit food lab, this kitchen has achieved such success that the owners now have outposts in Japan and Dubai. Here in Gotham, the space is comfy and the service, impressive.

Light and lovely chicken tortilla soup sees a pile of fried tortilla strips over a hearty broth bobbing with carrots, celery and shredded chicken. But breakfast for dinner is always a treat here, especially when golden Belgian waffles are served with warm maple butter and buttermilk-brined fried chicken for a flawless union of sweet and salt. Speaking of breakfast, it's cash-only during the day but credit cards are welcome at dinnertime.

4 Clinton St. (at Houston St.)
2 Av
(646) 602-6263 — **WEB:** www.clintonstreetbaking.com
Lunch daily Dinner Mon - Sat

PRICE: $$

CONGEE VILLAGE

Chinese • Family

MAP: B2

From the edge of Chinatown comes Congee Village, with its neon-etched sign that shines bright at night. Coveted for its fantastic cooking (check the front window for a slew of accolades), the menu also has a Cantonese focus. Service is basic and the décor kitschy at best, but it's clean, tidy and tons of fun.

This soothing namesake porridge comes in myriad forms— ladled into a clay pot with bits of crispy roasted duck skin, or mingled with pork liver and white fish to form an intense and rich flavor combination. Pair it with dunkable sticks of puffy deep-fried Chinese crullers for a satisfying contrast in texture. Less adventurous palates may deviate into such solid standards as sautéed short ribs and sweet onions tossed in a smoky black pepper sauce.

100 Allen St. (bet. Broome & Delancey Sts.)
Delancey St
(212) 941-1818 — **WEB:** www.congeevillagerestaurants.com
Lunch & dinner daily **PRICE:**

DIRT CANDY

Vegetarian • Trendy

MAP: B2

We all know that vegetables are good for us, but Dirt Candy shows us how good they can also taste. Chef Amanda Cohen's menu never hides the fact that you're eating vegetarian (and vegan) cuisine, but with her ethical approach and haute techniques, these simple-seeming eats are transformed into artistic bites. Robata-grilled sugar snap peas wrapped in yuba tastes as good as Peking duck, while the carrot slider is as tender and satisfying as a Big Mac. The vegetables aren't just for dinner either—they also star in desserts like hot chocolate, which incorporates mushroom cream, as well as cocktails that employ everything from cucumber to artichokes to popcorn.

The tasting menu ensures that you'll be able to sample a wide variety with five or nine courses.

86 Allen St. (bet. Broome & Grand Sts.)
Grand St
(212) 228-7732 — **WEB:** www.dirtcandynyc.com
Lunch Sat - Sun Dinner Tue - Sat **PRICE:** $$$$

CONTRA

Contemporary • Trendy

MAP: B2

Minimal, industrial and in harmony with the cool neighborhood, this is the kind of classic downtown spot that draws trendy millennials from afar. Seating is either intimate or cramped, and the music is lively or loud, all depending on your mood. Enthusiastic servers add to the room's energy.

Offering six courses for under $80, their prix-fixe menu is renowned not just for its ambition and creativity but also as one of good value. While the menu format may be fixed, dishes change frequently to reflect the young chefs' wide-ranging talents and contemporary flair. This kitchen really plays it up, presenting textures and ingredients in unusual, but appealing ways. Guinea hen, served in a light vin jaune sauce, is proof that simple can be spectacular. Whipped potato over a smoked date purée that is topped with fried kombu chips is equal parts fun and fantastic. Even dessert shows off a little sass: the elderflower granita with preserved celery, which imparts a dill pickle quality, is exceptional.

It's likely you won't recognize any names on Contra's wine list, hyper-focused on natural winemakers. Sip from a similar list and nibble on signature snacks next door at sibling Wildair.

---

138 Orchard St. (bet. Delancey & Rivington Sts.)

2 Av

(212) 466-4633 — **WEB:** www.contranyc.com

Dinner Tue - Sat

PRICE: $$$$

THE FLOWER SHOP ☺

American • Vintage

MAP: A2

First things first, The Flower Shop is more about Moscow Mules than mums, but judging by the bar packed at least two-people deep, that's just fine. Besides, the crowd is here to soak up the scene, which is a touch 70's nostalgic. Come for the drinks, but stay for the food and you'll be treated to some delicious pub grub.

This menu may be best described as gastropub-gone-global with eclectic offerings ranging from fries and wings to katsu chicken sandwiches. The Scotch eggs, with their crispy coating and ground beef meets soft-yolk interior, are particularly good. But don't fill up on these as the broccoli rabe tostada, featuring an impossibly crispy base smeared with thick ricotta, pickled chili and yuzu, is a clever trinity of heat, citrus and cream.

107 Eldridge St. (bet. Broome & Grand Sts.)
Grand St
(212) 257-4072 — **WEB:** www.theflowershopnyc.com
Lunch Sat - Sun Dinner nightly

PRICE: $$

GEM

Contemporary • Elegant

MAP: A2

Known as the "Justin Bieber of Food," Flynn McGarry has caused much ado on the local food scene. By seventh grade, he was committed to cooking, eventually apprenticing at well-known kitchens until he launched the pop-up Eureka in LA—which eventually moved to NY. With Gem, now he has his first brick-and-mortar spot, at the ripe old age of nineteen.

Come nighttime, this open kitchen boldly equipped with a small convection oven lights up with a merry crew cranking out ten or so courses over two seatings. The chef's unabashedly ambitious techniques with seasonal ingredients result in a remarkably vivid and mature culinary vision. Envision smoked cod with shaved green apple, or braised pork in a lettuce wrap with fish sauce and you'll start to get the picture.

116 Forsyth St. (bet. Broome & Delancey Sts.)
Grand St
N/A — **WEB:** www.gem-nyc.com
Dinner Tue - Sat

PRICE: $$$$

ICHIMURA AT UCHŪ ✿✿

Japanese • Intimate

MAP: B1

This glossy Japanese prodigy may be settled amidst generic bodegas and low-lying storefronts, but it is an absolute jewel of a spot. Envisioned by owner, Derek Feldman, the sushi bar is headed up by master chef, Eiji Ichimura, who prepares a culinary experience for up to 20 lucky diners nightly.

A sharply suited host ushers guests into an elegant space decked out in shades of gold. Designed by Scott Kester, walls are lined with textured coverings and the pale wood counter is armed with ten sienna-orange leather chairs. There are no tables and only two seatings per night—at 6:00 and 9:00 P.M.—ergo, it's important to be punctual as the first meal ends with just enough of a break to give the chef some time to set up for his second session.

A night in this master's presence is thrilling. The grit and noise from the outside will start to dim just as the soothing space and exquisite dishes begin to envelop you. Noodle-like baby squid is served in ponzu with a pinch of grated daikon for ace flavor, while slices of octopus are arranged with leeks and mustard for textural excellence. A delightfully savory monaka combining toasted nori, king crab and Hokkaido uni makes for a luxurious mouthful.

---

217 Eldridge St. (bet. Rivington & Stanton Sts.)

2 Av

(212) 203-7634 — **WEB:** www.uchu.nyc

Dinner Tue - Sat

PRICE: $$$$

IVAN RAMEN

Japanese • Colorful

MAP: C1

This delicious little ramen-ya couldn't have landed on a more fitting spot. It may appear rough around the edges, but the ultra-hip 'hood and its affinity for indie rock beats fit Ivan's scene to a tee. Then consider their sweet staff gliding within the snug space filled with packed seats, and realize how serious a treat this is. Solo diners head to the counter for a view of the action-packed kitchen, while others look for a seat from which to admire that mural of manga cutouts. Find them launching into pickled daikon with XO sauce and sesame seeds for a 'lil crunch and whole 'lotta flavor. Displaying a flair for non-traditional ingredients, paitan ramen with tender chicken confit in a chicken-kombu broth makes for a singular, savory and tasty highlight.

25 Clinton St. (bet. Houston & Stanton Sts.)
Delancey St
(646) 678-3859 – **WEB:** www.ivanramen.com
Lunch & dinner daily

PRICE: $$

KATZ'S

Deli • Delicatessen

MAP: B1

One of the last-standing, old-time Eastern European spots on the Lower East Side, Katz's is a true NY institution. It's crowded, crazy and packed with a panoply of characters weirder than a jury duty pool. Tourists, hipsters, blue hairs and everybody in between flock here, so come on off-hours. Because it's really that good.

Walk inside, get a ticket and don't lose it (those guys at the front aren't hosts—upset their system and you'll get a verbal beating). Then pick up your food at the counter and bring it to a first-come first-get table; or opt for a slightly less dizzying experience at a waitress-served table.

Nothing's changed in the looks or taste. Matzo ball soup, pastrami sandwiches, potato latkes—everything is what you'd expect, only better.

205 E. Houston St. (at Ludlow St.)
2 Av
(212) 254-2246 – **WEB:** www.katzsdelicatessen.com
Lunch & dinner daily

PRICE:

KIKI'S

Greek • Rustic

MAP: A3

This is where to find excellent home-style Greek cooking at unbeatable prices. Everything tastes fundamentally right and good, from the perfectly tender braised and grilled octopus to those moist and smoky lamb chops—the aromas alone guarantee that you will dine well here. Start with a superb spanakopita that balances flaky phyllo with just the right amount of chopped spinach, dotted with onion and feta. Saganaki entices with salty and springy Greek cheese wrapped in pastry that manages to stay crisp beneath a rich drenching of honey and sesame seeds.

The tavern-like space feels attractively dark, cozy, fills up quickly and doesn't take reservations, so expect a wait. The servers and staff are a stylish and laid-back mirror image of the neighborhood.

130 Division St. (at Orchard St.)
East Broadway
(646) 882-7052 – **WEB:** N/A
Lunch & dinner daily

PRICE: $$

LE TURTLE

Contemporary • Trendy

MAP: A1

Experience and style converge at this beautiful destination and instant favorite of the cool kids in town. The cuisine is not only as attractive as the setting, but sophisticated flavors ensure its success. The kitchen is operating at a high level experimenting with foams, gels and powders with good results. Begin with the meaty and savory mushrooms, buoyed by a white yuzu kosho foam and a hit of acidity thanks to lemon gel cubes. Duck, glazed in lavender honey, is served over a black porridge mixed with stracciatella cheese and squid ink that is positively addictive. Every flavor is perfectly complementary in the dense and buttery hazelnut financier, from the chewy caramelized edges to the quenelles of lemon yogurt sorbet and pear purée.

177 Chrystie St. (at Rivington St.)
Bowery
(646) 918-7189 – **WEB:** www.leturtle.fr
Dinner nightly

PRICE: $$

LIL GEM

Lebanese • Cozy

MAP: C1

This is a charming little button of a place, filled with high-tops and cushy banquettes that feel like they're closing in on the open kitchen. The Lebanese cooking turned out of the kitchen has a clear, chef-driven perspective that never shies away from spice; occasionally it rips with heat. Expect to feast on a spectrum of dips, shawarma and larger plates like ribeye seasoned with Aleppo pepper and coffee or whole duck spiced with cardamom. Babaganoush may appear dainty, but delivers intensely smoky flavors that almost conjure hickory barbecue. Don't miss out on Brussels sprouts, coated with caramelized pecans and pomegranate molasses.

It's important to arrive here early as this is the kind of kitchen that is prone to running out of favorite dishes.

29 Clinton St. (bet. Houston & Stanton Sts.)
Essex St
(646) 368-1392 — **WEB:** www.lilgemnyc.com
Lunch Sat - Sun Dinner nightly **PRICE:** $$

MISSION CHINESE

Chinese • Trendy

MAP: B3

Welcome to Danny Bowien's raucous, Sichuan-esque New York outpost of the San Francisco original. Long lines—often starring celebrities and nightlife VIPs—are to be expected.

Once inside, everything about this space can seem disorienting—from the bar's UV backlighting to the dizzying hall of mirrors downstairs. That said, this is a totally unique experience combining Sichuan spices with dishes unknown to the province—think steak tartare or hot cheese pizza. The kitchen is clearly having fun, and that is A-OK, as they pull it off in a way that never feels gimmicky. Just remember to pay attention to the prices (like the $100 duck). The smoky, fatty kung pao pastrami with potatoes, dried peppers and peanuts could even give Katz's a run for its money.

171 East Broadway (bet. Jefferson & Rutgers Sts.)
East Broadway
(917) 376-5660 — **WEB:** www.missionchinesefood.com
Lunch Sat - Sun Dinner nightly **PRICE:** $$$

MR. TAKA

Japanese • Minimalist

MAP: B1

When the chef of a successful Tokyo ramen-ya opens a spot in NY, success is virtually guaranteed. Mr. Taka may seem small and simple, but the food is fun and distinctive. Don't expect a conversation, since people dig in to these steaming bowls and barely come up for air.

The cooking here is a delicious break from tradition, thanks to ramen that ranges in toppings from avocado to the richest slice of pork belly on this side of the Pacific. The spicy Tonkatsu ramen, from its glistening pork and its springy noodles to its zesty homemade chili oil and black garlic oil, is the ultimate antidote to winter. Other highlights include the karage bun with juicy chicken slathered in a fiery chili mayo and encased in a crispy fried exterior.

170 Allen St. (bet. Stanton & Rivington Sts.)
2 Av
(212) 254-1508 — **WEB:** www.mrtakaramen.com
Lunch & dinner daily **PRICE:**

RUSS & DAUGHTERS CAFE

Deli • Delicatessen

MAP: B2

From white-jacketed servers to that pristine counter, this updated yet model LES café channels the very spirit and charm of its mothership, set only blocks away. The adept kitchen follows suit, taking the original, appetizing classics and turning them on their heads to form an array of proper and profoundly flavorful dishes.

Regulars perch at the bar to watch the 'tender whip up a cocktail or classic egg cream, while serious diners find a seat and get noshing on hot- and cold-smoked Scottish salmon teamed with everything-bagel chips. The result? A thrilling contrast in flavor and texture. Caramelized chocolate babka French toast is crowned with strawberries for a sweet-savory treat; and "eggs Benny" with salmon, spinach and challah never fails to peg a bruncher.

127 Orchard St. (bet. Delancey & Rivington Sts.)
Delancey St
(212) 475-4881 — **WEB:** www.russanddaughterscafe.com
Lunch & dinner daily **PRICE:** $$

SPICY VILLAGE

Chinese • Simple

MAP: A2

People are lining the sidewalks just to step inside this bare-bones spot that can feel as comfortable (read: cramped) as a rush-hour commuter train. Barely 20 people can fit inside, but the lightning-quick staff knows how to turn tables, so waits are bearable. Still, this Henan (central China) favorite leaves no one disappointed, even if they aren't sweating with the sinus-clearing numbness of its Sichuan competitors.

Big tray chicken is the signature order, and it is a hearty, filled-to-the-brim platter of bone-in meat and potatoes in ruby-red chili oil. But the real highlight is beneath all of that, in the exceptional noodles that seem to invite diners to slurp and tug their way through these dishes. Whatever you do, don't miss the spicy pork dumplings.

68 Forsyth St. #B (bet. Eldridge & Forsyth Sts.)
Grand St
(212) 625-8299 — **WEB:** www.spicyvillageny.com
Lunch & dinner Mon - Sat

PRICE:

THE STANTON SOCIAL

Fusion • Elegant

MAP: B1

This stylish downtown looker has been going strong for over a decade now. Unlike the hip spots that burn brightly then fade, The Stanton Social still has the stuff—best evidenced, perhaps, by the throngs of beautiful young things that fill its seats every weekend. That said, it's not so cool that you won't see a family with kids squeaking through the door for an early dinner.

Inside the generous space, you'll find tall, dark booths that could double as private rooms. The thumping music and dim lights give it a clubby vibe, as do the bar and lounge upstairs. The food is eclectic and playful, with shareable items including mini crispy fish tacos, a whimsical play on that Chinese-American standby, beef and broccoli and a signature beef Wellington.

99 Stanton St. (bet. Ludlow & Orchard Sts.)
2 Av
(212) 995-0099 — **WEB:** www.thestantonsocial.com
Lunch Sat - Sun Dinner nightly

PRICE: $$

TANG HOT POT

Chinese • Brasserie

MAP: A2

As evident by the crowds that file in until its doors close, this spot is truly very hot. The sleek restaurant is narrow and tiny, but with such high ceilings you'll feel like you're in a grand hall. Don't bother with starters or cold items here. Instead get your boil on, since within a few seconds of ordering you'll have a bevy of flavorful, full-bodied broths bubbling away. The tang pot blends a spicy beef tallow broth with serious kick and a non-spicy pork bone version for a perfect combination. These ingredients are top-notch, especially the beef ribeye and Japanese Kobe. Noodles, tofu, vegetables and sesame paste round it out.

Make sure to come with a crew here as you will need an army to partake in all the flavor fun—and to share the spoils.

135 Bowery (bet. Broome & Grand Sts.)
Grand St
(917) 421-9330 – **WEB:** www.tanghotpotnyc.com
Lunch Fri - Sun Dinner nightly **PRICE:** $$

UNA PIZZA NAPOLETANA

Pizza • Minimalist

MAP: B1

At long last, pizza maestro Anthony Mangieri returns with this highly anticipated spot, decked out with an airy black- and white-tiled hall and a glass-front open kitchen.

The chef tends to the wood-burning oven out of which 12-inch Neapolitan-style pies spring. And what glorious pies these are—with fluffy edges, papery crusts and toppings ranging from bubbly gumdrops of mozzarella di bufala and sweet tomato sauce to peppery arugula and smoked mozzarella. These creations are the draw, but starters and desserts deserve equal billing. Lobster tartare plates al dente chickpeas with minced lobster in a refreshing pepperoncino verde for a delightful appetizer. Then, panna cotta spiked with a cherry purée and finished with olive oil and balsamic, is pure bliss.

175 Orchard St. (bet. E. Houston & Stanton Sts.)
2 Av
(646) 692-3475 – **WEB:** www.unapizza.com
Dinner nightly **PRICE:** $$

YOPPARAI

Japanese • Cozy

MAP: C2

Guests ring a buzzer to gain access to this clandestine izakaya. Inside, you'll find a stylish, serene cubby hole—reservations are a must on popular nights—where every point of your experience has been thoughtfully considered, from the two-person bar stools to the kimono-clad servers with answers at the ready. Two chefs perform their magic in view: one works the grill station while the other tackles sashimi and steamed dishes. A small kitchen in the back pushes out occasional items as well. The menu offers barbecue dishes, robata specials, as well as other seasonal delights. But you'll have the most fun ordering a little of everything—each new presentation is truly an artful revelation.

Housed just down the block, Azasu is the modern and much loved sibling.

151 Rivington St. (bet. Clinton & Suffolk Sts.)
Delancey St
(212) 777-7253 — **WEB:** www.yopparainyc.com
Dinner Mon - Sat

PRICE: $$$

Look for our symbol spotlighting restaurants with a notable beer list.

MIDTOWN EAST

An interesting mix of office buildings, hotels, high-rises and townhouses, Midtown East is one of the city's most industrious areas. Home to the iconic Chrysler Building and United Nations Headquarters, the vibe here is perpetually abuzz with suits, students and old-timers wandering its streets. Whether it's that reliable diner on the corner, a gourmet supermarket or fine-dining establishment, this neighborhood flaunts it all. Residents of neighboring Beekman and Sutton Place are proud of their very own cheese shop (**Ideal Cheese**); butcher (**L. Simchick Meats**); bagel and lox shop (**Tal Bagels**); and—to complete any dinner party—renowned florist (**Zeze**). While **Dag Hammarskjöld Plaza Greenmarket** is for the most part dwarfed by Union Square, come Wednesdays it presents just the right amount of produce to feed hungry locals. Then sample a bit of chic at Paris-based café, **Rose Bakery**, set inside the very haute and hip Dover Street Market. It may be tucked behind a soaring cement column sheathed in colorful macramé, but turn a corner to find display cases filled with vibrant salads and tempting sweets.

GRAND CENTRAL TERMINAL

Built by the Vanderbilt family in the 19th century, **Grand Central Terminal** is a 21st-century food sanctuary. An ideal day at this titanic and particularly gorgeous train station may begin with a cup of coffee from **Joe's**. Later, stop by one of Manhattan's historic sites, the **Grand Central Oyster Bar & Restaurant**, nestled into the cavernous lower level. This gorgeous seafood respite proffers everything from shellfish stews and pristine fish dishes, to an incredible raw bar and so much more. Then take a turn—of taste—and head to **Neuhaus**, venerable chocolatiers who craft their delicacies from exceptional ingredients. Others may stop by family-owned and renowned **Li-Lac Chocolates** for such nostalgic confections as dark chocolate-covered pretzels or beautifully packaged holiday gift sets. Of course, no trip to this Terminal is complete without a visit to the "whispering gallery" where low, ceramic-tiled arches make whispers sound more like shouts. Just beyond, the loud dining concourse hums with lunch stalls ranging from **Café Spice** for Indian or **Eata Pita** for Middle Eastern. **Mendy's** is midtown's go-to for everything kosher, including pastrami and brisket mingled with more eats. Finish with the sweetest treats—maybe those legendary red velvet cupcakes—at the Terminal's very own **Magnolia Bakery** outpost. Moving on to the market, Eli Zabar has expanded his empire, and

continues to present the freshest fruits and vegetables at **Eli Zabar's Farm to Table**. But, for an impressive assortment of pastries and cakes, **Eli Zabar's Bread & Pastry** is your best bet. In addition to its myriad fishmongers, butchers and bakers, home cooks and top chefs are likely to find the best selection of spices here—at one of the market's better-kept secrets, **Spices and Tease**, specializing in exotic blends and a host of unique teas. But, if you're among hungry hordes with time to spare, make sure to visit one of the several prized restaurants situated beneath Grand Central's celestial ceiling for a stellar feast. Finally, if the scene in the Terminal is too corporate for your liking, then head on over to **Urbanspace Vanderbilt**. This lively food hall may exist in the heart of a commercial center, but it boasts over 20 cutting-edge culinary concepts.

JAPANTOWN

Trek a few blocks east of Lexington to find a very sophisticated Japantown, where izakaya and restaurants are scattered among hostess clubs. While salarymen frequent old-world hangouts like **Riki** and **Lucky Cat** for Japanese specialties, **BentOn Cafe** is a favored retail outpost for its daily changing bento boxes at terrific value. Expats with ladies in tow linger over the Japanese-Italian fusion at **Aya**, just as yuppies gather for a light bite from **Cafe Zaiya** or **Dainobu** (both bustling deli-cum-markets). **Sakagura's** sake collection may be impressive and extensive, but then so is the roster of comforting noodle soups at **Nishida Shoten**. **Hinata Ramen** is another all-time draw for steaming bowls of ramen, while red meat fiends join the lines outside **Katsu-Hama** or **Yakiniku Gen** for delicious grilled eats. Looking to impress your out-of-town guests? Plan a Japanese-themed evening by stocking up on ceramics, cookware and authentic produce from specialty emporium, **MTC Kitchen**. A few blocks south, younger and quieter Murray Hill has its own distinct vibe. Here, fast-casual finds thrive thanks to thirty-somethings sating late-night cravings. **The Kitano**, which is among a handful of Gotham's Japanese-owned boutique hotels, continues to lure thanks to its sleek vibe, live tunes at **JAZZ at Kitano** and kaiseki cuisine served at their very own subterranean hot spot, **Hakubai**.

SWEETS AND SPIRITS

Slightly north, owner and pastry chef, Stéphane Pourrez, brings French flair and baked treats to **Éclair** on 53rd Street. Presenting a lineup of pastries, cakes, macarons and of course, those eponymous eclairs, this sweet midtown spot also houses some of the flakiest croissants in town. Settled just steps away, make sure to lounge with the locals as you savor some fine wine, cheese, charcuterie and Mediterranean-inspired small bites at petite **Pierre Loti**.

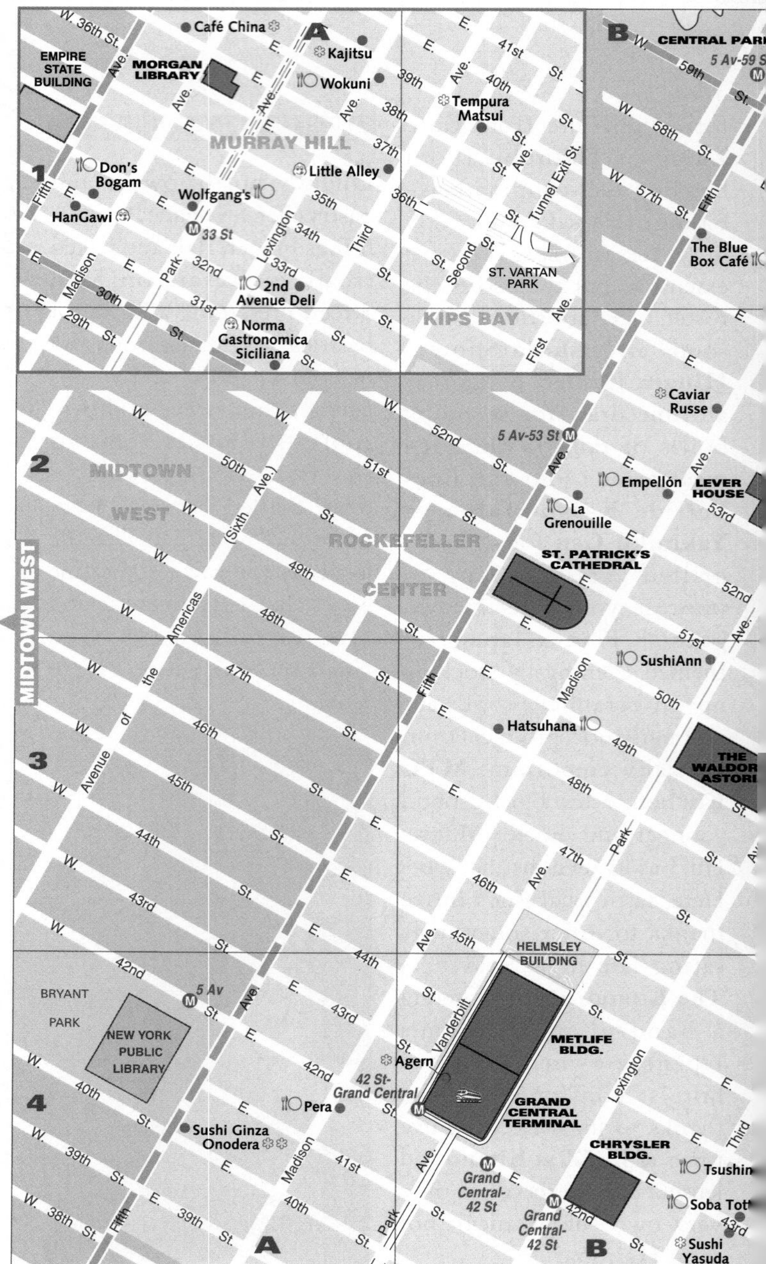

MIDTOWN WEST
A
B
1
2
3
4
EMPIRE STATE BUILDING
MORGAN LIBRARY
Café China
Kajitsu
Wokuni
Tempura Matsui
MURRAY HILL
Don's Bogam
HanGawi
Wolfgang's
Little Alley
33 St
2nd Avenue Deli
Norma Gastronomica Siciliana
ST. VARTAN PARK
KIPS BAY
CENTRAL PARK
5 Av-59 St
The Blue Box Café
Caviar Russe
5 Av-53 St
Empellón
LEVER HOUSE
La Grenouille
ST. PATRICK'S CATHEDRAL
MIDTOWN WEST
ROCKEFELLER CENTER
SushiAnn
Hatsuhana
THE WALDORF ASTORIA
HELMSLEY BUILDING
METLIFE BLDG.
BRYANT PARK
NEW YORK PUBLIC LIBRARY
5 Av
Agern
42 St-Grand Central
Pera
GRAND CENTRAL TERMINAL
Sushi Ginza Onodera
Grand Central-42 St
CHRYSLER BLDG.
Tsushin
Soba Tot
Sushi Yasuda

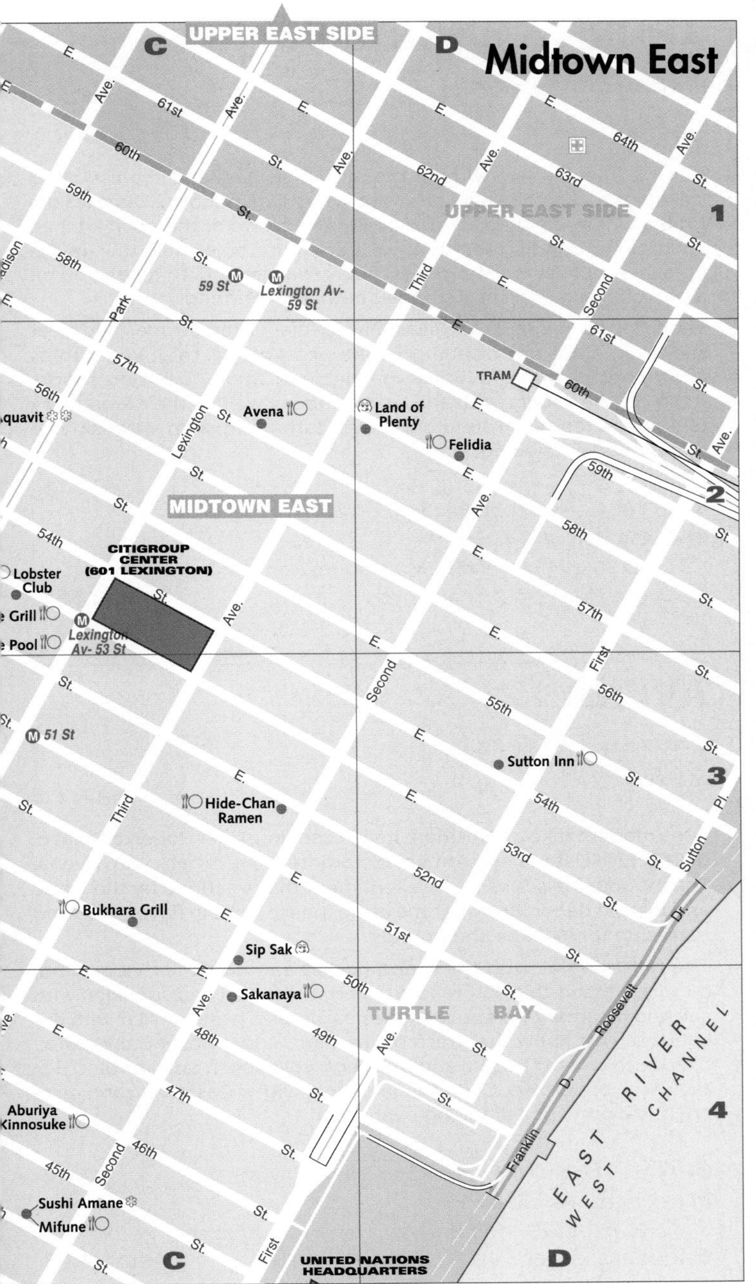
Midtown East
UPPER EAST SIDE
MIDTOWN EAST
TURTLE BAY
CITIGROUP CENTER (601 LEXINGTON)
UNITED NATIONS HEADQUARTERS
EAST RIVER WEST CHANNEL
TRAM
59 St
Lexington Av-59 St
Lexington Av-53 St
51 St
Aquavit
Avena
Land of Plenty
Felidia
Lobster Club
Grill
Pool
Sutton Inn
Hide-Chan Ramen
Bukhara Grill
Sip Sak
Sakanaya
Aburiya Kinnosuke
Sushi Amane
Mifune
Park Ave.
Lexington Ave.
Third Ave.
Second Ave.
First Ave.
Sutton Pl.
Franklin D. Roosevelt Dr.
E. 64th St.
E. 63rd St.
E. 62nd St.
E. 61st St.
E. 60th St.
E. 59th St.
E. 58th St.
E. 57th St.
E. 56th St.
E. 55th St.
E. 54th St.
E. 53rd St.
E. 52nd St.
E. 51st St.
E. 50th St.
E. 49th St.
E. 48th St.
E. 47th St.
E. 46th St.
E. 45th St.
C
D
1
2
3
4

ABURIYA KINNOSUKE

Japanese • Cozy

MAP: C4

Call it a trip to Tokyo without the tariff. This dark and sophisticated izakaya is tucked down a side street in bustling midtown. Once inside, grab an intimate table for two or join the crowd at the open kitchen counter surrounding the smoky robata grill. The waiters talk up the omakase, but it's worth trusting your own instincts to guide you on a personalized tour through their authentic offerings.

The sukiyaki is a must-try seasonal special of tender marbled beef served in a hot pot bobbing with a beaten egg, tofu, vegetables and noodles. Other favorites may include smoky bamboo shoots fresh off the robata with shaved bonito; as well as their legendary tsukune, a tender ground chicken meatball brushed with teriyaki and dipped in raw egg.

213 E. 45th St. (bet. Second & Third Aves.)
Grand Central - 42 St
(212) 867-5454 — **WEB:** www.aburiyakinnosuke.com
Lunch Mon - Fri Dinner nightly **PRICE:** $$$

AVENA

Italian • Elegant

MAP: C2

For a modern take on Northern Italian cooking, Chef Roberto Deiaco, of East 12th Osteria and Armani Ristorante fame, is back with Avena. The mood here is fuss-free—a sentiment that's echoed by the white and marble décor. But what the atmosphere lacks in flavor, the food makes up for in leaps and bounds.

The feast begins with the bread basket and its addictive carta di musica, a tissue-thin flatbread brushed with butter and sprinkled with salt and rosemary to represent musical notes. Those familiar with the chef's talents know that fresh pasta reigns supreme, and the ravioli filled with creamy ricotta and quail egg yolk doesn't disappoint. For the carnivore crowd, Colorado lamb loin with a Castelveltrano olive crust is worthy of a standing ovation.

141 E. 57th St. (bet. Lexington & Third Aves.)
Lexington Av - 59 St
(212) 752-5323 — **WEB:** www.avenarestaurant.com
Lunch & dinner daily **PRICE:** $$$

AGERN 

Scandinavian • Contemporary décor

MAP: B4

Even before disciples of the New Nordic creed started making pilgrimages to Copenhagen's Noma restaurant, it was clear that the winds of culinary change were blowing in from that direction. The ethos that has made the cooking in Scandinavia so influential—fierce adherence to seasonality and respect for nature's larder—may not seem particularly ground-breaking but for many a chef and restaurateur it prompted some sort of epiphany. The good news is that, thanks to the great Dane Claus Meyer, you don't need to fly there to find out more.

Agern is hidden at the Vanderbilt Hall end of Grand Central Terminal but has been designed with such understated elegance that you quickly forget where you are. The restaurant also leads into the Nordic-themed "Great Northern Food Hall" so it won't be long before everyone in this part of town is in cable-knit sweaters, discussing their own understanding of "hygge."

Ingredients like havgus, söl and ymer may not be familiar to all; nor perhaps will be the liberal use of techniques like pickling, fermenting or smoking. But, under the aegis of Icelandic chef Gunnar Gíslason, the kitchen uses these methods to deliver sharper, more defined and more natural flavors.

---

89 E. 42nd St. (at Vanderbilt Ave.)

Grand Central - 42 St

(646) 568-4018 — **WEB:** www.agernrestaurant.com

Lunch Mon - Fri Dinner Mon - Sat **PRICE: $$$$**

AQUAVIT ✿✿

Scandinavian • Design

MAP: C2

No detail goes unnoticed at this sleek beauty, where black-suited servers line the dining room. The overall design of Aquavit is clean and contemporary—with dark floors, wood tabletops and high-backed leather chairs. Courses are plated on beautiful dishware; expect wood boxes, slate platters and glazed earthenware.

The kitchen does many things well, but what makes it one of the more unique in the city is Chef Emma Bengtsson's ability to take bold Scandinavian flavors like dill, lingonberry, smoke or brine and soften them into balanced, whimsical and elegant dishes. Take for example, a sheet of raw Colorado Wagyu draped over pickled leeks and carefully strewn with pumpernickel croutons. Then delicately cooked Dover sole is plated with crisp apple, parsnip, and excellently seasoned pork cheek ragù for a veritable study in harmonious flavors.

Finally, opt for the namesake aquavit, offered in house-made flavors like anise-caraway-fennel or fig-cardamom, to team with such treats as a "nest" of honey tuile threads cradling three small "eggs" composed of white chocolate and frozen goat cheese. Pure bliss, indeed.

If you find yourself across the pond, visit the one-starred sister in London.

---

65 E. 55th St. (bet. Madison & Park Aves.)

5 Av - 53 St

(212) 307-7311 – **WEB:** www.aquavit.org

Lunch Mon - Fri Dinner Mon - Sat

PRICE: $$$$

THE BLUE BOX CAFÉ

Contemporary • Elegant

MAP: B1

Unsurprisingly, once you arrive at this café tucked into the fourth floor of Tiffany's flagship store, everything starts to resemble an actual "blue box," complete with walls, plush leather banquettes and armchairs all boasting the company's trademark robin's-egg hue. Suited elevator attendants politely usher diners into this dining room, whose prime corner location offers glorious city views.

Tables laid with custom china are usually groaning with breakfast service, which extends to lunch, and finally, afternoon tea. The latter is sure to become a cult favorite thanks to its three-tiered silver stand stocked with sweet and savory scones, dainty finger sandwiches and confections, like a petit four enrobed in—you guessed it—Tiffany blue fondant.

727 Fifth Ave. (at 57th St.)
5 Av - 59 St
(212) 605-4270 — **WEB:** www.tiffany.com
Lunch daily

PRICE: $$

BUKHARA GRILL

Indian • Simple

MAP: C3

In NYC's ever-expanding realm of Indian dining, Bukhara Grill has stood the test of time with excellence. Glimpse their expert chefs who seem contentedly trapped behind a glass kitchen wall. Featuring a noisy and yuppie set, this tri-level space is decorated (albeit oddly) with clunky wooden booths, closely set tables and private rooms.

Peek into the kitchen for a whiff of tandoori treats and Mughlai specialties. Dahi aloo papri (spicy potatoes and chickpeas tossed in yogurt and tamarind) is a predictable yet perfect starter. The signature, wickedly creamy dal Bukhara will have you coming back for more (tomorrow). Even if the service may range from sweet to clumsy, hand-crafted breads meant to sop up the likes of sarson ka saag remain a crowning glory.

217 E. 49th St. (bet. Second & Third Aves.)
51 St
(212) 888-2839 — **WEB:** www.bukharany.com
Lunch & dinner daily

PRICE: $$$

CAFÉ CHINA ✿

Chinese • Chic

MAP: A1

Blink and you'll miss its nondescript façade, but what a shame, for Café China is a little journey into the intense pleasures of Sichuan cuisine by way of midtown. Inside find a long and narrow space outfitted with seductive portraits of 1930s Shanghai starlets, bright red chairs, bamboo planters and a dominating marble-and-wood bar.

After struggling with their on-again-off-again popularity, this kitchen is back on track, creating Sichuan dishes with great aplomb. Their particular strength lies in the elegant and effortless contrast of complex flavors, even when the prep is decidedly simple—as evidenced by the steamed eggplant or the deliciously tender tea-smoked duck. Pickled vegetables achieve harmonious balance between sour and fiery notes; sliced conch pairs perfectly with that ubiquitous mouth-tingling chili oil; and tender pork dumplings arrive atop a delicious bath of soy sauce, and of course, more chili oil.

The use of such top-quality ingredients as in the Chungking chicken special, alternately tender and crispy with dried chillies and sesame seeds; or even in the lamb coated with smoky cumin and fried to perfection is yet another instance of the feat of this kitchen.

---

13 E. 37th St. (bet. Fifth & Madison Aves.)

34 St - Herald Sq

(212) 213-2810 — **WEB:** www.cafechinanyc.com

Lunch & dinner daily **PRICE: $$**

CAVIAR RUSSE ✿

Contemporary • Luxury

MAP: B2

No playful pun, no name-check for grandma, no oblique reference to a geographical landmark—whoever christened this restaurant clearly wanted to attract a certain type of customer. This is not the place where you should order by pointing vaguely at the menu—that way lies trouble because you may find yourself having to re-mortgage your apartment to pay for the 250 grams of Osetra caviar you've just inadvertently requested. Best leave that section of the carte to the oligarchs and retired dictators and concentrate on the main menu. Here you will find contemporary dishes of surprising delicacy and precision, with a pleasing bias towards wonderful seafood and shellfish, such as scallops with ricotta gnudi or delicious bluefin tuna with uni and asparagus.

You get buzzed in at street level, which adds a bit of mystery to proceedings. Up the stairs and you'll find yourself in a lavish little jewel box, with colorful murals on the wall, Murano chandeliers hanging from an ornate ceiling, and semi-circular booths. The only thing missing is James Bond's nemesis drumming his fingers on the table in the corner.

For more plush fun in the sun, there is a seriously posh outpost at The Four Seasons Tower in Miami.

---

538 Madison Ave. (bet. 54th & 55th Sts.)

5 Av - 53 St

(212) 980-5908 — **WEB:** www.caviarrusse.com

Lunch daily Dinner Mon - Sat **PRICE: $$$$**

DONS BOGAM

Korean • Contemporary décor

MAP: A1

At Dons Bogam, the food is fantastic and service indulgent. So, reserve ahead as every seat is filled—from the festive bar up front right down to those two-tops sporting blazing grills. Make no mistake: this is no average K-town joint. Inside, a top-notch venting system lets diners enjoy a smoke-free evening of exceptional grilled meats. Start with fried pork mandu, which are crisp, on-point and extra divine. Wonderfully flaky buchu gochu pajeon is studded with chives for perfect flavor; while pork belly marinated in red wine is smoky and supremely tender.

For the ultimate payoff, opt for the memorable beef platter. It features thinly sliced maeun and yangnyeom galbi set beside king trumpet mushrooms that are meaty and mouthwatering in their own right.

17 E. 32nd St. (bet. Fifth & Madison Aves.)
33 St
(212) 683-2200 – **WEB:** www.donsbogam.com
Lunch & dinner daily

PRICE: $$

EMPELLÓN

Mexican • Contemporary décor

MAP: B2

Buttoned-up midtown gets a much-needed shot in the arm compliments of Chef Alex Stupak's lively flagship from his popular Empellón family. This colorful and multi-level space offers a first floor outfitted with a generous bar area and prime view of the bustling open kitchen. On the mezzanine level, find a more intimate dining space.

The menu bears the chef's signature creative flair, offering a range of small bites, tacos and shareable large plates. Sample the clever spins on salsa, like a wickedly good smoky cashew version that arrives along with the sampler starter; or the irresistible lamb sweetbread tacos with a flutter of white onion and bright cilantro. Stupak is also a serious pastry chef and his talent shows in desserts, like the «avocado.»

510 Madison Ave. (entrance on 53rd St.)
51 St
(212) 858-9365 – **WEB:** www.empellon.com
Lunch & dinner daily

PRICE: $$

FELIDIA

Italian • Family

MAP: D2

Cookbook author, television series host and restaurateur Lidia Bastianich has been behind her flagship restaurant and greeting customers since 1981. Felidia's service is professional yet charming, and the elegant décor inspires dressing up for dinner. Wine connoisseurs will rejoice at the exceptional list, which offers a vast collection of Italian choices.

The family-style lunch prix-fixe is a crowd-pleaser, featuring such signature pastas as cacio e pere ravioli bathed with black pepper and pecorino. Massive portions of scallops, squid and lobster star in the grigliata drizzled with lemon vinaigrette. Rely on Lidia to deliver a cannoli that lives up to its true potential—narrow tubes filled with lemony ricotta cream spilling into the center of the plate.

243 E. 58th St. (bet. Second & Third Aves.)
Lexington Av - 59 St
(212) 758-1479 — **WEB:** www.felidia-nyc.com
Lunch Mon - Fri Dinner nightly **PRICE:** $$$$

THE GRILL

American • Vintage

MAP: C2

Once the power crowd's club of choice for dining and dishing, this stallion in the former Four Seasons (now run by Major Food Group) belongs to a rarefied crowd of iconic NYC addresses. After undergoing a stylish makeover, this incarnation is once again the favored watering hole of the well-heeled. The Grill is a grandiose scene, with flashy service to match (tableside presentations are plentiful). Over in the kitchen it's all-American, with a menu of beloved classics. Crab cakes topped with pan-fried potatoes are a highlight; while crispy duck is especially indulgent, featuring shatteringly crunchy skin and silky fat gushing with flavor.

For dessert, a chiffon cake layered with lemon curd and frosted with buttercream tastes of the good times gone by.

99 E. 52nd St. (bet. Lexington & Park Aves.)
51 St
(212) 375-9001 — **WEB:** www.thegrillnewyork.com
Lunch Mon - Fri Dinner Mon - Sat **PRICE:** $$$$

HANGAWI

Korean • Cozy

MAP: A1

Beyond an ordinary façade lies this serene, shoes-off retreat with traditional low tables, Korean artifacts and meditative music. While wine and beer are available, a pot of royal green tea from Mt. Jilee is a more apt pairing considering the soothing setting.

HanGawi is a soft-spoken, vegetarian-only restaurant that cares about what you eat and how you feel. The ssam bap offers a fun DIY experience with a long platter of fillings. Dark leafy lettuce and thin, herbaceous sesame leaves are topped with creamy slices of avocado, crunchy bean sprouts, pickled daikon, carrot, cucumber, radish and three rice options—white, brown and a nutty, purple-tinged multigrain. Topped with miso ssam sauce, each bite is a fresh burst of uplifting textures.

12 E. 32nd St. (bet. Fifth & Madison Aves.)
33 St
(212) 213-0077 — **WEB:** www.hangawirestaurant.com
Lunch Mon - Sat Dinner nightly **PRICE: $$**

HATSUHANA

Japanese • Elegant

MAP: B3

It's been around since the beginning of time (in NYC Japanese restaurant years) but this is no lesser a destination for excellent sushi. With a retro décor that spans two floors and a business that's run like a machine, Hatsuhana is a go-to for corporate dining.

Though the rave reviews came decades ago, their traditional Edomae sushi still holds its own. Fish is top quality, the army of chefs have solid knife skills and rice is properly prepared. This reliability draws a host of regulars who develop relationships with the itamae. Stick to the counter and go omakase: the sushi will be surprisingly impressive with accommodations for the spicy tuna set. At lunch, the "Box of Dreams" is an aptly named must-order.

17 E. 48th St. (bet. Fifth & Madison Aves.)
47-50 Sts - Rockefeller Ctr
(212) 355-3345 — **WEB:** www.hatsuhana.com
Lunch Mon - Fri Dinner Mon - Sat **PRICE: $$$**

HIDE-CHAN RAMEN

Japanese • Simple

MAP: C3

Nothing nourishes like ramen and nothing divides opinion more than ramen, as every self-respecting foodie seems to have an incontestable opinion about where to find the best. Hide-Chan, a franchise of a Japanese chain, is certainly a worthy candidate, as the prices are keen and it's perennially busy. It's on the second floor of a nondescript building—a fact you'll no doubt be aware of as you'll probably be queuing on the staircase.

The specialty is tonkatsu ramen, which is based on pork bones and originated in Fukuoka where it's referred to as Hakata ramen. The cloudy, rich broth will leave you feeling invigorated, especially if you opt for firmer noodles with a little bite. Start with homemade gyoza with their authentically sticky bottoms.

248 E. 52nd St. (bet. Second & Third Aves.)
Lexington Av - 53 St
(212) 813-1800 — **WEB:** www.hidechanramen.nyc
Lunch & dinner daily **PRICE:**

LA GRENOUILLE

French • Romantic

MAP: B2

La Grenouille is a bastion of old-world glamour and manners with an exorbitant budget for floral arrangements. Although this storied enclave still attracts a devoted following, there's always room for locals, newbies and blinged-out tourists. Everyone looks good in this lavish space, where red velvet banquettes, polished wood veneer and softly lit tables bathe the room with rose and apricot hues.

Classic and classy, this French cuisine deserves high praise. Delicate ravioli is stuffed with chopped lobster hinting of tarragon and dressed with creamy, tart beurre blanc; an exquisitely tender-seared beef filet arrives with pommes Darphin and a lick of perfect sauce au poivre; and for dessert, the île flottante is heaven under a cloud of spun caramel.

3 E. 52nd St. (bet. Fifth & Madison Aves.)
5 Av - 53 St
(212) 752-1495 — **WEB:** www.la-grenouille.com
Lunch & dinner Tue - Sat **PRICE:** $$$$

KAJITSU ✿

Japanese • Elegant

MAP: A1

It's the way of the modern world that we think of the changing of the seasons more in terms of our wardrobe rather than our food—but a meal at Kajitsu could change that. This Japanese vegan restaurant serves shojin cuisine based on the precepts of Buddhism—if you're in search of an antidote to the plethora of steakhouses in the city, this is it. The traditionally decorated space on the second floor is a sanctuary of peace and tranquility and offers table or counter seating and service that is as charming as it is earnest.

Such is the skill of the kitchen you'll forget in no time about the absence of fish or meat. It's all about balance, harmony and simplicity—and allowing the ingredients' natural flavors to shine, whether it's the delicate onion soup with mizuna and potato, or the visually arresting hassun which could include everything from mountain yam to burdock root.

Your period of contemplation and newfound respect for your fellow man may come to a juddering halt when you find yourself back on Lexington but, for a few moments at least, you'll feel you connected with nature.

---

125 E. 39th St. (bet. Lexington & Park Aves.)

Grand Central - 42 St

(212) 228-4873 — **WEB:** www.kajitsunyc.com

Dinner Tue - Sun

PRICE: $$$

LAND OF PLENTY

Chinese • Contemporary décor

MAP: D2

Why do they call it Land of Plenty? Perhaps it's because of the abundant flavors in Chongqing noodles puddled in a chili oil broth with ground pork, peanuts and sesame seeds; or bean curd bathed in...yes...more chili oil with toasted peanuts and Sichuan peppercorns. Then imagine green snow pea sprouts dusted with salt and garlic, or pork dumplings swimming in a soy- peanut- and chili-bath that's spicy, sweet and salty at once. And know that these are just a few of the plentiful reasons.

Though the focus here is definitely the food, this fiery haven feels more elegant than the other Sichuan spots in midtown. Tucked into a sleek, subterranean space, the décor features marble floors and mosaic-tile walls. A professional service staff helps further set the tone.

204 E. 58th St. (bet. Second & Third Aves.)
59 St
(212) 308-8788 — **WEB:** www.landofplenty58.com
Lunch Mon - Fri Dinner nightly **PRICE: $$**

LITTLE ALLEY

Chinese • Contemporary décor

MAP: A1

Thank Chef Yuchun Cheung for brightening Murray Hill by way of authentic regional dishes from China, with an emphasis on Shanghai. This cooking is accomplished, serious and high quality, but one could still make a very enjoyable meal by just focusing on appetizers and dumplings alone. Signatures, and fittingly so, include toothsome slices of pig's ear seasoned with chili oil, peppercorns and cilantro for freshness. Also explore dim sum, featuring pork- and crab-soup dumplings or caramelized, juicy and puffy pork buns. The Chinese sausage fried rice is a fragrant and wholly delicious treat.

The attractive interior is festooned with wood furniture, dark walls, cozy lighting and a small bar up front. Younger crowds lend the space a lively appeal.

550 Third Ave. (bet. 36th & 37th Sts.)
33 St
(646) 998-3976 — **WEB:** www.littlealley.nyc
Lunch & dinner daily **PRICE: $$**

LOBSTER CLUB

Japanese • Trendy

MAP: C2

The Lobster Club marks the third act in the revamping of the old Four Seasons dining room, housed within the landmark Seagram Building. The interior now looks like a mod Japanese brasserie, thanks to a white onyx bar counter, pink and chartreuse upholstery, as well as walls hung with bold artwork.

Chef Tasuku Murakami's menu may be sizable, but it repeatedly returns to Japan for inspiration. Sample an array of teppanyaki, such as scallops, first grilled, then brushed with savory sauce and toasted sesame seeds; or charred vegetables like king oyster mushrooms and shishito peppers. Other favorites include seafood mains like gently cooked black bass in an herbaceous yuzu sauce.

Japanese whisky aficionados should head to the bar; it pours more than 30 labels.

98 E. 53rd St. (bet. Lexington & Park Aves.)

51 St

(212) 375-9001 — **WEB:** www.thelobsterclub.com

Lunch Mon - Fri Dinner Mon - Sat **PRICE:** $$$

MIFUNE

Japanese • Contemporary décor

MAP: C4

Two superstar chefs arrive in one package with the elegant Mifune and omakase bar, Sushi Amane, which is located downstairs. Chef Hiroki Yoshitake presents delicious, contemporary Japanese cuisine here at Mifune, in a space featuring cement walls, blonde wood and cozy backlighting.

Alongside tempura, rice dishes, and other delightful entrées, this menu also offers a daily selection of sashimi. Tender smoked butterfish arrives with shaved radish rounds, nasturtium leaves and a bright chimichurri-like sauce made from garlic, herbs and oil. Then, grilled chicken Yuan-style appears in a mini cast-iron skillet, brushed with an irresistible teriyaki-based sauce, and paired with knobs of tender, buttery potatoes, snap peas and frizzled leeks.

245 E. 44th St. (bet. Second & Third Aves.)

Grand Central - 42 St

(212) 986-2800 — **WEB:** www.mifune-restaurant.com

Dinner Mon - Sat **PRICE:** $$$

NORMA GASTRONOMIA SICILIANA

Italian • Osteria

MAP: A2

To think of these arancini as mere "rice balls" is a slight on Sicilian cuisine; they are so much more. Nowhere else in the city will you dine on such crisp, classic beauties—filled with ragù, peas, mozzarella and rice cooked in chicken stock, then presented in a pool of light tomato sauce. Rest assured though as the menu goes on to list other authentic and deliciously rendered items, including the 'rianata pizza of Trapani.

The rustic space is filled with old, crackle-glazed platters that probably held the exact style of the rich anelletti al forno, back in the Old Country. Before you leave, stock up on specialty ingredients that are strategically displayed for sale. Wine bottles racked up along the walls hint at a lengthy and noteworthy selection.

438 Third Ave. (bet. 30th & 31st Sts.)
33 St
(212) 889-0600 – **WEB:** www.normarestaurant.com
Lunch & dinner daily **PRICE:** $$

PERA

Turkish • Contemporary décor

MAP: A4

For flavorful Turkish food infused with contemporary influence, Pera serves to please. Lunch does big business in this attractive dining room, layered in a chocolate-brown color scheme and packed with corporate types as well as visitors looking for a sleek place to sojourn mid-day. Acoustics can be loud, but with food so fine, you'll want to stay awhile.

Dinner is more low-key but the menu always brims with simple, good quality and slightly renovated plates like warm hummus with pastirma; lentil and bulgur tartare; or watermelon chunks tossed with salty feta, tomatoes and olive oil. A forkful of their model and deliciously tender chicken adana with a side of addictively crispy fries has wide appeal and makes for a fitting feast—at all times.

303 Madison Ave. (bet. 41st & 42nd Sts.)
Grand Central - 42 St
(212) 878-6301 – **WEB:** www.peranyc.com
Lunch Mon - Fri Dinner nightly **PRICE:** $$

THE POOL

Seafood • Vintage

MAP: C2

Set within the Seagram Building and once part of the venerated Four Seasons restaurant, this iconic dining room has been reinvented by the team behind Carbone and ZZ's Clam Bar. Beneath ceilings that reach for the sky, the imposing arena is structured around a marble pool surrounded by elaborate flower planters that are replaced weekly. Shimmering beads obscure the windows of a space decked out with walnut paneling, blue banquettes and custom Knoll armchairs.

The menu spotlights seafood, including classics like whole fish deboned tableside, crudo, as well as a lavish caviar service. Don't miss the tome of Chateau d'Yquem as it showcases bottles that date back to 1811, and represents one of the best collections in the country, if not the world.

99 E. 52nd St. (bet. Lexington & Park Aves.)
Lexington Av - 53 St
(212) 375-9001 — **WEB:** www.thepoolnewyork.com
Dinner Mon - Sat **PRICE:** $$$$

SAKANAYA

Japanese • Simple

MAP: C4

Sit at the L-shaped counter to best appreciate the skills of Chef Shigeru Nishida as he prepares nigiri with the fluid movements of a seasoned practitioner. You're in his hands for the evening as he offers just two omakase menus—the difference being that the more expensive one comes with an added sashimi course.

The chef sticks to a fairly traditional Edomae style and uses a variety of sources for his fish. Uni may be from Hokkaido but the shrimp is from Canada; tuna from Spain; salmon from Scotland; and the rice hails from California. The menus are good value as they include appetizers, around ten pieces of sushi, chawanmushi, red miso soup and dessert. If, for some bizarre reason, you're still not sated then go next door to the chef's ramen shop, Nishida Sho-ten.

304 E. 49th St. (bet. First & Second Aves.)
51 St
(212) 339-0033 — **WEB:** www.sakanayany.com
Lunch Mon - Fri Dinner Mon - Sat **PRICE:** $$$$

2ND AVENUE DELI

Deli • Neighborhood

MAP: A1

While the décor may be more deli-meets-deco and there's a tad less attitude, this food is every bit as good as it was on Second Avenue. Ignore the kvetching and know that this is a true Jewish deli filled with personality, and one of the best around by far.

The menu remains as it should: kosher, meat-loving and non-dairy with phenomenal pastrami, pillowy rye, tangy mustard, perfect potato pancakes and fluffy matzo balls in a comforting broth. Have the best of both worlds with the soup and half-sandwich combination.

Carve a nook during midday rush, when in pour those crowds. The deli also does takeout (popular with the midtown lunch bunch), and delivery (grandma's latkes at your door). Giant platters go equally well to a bris or brunch.

162 E. 33rd St. (bet. Lexington & Third Aves.)
33 St
(212) 689-9000 — **WEB:** www.2ndavedeli.com
Lunch & dinner daily **PRICE:**

SIP SAK

Turkish • Simple

MAP: C3

Tucked inside a charming, bistro-like setting with pressed-tin ceilings and cool white marble-top tables, this neighborhood favorite just keeps getting better with age. Owner Orhan Yegen runs a tight ship, directing his staff and kitchen as they entice diners with a meze of citrusy olives, delicious hummus, garlicky cacik and creamy tarama.

Kick things off with a starter of plump shrimp cooked in a downright addictive garlic and parsley sauce; or tuck into an equally earthy Greek salad with a Turkish twist featuring pickled cabbage, crumbled feta and a poached artichoke heart filled with dilled fava beans. For dinner, skip the seafood and opt for fragrant and hearty lamb meatballs, served over rice pilaf with a grilled tomato and pile of mixed greens.

928 Second Ave. (bet. 49th & 50th Sts.)
51 St
(212) 583-1900 — **WEB:** www.sip-sak.com
Lunch & dinner daily **PRICE:** $$

SOBA TOTTO

Japanese • Simple

MAP: B4

It's a jam-packed lunchtime operation here at Soba Totto, where business folks gather and quickly fill the popular space. As the name suggests, everyone arrives in droves for the tasty homemade soba. Dinnertime brings a mellower vibe, and a crowd of beer- and sake-sipping patrons ordering tasty plates of spicy fried chicken and yakitori galore.

Midday features several varieties of lunch sets. Tasty appetizers may unveil a salad of assorted pickles and simmered daikon in a sweet ginger dressing. Skip over the fried seafood in favor of the soba totto gozen set, which includes the wonderful noodles in fragrant dashi; or try one of the many delicious dons topped with tasty tidbits like sea urchin and salmon roe or soy-marinated tuna, grated yam and egg.

211 E. 43rd St. (bet. Second & Third Aves.)
Grand Central - 42 St
(212) 557-8200 — **WEB:** www.sobatotto.com
Lunch Mon – Fri Dinner nightly **PRICE:** $$

SUSHIANN

Japanese • Contemporary décor

MAP: B3

Step through the serene, bamboo-filled entrance and into this dedicated sushi den. The mood is respectfully formal yet friendly, thanks to the focused kitchen staff who are happily interacting with guests. Just arrive with a sense of what (and how much) you'd like to eat and insist upon the omakase.

Let the day's catch dictate your meal and take a seat at the counter, where only the glassed-in display of fish and mollusks separates you from this team of skilled, disciplined chefs. The omakase may be wildly varied depending on the day (and your chef), but high standards are always maintained and each morsel is treated with integrity. A final sashimi course may reveal a glistening array of mild giant clam, firm tai and tuna that melts in the mouth.

38 E. 51st St. (bet. Madison & Park Aves.)
51 St
(212) 755-1780 — **WEB:** www.sushiann.net
Lunch Mon – Fri Dinner Mon – Sat **PRICE:** $$

SUSHI AMANE ✿

Japanese • Intimate

♿ **MAP:** C4

If you've eaten at Mifune and wondered why you saw some customers with expectant grins being ushered downstairs, it's because they were lucky enough to secure reservations at Sushi Amane.

Behind the soft and silky wood counter, with seating for just eight, stands the confident figure of Chef Shion Uino. He looks young because he is young, but then again he started early and garnered over eight years' experience at the highly garlanded Sushi Saito in Tokyo before setting sail for NYC. His experience is evident in the number of dishes served before the nigiri, which may include creamy uni from different regions of Japan; delicious hairy crab served in its shell; steamed scallop wrapped in nori; and tender abalone.

When it comes to the nigiri, the chef also shares his alma mater's attention to detail and insistence on consistency. Each piece is given just a light brush of nikiri so that the focus remains on its natural flavor, whether that's the silvery kohada, luminous white squid or the golden anago. The rice, at slightly above body temperature, leaves a lasting impression. There are two seatings—at 6.00 and 8.30P.M—and as diners are served together it's important to arrive on time.

---

245 E. 44th St. (bet. Second & Third Aves.)

Grand Central - 42 St

(212) 986-2800 — **WEB:** www.mifune-restaurant.com

Dinner Mon - Sat **PRICE: $$$$**

SUSHI GINZA ONODERA ✿✿

Japanese • Contemporary décor

MAP: A4

Japanese cuisine is often prone to reinterpretation so traditionalists, albeit fiscally unencumbered ones, will like this Edomae sushi restaurant. It certainly looks quite grand in its midtown spot—a location that makes sense as Fifth Avenue and Ginza are pretty similar places. The restaurant is also impressive inside, thanks largely to the 16 seater L-shaped cypress counter that's the focus of the room.

The only real decision you need to make is how many pieces of nigiri you want. Once you've done that and chosen some sake, sit back and watch the chefs make each one with quick, deft movements before placing them individually in front of you. Much of the fish is flown in from Tokyo's Tsukiji market while the white rice is from Niigata Prefecture and is seasoned with two types of red vinegar, hence its dark hue. It's cooked firm, so that each grain is clearly discernible in the mouth—a feature of great sushi.

The nigiri follows the traditional path of starting with lighter fish and progressing through to stronger flavors, with each piece lightly brushed with nikiri. Highlights include salmon roe, succulent aji (horse mackerel) and squid, which comes dressed with a little Hokkaido uni.

---

461 Fifth Ave. (bet. 40th & 41st Sts.)

42 St - Bryant Pk

(212) 390-0925 — **WEB:** onodera-group.com

Lunch & dinner Mon - Fri

PRICE: $$$$

SUSHI YASUDA ✿

Japanese • Contemporary décor

♿

MAP: B4

There is a Spartan appearance to this sushi temple, where honey-toned bamboo slats are by far the warmest decorative feature. Reservations require confirmation and punctuality, but to sushi-loving diehards, this is just the cost of admission.

Avoid the tables packed with suits (this is midtown, after all) and request a seat at the sleek counter—it's where the magic happens. Your experience here depends entirely on the soft-spoken, attentive and very focused itamae working before you, as his signature style will guide your meal. Their mission is to ensure that each diner receives a wide variety of fish that has just been cut, formed and dressed moments before it is eaten.

The kitchen lives up to its hype by ignoring new wave trends in favor of serving classically assembled and spectacularly pristine sushi. Every item is handled with the utmost care, especially the progression of sashimi highlighting the ample textures of mackerel, tuna and salmon. Outstanding clams and scallops are seasoned with a touch of lemon and sea salt flakes to enhance their natural taste; while nigiri featuring Maine and Japanese uni tastings underscore the subtle differences in flavor.

---

204 E. 43rd St. (bet. Second & Third Aves.)

Grand Central - 42 St

(212) 972-1001 — **WEB:** www.sushiyasuda.com

Lunch Mon - Fri Dinner Mon - Sat **PRICE: $$$$**

SUTTON INN

American • Neighborhood

MAP: D3

This American bistro flies a bit under the radar, but has all the fixings of a local gem. It's exceptionally quaint and cozy; the guests are chatty; the vibe is laid-back; and the dishes flaunt a delicious interplay between ingredient quality and notable talent.

For all of its decidedly homey touches however, Chef Scott Grewe is a young talent who clearly has some creative muscles to flex. Need evidence? Look no further than the tomato jam or curried cauliflower. Then dive into a mouthwatering bowl of chilled corn soup garnished with roasted poblanos and Gouda; or a fillet of bluefish, roasted to crispy-outside-tender-inside precision, and served over nutty wild rice. A deconstructed key lime pie perfectly epitomizes the inventive vision of this kitchen.

347 E. 54th St. (bet. First & Second Aves.)
Lexington Av - 53 St
(646) 370-3045 — **WEB:** www.suttoninnrestaurant.com
Dinner Mon - Sat **PRICE:** $$$

TSUSHIMA

Japanese • Simple

MAP: B4

A shiny black awning marks the entrance to this slightly antiseptic yet considerably authentic sushi bar. A few rooms done in traditional Japanese style provide seating choices at this den, which hums with business groups on the run and neighborhood dwellers seeking fantastic value lunches as well as terrific quality sushi in the evening.

Choose to dine at their beloved counter or at a table in the well-lit dining room, attended to by speedy servers. Then, dive in to generously sized lunch specials featuring perhaps a colorful chirashi, headlining yellowtail, salmon, tamago and amberjack set deftly over well-seasoned sushi rice. Sticky glazed eel, nicely grilled and plenty fatty, is an absolute must, as is the impressive omakase for dinner.

210 E. 44th St. (bet. Second & Third Aves.)
Grand Central - 42 St
(212) 207-1938 — **WEB:** www.tsushimanyc.com
Lunch & dinner daily **PRICE:** $$

TEMPURA MATSUI

Japanese • Elegant

MAP: B1

If anything indicates the strength of New York City's Japanese restaurants, it is the growing number of authentic establishments that seem like they could be sitting just as happily in Ginza as they do in midtown Manhattan.

Tempura Matsui is such a place, as it skillfully demonstrates why tempura is a celebrated Japanese cuisine type in its own right. The prized seats are at the counter, especially if you want to see these craftsmen at work.

The chefs use a mix of sesame and cottonseed oils; and the gently bubbling pot is refreshed and replenished regularly. Equally important, the batter is used sparingly so that the ingredients taste truly of themselves. You'll start with a parade of seasonal dishes including tofu with uni, before having some beautifully arranged sashimi. It is then time for the main event, which begins in the traditional way with crispy shrimp legs. The ingredients and fish turned out of this kitchen usually vary according to the seasons, but could include the likes of wonderfully tender squid, succulent Hokkaido scallop, plump matsutake, as well as subtly sweet onion. And be sure to end with tencha, with its mellow, delicious and deeply flavorful broth.

---

222 E. 39th St. (bet. Second & Third Aves.)

Grand Central - 42 St

(212) 986-8885 — **WEB:** www.tempuramatsui.com

Lunch Tue - Fri Dinner Tue - Sun **PRICE: $$$$**

WOKUNI

Japanese • Tavern

MAP: A1

This smart izakaya is the stateside outpost of a well-known and beloved restaurant group—renowned for serving tiger blowfish and other such derring-do. Dishes here may be decidedly more tame, but Wokuni is a welcome arrival for adventurous locals craving sushi, skewers and other bites. The menu's broad reach focuses on nicely crafted sashimi, such as buri (seasonal yellowtail) arranged with little more than a pinch of wasabi, as well as cooked items like corn tempura. Grilled offerings include black cod marinated in saikyo miso, yakitori and washu sirloin flambéed with brandy.

The dining room features small booths, dark tables and a popular bar area. It combines the soothing colors often used in Japanese restaurants with an edgier, industrial look.

325 Lexington Ave. (bet. 38th & 39th Sts.)
Grand Central - 42 St
(212) 447-1212 — **WEB:** www.wokuninyc.com
Lunch Mon – Sat Dinner nightly **PRICE:** $$

WOLFGANG'S

Steakhouse • Historic

MAP: A1

Wolfgang's is no stranger to the bustling New York steakhouse scene. From the lunch hour business crowd to the lively, post-work bar scene, this dining room jams in locals and tourists alike—each coming for the classic fare and precise Manhattans. The service can be gruff at times, but they have a good track record of squeezing you into a table or perch at the bar without a reservation.

Once seated, the bone-in Porterhouse, cooked rare, is the only way to go. It arrives sizzling in its own fat, perfectly seasoned. Save space for a slice of bacon—a must-order appetizer—creamed spinach and crispy German potatoes with yet more salt and fat (at this point, why not?). Just beware: while dishes are sized to share, they're priced like Maseratis.

4 Park Ave. (at 33rd St.)
33 St
(212) 889-3369 — **WEB:** www.wolfgangssteakhouse.net
Lunch & dinner daily **PRICE:** $$$$

ROASTERS
COFFEE
FROM COPENHAGEN
TO NEW YORK
COFFEE
TEA
NORTHERN FOOD HALL
ALMANAK

MIDTOWN WEST

More diverse than its counterpart (Midtown East) but still rather gritty in parts, Midtown West presents a unique blend of tree-lined streets and ethnic enclaves amid glitzy glass-walled towers. It is also home to numerous iconic sights, including now well-known **Restaurant Row**—the only street in all five boroughs to be proudly advertised as such. The fact that it resides in an area called Hell's Kitchen and highlights an impressive range of global cuisines is sealing evidence of this nabe's devotion to good food.

EAT THE STREETS

Also referred to as "Clinton," Hell's Kitchen is a colorful mosaic of workaday immigrants, old-timey residents and young families. Gone are the Prohibition-era dens, which are now replaced by swanky restaurants, boutique hotels and hip bars. **Little Brazil**, which is set only steps away from bustling Sixth Avenue, showcases samba and street food every summer on Brazilian Day. And speaking of the same nation, tourist-centric **Churrascaria Plataforma** is an all-you-can-eat Brazilian steakhouse showing off their wares via waiters armed with skewers of succulent roasted meat. Midtown may be choked by cabs and corporate types on the go, but in true Big Apple-style, these residents demand (and streets oblige with) outstanding eats in varying venues. Under the guidance of the Vendy Awards and the blog—Midtown Lunch—

discover a changing lineup of speedy and satisfying street food stalls, as well as delis stocked with everything from Mexican specialties and dried chilies to farm-fresh produce. Those in a hurry hustle over to **Tehuitzingo** for over 12 types of tacos, but if seeking a more reliable scene, find a seat at **Tulcingo del Valle** where tortas are turned out alongside burritos and burgers. Similarly, find carnivores reveling over those perfectly pink patties laced with crispy fries at Le Parker Meridien's **burger joint**. On the beat for more meat? Then head on over to the wilds of **K-town** for smoky, succulent 'cue, as well as a host of other food. This dark horse-like quarter has been known to sneak up and surprise. Its instant and unapologetically authentic vibe owes largely to the prominence of aromatic barbecue joints, karaoke bars and of course, grocers hawking everything from fresh tofu to handmade mandu.

Shop till you drop at Bergdorf Goodman; then cool your heels over caviar and croissants at the *très* chic **Petrossian**. Otherwise, stir things up in Times Square, with a martini and small bite from the stately **Charlie Palmer at the Knick**, comfortably situated in the Knickerbocker Hotel.

Switching gears from specialty spots to mega markets, **Gotham West Market** is one of Manhattan's most favored gourmet feats. Settled along Eleventh Avenue, this culinary complex cradles a number of chef-driven stalls and artisanal purveyors offering tapas, charcuterie, sammies and everything in between. Of special note is the first stateside outpost of **Ivan Ramen Slurp Shop**, where the rockstar chef's global fans slurp down bowlfuls of wispy rye noodles in a sumptuous broth. If you have time, swing by **Corner Slice** for a simple, airy and assertive pie, lashed with tomato sauce, garlic and Sicilian oregano. **City Kitchen** is yet another formidable bazaar featuring a rustic-industrial setting and outfitted with kiosks from **ilili Box**, **Gabriela's Taqueria**, **Luke's Lobster**, **Dough** and more. Of course, cached beneath the graceful Plaza hotel is the tastefully decorated **Plaza Food Hall**. Here, a dizzying array of comestibles is on full display and makes for a fine attraction—or distraction! Curated by mega-watt personality, Todd English, this 32,000-square-foot space is a perfect meeting spot to sip, savor and shop. Beginning with caviar, lobster rolls or sushi; and closing with coffee or cupcakes, it's a veritable tour de force that typifies the city's culinary elite.

FOOD FIXES

A few steps west and Gotham City's eclectic identity reveals yet another facet, where Ninth Avenue unearths a wealth of eats. A wonderful start to any day is practically certified at **Amy's Bread**, where fresh-baked baguettes lend countless restaurant kitchens that extra crumb of culture. But, it is their famously colorful cakes and cookies that tempt passersby off the streets. Across the way, **Poseidon Bakery** is golden for Greek sweets. It is also the last place in town that still crafts their own phyllo dough by hand—a taste of the spanakopita will prove it. Then, even though its moniker depicts another district, **Sullivan Street Bakery**'s one and only retail outlet is also housed along this midtown corridor—a location so perilously far west in the Manhattan mindset that its success is worth its weight in gold. Just as Jim Lahey's luxurious loaves claim a cult-like following, so do the fantastic components (a warm Portuguese-style roll?) at **City Sandwich**. New

Yorkers in the know never tire of the lure behind **La Boîte**'s spice blends, or the sumptuous cured meats and formaggi found at **Sergimmo Salumeria**. Find more such salty goodness at veteran butcher, **Esposito Meat Market**, proudly purveying every part of the pig alongside piles of offal. Thirsty travelers should keep heading further south of Port Authority Bus Terminal to uncover yet another enclave rich with restaurants and food marts. Here, foodies start their feasting at **International Grocery** proffering such pleasures as olives, oils, spices and spreads. But, among their outstanding produce, make sure to sample the renowned taramosalata (as if prepared by the gods atop Mount Olympus themselves).

TIME WARNER CENTER

Finally, no visit to this district is complete without paying homage to the epicurean feat that is the **Time Warner Center**. Presiding over Columbus Circle, high-flying chefs indulge both themselves and their pretty patrons here with ground-breaking success. Discover a range of savory and sweet spots indoors—from **Bouchon Bakery**'s colorful French macarons to the eye-popping style and sass of **Ascent Lounge**. Located on the fourth floor, **Center Bar** (brought to you by Michael Lomonaco) is yet another sophisticated perch for enjoying a champagne cocktail while taking in the views of Central Park. This is classic New York—only more glossy and glamorous than usual.

Midtown West
A
B
1
2
3
4
HUDSON RIVER
INTREPID SEA, AIR & SPACE MUSEUM
CIRCLE LINE FERRY TERMINAL
LINCOLN TUNNEL
495
JACOB K. JAVITS CONVENTION CENTER
Joe DiMaggio Hwy.
DEWITT CLINTON PARK
Legacy Records
Chef's Table at Brooklyn Fare
Mercato
Larb Ubol
Dyer Ave
Ninth
Tenth
Eleventh
Eighth
Seventh
34 St-Penn Sta
MADISON SQUARE GARDEN
CHELSEA
28 St
CENTRAL PARK
Central Park South
The Pond
57 St-7 Av
Molyvos
Indian Accent
Norma's
57 St
7 Av
Benoit
Broadway
Avenue of the Americas (Sixth Ave.)
Le Bernardin
MOMA
Il Gattopardo
Nusr-Et
Aldo Sohm Wine Bar
The Modern
5 Av-53 St
21 Club
Fifth Ave.
E. 53rd St.
W. 49th St.
ROCKEFELLER CENTER

UPPER WEST SIDE
C
D
Asiate
Porter House
Masa
TIME WARNER CENTER
CENTRAL PARK
59 St-Columbus Circle
Per Se
Marea
Central
Park
South
The Pond
UPPER EAST SIDE
1
Gloria
Casellula
Tori Shin
Danji
CARNEGIE HALL
57 St-7 Av
5 Av-59 St
57 St
MIDTOWN
WEST
Broadway
Ninth
Eighth
Seventh
(Sixth
Fifth
Chez Napoléon
Russian Samovar
Don Antonio by Starita
Gallagher's
50 St
7 Av
Kung Fu Little Steamed Buns Ramen
MOMA
Barbetta
49 St
RADIO CITY MUSIC HALL
5 Av-53 St
2
THEATER
DISTRICT
ROCKEFELLER CENTER
Hakkasan
Suzuki
Satsuki
47-50 Sts-Rockefeller Ctr
The Sea Grill
ST. PATRICK'S CATHEDRAL
42 St- Port Authority Bus Terminal
PORT AUTHORITY BUS TERMINAL
TIMES SQUARE
Times Sq
Aureole
db Bistro Moderne
MIDTOWN EAST
Madison
Park
Times Sq-42 St
Gabriel Kreuther
42 St-Bryant Pk
5 Av
BRYANT PARK
METLIFE BLDG.
GRAND CENTRAL TERMINAL
Lexington
3
GARMENT DISTRICT
Americas
Szechuan Gourmet
NY PUBLIC LIBRARY
Grand Central-42 St
Charlie Palmer Steak New York
42 St-Grand Central
MACY'S
CHRYSLER BUILDING
MIDTOWN EAST
Keens
HERALD SQUARE
Tonchin
Cho Dang Gol
Ai Fiori
34 St-Herald Sq
MURRAY HILL
Samwon Garden BBQ
EMPIRE STATE BUILDING
4
New Wonjo
Miss Korea
33 St
Third
Second
28 St
C
D

AI FIORI

Italian • Contemporary décor

MAP: C4

Elegantly accessed by a sweeping staircase (or elevator) in the Langham hotel's lobby, Ai Fiori stands proudly above its Fifth Avenue address. This perfect perch for pretty ladies with their deal-making beaus in tow is dominated by walls of windows and espresso-dark wood. The handsome marble bar and lounge furnished with tufted banquettes sets an ideal scene for a post-work drink; while large florals, leather chairs and square columns lure families into the formal dining room. Service is attentive, the linens are thick, chargers are monogrammed with a goldleaf "F" and every last detail is very, very lovely.

As one might expect of a Michael White restaurant, the menu boasts of Italian favorites mingled with contemporary flair. Pastas are masterful: begin with perfect squares of ricotta- and mascarpone-filled ravioli glazed with red wine and garnished with a deliciously mild and earthy sottocenere al tartufo. Fish courses can be even more enticing, as evidenced by a shining and perfectly seared piece of Atlantic halibut, crowned by yellow squash and purple radishes.

Desserts, like a Paris-Brest filled with hazelnut-praline cream, are almost too bright and beautiful to eat—well, almost.

---

400 Fifth Ave. (bet. 36th & 37th Sts.)

34 St - Herald Sq

(212) 613-8660 — **WEB:** www.aifiorinyc.com

Lunch Mon- Fri Dinner nightly

PRICE: $$$$

ALDO SOHM WINE BAR

Contemporary • Wine bar

MAP: A4

Step through this buffed metal doorway to find an oenophile's fantasy where Zalto stemware is stacked high and each polished glass is ready to be filled by one of the 200 selections brilliantly curated by Le Bernardin's super-star sommelier, Aldo Sohm. Over 40 wines on the list are offered by the glass.

A tailored crowd sits and sips—perhaps on an oversized U-shaped sofa, at a comfy counter or at one of a handful of tall tables. The scene is luxe but also comfortable, featuring crystal fixtures and a stylish array of bric-a-brac stacked high to the soaring ceiling. Tapas-sized snacks are designed for sharing with wine consumption in mind and include a plate of cheeses, charcuterie, harissa-roasted carrots or chicken drumstick prepared coq au vin-style.

151 W. 51st St. (bet. Sixth & Seventh Aves.)
50 St (Broadway)
(212) 554-1143 — **WEB:** www.aldosohmwinebar.com
Lunch Mon - Fri Dinner Mon - Sat **PRICE: $$**

ASIATE

Contemporary • Luxury

MAP: C1

Tucked inside the 35th floor of the swank Mandarin Oriental, Asiate boasts a breathtaking view with towering glass windows overlooking Central Park and that legendary Manhattan skyline. Magenta booths (with flowers on the table to match) add a bit of whimsy to the space; service is understated, but always professional.

Chef Mazen Mustafa heads this kitchen—where dinner might feature tender, faintly charred octopus paired with a slightly sweet piquillo sauce; and then move on to the terrific Ora King salmon, a signature from the chef. Cooked sous vide, it's served with a green sauce of avocado, sorrel and coconut, as well as a bit of charred white spring onion. Don't forgo the chocolate coulant, which is topped with a gold leaf and pure heaven to devour.

80 Columbus Cir. (bet. Broadway & Columbus Ave.)
59 St - Columbus Circle
(212) 805-8881 — **WEB:** www.mandarinoriental.com
Lunch & dinner daily **PRICE: $$$$**

AUREOLE ⅡO

Contemporary • Elegant

MAP: C3

Charlie Palmer's midtown behemoth is made up of two distinct areas so it's worth knowing which one's for you. The Liberty Room plays host to the after-work crowd, in for a drink to celebrate a promotion or just the end of another day. If you're coming to close a deal or impress the in-laws then ask for the inner sanctum of the more formal dining room, which comes with fewer braying suits.

The menu is a roll-call of luxury ingredients—from Maine lobster to Scottish salmon, Griggstown pheasant to Wagyu beef—and the kitchen ensures they're the focus of the plate, in dishes that are contemporary without being overwrought. Pastas, like garganelli with veal ragout or squid ink cavatelli, are a highlight. The impressive wine list is strong on burgundy.

135 W. 42nd St. (bet. Broadway & Sixth Ave.)
42 St - Bryant Pk
(212) 319-1660 — **WEB:** www.charliepalmer.com
Lunch Mon - Fri Dinner Mon - Sat **PRICE:** $$$$

BARBETTA ⅡO

Italian • Historic

MAP: C2

It doesn't get more old-world New York than this iconic Restaurant Row institution. Opened in 1906, Barbetta is a testament to proper dining out, where outerwear is mandatorily checked and servers waltz around good-looking guests as well as the hushed, gilded surrounds donning neatly pressed tuxedos. Perhaps unsurprisingly, the impossibly romantic patio has been the backdrop for countless marriage proposals.

The kitchen's Northern-influenced specialties are listed on thick cardstock, and each item is highlighted by the year of its addition to the menu. Linguine with pesto alla Genovese is as scrumptious today as it was in 1914; while luscious rabbit alla Piemontese, dating back to the Clinton era and braised in white wine and lemon, is equally divine.

321 W. 46th St. (bet. Eighth & Ninth Aves.)
50 St (Eighth Ave.)
(212) 246-9171 — **WEB:** www.barbettarestaurant.com
Lunch & dinner Tue - Sat **PRICE:** $$$

BENOIT

French • Bistro

MAP: A4

This Alain Ducasse bistro, housed in the venerable La Côte Basque space, may have been renovated in recent years, but it remains decidedly Old World in look, feel and taste. The setting remains a sight to behold, with its abundant framed mirrors, red velvet banquettes and oak paneled walls. In the front salon, two red wingback chairs are tilted in to face a working fireplace and make an idyllic spot for nibbling madeleines at the end of your meal.

To begin, peruse the menu of Chef Laëtitia Rouabah's classical French cooking, featuring the likes of leeks vinaigrette or foie de veau, while snacking on fresh gougères. Traditional desserts are a highlight, especially the crème caramel, flecked with vanilla beans and served in a generous pool of sauce.

60 W. 55th St. (bet. Fifth & Sixth Aves.)
57 St
(646) 943-7373 – **WEB:** www.benoitny.com
Lunch & dinner daily

PRICE: $$$

CASELLULA

American • Wine bar

MAP: C1

Fresh, soft-ripened, pressed, washed or blue—no matter what kind of cheese you prefer, Casellula is sure to have it. Better still, take advantage of their helpful tasting notes and try something brand new. Cheeses arrive with creative pairings like pickled fennel, lemon-zested hazelnuts and maybe even a glass of something from their vast wine list. Round out your meal with small plates of crostini or perhaps a hearty sandwich. For dessert, sweet potato cake is topped with brown sugar sauce and served with a scoop of butter pecan-ice cream for just the right amount of sweetness.

The cozy dining room is warm with flickering candles, wood tables and a delightful staff. It's also small and fills up quickly, so parties of two should make a reservation.

401 W. 52nd St. (bet. Ninth & Tenth Aves.)
50 St (Eighth Ave.)
(212) 247-8137 – **WEB:** www.casellula.com
Dinner nightly

PRICE: $$

CHARLIE PALMER STEAK NEW YORK

Steakhouse • Elegant

MAP: C3

Charlie Palmer has been a name in New York dining since his tenure at the River Café in the early 80s. Here, find the latest namesake, which makes an idyllic choice for anyone in the mood for solid steakhouse food. Servers seem to treat everyone like an old-time regular—a move that belies its young age. The royal-blue and white-dining room dons a rather striking décor within the Archer Hotel.

Meats are cooked to meticulous perfection, with a salty, peppery, garlicky crust that yields mouthwatering umami flavor. If you're going with a big group, order the tomahawk steak, which you can smell and hear sizzling in its giant cast-iron pan well in advance of its arrival at your table. Nothing goes better with this than the off-menu favorite—truffled fries.

47 W. 38th St. (bet. Fifth & Sixth Aves.)
Times Sq - 42 St
(212) 302-3838 — **WEB:** www.charliepalmersteak.com
Lunch & dinner daily **PRICE:** $$$$

CHEZ NAPOLÉON

French • Cozy

MAP: C2

Oh-so-popular and run by the Bruno family since 1982, this atmospheric bistro is not to be missed for its unapologetically creamy and butter-dreamy plates of traditional French cuisine. And despite the fact that their late, beloved Chef/grandmère (Marguerite Bruno) who steadily commanded the kitchen for an impressive tenure, is no longer with them, the scene remains busy as ever.

Take in the creaky wood floors and parchment-colored walls hung with French-themed jigsaw puzzles. Then indulge in chilled leeks dressed with the famous house vinaigrette; sautéed veal kidneys in mustard-cream sauce; and steak au poivre with black or green peppercorn sauce. Plan ahead when ordering so you have time (and space) for a classic dessert soufflé with crème anglaise.

365 W. 50th St. (bet. Eighth & Ninth Aves.)
50 St (Eighth Ave.)
(212) 265-6980 — **WEB:** www.cheznapoleon.com
Lunch Mon - Fri Dinner Mon - Sat **PRICE:** $$

CHEF'S TABLE AT BROOKLYN FARE ✿✿✿

Contemporary • Design

✿ ♿

MAP: B3

Unlike its original downtown Brooklyn location, excited diners must now navigate the labyrinth of Brooklyn Fare's grocery aisles to arrive at this illustrious, gorgeous and gleaming dining room. Inside, everything centers around the kitchen, shining with copper pans overhead, bright white tiles and fine stemware. Prime seats are located along the finely honed and brushed wood counter, though there is table seating.

Chef César Ramirez's dedication to his kitchen remains as unchanged as ever. He may be a visionary, but this cuisine refrains from being showy, keeping simplicity and astounding precision at the heart of each bite. Great wizardry is displayed in the sauces, which are consistently brilliant accents to high-level ingredients. One course may showcase a cut of near-translucent kinmedai in an electrifying blend of ginger and turnips. Cod is robata-grilled until it pulls apart with ease, then bathed in delicate vin jaune that is as smooth as butter, with a bit of earthy chanterelle cream. Delicate and fleshy, grilled quail beneath crackling skin is served with a duo of barbecue and mustard sauces of tremendous depth. Expect a generous hand with luxuries, like caviar, foie gras and uni.

---

431 W. 37th St. (bet. Ninth & Tenth Aves.)
34 St - Hudson Yards
(718) 243-0050 — **WEB:** www.brooklynfare.com
Dinner Tue - Sat

PRICE: $$$$

CHO DANG GOL

Korean • Family

MAP: C4

For a change of pace in bustling Koreatown, Cho Dang Gol offers the barbecue-weary an opportunity to explore some of this nation's more rustic cooking. Soft tofu is the specialty of the house and for fitting reason (it's downright delicious). But, bubbling casseroles and spicy stews are equally heartwarming.

The menu also offers favorites like flaky pajeon, satisfying bibimbap and marinated meats. A sautéed tofu trio with pork belly is stir-fried with glassy sweet potato noodles and kimchi, in an excellent sweet and spicy red pepper sauce.

The interior has a simple, homey appeal—its cozy dining room simply decorated with close-knit wood tables. The occasional burst of sound drifting down from the upstairs karaoke bar promises a little post-dinner fun.

55 W. 35th St. (bet. Fifth & Sixth Aves.)

34 St - Herald Sq

(212) 695-8222 – **WEB:** www.chodanggolnyc.com

Lunch & dinner daily **PRICE: $$**

DANJI

Korean • Contemporary décor

MAP: C1

Thanks to tall communal tables that practically fill the dining room, Chef Hooni Kim's Hell's Kitchen hot spot is both festive and bustling. Attractive and smartly designed, its silk panels, pottery and striking display of spoons are further enhanced by a flattering lighting scheme.

Equally impressive are the menu's myriad small plates, each of them a refreshing take on Korean specialties. Blocks of soft tofu are quickly deep-fried and boldly dressed with gochujang and a ginger-scallion vinaigrette. Poached daikon rings accompanied by bok choy are glazed with a dark and spicy sauce and stacked high for dramatic presentation.

Vegetarian highlights include spicy, crispy dumplings filled with tofu, vegetables and cellophane noodles.

346 W. 52nd St. (bet. Eighth & Ninth Aves.)

50 St (Eighth Ave.)

(212) 586-2880 – **WEB:** www.danjinyc.com

Lunch & dinner daily **PRICE: $$**

DB BISTRO MODERNE

French • Elegant

MAP: D3

Chef Daniel Boulud's midtown canteen is fashioned by Jeffrey Beers and dons a contemporary demeanor. The front lounge is abuzz with post-work and pre-theater gaggles, while well-behaved crowds in the back are seated in a walnut-paneled space dressed with mirrors and black-and-white photography.

Like its setting, the menu is inventive and unites classic bistro cooking with market-inspired creations. That lush pâté en croûte is a buttery pastry encasing layers of creamy country pâté, guinea hen and foie gras, dressed with huckleberry compote, toasted pine nuts and pickled enoki mushrooms. Wild rice-crusted fluke presented with Hawaiian blue prawn and sauce Américaine further demonstrates the kitchen's contemporary leanings.

55 W. 44th St. (bet. Fifth & Sixth Aves.)
5 Av
(212) 391-2400 — **WEB:** www.dbbistro.com
Lunch & dinner daily

PRICE: $$$

DON ANTONIO BY STARITA

Pizza • Cozy

MAP: C2

Don Antonio's knows its way around a pie. The namesake outpost, located in Naples, has been running strong since 1901. If that isn't enough street cred to send you running to this beloved midtown pizzeria, then the generous buzz surrounding Roberto Caporuscio's other NY venture, Kesté, will do the trick. This kitchen's signature is the Montanara Starita—a lightly fried pizza laced with house-made tomato sauce, smoked mozzarella and basil, then finished in the wood-fired oven. But really, who could stop there with treasures like the salsiccia e friarielli pizza to sample, highlighting crumbled fennel sausage, smoked mozzarella, rapini greens and a swirl of EVOO.

Filled with unique Sicilian varietals, this wine list is more thoughtful than it needs to be.

309 W. 50th St. (bet. Eighth & Ninth Aves.)
50 St (Eighth Ave.)
(646) 719-1043 — **WEB:** www.donantoniopizza.com
Lunch & dinner daily

PRICE: $$

GABRIEL KREUTHER ✿✿

Contemporary • Luxury

MAP: C3

Distinctively housed at the base of the Grace building, this dining room is modern, beautiful and elegant, with neutral grays and plush leather banquettes; it is also spacious and perfect for celebrating special occasions. Crockery and cutlery are notable—the salt cellar even resembles a gilt apple. Service oscillates between professional and relaxed, but it is always efficient—even your bag will have its own rack.

Dishes reflect global sensibilities with a strong creative edge. Nowhere is that more clear than in the precisely cut langoustine tartare, topped with a crispy tuile and wonderfully enriched with cauliflower cream. Foie gras arrives in myriad guises, perhaps as a seared lobe as rich as custard, surrounded by roasted quince, chestnuts and vanilla gastrique. Old-school luxuries extend right through to the cheese trolley. A cocktail list dedicated to the history of Bryant Park, which is located across the street, lends a sense of identity to this already impressive room. As an homage to the eponymous chef's Alsatian heritage, the wine selection prominently features rieslings, pinot blancs and gewürztraminers.

Stop by the lounge for inventive sips and simpler bites.

---

41 W. 42nd St. (bet. Fifth & Sixth Aves.)

42 St - Bryant Pk

(212) 257-5826 — **WEB:** www.gknyc.com

Lunch Mon - Fri Dinner Mon - Sat **PRICE: $$$$**

GALLAGHER'S

Steakhouse • Vintage

MAP: C2

A multi-million dollar renovation hasn't glossed over any of Gallagher's iconic character. Walls covered with photos of horses and jockeys harken back to the seasoned stallion's former proximity to the old Madison Square Garden. The menu's "other soup" is a sly reference held over from Prohibition days; and diners still walk past the window-fronted meat locker where slabs of USDA Prime beef are dry-aged.

Gallagher's fresh sparkle is exhibited by the display kitchen, set behind glass panes. The chefs here turn out contemporary-minded fare like hamachi crudo with a yuzu-jalapeño vinaigrette to go with choice cuts of meat grilled over hickory. The rib steak is a bone-in ribeye that arrives mouthwateringly tender with a side of warm and savory house sauce.

228 W. 52nd St. (bet. Broadway & Eighth Ave.)
50 St (Broadway)
(212) 586-5000 — **WEB:** www.gallaghersnysteakhouse.com
Lunch & dinner daily **PRICE: $$$**

GLORIA

Seafood • Minimalist

MAP: C1

Though dinner at Gloria doesn't come with a side of personal space (read: you'll likely be elbow-to-elbow with your neighbors as you dine), the tiny spot slays its Ninth Avenue competition with a trendy ambience, buzzing bar and terrific food crafted by Chef Diego Garcia.

The concise, seafood-centric menu, which offers just a handful of savory items and two desserts, reflects the chef's impressive background. Expertly charred octopus or red snapper served in a red wine béarnaise-inspired sauce both hint at Garcia's time at Le Bernardin, while a tres leches cake filled with thick cream is a nod to his Mexican heritage. No matter what you order, be sure to arrive with a fully charged phone, as these dishes practically beg to be shared on Instagram.

401 W. 53rd St. (bet. Ninth & Tenth Aves.)
50 St (Eighth Ave.)
(212) 956-0709 — **WEB:** www.gloria-nyc.com
Dinner Tue - Sat **PRICE: $$**

HAKKASAN

Chinese • Design

MAP: C2

If this sensual and sophisticated lair doesn't come to mind when you crave quality Cantonese cooking, it's high time you added it to the list. Behind its front door lies a long, moodily lit corridor that leads to a massive dining room, which, thanks to cobalt-blue glass, Carrara marble and mirrors, feels intimate despite its size.

The equally elegant menu includes such mouthwatering items as the wallet-friendly Hakka fried dim sum platter featuring roast duck-and-pumpkin, crispy prawn, as well as a seafood puff. The roast duck theme continues on, but this time the juicy bird is enhanced with an earthy and fragrant black truffle sauce. Sweet and sour pork tenderloin is yet another decadent surprise that syncs perfectly with the restaurant's luxe tenor.

311 W. 43rd St. (bet. Eighth & Ninth Aves.)
42 St - Port Authority Bus Terminal
(212) 776-1818 — **WEB:** www.hakkasan.com
Lunch & dinner daily **PRICE: $$$$**

IL GATTOPARDO

Italian • Elegant

MAP: B4

This leopard's take on Italian dining favors elegance over rusticity. Set within two Beaux Arts townhouses (once home to a Rockefeller family member), the restaurant is an understated sprawl of ivory walls contrasted against dark-stained floors and smoky mirrors.

The smartly attired staff attends to a buttoned-up crowd digging into pricey but pleasing fare like shaved artichoke salad with organic frisée, lemon, olive oil and bottarga di muggine.

Here, a golden-brown and crisp-skinned baby chicken arrives split into two neat halves, simply grilled with rosemary and lemon, and served with roasted potatoes. And like everything else at Il Gattopardo, the cassata Siciliana—with its candied fruit and bright green almond paste—is a dressed-up take on the classic.

13-15 W. 54th St. (bet. Fifth & Sixth Aves.)
5 Av - 53 St
(212) 246-0412 — **WEB:** www.ilgattopardonyc.com
Lunch & dinner daily **PRICE: $$$**

INDIAN ACCENT

Indian • Elegant

MAP: A3

Set inside the posh Le Parker Méridien hotel, Indian Accent offers gorgeously plated food with a decidedly modern spin. An outpost of the highly acclaimed original in Delhi, this space is sleek and exotic, with purple banquettes, brass details and a shimmering gold-accent wall. The service is polished and professional, with the knowledgeable staff carefully walking you through a customized prix-fixe menu selected from various parts of the carte.

Celebrated chef Manish Mehrotra heads the talented kitchen, serving up impressive starters like freshly griddled phulka paired with jackfruit, green chili sauce and micro sprouts. Perfectly tender sea bass is then served with herbed barley, trout roe and creamy coconut sauce for a display in contemporary couplings.

123 W. 56th St. (bet. Sixth & Seventh Aves.)
57 St
(212) 842-8070 — **WEB:** www.indianaccent.com
Lunch Mon - Sat Dinner nightly

PRICE: $$$

KEENS

Steakhouse • Historic

MAP: C4

It's not just carnivores who'll appreciate this most classic of steakhouses; Anglophiles, social historians, Scotch lovers and pipe smokers will also find themselves reveling in the immeasurably appealing atmosphere of Keens and its palpable sense of times past. Established in 1885, this midtown marvel suggests a Dickensian Gentleman's club, with its dark wood paneling and low ceiling lined with thousands of clay pipes, although these days the customers are mostly deal-making business types rather than extravagantly whiskered thespians.

Follow their lead and drape your jacket over the back of your chair, roll up your sleeves and attempt to gain control over a Porterhouse steak, dry-aged in-house, or finish their legendary mutton chop in one sitting.

72 W. 36th St. (bet. Fifth & Sixth Aves.)
34 St - Herald Sq
(212) 947-3636 — **WEB:** www.keens.com
Lunch Mon - Fri Dinner nightly

PRICE: $$$

KUNG FU LITTLE STEAMED BUNS RAMEN

Chinese • Simple

MAP: C2

Watch out Hell's Kitchen; watch out Flushing—with its lineup of traditional Chinese comfort food, including the best soup dumplings in town, this steamy joint kicks its competitors to the curb. Set among the neon lights of the Theater District, the ever-packed gem may showcase a noodle house-like vibe, but the staff is friendly and the cooking on-point at all times.

Hand-pulled and hand-cut noodles are stir-fried with mouthwatering accompaniments, while the dumpling variety is so great it's almost impossible to pick. Herb-spiked pork and shrimp wonton soup is well worth the 20-minute wait, allowing diners plenty of time to devour pan-fried Peking duck bundles, scallion pancakes stuffed with sliced beef or even steamed buns full of mushroom and bok choy.

811 Eighth Ave. (bet. 48th & 49th Sts.)
50 St (Eighth Ave.)
(917) 388-2555 — **WEB:** www.kfdelicacy.com
Lunch & dinner daily **PRICE:**

LARB UBOL

Thai • Simple

MAP: B3

The larb here really is good enough to be the restaurant's namesake as these spicy, crunchy, salty and herb-y salads sing with flavor. Yet Larb Ubol does much more with equal skill: the sheer size of their massive chicken wings defy nature, yielding enough crisp-skinned and chili-coated meat to satisfy any appetite. Yum moo krob mixes impossibly tender pork with abundant green chilies in a fish sauce dressing for a brilliant counterpoint in flavor; while kai jeow, a Thai-style omelet, is an unexpectedly comforting dish that highlights excellent technique. There may be a choice of three fillings, but the pickled garlic can't be beat.

The space itself is no more than basic; the location is, well, meh. Service is friendly, though not necessarily speedy.

480 Ninth Ave. (bet. 36th & 37th Sts.)
34 St - Penn Station
(212) 564-1822 — **WEB:** www.larbubol.com
Lunch & dinner daily **PRICE:**

LE BERNARDIN ✿✿✿

Seafood • Luxury

MAP: A4

When the definitive history of NYC's dining scene is written, Le Bernardin will have a chapter all to itself. Maguy Le Coze and Eric Ripert's icon has been entertaining the city's movers and shakers for over 20 years and its popularity remains undimmed.

As soon as you step inside you are enveloped in a warm embrace. Lunch is busy with those who know what they want and trust this well-oiled machine to deliver it in the time they have. Come at dinner for a more languid affair. The menu is divided into headings of "Almost raw," "Barely touched" and "Lightly cooked," but don't be fooled, these product-driven items have considerable depth. Seafood restaurants have no hiding place when it comes to cooking fish or crustaceans and this kitchen always hits its marks—whether that's poaching halibut, pan-roasting monkfish, baking striped bass or searing tuna.

While seafood remains Ripert's passion, his recent vegetarian tasting menu has been making waves with dishes like the Himalayan morel, spring pea and fava bean casserole or the warm artichoke panaché with vegetable risotto and Périgord truffle vinaigrette. Bid this spread adieu over coconut mousse with shavings of caramelized pineapple.

---

155 W. 51st St. (bet. Sixth & Seventh Aves.)

50 St (Broadway)

(212) 554-1515 — **WEB:** www.le-bernardin.com

Lunch Mon - Fri Dinner Mon - Sat **PRICE: $$$$**

LEGACY RECORDS

Mediterranean • Design

MAP: B2

Burrowed inside the Henry Hall Hotel in Hudson Yard, Legacy Records is hip personified—down to every last detail. Its art deco interior is defined by gold-accented trim, tile floors and burgundy leather-topped tables. Zalto glasses grace each of these tables indicating that wine is serious business here—the sommelier was recently crowned the best in the world. Cocktails are smartly divided into styles, namely light beginning, weightier middle or stout nightcap.

Winning drinks aside, dishes are remarkable and treated with great care. Pigeon with prosciutto is grilled for that perfect char; handmade pasta with beet and ricotta has a pop of color plus an explosion of flavor; and duck, aged for two weeks and glazed with spices and honey, is revelatory.

517 W. 38th St. (bet. 10th & 11th Aves.)
34 St - Hudson Yards
N/A — **WEB:** www.legacyrecordsnyc.com
Dinner Tue - Sat

PRICE: $$$$

MERCATO

Italian • Trattoria

MAP: B3

Italian hospitality with a Pugliese accent is on display at Mercato, a rustic trattoria in the western midtown hinterlands. The space is country-chic, with distressed wood tables, soft, exposed bulbs and vintage signs. The atmosphere is inviting and the menu is inspired by the classic dishes of Puglia, the birthplace of owner Fabio Camardi.

First get a drink in your hand, then start with fave e cicoria, a straightforward purée of fava beans and garlicky chicory greens. A well-rounded Italian meal must have pasta, so be sure to indulge in the likes of orecchiette with broccoli rabe and garlic, enhanced by anchovies and breadcrumbs. For something deeply satisfying, try the fennel-dusted porchetta with a hearty side of potato and green cabbage mash.

352 W. 39th St. (bet. Eighth & Ninth Aves.)
42 St - Port Authority Bus Terminal
(212) 643-2000 — **WEB:** www.mercatonyc.com
Lunch & dinner daily

PRICE: $$

MAREA

Seafood • Elegant

MAP: D1

Gorgeous and sophisticated Marea couldn't really be found anywhere other than Central Park South. Its urbane clientele ensures the atmosphere remains as elegant as ever and the restaurant keeps its side of the deal by providing expert, if at times erratic, service in a beautiful, light-flooded dining room dressed to the nines with high-gloss Indonesian rosewood.

Fish and shellfish are the stars of this culinary show and Italian the chosen language. The quality and condition of the fish are top-notch, but that would count for little if the chefs didn't get the cooking process spot on—and so they do.

Nothing commences a meal like crudo (and this kitchen offers around ten to choose from), but the sepia laced with olive oil, lemon rind, tossed soffritto and shavings of bottarga di muggine is a plate full of flavor. Other generously sized antipasti also make for great starter options; while house-made pastas are spot on and forever popular among the regulars. Looking for something different? Go for the grilled octopus, glossed in herbs, olive oil and served with smoked potatoes and pickled red onions; or halibut enriched by a bright butter sauce, smoked trout roe and roasted potatoes.

---

240 Central Park South (bet. Broadway & Seventh Ave.)
59 St - Columbus Circle
(212) 582-5100 — **WEB:** www.marea-nyc.com
Lunch & dinner daily

PRICE: $$$$

MASA ✿✿✿

Japanese • Luxury

MAP: C1

To taste what may be the continent's best sushi, experience the quiet, contemplative and very exclusive ceremony of Chef Masa Takayama's omakase. Everything here carries a certain weight, beginning with the heavy wooden door and carrying through to the bill. The room of course is as unchanging and calming as a river stone, set amid blonde hinoki wood and a gargantuan forsythia tree. Yes, you'll forget it's on the fourth floor of a mall.

Attention to detail is unsurpassed and at times it may seem like a bit much, but a reverential spirit is part of your meal here. Service displays the same smooth grace, with servers at-the-ready carrying their hot towels, fingerbowls, tea and bits of insight.

Awaken the palate with a sweet chunk of hairy crab meat dressed in citrusy yuzu beneath creamy tomalley. This may be followed by the chef's signature glass coupe of minced toro and a very fine—and very generous—pile of Osetra caviar. Maine uni is downright wondrous, served in its shell with caramelized custard and paper-thin, melting sheets of white truffle. The chef's selection of sushi is unrivaled; the rice is firm and temperate, garnishes are subtle, and quality of fish is supreme.

---

10 Columbus Circle (in the Time Warner Center)
59 St - Columbus Circle
(212) 823-9807 — **WEB:** www.masanyc.com
Lunch Tue - Fri Dinner Mon - Sat

PRICE: $$$$

MISS KOREA

Korean • Family

MAP: C4

24-hour access to delicious Korean food? Yes please, Miss Korea. Located in the heart of K-Town, this popular restaurant is guaranteed to have a line out the door during peak dinner hours, but once inside you'll find a fairly serene décor, with each of its floors dedicated to a unique aspect of Korean culture.

The first floor offers the most robust menu; the second floor is more intimate, with zen-like private dining rooms and a set menu featuring Imperial cuisine. Each floor is packed with blonde wooden tables fixed with grills. However, make sure to go for the outstanding clay pot galbi highlighting tender USDA Prime beef short ribs marinated on the bone for 24 hours, then cut tableside and grilled to heavenly perfection on the spot.

10 W. 32nd St. (bet. Broadway & Fifth Ave.)
34 St - Herald Sq
(212) 594-4963 — **WEB:** www.misskoreabbq.com
Lunch & dinner daily

PRICE: $$

MOLYVOS

Greek • Mediterranean décor

MAP: A3

The city has upped its Greek game in recent years, but Molyvos has more than earned its OG status—having served fresh Mediterranean cuisine to a loyal crowd for innumerable years. The secret to its longevity lies in the kitchen's simple and enjoyable food, smart service and casually elegant setting (tables covered with white cloth and a spare, rustic aesthetic).

Executive Chef Carlos Carreto oversees this menu. Among a host of delicious sounding (and tasting) items is the lamb pie, highlighting flaky, fried phyllo packed with tender shredded shank and a mild cheese sauce. Plush pillows of bougatsa filled with warm semolina custard will have you begging for more. The wine list is of particular note, starring some of the city's finest all-Greek vintages.

871 Seventh Ave. (bet. 55th & 56th Sts.)
57 St - 7 Av
(212) 582-7500 — **WEB:** www.molyvos.com
Lunch & dinner daily

PRICE: $$

THE MODERN ✿✿

Contemporary • Design

MAP: A4

It goes without saying that The Modern has one of the city's most prized locations, designed to capture the iconic feel of the MoMA in which it is seamlessly housed. Art enthusiasts have always appreciated its timeless and glorious surrounds; and thanks to an ambitious nip-tuck, they are sure to notice the improved acoustics, which facilitate quiet conversation and match the calm of the view over the sculpture garden. The state-of-the-art kitchen allows the team to grow into its full creative potential—both in the dining room and at the buzzy bar. But for a truly special experience, book the chef's table (complete with a multi-course tasting menu) inside the kitchen.

Chef Abram Bissell and crew are wowing these globe-trotting patrons with excellent food and warm, well-timed service. Appealing dishes showcase clean flavors and may include roasted cauliflower with crab butter, almond-cauliflower purée and crabmeat. The juicy milk-fed pork from Quebec is enriched with wine and butter for a gloriously decadent treat.

Banana bread pudding with Armagnac crème anglaise comes encased in a chocolate cylinder and is topped with banana ice cream for a treat that will leave you with sweet dreams.

---

9 W. 53rd St. (bet. Fifth & Sixth Aves.)

5 Av - 53 St

(212) 333-1220 — **WEB:** www.themodernnyc.com

Lunch & dinner Mon - Sat

PRICE: $$$$

NEW WONJO

Korean • Family

MAP: C4

New Wonjo offers a delightful 24-hour respite in this jam-packed quarter of K-town. The modest space is mighty popular for barbecue-seeking groups. These grills still use charcoal only, adding to the overall lure, though it's hands-on only during dinner. No matter the time, one can expect to find hordes of diners huddling around platters of marinated beef short ribs (kalbi) or thinly sliced pork belly (samgyupsal).

Non-barbecue delights include mandoo, chap chae and cochu pa jeon. Be sure to keep room for soups like ban gye tang—a soothing ginseng-infused broth with sticky rice- garlic- and jujubes-stuffed chicken. Gobdol bibimbap with minced beef, a runny egg and other spicy condiments is wonderfully flavorful but only incendiary upon request.

23 W. 32nd St. (bet. Broadway & Fifth Ave.)
34 St - Herald Sq
(212) 695-5815 — **WEB:** www.newwonjo.com
Lunch & dinner daily **PRICE:** $$

NORMA'S

American • Brasserie

MAP: A3

Serving heaping platters of breakfast well into the afternoon, Norma's may have been inspired by the humble diner but rest assured that she is no greasy spoon. Tables at this Le Parker Méridien dining room are bound to be filled with business types already dealing over the first meal of the day. Upscale touches include tables wide enough to accommodate a laptop beside your plate, a polished staff and gratis smoothie shots.

The menu adds personality with whimsically titled dishes like "Very Berry Brioche French Toast" or "Normalita's Huevos Rancheros." The Crunchy French Toast's outrageously over-the-top sweetness begins with a layering of crisped rice, gilded with a sprinkling of powdered sugar, ramekin of caramel sauce and individual bottle of maple syrup.

119 W. 56th St. (bet. Sixth & Seventh Aves.)
57 St
(212) 708-7460 — **WEB:** www.normasnyc.com
Lunch daily **PRICE:** $$

NUSR-ET 

Steakhouse • Chic

MAP: A4

Celebrity chef-driven ventures don't always pan out, but this one from Salt Bae is, well, worth its salt. He may be a meme but the food here is no joke. Walk through the oversized freezer-door entrance to arrive inside this clubby space, complete with a DJ spinning dance tunes. The theatrics are plentiful, even without Salt Bae.

"Meat sushi" is the first order of business, whereby a server arrives with a trolley, flamethrower and tender sirloin. Drama aside, it tastes great. The Ottoman steak is a massive 36 oz'er, marinated in mustard sauce, grilled on an open flame and carved tableside. It boasts a terrific char, texture and should be accompanied by amply sized sides. But nobody leaves without baklava—if only for the mind-boggling flips, slaps and flourishes.

60 W. 53rd St. (bet. Fifth & Sixth Aves.)
5 Av - 53 St
(212) 315-3660 — **WEB:** www.nusr-et.com.tr
Lunch & dinner daily **PRICE:** $$$$

PORTER HOUSE

Steakhouse • Contemporary décor

MAP: C1

This is a steakhouse in the moneyed Time Warner Center after all, so deals here are going down almost as quickly as those bottles of Château Margaux. Still, this isn't a suits-only haunt; in fact, the intuitive service makes everyone feel like a bigwig. And the Central Park views are worthy of the price tag alone.

The food is straightforward, featuring crab cakes with horseradish-mustard sauce and charred cowboy rib steak. But, don't shy away from other equally surprising items, including sweet, slightly al dente corn bathed with a delightfully rich and creamy sauce. South Carolina coconut cake is one fluffy layer after another topped with a smooth and not-too-sweet icing as well as a heap of shaved coconut for just the right bit of crunch.

10 Columbus Circle (in the Time Warner Center)
59 St - Columbus Circle
(212) 823-9500 — **WEB:** www.porterhousenewyork.com
Lunch & dinner daily **PRICE:** $$$$

PER SE 

Contemporary • Luxury

MAP: C1

An experience at Thomas Keller's Per Se is one to be savored, treasured, recounted and remembered. Once you've been welcomed by the charming team, the somewhat incongruous feeling of riding an escalator up to such a place will soon be forgotten, as will the Time Warner Center itself.

However, even with those stunning cityscape views afforded by the large windows—and the clever design of the room whereby all tables get to look out—your attention won't stray far from the plate in front of you. Such is the appeal of the dishes.

There are two tasting menus, one of which is vegetarian. They do offer alternatives using extra-lavish ingredients at eye-wateringly expensive supplements but unless you're richer than Croesus, you really needn't consider them as the "standard" dishes provide all the flavor and luxury you'll need. Just put yourself in the chef's hands and enjoy a meal that is balanced, varied and as seasonal as it gets. The kitchen's sourcing is legendary and will make you think again about ingredients you consider familiar. For instance, the milk-poached poularde is so exceptionally succulent and flavorsome that any chicken you subsequently sample will seem a disappointment.

---

10 Columbus Circle (in the Time Warner Center)

59 St - Columbus Circle

(212) 823-9335 – **WEB:** www.perseny.com

Lunch Fri - Sun Dinner nightly

PRICE: $$$$

RUSSIAN SAMOVAR

Russian • Historic

MAP: C2

Which came first: the vodka or the celebs? It's hard to say when it comes to this hot spot, which caters to hockey players, Russian intelligentsia and vodka aficionados alike. Our bets are on that beautiful vodka selection, available in all kinds of flavors, qualities and sizes (shot, carafe, or bottle).

Nestled into the bustling Theater District, Russian Samovar is both quirky and elegant—with low lighting, glass panels and musicians tickling the piano and violin. The service staff is attentive, sweet and can walk you through delicious fare like fresh salmon-caviar blini, prepared tableside; pelmeni, tender veal dumplings served with sour cream and honey mustard; or beef stroganoff, whose rich and buttery noodles need no introduction.

256 W. 52nd St. (bet. Broadway & Eighth Ave.)
50 St (Broadway)
(212) 757-0168 — **WEB:** www.russiansamovar.com
Lunch Tue - Sun Dinner nightly **PRICE:** $$

SAMWON GARDEN BBQ

Korean • Elegant

MAP: C4

Koreans have long flocked to Samwon Garden BBQ, as it was founded in Seoul in 1976. This incarnation in midtown is a welcome surprise and serves as the first outpost in the States. The three-story haunt hums with constant K-Pop beats and the service is friendly but astute. As expected, it's known for its barbecue (that signature galbi, with its tenderness and perfect blend of salt and sweet, is a can't-miss). However, appetizers here are also a hit. Try the fried skate wings in a homemade buffalo sauce with a distinct kick, or tuck in to the fluffy goodness of an egg and mushroom soufflé, rising up on a black cauldron.

Gas-powered grills mean the space is free of smoke (and smells), though it's a trade-off, since meats here have minimal sear.

37 W. 32nd St. (bet. Fifth & Sixth Aves.)
33 St
(212) 695-3131 — **WEB:** www.samwongardenbbq.com
Lunch & dinner daily **PRICE:** $$

SATSUKI ✿

Japanese • Minimalist

MAP: C2

The unique nature of this marvel begins with its layout. Descend to the lower level and first encounter the opulent Three Pillars bar. Then comes the elegant Suzuki dining room, and finally reach your goal at Satsuki. This omakase-only counter seats no more than ten guests in an utterly tranquil shrine dedicated to upscale Japanese cuisine.

Feasts begin with the presentation of a wooden box, displaying the seafood that will soon become your meal. Each component of this sushi is prepared with paramount care, right down to the blend of vinegars that season the rice. The selection of fish may sound familiar—shrimp, cuts of tuna, uni—but demonstrates the careful craftsmanship of Chef Toshio Suzuki, who spent an age honing his skills at Sushi Zen. A trio of sashimi is served with three distinct sauces for dipping. This is followed by a simmered dish, like braised monkfish liver with sesame salt. When the parade of sushi arrives, each morsel strives to outdo the last. Meals culminate as the chefs coax layers of flavor from petals of Hokkaido uni with a hint of wasabi, wonderfully mild needlefish and fatty tuna from Spain.

Handrolls in crisp nori make for a superb conclusion.

---

114 W. 47th St. (bet. Sixth & Seventh Aves.)

47-50 Sts - Rockefeller Ctr

(212) 278-0010 — **WEB:** www.suzukinyc.com

Dinner Mon - Sat

PRICE: $$$$

THE SEA GRILL

Seafood • Elegant

MAP: D2

This seafood-centric grill looks onto the iconic Rockefeller Center ice-skating rink and is framed by a wall of windows. Inside, find a cool aqua-accented space that inspires dressing up. Yes, tourists flock here after a spin on the ice, but it is also popular among business crowds—especially at lunch when the bar is bustling with sharp suits munching on lobster tail with a martini on the side.

The food itself is light and fresh. In-season you may find soft-shelled crab, served alongside a seaweed salad with citrus-marinated hearts of palm. The Northeast supplies many local seafood choices, such as the Block Island golden snapper a la plancha, with tangy cherry-tomato vinaigrette. Dependable and familiar classics like jumbo lump crab cakes are also on offer.

19 W. 49th St. (bet. Fifth & Sixth Aves.)
47-50 Sts - Rockefeller Ctr
(212) 332-7610 — **WEB:** www.patinagroup.com
Lunch & dinner Mon - Sat

PRICE: $$$

SUZUKI

Japanese • Chic

MAP: C2

In typical Japanese fashion, Suzuki nails minimalist chic. The simple elegance doesn't end with its high design. Also noticeably uncluttered is the dining room, so if you're looking for a "scene," venture elsewhere.

The carte here spins to the season and is a study in fine-dining. Artful creations include a vegetarian variety, but those in the know may pass on that menu, order Chef Takashi Yamamoto's version of kaiseki and let him show off his skills. Wanmori impresses with its exceptional consommé and delicate dumpling; top-quality sashimi is nicely plated; and baby ayu tempura elevates the Saikyo miso-marinated grilled rainbow trout. Kurobuta pork belly served Yamato-style with eggplant and red paprika is delicious despite its less-than-dazzling appearance.

114 W. 47th St. (bet. Sixth & Seventh Aves.)
47-50 Sts - Rockefeller Ctr
(212) 278-0010 — **WEB:** www.suzukinyc.com
Lunch Mon - Fri Dinner Mon - Sat

PRICE: $$$$

TABOON

Middle Eastern • Chic

MAP: C1

Taboon's namesake brick-walled, wood-fired oven is burning a bit brighter these days since Chef Efi Nahon has returned to Hell's Kitchen's finest Middle Eastern dining room. That oven not only provides a heartwarming welcome and sets the whitewashed interior aglow, but it is also responsible for baking an incredible plank of bread that is alone worth a trip here.

Bring friends because this midtown marvel's menu is best enjoyed by grazing the list of zesty meze like house-made scallop and crab sausage shakshuka with poached quail egg, or a wild mushroom bread pudding with creamy taleggio and romesco. Vegetables aren't spared the flames either, as evident in a luscious and healthy pile of roasted broccolini splashed with orange oil.

773 Tenth Ave. (at 52nd St.)
50 St (Eighth Ave.)
(212) 713-0271 — **WEB:** www.taboononline.com
Lunch Sun Dinner nightly

PRICE: $$

TONCHIN

Japanese • Minimalist

MAP: C4

Finally, the beloved ramen chain of Tokyo has landed in New York. Ramen tops every table here, and those in the know have probably ordered the classic tonkatsu, or maybe the smoked dashi ramen. All noodles are made in-house and have just as much authenticity, spring and bounce as their Tokyo-based counterparts. Sides also flaunt unique refinement, including those crisp-seared gyoza filled with tender pork, ginger, scallions, and served with spicy chili oil as well as ramen that arrives sizzling in a cast-iron pan. The chicken wings are pitch-perfect, glazed in teriyaki with pink peppercorn and a bit of lime.

Inside, the décor is sleek, donning high ceilings, concrete floors and everything necessary to make it a slam-dunk among the midtown lunch crowds.

13 W. 36th St. (bet. Fifth & Sixth Aves.)
34 St - Herald Sq
(646) 692-9912 — **WEB:** www.tonchinnewyork.com
Lunch & dinner daily

PRICE: $

TORI SHIN

Japanese • Trendy

MAP: C1

Featuring a manifold of rooms including a sunken area with close-quartered tables and a mezzanine with gold leaf walls, it is Tori Shin's enclosed (read: select) counter that retains the X factor. Packed with a mix of expense account crowds and casual walk-ins, this labyrinth of a restaurant exudes a lively energy, as does its chefs who can be seen fanning charcoal over a sizzling grill. What emerges is a host of skewers best ordered as part of the omakase.

The kitchen's focus is on such organically raised chicken parts as tenderloin with wasabi; boneless thighs with bell peppers; and smoky ribs with yuzu kosho. This worthy progression is then tailed by seaweed-seasoned sushi rice for a harmonizing feast. Shiso ice cream makes a fine denouement.

362 W. 53rd St. (bet. Eighth & Ninth Aves.)
50 St (Eighth Ave.)
(212) 757-0108 — **WEB:** www.torishinny.com
Dinner nightly

PRICE: $$$

---

21 CLUB

American • Historic

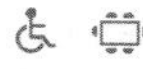

MAP: A4

This fabled institution has been in business for over 85 years, and there's nothing slowing it down. Once a speakeasy, 21 Club has wined and dined everyone, from movie stars and music moguls to moneyed locals. Add to that its lantern-holding jockeys, townhouse exterior, leather- and wood-paneled dining room and know this is a classic through and through. Gentlemen, don't forget to don your jackets here.

The menu is a perfect accompaniment to the setting featuring "Clayton's jumbo lump crab meat" dabbed with mustard and topped with cucumber; or splendid oxtail ravioli in a rich bone marrow-brown butter sauce. The Dutch apple pie with cheddar crumble and sarsaparilla ice cream offers a delightful contrast in taste and texture and will guarantee your favor.

21 W. 52nd St. (bet. Fifth & Sixth Aves.)
5 Av - 53 St
(212) 582-7200 — **WEB:** www.21club.com
Lunch Mon - Fri Dinner Mon - Sat

PRICE: $$$

SHALL BE THE
STABILITY OF THY

SOHO & NOLITA

SoHo (or the area South of Houston) and Nolita (North of Little Italy) prove not only that New York City has a penchant for prime shopping and divine dining, but that the downtown scene lives on now more than ever.

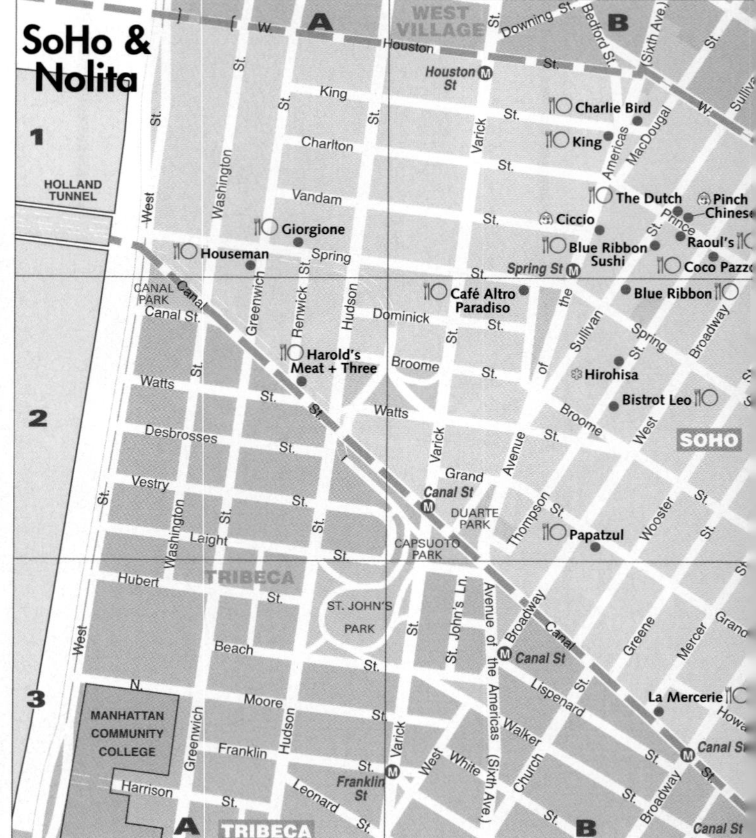

SHOPPING CENTRAL

Halfway through the 20th century, SoHo's cast-iron structures gave way to grand hotels, theaters and commercial establishments. Thanks to such large-scale development, housing costs soared and artists absconded to adjoining Chelsea. Yet, these streets remain true to their promise of sun-drenched restaurants and sleek cafés filled with wine-sipping sophisticates, supermodels and tourists. Locals fortunate enough to live in SoHo's

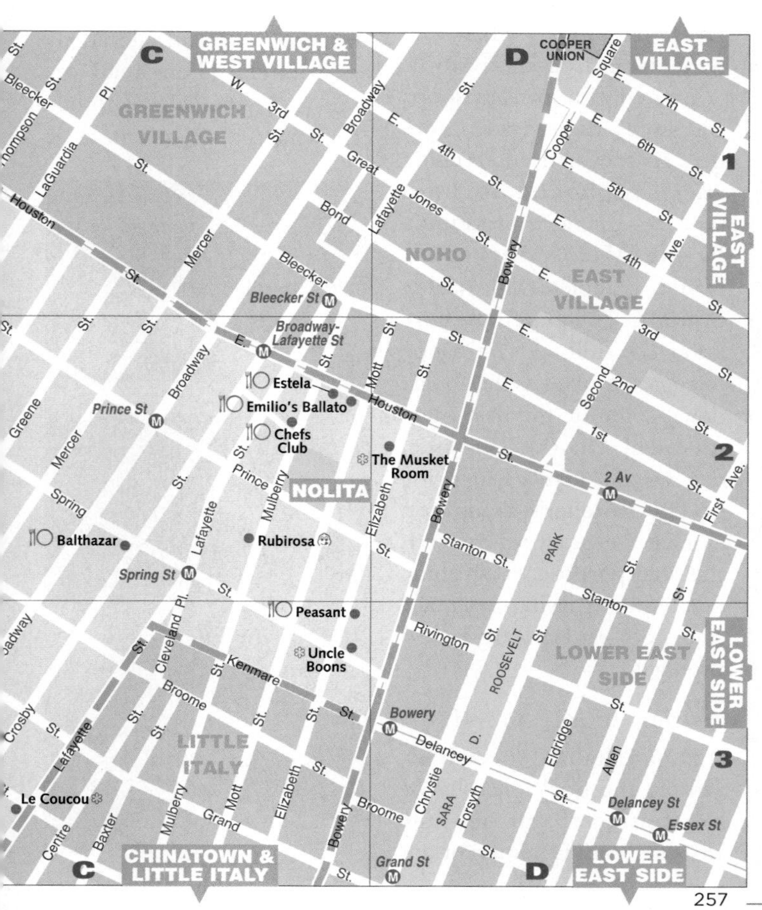

pricey condos know to stock up on cheese and meats from **Despaña**—they even prepare a traditional tortilla Española for you with advance notice. **Broome Street Bar** is beloved for burgers (served on pita) as well as desserts, which must be followed by a fantastic selection of sips at **Despaña Vinos y Mas**—the wine boutique next door. Scatttered with specialty shops and stores, these residents are here to stay, and entertaining guests is bound to be a breeze—after a visit to **Pino's Prime Meat Market** of course, complete with quality options. The butchers here know the drill and are happy to engage rookies as they break down some of the best game in town. On the flip side, vegetarians take great pride in **The Butcher's Daughter**, a meat-free emporium with the sole purpose of treating, cutting and carving regionally sourced and plant-based products.

When in the mood for regional Italian specialties, sample the brick oven-baked prosciutto rolls at old-time treasure, **Parisi Bakery**; or opt for the specialty sandwiches (featuring over 40 different varieties) at **Alidoro**. Sugar junkies find their fix at **Vosges Haut-Chocolat**, where sweets reach new heights of innovation. Try the "absinthe truffles" filled with Chinese star anise, fennel, dark chocolate and absinthe for a truly decadent experience. Then head on over to **MarieBelle**, another renowned cocoa queen, as it

combines exotic ingredients and precise methods to create precious "chocolate jewels." For the Big Apple's most cherished cheeses, coffees and other condiments, the original Broadway location of **Dean & Deluca** is always buzzing with locals, food lovers and hungry office workers. And of course, for bagels in their best form, **Black Seed Bagels** on Elizabeth Street is an eternal dream. Office types may wait until the clock strikes happy hour, before sampling the stellar selection of sips at **City Winery**. Located over on Hudson Square and equipped with barrels, storage and expertise, this is a bona fide destination for oenophiles, who can even make their own private-label wine. But if sweet is your favorite way to seal a meal, then follow your nose to **Little Cupcake Bakeshop** on Prince Street or **Maman** (the Center Street location) for comforting French baked goodies. Meanwhile, home shoppers frequent **Global Table** for its international accessories with simple lines and vivid finishes. Avoid those inevitable hunger pangs after a shopping spree by visiting **Smile to Go**—a quiet spot set blocks from humming Canal Street that serves big breakfasts and light lunch bites.

NIGHTS OUT IN NOLITA

Nolita may have been an integral part of Little Italy back in the day, but today it is its own distinctive district and explodes with swanky boutiques, sleek restaurants, as well as hip bars. Located farther east than tourist-heavy SoHo, this neighborhood is also home to slightly cooler (read: cosmopolitan) groups. Not unlike its name, Nolita's eclectic residents shun the typical nine-to-five drill and reject SoHo's sceney hangouts in favor of more intimate spots that invariably begin with the word "café."

At the top of this list is **Café Habana**, offering that ubiquitous diner vibe and four square meals a day—breakfasts typically include sunny-side-up eggs topped with salsa verde and salsa ranchera. Amazing Mexico City-style corn-on-the-cob is also available for takeout next door at **Habana To Go**; while **Cafe Gitane** is an exquisite hipster hangout, well-tread at all times for wonderful French-Moroccan cooking and a litany of stirring cocktails. The ethos in Nolita is simple yet resolute—to do a single thing very well. This may have been inspired by **Lombardi's** on Spring Street, which claims to be America's very first pizzeria (founded in 1905). The fact that they still serve these coal oven-fired delicacies by the pie (not the slice) clearly hasn't been bad for business, and lines continue to snake out of the door (if not the block) at all hours. Hopping continents from Italy to the Asian Southeast, the décor and service at **Uncle Boons Sister** may be rudimentary at best, but this quick-serve spinoff of the original is perpetually packed for its creative food. A trail of starving diners points to a booming take-out business.

Top off this plethora of eats at the aromatic and always-alluring **Dominique Ansel Bakery**. Formerly an executive pastry chef at Daniel, Chef Ansel is now fulfilling his own dessert dreams with a spectrum of specialty cakes, tarts, cookies and pastries. For a taste of such sweet bliss, follow instructions and eat the made-to-order "Magic Soufflé" piping hot. Desserts are best matched with coffee, so head on over to **La Colombe**—a Philadelphia-based roaster located nearby on Lafayette Street. If date-night duos aren't closing the deal here over one of their eco-friendly blends, then find them sweetening things up at **Rice To Riches**, which brings comfort food to this edgy nook in bowls of creamy

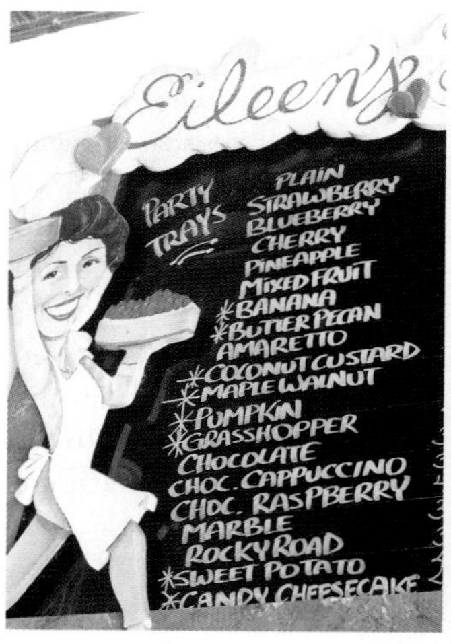

rice pudding. The fact that these treats are appended with quirky names like "Sex Drugs and Rocky Road" or "Fluent in French Toast" adds to this sugar den's supreme appeal.

Cheesecake addicts take note: **Eileen's Special Cheesecake** bears the moniker "special" for good reason. Embellished with fruit toppings and fun flavors, like amaretto or coconut custard, Eileen's divine creations continue to control the downtown scene, chasing those Junior's fans back to Brooklyn. Of course, one of the greater challenges that this neighborhood poses is the decision of where to end the day—or night. But, savvy locals know full well that tucked into these vibrant streets are scores of snug bars, each with its own sleek city feel. Originally a speakeasy during the Prohibition era, today **Fanelli Cafe** is one of the city's oldest establishments offering a range of simple pub grub, beers and cocktails. But revelers looking to end the night with a bit of delight must make their way to **Sweet & Vicious**, as it pours concoctions that promise to leave you starry-eyed. Between these countless dinners and drinks, Nolita also caters to New York City's culinary elite by virtue of its numerous wholesale kitchen supply stores—all of which are settled and thriving along the Bowery.

BALTHAZAR

French • Brasserie

MAP: C2

As ageless as its beautiful patrons, the brassy and mirrored Balthazar should be called "quintessentially SoHo" because it invented the term. One of the benchmark brasseries from serial restaurateur Keith McNally, the attractive space is housed in a former tannery. Those whiffs of leather have been replaced by red awnings, scents of pastries and an excellent oyster-filled raw bar completing its Parisian transformation.

It seems as though every other table is topped with their bestselling steak frites—hardly a value but expertly prepared and served with a heaping side of fries. On the delicate side, sautéed skate is served with sweet raisins and tart capers; while silky beef tartare with shallots, herbs and Worcestershire spreads just like butter.

80 Spring St. (bet. Broadway & Crosby St.)
Spring St (Lafayette St.)
(212) 965-1414 — **WEB:** www.balthazarny.com
Lunch & dinner daily

PRICE: $$$

BISTROT LEO

French • Brasserie

MAP: B2

Snuggled within the chic Thompson hotel, Bistrot Leo echoes its stylish attitude but infuses it with a decidedly French flair. Inside, the look is brasserie to a tee, starring marble-topped tables, banquettes, frosted globe sconces and checkered floors. The bar is a hot spot, but slide in to a cozy banquette to enjoy Chef Brian Loiacono's well-executed French cooking. He is an alum of some of the best French kitchens in town, so diners can expect classic cooking that doesn't raise eyebrows. From a cold English pea soup with crème fraîche for a bit of tang and sweet carrots Vichy with tart yogurt and rare Timut peppercorn, to spot-on salmon en papillote, these dishes aren't edgy, but they are excellent.

Save a fork to stick into the terrific banana pain perdu.

60 Thompson St. (bet. Spring & Broome Sts.)
Canal St
(212) 219-8119 — **WEB:** www.bistrotleo.com
Lunch & dinner daily

PRICE: $$$

BLUE RIBBON

Contemporary • Bistro

MAP: B2

Blue Ribbon stays open until the wee hours, serving somewhat simple but particularly memorable food to SoHo's stylish set. Moreover, this unaffectedly warm and very classic bistro boasts zero pretense and deserves all praise that comes its way. Its décor may have stayed the same through the years—think timeless—but those bar seats remain a hot ticket.

This "chef's canteen," as it is typically hailed, is well-tread for masterpieces like fresh shucked oysters; smoked trout salad tossed with sour cream and zippy horseradish; or matzo ball soup—enjoyable, aromatic, and full of root vegetables. Fried chicken with mashed potatoes takes home the gold medal for comfort classics, while banana-walnut bread pudding with caramel sauce is the very essence of decadence.

97 Sullivan St. (bet. Prince & Spring Sts.)
Spring St (Sixth Ave.)
(212) 274-0404 — **WEB:** www.blueribbonrestaurants.com
Dinner nightly **PRICE:** $$$

BLUE RIBBON SUSHI

Japanese • Minimalist

MAP: B1

Set just below street level and down the block from its eldest sibling, Blue Ribbon Sushi is an inviting spot to watch the masters at work. A sushi bar dominates the space, with colorful sake bottles and premium spirits on display. The low, wood-covered ceilings and polished tables provide an intimate setting, while the counter is a prime perch for a solo diner.

The staff may point to Americanized options, but it's best to trust the expert chefs and go with the omakase. The menu divides itself into Taiheiyo ("Pacific") offerings, like the kohada, spotted sardine or a sweet and briny giant clam; and Taiseiyo ("Atlantic"), perhaps featuring fluke fin or a spicy lobster knuckle. Maki tempts with the karai kaibashire, with spicy minced scallop and smelt roe.

119 Sullivan St. (bet. Prince & Spring Sts.)
Spring St (Sixth Ave.)
(212) 343-0404 — **WEB:** www.blueribbonrestaurants.com
Lunch & dinner daily **PRICE:** $$$

CAFÉ ALTRO PARADISO

Italian • Contemporary décor

MAP: B2

Everything about this often-packed "café" is thoroughly warm and welcoming, thanks to Chef Ignacio Mattos' desirably personal cuisine. His flavors are elegant but surprisingly new, as found in the piatto di antipasti, which reveals an array of classic affettati. Then arrives the beef carpaccio, properly seasoned and almost heady with truffle essence. When paired with truffle-infused potatoes, it is transformed into a delicious, dazzling and hearty feat. One of the kitchen's main highlights includes the pici al nero di seppia, bathed with a heartwarming tomato and basil ragù that is perfectly twirled around long strands of semolina pasta.

Fans of Chef Mattos' delightfully healthy cooking can also mosey up to Flora Bar, his Upper East Side outpost.

234 Spring St. (bet. Sixth Ave. & Varick St.)
Spring St (Lafayette St.)
(646) 952-0828 — **WEB:** www.altroparadiso.com
Lunch Tue - Sat Dinner nightly

PRICE: $$

CHARLIE BIRD

Italian • Contemporary décor

MAP: B1

Of all the out-of-the-way restaurants that dot this stretch of SoHo, none are hipper than Charlie Bird. You'll be greeted by a blast of beats upon entry, where a long bar leads to the cool brick-lined dining space armed with leather seats.

From there, things just take off: along with a clever menu, upbeat service, and a thoughtful wine list brimming with interesting old-world selections, the kitchen delights long before Chef/co-owner Ryan Hardy's renowned pastas hit your palate. These may include rigatoni with fennel-roasted suckling pig; or spaghetti alla carbonara formed into a nest and topped with buttery spring onions, smoked bacon and a bright yellow duck egg. A warm chocolate budino with olive oil ice cream is insanely creamy and utterly dreamy.

5 King St. (entrance on Sixth Ave.)
Houston St
(212) 235-7133 — **WEB:** www.charliebirdnyc.com
Lunch & dinner daily

PRICE: $$$$

CHEFS CLUB

Contemporary • Design

MAP: C2

Chefs Club (by Food & Wine) is visually stunning, featuring a state-of-the-art open kitchen with a striking blue-tile backdrop; a sensational modern bar; and lots of loud music to set the mood. The concept is particularly innovative, with chefs and menus that are beyond prediction.

The only "known" is that meals are often as intellectually satisfying as appetite satiating. Case in point? A recent showcase of the foods of the African diaspora, which included a spicy rice bowl with sweet butternut squash, tart yogurt, and creamy egg; fiery roti with three dipping sauces you'd want to swim in; and jerk chicken with a tamarind glaze. The melting pot mentality is best seen in the udon, which gets a West African twist with braised goat and peanut sauce.

275 Mulberry St. (bet. Houston & Jersey Sts.)
Broadway - Lafayette St
(212) 941-1100 — **WEB:** www.chefsclub.com
Dinner nightly

PRICE: $$$$

CICCIO

Italian • Trattoria

MAP: B1

Chef/owner Giacomo Romano defines this brilliant little restaurant as an alimenteria—a place where patrons can find ever-changing temptations day or night. This may mean hearty ribollita for lunch or satisfying pasta for dinner. The sunny space is a former antique store that fashions a raw look through whitewashed brick walls and blonde wood tables.

Simple, unpretentious food is the focus here, as seen in dishes like insalata di carota, mixing sweet roasted carrots, peppery arugula and pumpkin seeds—grab wedges of bread to soak up its citrusy vinaigrette. Fresh pasta is a must and the pappardelle verdi in a creamy Gorgonzola sauce, for instance, is delicious.

Stop by the sliver of an annex next door to pick up a frittata, sandwich or sweet to go.

190 Sixth Ave. (bet. Prince & Vandam Sts.)
Spring St (Sixth Ave.)
(646) 476-9498 — **WEB:** www.ciccionyc.com
Lunch Mon - Fri Dinner nightly

PRICE: $$

COCO PAZZO

Italian • Contemporary décor

MAP: B1

You can't keep a good man down, unless it's Pino Luongo and by "down" you mean downtown. Chef Luongo is a legend and though his Upper East Side Coco Pazzo closed over a decade ago, it has reemerged Phoenix-like in this area South of Houston. Settled at the base of a so-SoHo tenement, the elegant space with steel-casing windows and Venetian plaster delivers on its promise of Italian flavor.

Fans of this cuisine are bound to discover a host of favorites on the succinct menu. Shaved artichokes with parmesan make for a light starter; while Coco Sette—a pleasing dish comprised of chickpeas, lentils, vegetables and beans over chewy farro—warrants digging into. Charred octopus is elevated to memorable status with the addition of soft potatoes and burrata.

160 Prince St. (at Thompson)
Spring St (Sixth Ave.)
(917) 261-6321 – **WEB:** www.cocopazzonyc.com
Dinner nightly **PRICE:** $$$

THE DUTCH

American • Brasserie

MAP: B1

Buzzy and beloved since day one, Chef Andrew Carmellini's The Dutch quickly became a major hit and SoHo institution. Its primo corner windows open on to the sidewalk, tempting guests inside with a stocked oyster bar, cozy banquettes and sharply dressed service staff.

The menu is just as seductive as the space, familiar but with fresh updates. Highlights include a roundabout take on the plump fried oyster po' boy, made here with mustard-pickled okra remoulade. Tasty pastas refresh the menu consistently; you might find black rigatini tossed with tender squid and spicy pork sausage, finished with fiery breadcrumbs. Desserts are divine, with fresh pies made daily, such as salted lime with passion fruit, nata de coco and coconut sorbet.

131 Sullivan St. (at Prince St.)
Spring St (Lafayette St.)
(212) 677-6200 – **WEB:** www.thedutchnyc.com
Lunch & dinner daily **PRICE:** $$$

EMILIO'S BALLATO

Italian • Vintage

MAP: C2

This unassuming Houston St. standard is an unsung hero, even if many walk past Emilio's gold- and red-etched window and write it off as some run-of-the-mill red-sauce joint. Step inside the narrow, weathered space, where owner Emilio Vitolo and son, Anthony, offer each guest a personal welcome and a genuine Italian-American experience.

The menu is filled with pasta classics like Roman cacio e pepe, tossed with sharp pecorino cheese and freshly ground black pepper. Signature specialties include pollo Emilio, a delicately breaded chicken cutlet draped in lemon-caper sauce; and plump clams oreganata speckled with garlicky breadcrumbs. Crisp cannoli shells filled with vanilla- and cinnamon-tinged ricotta cream rival any other version found from Palermo to Siracusa.

55 E. Houston St. (bet. Mott & Mulberry Sts.)
Broadway - Lafayette St
(212) 274-8881 – **WEB:** N/A
Lunch & dinner daily

PRICE: $$

ESTELA

Contemporary • Trendy

MAP: C2

Half a decade into its tenure as a downtown darling, Estela still feels as hip and relevant as ever. What's the secret to its continued "It Place" appeal? It's a playful little spot that's also ideal to meet friends for a night of bites and bevvies. And no matter how packed this narrow room gets, Chef Ignacio Mattos' cooking is remarkable, inventive and unwavering.

Make your way inside the cozy alcove to peruse a menu that spins to the season, but if you spot the fried arroz negro, don't skip it. Ever. Dinner may kick off with succulent marinated mussels, followed by ricotta- and Pecorino Sardo-dumplings. Your meal will hit a crescendo with the seemingly simple but utterly delicious grilled pork collar—caramelized to perfection and topped with daikon.

47 E. Houston St. (bet. Mott & Mulberry Sts.)
Broadway - Lafayette St
(212) 219-7693 – **WEB:** www.estelanyc.com
Lunch Fri - Sun Dinner nightly

PRICE: $$$

GIORGIONE

Italian • Contemporary décor

MAP: A1

Before setting foot inside this far-west and well-loved Italian institution in SoHo, know that you should save room for their desserts—imagine poached pears, tiramisu or a slice of their daily crostata. This is an important starting point, because there are plenty of other wonderful dishes vying for your attention along the way. Regional specialties include Sicilian veal and beef meatballs with raisins and pine nuts in an excellent tomato sauce. Many also come here for the pastas, like ricotta cavatelli with wilted arugula and smoky bacon cubes. A front row seat at the oyster bar is just as rewarding.

The interior is something of a love letter to Sophia Loren—maybe as an attempt to remind us of the beauty in eating carbs? The location is equally iconic.

307 Spring St. (bet. Greenwich & Hudson Sts.)
Spring St (Sixth Ave.)
(212) 352-2269 — **WEB:** www.giorgionenyc.com
Lunch Mon - Fri Dinner Mon - Sat **PRICE:** $$

HAROLD'S MEAT + THREE

Contemporary • Chic

MAP: A2

This cool dude brings the global comfort food of Chef Harold Moore downtown to the Arlo Square Hotel dining room. With a separate bar, courtyard seating, as well as an open layout, the vibe is au courant and family friendly.

The menu concept simply involves choosing a meat or protein along with three accompanying side dishes. However, the chef's skill and international touches mean that options include the likes of Sichuan-style pork chop, steak au poivre or fish with green curry. Sides unveil broccoli-rice casserole or smoky campfire leeks. For a few extra dollars, diners can visit the salad bar, freshly lined with lettuces, bocconcini and house-made dressings to snack on while they wait. It also displays tempting layer cakes for dessert.

2 Renwick St. (at Canal St.)
Canal St (Varick St.)
(212) 342-7000 — **WEB:** www.haroldsmeatandthree.com
Lunch & dinner daily **PRICE:** $$

HIROHISA ✿

Japanese • Minimalist

♿

MAP: B2

There's nothing like a discreet entrance to raise expectations—and Hirohisa is nicely concealed on Thompson Street. When you do find it, you enter into a stylish, beautifully understated and meticulously laid out room that looks like a page from Wallpaper magazine. It's run with considerable charm by an unobtrusive and very courteous Japanese team.

The two-page menu is easy to decipher with clear headings. However, you might just be better off giving in and letting the chefs decide by going for the balanced and seasonal dishes from the seven- or nine-course omakase. Two things will quickly become clear: the ingredients are exceptional and the technical skills of the team considerable. This is food that is as rewarding to eat as it is restorative. Standouts include the lingering, complex flavors of Kumamoto oysters wrapped in Wagyu beef carpaccio and topped with Maine sea urchin, perfectly grilled Japanese kinki or anything with their homemade tofu.

There are tables available, but it's so much more satisfying to sit at the counter and engage with the smiling chefs—this way, you may even find that there are a few more dishes in their repertoire than they advertise.

---

73 Thompson St. (bet. Broome & Spring Sts.)

Spring St (Sixth Ave.)

(212) 925-1613 — **WEB:** www.hirohisa-nyc.com

Lunch Mon - Fri Dinner Mon - Sat **PRICE: $$$**

HOUSEMAN

American • Contemporary décor

MAP: A1

Just around the corner from the legendary Ear Inn, you'll find this amazing offering courtesy of Chef/owner Ned Baldwin. Sporting a small, but sharply designed interior by Louis Yoh, replete with schoolhouse chairs and reclaimed bowling alley wood tables, Houseman's menu is constantly changing and isn't extensive. But each dish is extremely well-sourced—not to mention well-executed.

Kick things off with a grilled tomato salad, bursting with herbs, salty feta and smoky shishito peppers. Then linger over a superbly fresh, slashed and fried whole black sea bass, laced with a tarragon-forward sauce; or excellent, beer-braised sausage links, made in house and served with mustard greens, melted leeks and sprinkled with crunchy breadcrumbs.

508 Greenwich St. (bet. Canal & Spring Sts.)
Spring St (Sixth Ave.)
(212) 641-0654 — **WEB:** www.housemanrestaurant.com
Lunch Mon - Fri Dinner nightly **PRICE: $$**

KING

Mediterranean • Chic

MAP: B1

It's still a fresh face on the SoHo dining scene, but King boasts a rare coziness that restaurants can take ages to acquire. The popular bar area leads to an intimate rear dining space lined with blonde wood mirrors.

Chef/owners Clare de Boer and Jess Shadbolt met while working at London's esteemed River Café, then banded together with Annie Shi to open King. The talented kitchen brings a deft touch to their brief, daily-changing menu, pulled straight from the greenmarket. A tangle of warm green and wax beans are tossed with torn mint, nutty parmesan and exquisite extra virgin olive oil. Flaky halibut is seasoned with restraint, then cooked to succulent perfection and plated with fresh-from-the-market wilted spinach and zucchini trifolati.

18 King St. (at Sixth Ave.)
Houston St
(917) 825-1618 — **WEB:** www.kingrestaurant.nyc
Lunch Mon - Fri Dinner nightly **PRICE: $$$**

LA MERCERIE

French • Design

MAP: B3

This hot spot is sequestered into the opulent emporium by noted interior design firm, Roman and Williams. It's all in the family here, where the principals have partnered with Stephen Starr—the prolific restaurateur behind neighboring Le Coucou—and the chef, Marie-Aude Rose happens to be married to Le Coucou's very own Daniel Rose.

You'll find the café on one end of the boutique, lined with powder-blue banquettes and tables prettified by delicate blooms. The open kitchen is a sight unto itself, with sage-green tiles and gleaming cookware. The morning menu offers "eggscellent" dishes and pastries, while dinner pairs classic French food with enticing sips. Don't miss the heartwarming bœuf bourguignon united with crispy lardons and soft pearl onions.

53 Howard St. (at Mercer St.)
Canal St (Lafayette St.)
(212) 852-9097 – **WEB:** www.lamerceriecafe.com
Lunch & dinner daily

PRICE: $$

PAPATZUL

Mexican • Simple

MAP: B2

Sangria and salsas are a heavenly match at SoHo's favorite cantina, where a boisterous crowd devours delightful Mexican cuisine. Decorated with masks and classic movie posters, Papatzul is abuzz with drinking buddies getting friendly with the bar's offerings and tables of friends scooping up every last drop from the signature salsa assortment—five varieties, each inspired by a different region of the country.

The talented kitchen churns out tacos and enchiladas at a steady clip. You can't go wrong with an order of enchiladas San Miguel, a creative rendition that stuffs salsa roja-soaked tortillas with sautéed kale, roasted sweet cherry tomatoes and creamy goat cheese. If you still have room, go for the chocolate flan with cinnamon ice cream.

55 Grand St. (bet. West Broadway & Wooster St.)
Canal St (Varick St.)
(212) 274-8225 – **WEB:** www.papatzul.com
Lunch & dinner daily

PRICE: $$

LE COUCOU ✿

French • Romantic

MAP: C3

Chef Daniel Rose made a name for himself when he opened Spring, his popular Paris bistro. Back here in the States, France's favorite American expat partners with Philadelphia-based restaurateur Stephen Starr, to create a white-hot scene that's part classic, part cool.

Patrons linger late into the night amid plush velvet chairs and custom chandeliers, enjoying exceptional service and a view of the bustling open kitchen. This menu is unapologetically French, though Rose infuses his classics with a strong dose of personality, making powerful traditional dishes that may have fallen by the wayside relevant again. For instance, a selection of "gourmandises" (or more indulgent delicacies) showcases such exemplary classics as pike quenelles or sautéed sweetbreads. The latter achieves prominent flavor when paired with tomato crème, and may be tailed by beef cheek and foie gras terrine in a pitch-perfect sherry vinaigrette.

In closing, a venerated rabbit dish is exceptional under the chef's lead, presented as three acts: gently braised legs in a clear consommé with an array of vegetables; stuffed saddle drizzled with a rustic pan sauce; and the rest matched with delicious mustard-enrobed cabbage.

---

138 Lafayette St. (at Howard St.)

Canal St (Lafayette St.)

(212) 271-4252 – **WEB:** www.lecoucou.com

Lunch & dinner daily

PRICE: $$$

THE MUSKET ROOM ✿

Contemporary • Design

MAP: D2

New Zealander Matt Lambert appears to be on a mission to debunk some stereotypes and defy a few expectations about his homeland. For a chef who was raised in a country famous for its rugged terrain and affinity for game, his contemporary cuisine is surprisingly subtle and thoughtful.

His warm and inviting room fits seamlessly into this neighborhood, featuring a 20-foot walnut timbered bar and lime-washed, exposed brick walls. Sure, the space is rustic, but in a stunning, well-designed way. Service is relaxed but practiced and informed, which complements the nature of the menu.

Lambert's cuisine shows a mastery of all the modern culinary techniques, and his ingredients are sourced locally—sometimes as near as the restaurant's back garden. Kick things off with the impossibly addictive monkey bread sprinkled with black Maldon sea salt and served with homemade Finger Lakes butter. Next up, tender mackerel paired with celery ribbons, pear and jalapeño; or smoked Hudson Valley foie gras coupled with beet and Manuka honey cake. Regulars know to save room for such stellar desserts as the passion fruit pavlova, which is presented as a beautiful meringue filled with passion fruit curd.

---

265 Elizabeth St. (bet. Houston & Prince Sts.)
Broadway - Lafayette St
(212) 219-0764 — **WEB:** www.themusketroom.com
Dinner nightly

PRICE: $$$

PEASANT

Italian • Rustic

MAP: C3

Year after year, Peasant hits it out of the park. From the mouthwatering Italian food and the spot-on service, to the utterly charming osteria spirit, Frank DeCarlo's ode to the Italian gathering spot is the essence of easy excellence. This décor is charmingly rustic—picture whitewashed walls, bare wood tables and a bustling wine bar downstairs.

Kick things off with ricotta and otherworldly bread, fresh from the visible centerpiece hearth—which is the main method of cooking and sets this spot apart. But save room for house-made lasagna with braised rabbit ragù, creamy béchamel and sweet root vegetables; tender razor clams in a fragrant white wine broth; succulent porchetta studded with garlic and rosemary; or stewed and chewy trippa alla Romana.

194 Elizabeth St. (bet. Prince & Spring Sts.)
Spring St (Lafayette St.)
(212) 965-9511 — **WEB:** www.peasantnyc.com
Dinner Tue - Sun — **PRICE:** $$

PINCH CHINESE

Chinese • Contemporary décor

MAP: B1

Go ahead and pinch yourself—you're not dreaming. Pinch Chinese is really that good. The décor, featuring red metal chairs and birch countertops, is straight-up SoHo, but the food tastes like you're in the heart of Flushing.

The glass-paneled kitchen complete with mask-wearing chefs can veer a bit lab-like, but don't worry, as they're busy making soup dumplings in there. These superlative gems are works of art that taste even better than they look. Pan-fried beef dumplings flaunt just the right balance of crust and chew, while fried rice heaped with bay scallops, blue crab and shrimp is far from your corner takeout joint's usual rendition. Roast duck, carved tableside by the white jacket- and surgeon mask-wearing chef, is a crisp and tender revelation.

177 Prince St. (bet. Sullivan & Thompson Sts.)
Spring St (Sixth Ave.)
(212) 328-7880 — **WEB:** www.pinchchinese.com
Lunch & dinner daily — **PRICE:** $$

RAOUL'S

French • Vintage

MAP: B1

In a city that changes faster than you can go from uptown to down, Raoul's (open since the 1970s) is a stalwart—here long before SoHo was a brand name. Once inside, order a cocktail and admire the art-filled walls; it's a veritable walk through memory lane for the bohemian set.

This is a place where diners return for consistently well-prepared French-American cooking. The kitchen has a delicate touch, lifting standards like a rack of lamb with oyster mushrooms or octopus with chickpea purée above the everyday. Chilled corn soup with tender chunks of lobster and creamy avocado is a perfect summer opener, while plats principaux unites seared halibut with zucchini and wild garlic risotto with freshly shelled fava beans for a simple and delicious dish.

180 Prince St. (bet. Sullivan & Thompson Sts.)
Spring St (Sixth Ave.)
(212) 966-3518 — **WEB:** www.raouls.com
Lunch Sat - Sun Dinner nightly **PRICE:** $$$

RUBIROSA

Italian • Osteria

MAP: C2

Push through the dark red velvet curtain into Rubirosa's narrow, dimly lit dining room to discover how very cool nonna can be. Although it may be loud and cramped with the requisite 80's tunes blaring overhead, this adept Italian-American kitchen is bright with classic dishes and an heirloom Staten Island pizza recipe that's 57-years-old and counting.

The classic pie balances a crispy, cracker-thin crust with tart tomato sauce and oven-browned spots of salty, melting mozzarella. And the handmade pastas are highly recommended—you can't go wrong with a bowl of chewy chittara and its three hefty and hearty meatballs. Half portions allow diners to enjoy more of the favorable cooking here, and gluten-free pasta and pizza ensure everyone can enjoy it.

235 Mulberry St. (bet. Prince & Spring Sts.)
Spring St (Lafayette St.)
(212) 965-0500 — **WEB:** www.rubirosanyc.com
Lunch & dinner daily **PRICE:** $$

UNCLE BOONS

Thai • Trendy

MAP: C3

Can't fit in a trip to Thailand? No problem. This transporting little gem—compliments of talented husband-wife duo Matt Danzer and Ann Redding—brings the Northern Thai experience stateside with creative cuisine and whimsical drinks—Singha beer slushies anyone?

Tucked along the eastern edge of Spring Street, the dining room is den-like. A vibrant crowd keeps the place popping all night, as does the gentle stream of Thai pop music in the background. Though tables are mini, the kitchen feels immense in its creative vision—a window into where the magic happens offers views of a slow-rotating rotisserie and crackling embers.

Danzer and Redding's offerings are certainly rooted in this nation's cuisine, but they give each dish a unique spin thereby infusing vibrant flavor into small plates, large plates, "charcoal-grilled goodies," desserts and drinking snacks. Laab neuh gae is a spicy chopped lamb salad with a wonderfully sour dressing; and Thai-style blood sausage cooked in banana leaf has an intriguing flavor. For an epic end, go for grilled pork jowl, topped with watermelon radish, salted duck yolk and a shake of sawtooth herb.

The 12-seat Uncle Boons Sister on Mott Street is equally popular.

---

7 Spring St. (bet. Bowery & Elizabeth St.)

Bowery

(646) 370-6650 – **WEB:** www.uncleboons.com

Dinner nightly

PRICE: $$

FENDI
TASCHEN
Dior

TRIBECA

DRINK AND DINE

TriBeCa is an established commercial center sprinkled with haute design stores, warehouses-turned-lavish lofts and trendy drink-cum-dining destinations. Quite simply, this "triangle below Canal Street" is a cool place to eat, and its affluent residents can be seen splurging in restaurants whose reputations precede them. Of course that isn't to say that the area's famously wide, umbrella-shaded sidewalks aren't cramped with more modest hangouts. In fact, **Puffy's Tavern** is a favored neighborhood watering hole equipped with small bites, hearty sandwiches and five flat-screens for those happy-hour crowds. Over on West Broadway, **Square Diner** is a local institution that takes you back in time thanks to its red vinyl booths and ubiquitous diner counter scattered with the staples. Like every other Manhattan neighborhood, TriBeCa claims its own culinary treasures. For instance, **Bubby's** is a gem for comfort food—imagine bacon-wrapped meatloaf—while **Zucker's Bagels & Smoked Fish** flaunts an updated décor and floors patrons with a taste of bubbe's best. Then **Dirty Bird To Go** delivers fresh, all-natural chicken in its many glorious

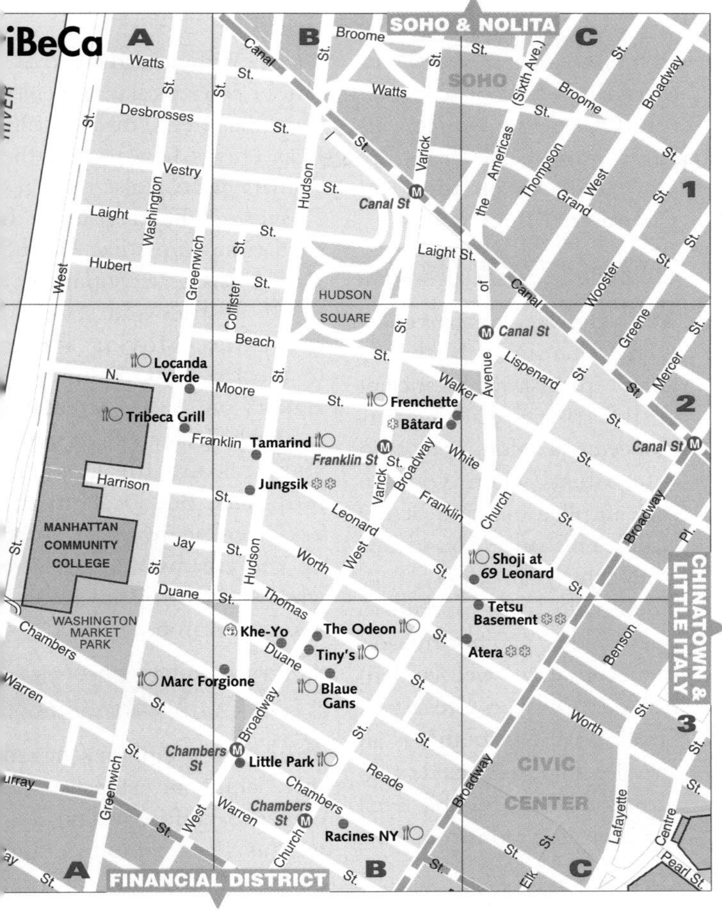

forms—join its endless line of fans to try either the buttermilk-fried bird or slow-roasted rotisserie. And over on North Moore Street, **Smith & Mills** continues to make waves as a cocoon for sumptuous eats accompanied by spectacular drinks. In keeping with its cutting-edge reputation, TriBeCa also offers a gourmet experience for all types of palates and price tags. More specifically, go to **Grand Banks**, which bobs along the Hudson River, as it is a summer special for seasonal oysters or a lobster roll. Of course, winter calls for a range of first-rate vino that can be found at **Chambers Street Wines**.

BATHS & BAKERS

Work off a hangover at AIRE Ancient Baths, a luxury spa inspired by ancient civilizations and water-induced relaxation. They even offer rituals where you can soak in olive oil, cava or red wine. The only downside? You can't drink any of it! Then, take your appetite to one of this neighborhood's numerous (and well-lauded) bakeries. Over on Greenwich Street, posh **Sarabeth's** is an award-winning jam maker who turned this once humble retail store into the monstrous hit it is today. With such an impressive carte of cookies, cakes, preserves and other treats, this specialty chain knows how to play the culinary game. It also manages to successfully keep up with solid competitors like **Duane Park Patisserie**, popular for pretty pastries and seasonal specialties. Moving across to the Far East, **Takahachi Bakery** on Murray Street is a modestly decorated but must-visit treasure for Japanese refreshers. But locals in the know come here to slurp up the creamy matcha latte while snacking on at least one sakura macaron.

AROUND THE WORLD

Korin is a culinary haven that flaunts an extensive and exquisite knife collection, as well as sleek tableware and gorgeous kitchen supplies. Not only do these products shine in many fine-dining establishments, they also bring to life the essence of food art. Even top chefs come here to get their blades worked on or to order a specific knife, while home cooks might opt for those attractive gift sets that are guaranteed to excite a friend or impress a colleague.

Before this area became associated with top films from varying genres, director Bob Giraldi shot his mob- and food-themed movie *Dinner Rush* at famed eatery, **Gigino Trattoria**. However, thanks to the annual Tribeca Film Festival, a springtime extravaganza created by Robert DeNiro to revitalize the area after 9/11, TriBeCa is now the official home of twelve days of great films and community camaraderie. In fact, scores of locals, tourists and film buffs collect here every year to see the movies and share their views and reviews at hot spots like **Nish Nush**, a sidewalk show-stopper incorporating authentic Israeli hummus and crispy falafel into sandwiches, hearty platters and healthy salads. Not in the mood for nourishing eats? Then saunter over to the heavenly retreat, **Baked**. While the mothership continues to flourish in Red Hook, this considerably larger venture in TriBeCa continues to draw crowds for its breakfast, brownies, sandwiches and cookies.

Carb junkies craving bread in its best form (maybe even flatbread pizza?) can be found relishing the loaves at historic **Arcade Bakery**, settled on Church Street. And while on the topic of laudable tenants in this area, Chef David Bouley and team are the responsible parties behind **Bouley Botanical**, a resourceful event space that is designed to entice the senses and committed to celebrating every occasion in style. This greenhouse-inspired venue is famously outfitted with state-of-the-art sound and lighting equipment, as well as an impressive exhibition kitchen.

ATERA

Contemporary • Design

MAP: C3

Counter dining can sometimes mean lots of elbows and competitive eaters who enjoy flaunting their food knowledge in front of others. Fortunately, the three-sided counter here at Atera is large enough to ensure you're sufficiently far from your fellow diners as well as a certain level of privacy while still letting you enjoy the communal, immersive experience.

Things are certainly more grown-up and a little less rock-n-roll here than in similarly styled places: there's barely a tattoo in sight and the soundtrack appears to have been chosen by someone who doesn't care that much for music. But, it is needed because there can be pauses in conversation when everyone is facing forward.

Danish chef Ronny Emborg and his multi-national team serve up a nightly menu of around 20 courses, progressing from the light and subtle to the rich and robust. There may be plenty of tweezer action from the chefs as they plate up their beguiling creations, but they know that there's nowhere to hide when food is this precise and delicate. Dishes also deliver on the promise that their beauty suggests, whether that's the creamy scallop with crisp celery or the succulent loin of lamb with snap peas.

---

77 Worth St. (bet. Broadway & Church St.)
Chambers St (Church St.)
(212) 226-1444 — **WEB:** www.ateranyc.com
Dinner Tue - Sat

PRICE: $$$$

BÂTARD

Contemporary • Chic

MAP: B2

The space has long been home to some of TriBeCa's favorite restaurants and Bâtard is no exception. Chef Markus Glocker has been at the helm since the very beginning and he continues to impress with his contemporary European cooking that is noticeably influenced by his Austrian background and upbringing.

Dishes are very precise and look quite delicate on the plate. But like a good featherweight they pack more of a punch than you're expecting. You'll discern his roots in such delightful preparations as the octopus terrine garnished with a slab of ham hock slathered in house-made mustard and dressed with pastrami spices. Narrow ribbons of tagliatelle arrive perfectly al dente and twirled into a neat cylinder, dressed with a mushroom-cream sauce and crowned by deliciously earthy shiitakes. A wedge of deep-green pistachio cake arranged with petals of caramelized pineapple, dusted with crushed brittle and donning a brown butter parfait makes a rich and nutty finale.

Thankfully, the space remains unchanged, comfortable and the atmosphere grown-up yet animated, filled no doubt with a bevy of regulars. Service often lacks coordination or direction, but you're here for the food, so don't fret.

---

239 West Broadway (bet. Walker & White Sts.)

Franklin St

(212) 219-2777 — **WEB:** www.batardtribeca.com

Dinner Mon - Sat

PRICE: $$$$

BLAUE GANS

Austrian • Bistro

MAP: B3

This unbridled Viennese-style café feels almost smoky and well-worn, but never out of touch. Its walls are papered with vintage movie posters, while banquettes and tables dominate the dining space.

Blaue Gans' strong and loyal following (an increasingly rare feat in this city) is comprised of locals engaging in familiar banter at the bar or communal table. Everyone is here for the comfort-leaning Austrian cooking. Crêpes, for instance, stuffed with creamy smoked trout are offset by the crunchy balance of green apple and a smear of chive-flecked horseradish cream. Other classic treasures include pork Jäger schnitzel with mushrooms, bacon and herbed spätzle; or classic kavalierspitz accompanied by creamed spinach and sweet-tart apple horseradish.

139 Duane St. (bet. Church St. & West Broadway)
Chambers St (West Broadway)
(212) 571-8880 — **WEB:** www.kurtgutenbrunner.com
Lunch & dinner daily

PRICE: $$

FRENCHETTE

French • Bistro

MAP: B2

Zinc bar, marble floors, burgundy leather banquettes—it's textbook brasserie with a smattering of art deco finesse. Frenchette arrives courtesy of Riad Nasr and Lee Hanson, veterans of some of the city's most beloved brasseries, and this duo has perfected their Parisian-laced panache.

Crusty bread and excellent butter are the first signs that this buzzy spot is worth a visit for more than just people watching. Begin with brouillade, a plate filled with scrambled eggs framing a pool of Peconic snails and—you guessed it—garlic butter. Traditional sweetbreads sport a crisp shell masking the smooth interior and are served in a savory jus studded with poached crayfish and spring peas. Savor a flaky mille feuille before bidding this delightful kitchen adieu.

241 W. Broadway (bet. Walker & White Sts.)
Franklin St
(212) 334-3883 — **WEB:** www.frenchettenyc.com
Dinner nightly

PRICE: $$$

JUNGSIK

Korean • Contemporary décor

MAP: B2

Cool, chic and completely urbane, Jungsik is the epitome of contemporary elegance. Inside the large and neatly partitioned space, find rich browns and ivory furnishings with flattering lighting that is just bright enough to see your food clearly. The chairs are deep and tables well spaced, but request a plush corner banquette for maximum comfort. Even the place settings show sculptural beauty through dark pottery and white porcelain. The ambience is fairly quiet and somewhat reflective.

The modern cuisine is confident, complex and happens to be leaning much more toward Europe than Korea of late. No matter—the cooking remains profoundly enjoyable. At the same time, the most inspired dishes are the ones that retain their heritage. Prime examples include the delicate mandoo filled with foie gras, draped in Wagyu beef, and set in a soulful Wagyu broth. Tuna kimbap may look like a cigar, but it is a crispy treat filled with black truffle rice, tuna and Korean mustard. Oh, and the octopus braised in dashi could very well be the best you've ever had.

Artful desserts include black raspberry and coconut sorbet with crumbles of spinach cake, yuzu meringue and perfect berry slices.

---

2 Harrison St. (at Hudson St.)

Franklin St

(212) 219-0900 – **WEB:** www.jungsik.com

Dinner Mon - Sun

PRICE: $$$$

KHE-YO

Lao • Rustic

MAP: B3

This Laotian hot spot serves up vibrant family-style plates brimming with tart and spicy notes that pack a punch—make that a Bang Bang, actually, as in the house sauce of mixed chilies, cilantro, fish sauce and garlic served to diners as a welcome, along with a basket of sticky rice.

The food is worth braving the wait and decibel levels, so sip a craft brew or cocktail before digging in. Start with a plate of wide rice noodles and bits of slow-cooked pork in a coconut-rich yellow curry garnished with herbs, bean sprouts and slivered banana blossom. Banana leaf-steamed red snapper is another beautifully prepared item, paired with crisped artichoke hearts, Chinese broccoli and more of that sauce. Bright and bitter grapefruit sorbet is a fitting finish.

157 Duane St. (bet. Hudson St. & West Broadway)
Chambers St (West Broadway)
(212) 587-1089 — **WEB:** www.kheyo.com
Lunch & dinner daily **PRICE:** **$$**

LITTLE PARK

American • Contemporary décor

MAP: B3

Little Park flaunts that upscale downtown feel that TriBeCa seems to have trademarked. Yet Chef Min Kong delivers a personal and unique cuisine that distinguishes it from other Andrew Carmellini restaurants. Here, vegetables are often spotlighted, with meat and seafood serving as accents. This means that the harmonious flavors of beet tartare with rye crumbs and smoked trout roe are just as impressive as the equal parts playful and thrilling Sullivan County chicken, starring a savory garam masala-infused tamarind sauce. Masterful desserts include the frozen Meyer lemon "fluff" with meringue and orange sorbet.

The bar is perpetually buzzing as the bold cocktail program operates on a high level, so diners looking for peace and quiet should steer clear.

85 West Broadway (at Chambers St.)
Chambers St (West Broadway)
(212) 220-4110 — **WEB:** www.littlepark.com
Lunch & dinner daily **PRICE:** **$$$**

LOCANDA VERDE

Italian • Trendy

MAP: A2

This ever-trendy yet refined Italian ristorante is as much coveted for its gorgeous setting as its lineup of rustic, tasty fare. The ambience is always abuzz and everyone looks beautiful amid low lights, a long bar and walls adorned with wine bottles.

Breakfast verges on divine—think lemon pancakes and apple cider doughnuts. Bare tables are packed throughout the day with a stylish crowd waxing poetic about crostini topped with blue crab and jalapeño. Also try terrific house-made pastas such as pappardelle with lamb Bolognese, finished with a dollop of sheep's milk ricotta, or paccheri dressed in "Sunday night ragù." No one should leave without sampling superb sweets, like the apple and concord grape crostata with rosemary-hazelnut brittle and brown butter gelato.

377 Greenwich St. (at N. Moore St.)
Franklin St
(212) 925-3797 — **WEB:** www.locandaverdenyc.com
Lunch & dinner daily

PRICE: $$$

MARC FORGIONE

American • Rustic

MAP: B3

This eponymous restaurant is dark, sexy and attracts an endless stream of downtown denizens. Abundant candles produce more atmosphere than light for the room clad in exposed brick and salvaged wood. Aloof servers dressed in black seem to disappear into the background.

The innovative American food excites with bold flavors, as in barbecued oysters sprinkled with pancetta powder. Montauk fluke en croute, set over roasted cauliflower, hazelnuts and capers topped with a buttery panel of toast, is dressed with sauce proposal—so named because the rich brown butter and golden raisin emulsion is said to have earned the chef a few romantic offers. It is delicious, but Chef Marc Forgione deserves equal affection for those amazing butter-glazed potato rolls.

134 Reade St. (bet. Greenwich & Hudson Sts.)
Chambers St (West Broadway)
(212) 941-9401 — **WEB:** www.marcforgione.com
Dinner nightly

PRICE: $$$

THE ODEON

American • Brasserie

MAP: B3

It's easy to see why The Odeon has been a part of the fabric of TriBeCa life for so long. Like watching a re-run of Seinfeld, it is reassuringly familiar, classically New York and, even when you know what's coming next, still eminently satisfying. The menu is a roll-call of everyone's favorites, from chicken paillard to beet salad, burgers to cheesecake. Cocktails are well made and beers carefully poured. Dishes are executed with sufficient care and portions are of manageable proportions.

The room comes with an appealing art deco feel and the terrace at the front pulls in the occasional passerby. Service is personable and willing too, although after all this time the place could probably run itself.

145 West Broadway (at Thomas St.)
Chambers St (West Broadway)
(212) 233-0507 – **WEB:** www.theodeonrestaurant.com
Lunch & dinner daily **PRICE: $$$**

RACINES NY

French • Wine bar

MAP: B3

Big names like Sommelier-turned-Partner Pascaline Lepeltier and Chef Paul Liebrandt (who took a turn at these stoves) have taken residence at Arnaud Tronche's wine bistro-a-vin, which cuts an elegant figure with a marble bar and floral ensembles. Throw in low lighting and a tony address—and you have quite the operation.

The service can be off at times, which is a shame because Racines NY has an ace, even affordable, wine list that bears discussion. As for the food, you'll pay for all that sexy ambience a little more than the cuisine currently merits. Yet, the «Flavors of Summer» with eggplant, peas and morels makes for a pretty bite, while Berkshire pork with grilled prawns is a hearty delight. A chocolate confection with sesame tuile is a deal sealed.

94 Chambers St. (bet. Broadway & Church St.)
Chambers St (West Broadway)
(212) 227-3400 – **WEB:** www.racinesny.com
Dinner Mon - Sat **PRICE: $$$$**

SHOJI AT 69 LEONARD

Japanese • Minimalist

MAP: C2

Come here to experience a unique style of Japanese dining called "kappo," which leaves your meal entirely to the chef's discretion. It may be less refined than the traditional kaiseki, but you will forget that when you begin to taste these ambitious compilations (with prices to match).

A dedication to seasonal ingredients sourced locally and from Japan makes this style of cooking truly distinct. Sashimi courses may move from bluefin tuna in sweet miso and mustard dressing, to rich winter yellowtail with grated purple daikon and tangy yuzu juice. Then that last fish returns, koji-marinated, grilled and set over braised chrysanthemum greens. This chef may not be from Japan, but he spent a whole decade there, refining his technical skills.

69 Leonard St. (bet. Broadway & Church St.)
Franklin St
(212) 404-4600 – **WEB:** www.69leonardstreet.com
Dinner Mon - Sat **PRICE: $$$$**

TAMARIND

Indian • Contemporary décor

MAP: B2

Building Tamarind cost a cool five million, and it shows—every inch of this soaring space oozes with grandeur. With its classic TriBeCa edifice and gorgeous marble bar (an ideal perch for post-work indulgence), the glass-fronted behemoth draws a posh crowd of Wall Streeters and well-heeled locals.

Most impressive of all is the sleek display kitchen, outfitted with a gleaming tandoor that turns out exceptional Mughlai food like sirkha gosht (lamb in a fiery chili and coriander chutney). Malai halibut, roasted then blanketed in a coconut-ginger sauce with toasted cumin seeds, is a standout. While service is mediocre at best and the kitchen may fall behind at peak times, mains like kolambi pola (prawns in a coconut-and-chili curry) make up for any gaffes.

99 Hudson St. (at Franklin St.)
Franklin St
(212) 775-9000 – **WEB:** www.tamarindrestaurantsnyc.com
Lunch & dinner daily **PRICE: $$$**

TETSU BASEMENT ✿✿

Japanese • Chic

MAP: C3

Tucked below Masa Takayama's TriBeCa robatayaki, Tetsu Basement exudes that cherished clandestine vibe, but rest assured, as this sexy hot spot is no secret. From his popular offering upstairs to his heavily lauded fine dining sushi temple in the Time Warner Center, you can't keep a lid on Masa's enormous talent.

And so it goes with his latest offering, which aims to bring his singular dedication to purity and unparalleled quality to a meat-focused kaiseki menu. The restaurant—a dark, masculine lair filled with wrought-iron, exposed brick and a 22-foot-long African Bubinga wood countertop—is brimming with intimacy and date-night possibility. The chef himself is often on hand, bantering with guests or jumping behind the grill to fashion a dish just so.

Plates are modest yet exquisite, with top sourcing rendering complicated recipes unnecessary. Tender venison tenderloin is simply paired with dashi, cilantro oil and toasted rice powder; just as a plump scallop, scored precisely, is sizzled on the teppanyaki grill to caramelized excellence. A pristine cut of Ohmi beef is then perfectly seared, topped with salt, and presented with a dab of wasabi and garlic paste for a luxurious finale.

---

78 Leonard St. (bet. Broadway & Church St.)

Franklin St

(212) 207-2370 — **WEB:** www.tetsunyc.com

Dinner Tue - Fri

PRICE: $$$$

TINY'S

American • Vintage

MAP: B3

The name says it all—Tiny's is indeed tiny, but in that old New York, wood-burning fire and pressed-tin ceiling kind of way. Enter this narrow Federal-style home (c. 1810) and sidle up to the beautiful people along the pew seats that overlook a poster of the Marlboro Man. Alternatively, head on up to the suitably named Bar Upstairs.

The setting is so rich with character that one could simply be satisfied by Tiny's fine burger, featuring dry-aged rib-eye and a side of cheddar tater tots. However, this is a surprisingly ambitious kitchen turning out some very clever dishes. The wild Coho salmon for example, is grilled to specification and plated with vadouvan-spiced beurre blanc; while the vanilla flan slicked with cold caramel syrup makes a wonderful finale.

135 West Broadway (bet. Duane & Thomas Sts.)
Chambers St (West Broadway)
(212) 374-1135 — **WEB:** www.tinysnyc.com
Lunch & dinner daily

PRICE: $$

TRIBECA GRILL

Contemporary • Brasserie

MAP: A2

Beckoning business titans day and night, this corner restaurant is a destination for its big, bright dining room with well-spaced tables. Wall-to-wall windows overlook two quintessential TriBeCa streets, while exposed brick, moody artwork and a spectacular bar smack in the center of the room complete the refined vibe.

Gigantone, large tubular pasta loaded with braised short rib Bolognese beneath a dollop of fresh sheep's milk ricotta, makes a rich start to any meal. The decadence continues with seared scallops over creamy carrot risotto, topped with a truffled-Madeira vinaigrette and brought over the top with a few fragrant shavings of black truffle. Desserts are as classic as the space; try the banana tart with malted chocolate and pecan ice cream.

375 Greenwich St. (at Franklin St.)
Franklin St
(212) 941-3900 — **WEB:** www.myriadrestaurantgroup.com
Lunch Sun - Fri Dinner nightly

PRICE: $$$

UPPER EAST SIDE

Famously expensive and exceptionally charming, the Upper East Side is flanked by lush Central Park on one side and the East River on the other. If watching barges and boats bob along the river from a dense metropolis doesn't sound like a perfect paradox, know that this prime area is predominantly residential and home to iconic addresses, like Gracie Mansion. Closest to the park are posh diners catering to expats with expense accounts. But walk a few steps east and discover young families filling the latest sushi-ya, artisanal pizzeria, cheese shop or hot sidewalk spot where they can dig into salads, soup and other types of gooey goodness—imagine panini-pressed ciabatta rolls stuffed with Iowa cheddar and locally sourced pickles from Brooklyn, obviously! There is no shortage of sips here, either. Along First and Second avenue, classic Irish pubs are packed with post-grads who keep the party alive well through happy hour and into the wee hours.

SHOPPING CENTRAL

The most upper and eastern reaches of this neighborhood were originally developed by famous families of German descent. While here, make sure to join the queue of carnivores at **Schaller & Weber** as they hover over Austro-German specialties, including wursts for winter steaming or summer grilling, as well as a plethora of pungent mustards to accompany them. This area also boasts

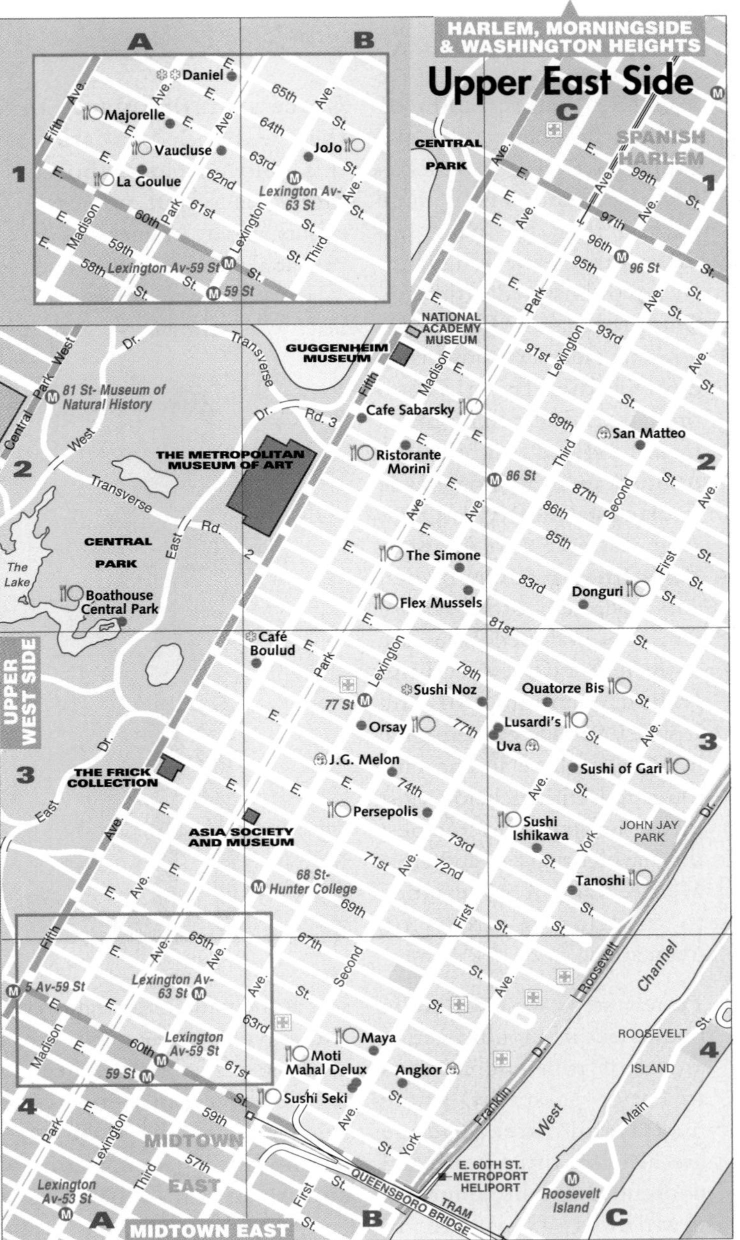

HARLEM, MORNINGSIDE & WASHINGTON HEIGHTS
Upper East Side
Daniel
Majorelle
Vaucluse
La Goulue
JoJo
Lexington Av-63 St
Lexington Av-59 St
59 St
CENTRAL PARK
SPANISH HARLEM
96 St
NATIONAL ACADEMY MUSEUM
GUGGENHEIM MUSEUM
81 St- Museum of Natural History
Cafe Sabarsky
San Matteo
THE METROPOLITAN MUSEUM OF ART
Ristorante Morini
86 St
CENTRAL PARK
The Lake
The Simone
Flex Mussels
Donguri
Boathouse Central Park
Café Boulud
UPPER WEST SIDE
Sushi Noz
Quatorze Bis
77 St
Orsay
Lusardi's
Uva
J.G. Melon
Sushi of Gari
THE FRICK COLLECTION
Persepolis
Sushi Ishikawa
JOHN JAY PARK
ASIA SOCIETY AND MUSEUM
68 St-Hunter College
Tanoshi
5 Av-59 St
Lexington Av-63 St
Lexington Av-59 St
59 St
Maya
Moti Mahal Delux
Angkor
Sushi Seki
ROOSEVELT ISLAND
MIDTOWN EAST
E. 60TH ST. METROPORT HELIPORT
QUEENSBORO BRIDGE TRAM
Lexington Av-53 St
Roosevelt Island
MIDTOWN EAST

a greater concentration of gourmet markets than any other part of town. Each of these emporiums is more packed than the next and make processing long lines an art of inspired efficiency. The presence of **Fairway**, a gourmet sanctuary showcasing everything from fresh produce and glistening meats to seafood and deli bites, has made shopping for homemade meals a total breeze. And, with such easy access to **Agata & Valentina**, a family-owned and operated store whose famously cramped aisles are supplied with everything Italian, residents of the Upper East Side can't imagine living elsewhere in the city. Outfitted with delicious gift ideas, baskets and recipes, this haven brings an authentic Mediterranean experience to the vibrant streets of Manhattan.

Grace's Marketplace. In their expanded location, this beloved bazaar boasts more space, but no lesser quality, variety or guests at the prepared foods counter. Such a savory spectacle is bound to leave you starving, so grab a

A few steps west, **Citarella** pumps out its mouthwatering aroma of rotisserie chickens to entice passersby. Prime meats and rare produce are also on offer here, and contend with the abundant goodness available at

seat at their adjoining trattoria and devour some pasta or a whole pizza. At the head of the epicurean game and celebrated as the reigning champion of everything uptown is Eli Zabar and his ever-expanding empire. **E.A.T.** is a Madison Avenue treasure selling all things edible in its casual café. Thanks to its vast carte and appeal, other outposts (like mega-mart **Eli's**) have sprouted and continue to prosper in this quarter. Meanwhile, **Corner Café and Bakery** is a gem among nannies and mommies, who may arrive here with uniformed young ones in tow for a selection of salads, sammies and fro-yo to-go. Of course, every self-respecting foodie knows that **Kitchen Arts & Letters** flaunts the largest stock of food and wine publications in the country, and founder Nach Waxman is as good a source of industry insight as any other book or blogger in town.

SUPPER, SWEETS AND SIPS

In spite of such large-scale shopping, still there are smaller purveyors to patronize in this quarter. **Lobel's** and **Ottomanelli** is among the best butchers around; while **William Greenberg** continues to bake first-rate babka and Gotham City's

favorite black-and-white cookie. Just as **Ladurée**'s pastel-hued macarons bring a slice of the City of Lights to this glitzy enclave. **Two Little Red Hens** bakery is famous for their Brooklyn blackout cupcakes, while **Lady M's** cakes fit perfectly into its plush setting, right off Madison Avenue. And, switching from snacks to sips, thirsty revelers will appreciate **Bemelmans Bar** or **The Jeffrey**, a railcar-like space serving stellar libations and pub grub. But if in the mood for supper and a show, it doesn't get more classic than the storied **Café Carlyle**. Finally, balance things out at **Bar Pleiades**, which is yet another contemporary retreat, but just as elegantly uptown as one would expect with quilted walls and lacquer finishes.

ANGKOR

Cambodian • Regional décor

MAP: B4

Connoisseurs of Southeast Asian cuisine, take note: in a city that prides itself on ethnic eats, this fresh bistro offers one of the few true places for Cambodian food in Manhattan.

Inside, the stone-accented Angkor is lined in richly stained wood and filled with woven rattan furnishings and Buddha figurines. Owned by Minh and Mandy Truong, the husband-wife team who ran Chelsea's Royal Siam for 20 years, this menu certainly shares DNA with other Southeast Asian restaurants, offering classic items like grilled, marinated meat skewers, sour soups, spicy salads and curries. But there are also more unique items to be explored, like delicious stir-fried specialties from Siem Reap; or nyoam, a traditional Khmer noodle dish sauced with thick red fish curry.

408 E. 64th St. (bet. First & York Aves.)
Lexington Av - 63 St
(212) 758-2111 — **WEB:** www.angkornyc.com
Lunch Mon - Sat Dinner nightly

PRICE: $$

BOATHOUSE CENTRAL PARK

American • Historic

MAP: A2

The word "touristy" is mostly used pejoratively but there's no denying that sometimes visitors to the city know a good thing when they see one. Loeb Boathouse was built in 1954 and includes an outdoor bar and a restaurant whose glass wall folds away in the summer to give every table a great view of the lake. If you want to swap the chaos of the city and its cacophony of car horns for a couple of tranquil hours, then here's where to come.

The menu is a mix of American and European classics alongside less successful dishes of a more innovative persuasion. Try the robustly seasoned linguine with littleneck clams or Scottish salmon with chickpea purée.

While brunch and lunch are year-long affairs, dinner is only served during warmer months.

The Lake at Central Park (E. 72nd St. & Park Dr. North)
68 St - Hunter College
(212) 517-2233 — **WEB:** www.thecentralparkboathouse.com
Lunch & dinner daily

PRICE: $$$

CAFÉ BOULUD ✿

French • Elegant

MAP: B3

Taking its cue from classic French cuisine, Daniel Boulud's refined vision of food and beverage at the Surrey hotel is comprised of two spaces: the jewel box known as Bar Pleiades and this elegant, appealingly understated restaurant.

Inside, ritzy residents and in-the-know globetrotters dine in a well-groomed, secluded room furnished with plush carpeting, rich wood accents and mirrored surfaces. Sparkling elements atop beautifully laid tables set off the spot's conviviality, and gallant, smartly dressed servers display unwavering competence in their presentation of uniquely constructed and superb tasting compositions. Under the watch of Chef Aaron Bludorn, the kitchen makes culinary decisions that never disappoint. Peruse the menu divided into four distinctions ranging from the French classics and farmers' market-minded selections to seasonal offerings and globally inspired dishes. Classically done poulet rôti showcases evenly moist, crispy skinned chicken finished with a fragrant tarragon jus.

For dessert, an intricately layered crêpe cake is garnished with rhubarb gelée and kissed with ricotta sorbet. Finally, warm and springy madeleines—a house signature—send diners on their way.

---

20 E. 76th St. (bet. Fifth & Madison Aves.)

77 St

(212) 772-2600 – **WEB:** www.cafeboulud.com

Lunch & dinner daily

PRICE: $$$$

CAFE SABARSKY

Austrian • Brasserie

MAP: B2

This Museum Mile kaffeehaus is so authentic it may as well be set along Vienna's Ringstrasse. Instead, find it in a Beaux Arts mansion—which is also home to Serge Sabarsky and Ronald Lauder's Neue Galerie, replete with 20th-century Austrian-and-German art and design. Located across from Central Park, this gorgeous ground-floor den is clad in dark-stained wood with diners seated along a banquette covered in Otto Wagner fabric.

Stunning cakes and pastries are displayed on a marble-topped sideboard. But first, order one of Chef Kurt Gutenbrunner's traditional specialties, including the city's best wiener schnitzel or hearty Hungarian beef goulash with creamy, herbed spätzle. When it's time for dessert, try a wedge of the chocolate, almond and rum Sabarskytorte.

1048 Fifth Ave. (at 86th St.)

86 St (Lexington Ave.)

(212) 288-0665 — **WEB:** www.kurtgutenbrunner.com

Lunch Wed - Mon Dinner Fri - Sun **PRICE: $$**

DONGURI

Japanese • Neighborhood

MAP: C2

This cozy Yorkville hideaway has endured years of non-stop construction along Second Avenue and a more recent change in ownership and chef. Yet Donguri still perseveres as a highly recommendable venue. Service has lightened up of late, reflected in the genuine smiles of the small and gracious crew, but the cuisine's ethos remains very much unaltered.

Don't expect to dine on sushi here—there's more to Japanese cuisine after all, as evidenced by their home-style cooked dishes. Nightly specials posted on the wall direct your attention to options like fried soft-shell crabs so pleasingly crispy and plump they don't need anything else. Okay, a squeeze of lemon if you must. Rice bowls topped with the likes of yellowtail and scallion are yet another specialty.

309 E. 83rd St. (bet. First & Second Aves.)

86 St (Lexington Ave.)

(212) 737-5656 — **WEB:** www.donguriny.com

Dinner Tue - Sun **PRICE: $$**

DANIEL

French • Luxury

MAP: A1

Everyone needs a little pomp and circumstance now and then and, for these grand occasions, there will always be Daniel. This neo-classical citadel of Gallic sophistication will certainly impress your guests—the tables are impeccably dressed and a battalion of immaculately groomed staff runs it. They add some nice touches, like presenting you at the end of dinner with your own printed menu, as well as a box of canelé to take home for your doorman or babysitter. If you're a two, do express a preference for which type of table you want—sitting side by side instead of opposite each other isn't for everyone.

The main menu comes with a choice of six dishes per course, or you can take the decision-making out of the process altogether and go for the seven-course tasting menu with its wine pairings. The cooking is classically French but not rigidly so. That being said, there are no jarring flavors that can sometimes blight ambitious cooking.

This is certainly a kitchen with lots of technical skill: the partridge and quail pithivier with black truffle and spinach is a cleverly layered creation, while the dark chocolate and cranberry bavaroise is a construction that recalls the works of M.C. Escher.

---

60 E. 65th St. (bet. Madison & Park Aves.)

68 St - Hunter College

(212) 288-0033 – **WEB:** www.danielnyc.com

Dinner Mon - Sat

PRICE: $$$$

FLEX MUSSELS

Seafood • Neighborhood

MAP: B2

Presenting a focused menu of cleverly made, high-quality seafood, it's no surprise that this haven is still going strong. Inside, the setting is routinely packed to the gills, both up front where there is a bar and counter, as well as in the back dining room, adorned with an abundance of maritime-themed artwork.

Expect to taste plenty of the namesake bivalve, hailing from Prince Edward Island. Priced by the pound and steamed in no fewer than twenty globally inspired broths, they are best when paired with killer hand-cut skinny fries. Mussels No. 23 refers to the daily special, which features these mollusks in a fragrant bath of white wine, tomatillo salsa and spicy jalapeño. When coupled with shrimp and calamari, this does indeed make for a sweet treat.

174 E. 82nd St. (bet. Lexington & Third Aves.)
86 St (Lexington Ave.)
(212) 717-7772 – **WEB:** www.flexmusselsny.com
Dinner nightly **PRICE: $$**

J.G. MELON

American • Pub

MAP: B3

Posterity will remember J.G. Melon as a classic and coveted New York institution. Make your way into this cave set upon a cozy Upper East corner, where the timeless vibe and cheery staff make up most of its allure. Drinks are steadily churned out at a dark wood bar, so arrive early to avoid the hordes.

The focus at this multi-generational saloon is the burger—perhaps paired with a lip-smacking Bloody Mary at lunch? The warm toasted bun topped with meat cooked on a griddle to rosy pink is coupled with onions, pickles and crispy crinkle-cut fries. Be forewarned: you will go through the entire stack of napkins before finishing. Other simple pleasures include standards like salads, steaks and eggs. Seal the meal with a chocolate chip-studded layer cake.

1291 Third Ave. (at 74th St.)
77 St
(212) 744-0585 – **WEB:** www.jgmelon-nyc.com
Lunch & dinner daily **PRICE:**

JOJO

Contemporary • Chic

MAP: B1

The 90's are back and so is JoJo—famed chef, Jean-Georges Vongerichten's first New York restaurant. Like the very best facelift, this transformation has rid the space of its former fuddy-duddy feel and replaced it with a fresh, contemporary backdrop that beckons moneyed residents.

Good taste never goes out of style and diners hoping for a little culinary nostalgia will be rewarded here. The menu isn't groundbreaking (think: roast chicken and Maine lobster) but it is very well executed. The kitchen's daily menu invites patrons to enjoy a different classic nightly, though some dishes including the Peekytoe crab dumplings, are always on offer. Just one bite of the luxurious molten chocolate cake and memories of Y2K will come flooding back all the way.

160 E. 64th St. (bet. Third & Lexington Aves.)
77 St
(212) 223-5656 — **WEB:** www.jojorestaurantnyc.com
Dinner nightly **PRICE:** $$$

LA GOULUE

French • Bistro

MAP: A1

Like a doyenne who moves to a penthouse post-divorce, La Goulue is back on the scene. Just off Park Avenue, this quintessential French bistro has been the go-to for generations of Birkin bag-donning divas, and despite this move, it appears to have preserved much of its glorious past. Rediscover everything from the dark wood panels and front door, to their iconic cheese soufflé—on offer since 1972.

It's a see-and-be-seen scene, packed with suited gents and their lovely ladies. Everyone is supping on traditional favorites like a haricot vert salad, crisp, cool and slathered with white truffle dressing; followed by duck confit with a wonderfully tart cherry reduction. Flaky and buttery tarte Tatin is topped with crème fraîche for a crowning dessert.

29 E. 61st St. (bet. Madison & Park Aves.)
Lexington Av - 59 St
(212) 988-8169 — **WEB:** www.lagouluerestaurant.com
Lunch & dinner daily **PRICE:** $$$

LUSARDI'S

Italian • Osteria

MAP: C3

With its pumpkin-colored walls, dark woodwork and vintage posters, this beloved old-school mainstay offers a menu that relishes in decadent Northern Italian cooking. Picture an array of fresh pasta and veal, richly embellished with cream, authentic cheeses or truffle-infused olive oil.

The insalata bianca is a monotone-white and delightfully refreshing composition of shaved fennel, sliced artichoke hearts, chopped endive and slivered hearts of palm dressed with lemony vinaigrette and Parmigiano Reggiano, all singing with black pepper freshly ground tableside. Paccheri in salsa affumicata presents large pasta tubes draped with plum tomato sauce that has been enriched with creamy smoked mozzarella and strewn with bits of roasted eggplant.

1494 Second Ave. (bet. 77th & 78th Sts.)
77 St
(212) 249-2020 — **WEB:** www.lusardis.com
Lunch Mon - Fri Dinner nightly **PRICE:** $$$

MAJORELLE

French • Elegant

MAP: A1

Named for a French painter, Majorelle exudes timelessness from its elegant home in the Lowell Hotel. The charming winter garden patio, splendid flowers and subtle decorative accents that allude to Marrakech do not only recall the eponymous artist's love for the city, but also reflect the cooking.

Everything here is rooted in France but lovingly inspired by Morocco. Start with a classic harira soup, comprised of seasonal vegetables floating in a spicy tomato broth. Follow this with fresh roasted sea bass, its flesh tender and skin crisped, served with a wonderful sauce vierge of citrus and olives. Pleasant desserts highlight such favorites as soufflé au Grand Marnier, or a lovely tarte Tatin, thick with buttery and sweet caramelized apple confit.

28 E. 63rd St. (bet. Madison & Park Aves.)
Lexington Av - 63 St
(212) 935-2888 — **WEB:** www.lowellhotel.com
Lunch Tue - Sat Dinner Mon - Sat **PRICE:** $$$$

MAYA

Mexican • Colorful

MAP: B4

Upscale Mexican dining thrives at Chef Richard Sandoval's <I>muy</I> popular Maya. Slick with polished dark wood furnishings, vibrant tiled flooring and accent walls the color of a ripe mango, this is always a fun scene. Adding to the revelry is the Tequileria, Maya's bar with a serious focus on agave spirits.

Antojitos, such as squash blossom quesadillas and their trio of salsas, headline as starters. Tasty tacos are stuffed with smoked brisket and creamy chili slaw. Heartier dishes feature huitlacoche and wild mushroom enchiladas swathed in a creamy, fire-roasted poblano chile sauce. Especialidades like achiote-marinated carne asada with cactus-green bean salad and bacon-wrapped jalapeños display the kitchen's contemporary flair.

1191 First Ave. (bet. 64th & 65th Sts.)
68 St - Hunter College
(212) 585-1818 — **WEB:** www.richardsandoval.com
Lunch Sat - Sun Dinner nightly

PRICE: $$

MOTI MAHAL DELUX

Indian • Neighborhood

MAP: B4

This corner spot marks the first American location of a fine dining chain that began in Delhi and now boasts outposts throughout India. Here in NYC, Moti Mahal Delux offers two distinct seating areas: an earth-toned dining room and windowed sidewalk atrium.

Their Northern-leaning cuisine traces back to the kitchens of the Mughal Empire, which brought Muslim influences to the Indian subcontinent. Lunch is limited, while dinner is more rewarding, featuring tandoori preparations like anardana tikka—grilled chicken infused with a pomegranate and black pepper marinade. Delightful flavors abound through the brick-red mutton curry with spiced tomato, onion and ginger; paratha dusted with dried mint; as well as the mustard seed- and curry leaf-infused lemon rice.

1149 First Ave. (at 63rd St.)
Lexington Av - 63 St
(212) 371-3535 — **WEB:** www.motimahaldelux.us
Lunch & dinner daily

PRICE: $$

ORSAY

French • Bistro

MAP: B3

Its classic art nouveau styling makes this popular French brasserie de luxe infinitely more 7th arrondissement than Upper East Side. The efficient service is overseen by managers armed with authentic French accents and highly skilled in the art of flirting and flattery—the immaculately coiffured Orcéens may be a sophisticated bunch of customers but they expect a generous side order of Gallic charm to go with their classic French cuisine.

All the favorites are here, from escargots to lobster bisque, quenelle Lyonnaise to île flottante, and the kitchen prepares them with a healthy respect for tradition. There are also plenty of salads for those who've given up wondering how French women can eat this kind of food without ever going to the gym.

1057 Lexington Ave. (at 75th St.)
77 St
(212) 517-6400 – **WEB:** www.orsayrestaurant.com
Lunch & dinner daily
PRICE: $$$

PERSEPOLIS

Persian • Elegant

MAP: B3

Silky-smooth spreads, homemade yogurt, grilled meats and fragrantly spiced stews have solidified Persepolis' reputation as one of the city's finest Persian restaurants. Linen-draped tables, spacious banquettes and big windows facing Second Avenue fashion a look that inspires dressing up (or not). Service is always gracious, if at times too earnest.

The kitchen shines with its eggplant halim, a creamy, steaming roasted eggplant and onion dip with tender lentils and a dollop of yogurt on top. A kebab duo of saffron-tinged chicken and grilled beef are both succulent successes, served with basmati rice flecked with sour cherries. For dessert, try the tart-sweet Persian lemon ice studded with bits of rice noodles and doused in a deep red cherry syrup.

1407 Second Ave. (bet. 73rd & 74th Sts.)
77 St
(212) 535-1100 – **WEB:** www.persepolisnewyork.com
Lunch & dinner daily
PRICE: $$

QUATORZE BIS

French • Cozy

MAP: C3

Savoring a meal at this ever-charming bistro is like taking a break from the constant evolution that is life in New York City, where tastes change faster than you can tweet. The red-lacquer façade, claret-velvet banquettes and sophisticated clientele are all much the same as when Quatorze Bis opened over 25 years ago.

Though the ambience's timeless appeal is noteworthy, the traditional French cooking is their key to success. Frilly chicory, drizzled with hot bacon fat and red wine vinegar and pocked with lardons, croutons and shallots makes for a very hearty, très French salad. Seafood sausage is plump and studded with sweet red pepper and pine nuts. Daily specials keep the menu fresh, with dishes like striped bass served beside a creamy sorrel sauce.

323 E. 79th St. (bet. First & Second Aves.)
77 St
(212) 535-1414 – **WEB:** www.quatorze.nyc
Lunch Tue - Sun Dinner nightly **PRICE:** $$$

RISTORANTE MORINI

Italian • Osteria

MAP: B2

Altamarea Group's prime Madison Avenue corner boasts a lively street-level lounge and second story window-lined dining room where even children in tow are properly attired for lunch. Despite the high-rent address, Ristorante Morini offers an economical lunch prix-fixe, as well as a family-style Sunday supper.

Slick Italian dining is the draw here, as demonstrated by the likes of bocconcini (chicken meatballs) infused with eggplant and fennel seed, baked with tomato sauce, and garnished with basil, breadcrumbs and more eggplant. Spaghetti vongole tossed with steamed clams, leeks and a white wine sauce flaunts luxurious texture from a swirl of butter; while desserts like vanilla bean gelato dressed with a shot of espresso and amaro are nothing short of luxurious.

1167 Madison Ave. (bet. 85th & 86th Sts.)
86 St (Lexington Ave.)
(212) 249-0444 – **WEB:** www.ristorantemorini.com
Lunch & dinner daily **PRICE:** $$$

SAN MATTEO

Italian • Simple

MAP: C2

This tiny pizzeria has made a big splash with its panuozzo, a regional specialty hailing from Campania that's a cross between a calzone and panino. The puffy plank of tender, salted dough emerges from San Matteo's hand-built, wood-fired oven crusty and smoke-infused before being sliced and stuffed with first-rate ingredients (highlights include the ortolano's fresh, house-made mozzarella, grilled eggplant, roasted sweet peppers and baby arugula).

The room is graciously attended to and perpetually crowded with neighborhood folks stuffing their faces. In addition to the appetizing house signature, other favorites feature bright salads such as escarole with Gaeta olives, capers and gorgonzola; Neapolitan-style pizza; or the day's special baked pasta.

1739 Second Ave. (at 90th St.)
86 St (Lexington Ave.)
(212) 426-6943 — **WEB:** www.sanmatteopanuozzo.com
Lunch Fri - Sun Dinner nightly **PRICE:**

THE SIMONE

Contemporary • Elegant

MAP: B2

Chef Chip Smith and wife Tina Vaughn prove hospitality isn't dead at their posh dining room, where genuine service and excellent cuisine have Upper East Siders giddy. Menus ask diners to refrain from cellphone usage, proving that this is an endearingly old-school spot despite its young age. And the bonhomie present sets the perfect tone for astute cooking. Agnolotti filled with parsnip purée and garnished by crunchy hazelnuts boasts an impeccable start. Then savor a cylinder of flounder, luxuriously scented with Perigord black truffle and served alongside shaved carrots formed into a gratin-like cake and frilled with breadcrumbs.

For a true-blue finish, try the Alsatian apple tart topped with torched custard and a single scoop of prune-Armagnac ice cream.

151 E. 82nd St. (bet. Lexington & Third Aves.)
86 St (Lexington Ave.)
(212) 772-8861 — **WEB:** www.thesimonerestaurant.com
Dinner Mon - Sat **PRICE:** $$$

SUSHI ISHIKAWA

Japanese • Minimalist

MAP: C3

After honing his skills at the New York outpost of O Ya, Chef Don Pham has made his way to this quiet residential stretch of the Upper East Side, where he delivers a profoundly solid and wallet-friendly omakase each night. This space is minimalist and very pleasant, largely thanks to the chef's charming presence, as he informs counter guests of the provenance of each morsel of fish—most often sourced from Japan.

Meals arrive primarily as a parade of nigiri, presented one piece at a time on a ceramic slab with chopped bits of pickled ginger. Highlights may reveal torched barracuda or shima-aji with a spicy dab of chilies. That procession may be broken up with delicious small plates, such as smoked bonito with shaved summer truffles and ponzu sauce.

419 E. 74th St. (bet. First & York Aves.)
77 St
(212) 651-7292 — **WEB:** www.ishikawanyc.com
Dinner Mon - Sat

PRICE: $$$$

SUSHI OF GARI

Japanese • Cozy

MAP: C3

There is a great deal that appears simple here, but there is much more that is not. The room, itself, is a minimally decorated space of pale wood, bright lights and a few ikebana arrangements that it almost feels sterile. However, few seem to take note. It is no secret that when you make a reservation here, request the counter and go for the omakase, because precise plating, skilled knife work and renowned sushi is where everyone's attention remains.

The kitchen's skill shines with dishes that showcase their unique creativity. Signature dishes include lean, ruby-red slices of tuna wrapped around creamy tofu dressed with spicy sesame oil, or salmon nigiri with piping-hot sautéed tomato.

Dining here requires advance planning, but they also offer takeout.

402 E. 78th St. (bet. First & York Aves.)
77 St
(212) 517-5340 — **WEB:** www.sushiofgari.com
Dinner Tue - Sun

PRICE: $$$$

SUSHI NOZ ✿

Japanese • Luxury

MAP: B3

Set on a tree-lined street in the Upper East Side, Sushi Noz may blend in with its surrounds, but glide past the sliding door and suddenly you're no longer in New York. Every detail has been painstakingly selected (and imported) to recreate an intimate Japanese refuge and the result is breathtaking. The 200-year-old hinoki sushi counter, for instance, is not only the heart of the room but it's also a design centerpiece; aged for 40 years in Chef Nozomu Abe's hometown of Hokkaido, it's soft, smooth and stunning.

There is a clear element of luxury coursing through the veins of this hideaway, and the eight seats at the counter only magnify the exclusivity quotient. While the omakase often resembles a generous gift from the chef, this rendition feels like every bite has been designed solely for you.

Diners are in for a treat as this culinary guru seasons rice, deftly slices fish and sears fatty tuna collar under the blazing-hot binchotan. His parade unveils several otsumami and pieces of Edo-style nigiri—smoked, seared and torched to deliver maximum flavor. Otsumami, or "snacks," are perhaps a misnomer, as these masterfully primed plates containing pristine ingredients are an absolute highlight.

---

181 E 78th St. (bet. Lexington & Third Aves.)

77 St

(917) 338-1792 — **WEB:** www.sushinoz.com

Dinner Mon - Sat

PRICE: $$$$

SUSHI SEKI

Japanese • Neighborhood

MAP: B4

A local standby that doesn't actually look like much, Sushi Seki combines exceptional sushi and sashimi with a casual vibe that keeps neighborhood loyalists packed in for late-night dinners and takeout. It may seem like a simple restaurant for a very good spicy tuna roll, but their unique omakase is what makes it a worthy favorite. Dedicated itamae bring quality and creativity to each bite. Sample toro chopped with ginger that is at once tender, rich and crunchy over rice; or a slice of fatty salmon with avocado sauce. But, for a true treat, go for their signature hand roll of toasted nori surrounding chopped juicy scallop with crunchy tempura flakes, tobiko and spicy mayo.

An expanded location in Hell's Kitchen offers an attractive array of seating options.

1143 First Ave. (bet. 62nd & 63rd Sts.)
Lexington Av - 59 St
(212) 371-0238 — **WEB:** www.sushiseki.com
Dinner Mon - Sat

PRICE: $$

TANOSHI

Japanese • Simple

MAP: C3

Tanoshi isn't exactly the "sushi and sake bar" that the awning lists. It is BYO, so no sake, and a clipboard posted outside the door lists reservations for their two distinct dining rooms (the right side is nicer).

Settle into Chef Toshio Oguma's true expression of Edomae sushi, as you forgive the lacking service and ambience. Lunch is a limited affair, so come for dinner when it is omakase-only, with the exception of a few handwritten specials. But all that is second to the sushi, which is crafted from loosely formed mounds of warm, akazu-seasoned rice and topped with perfect fish. Highlights include New Zealand king salmon that melts in the mouth, tender amberjack with marinated cherry leaf, as well as bigeye tuna crowned with wisps of kelp.

1372 York Ave. (bet. 73rd & 74th Sts.)
77 St
(917) 265-8254 — **WEB:** www.tanoshisushinyc.com
Lunch & dinner Mon - Sat

PRICE: $$$

UVA

Italian • Rustic

MAP: C3

Perpetually packed and always pleasing, this cousin of elegant Lusardi's is a rocking, rustic good time. Votive-filled nooks and fringed sconces cast a flattering light on the inviting room furnished with straw-seat chairs and wooden tables laden with wine bar-themed small plates.

Cheeses, meats and salads are fine ways to start. The insalata di manzo is a tasty hybrid of all three—shaved lean beef topped with peppery young arugula, nutty parmesan and pickled mushrooms. Join the crowds at the start of the week for Meatball Mondays offering three courses revolving around...you guessed it. Sample the hearty beef meatball ravioli garnished with sliced artichoke hearts, silky smooth tomato sauce and a drizzle of extra virgin olive oil.

1486 Second Ave. (bet. 77th & 78th Sts.)
77 St
(212) 472-4552 – **WEB:** www.uvanyc.com
Lunch Sat - Sun Dinner nightly

PRICE: $$

VAUCLUSE

French • Elegant

MAP: A1

There is no shortage of good looks in this part of town and Michael White's Vaucluse fits in nicely. It's certainly an impressive space, donning neutral hues. It's also a big space, with a bar that divides two dining rooms—the upper level one is less formal, and the lower level, which has a more animated air. Regardless of where you sit, service is ace and one of the highlights of dining here.

The name refers to a department in France's southwest; and the menu boasts of classical brasserie fare. There is a lot of choice on offer—bouillabaisse, grillades, fruits de mer and other familiar meat or fish plates. The kitchen reveals its confidence by ensuring that dishes are never overcrowded. Desserts, like Paris-Brest or crème brûlée, are revelatory.

100 E. 63rd St. (at Park Ave.)
59 St
(646) 869-2300 – **WEB:** www.vauclusenyc.com
Lunch Sun - Fri Dinner nightly

PRICE: $$$

UPPER WEST SIDE

The Upper West Side is the epitome of classic New York. Proudly situated between Central Park and the Hudson River, this family-friendly neighborhood is one of the Big Apple's most distinct and upscale localities that has a near-religious belief in its own way of doing things. Whether that's because these charming streets cradle some of the cutest cafés in town, or that life here means constantly tripping over culture vultures destined for world-renowned Lincoln Center, residents here cannot imagine playing house elsewhere. On the heels of this famed institution is **Dizzy's Club Coca-Cola**—one of the better places to spend a night on the town. From its alluring vibe and exceptional jazz talent, to a stellar lineup of Southern food, audiences seem entranced by this imposing home to America's creative art form. The Upper West Side is also considered

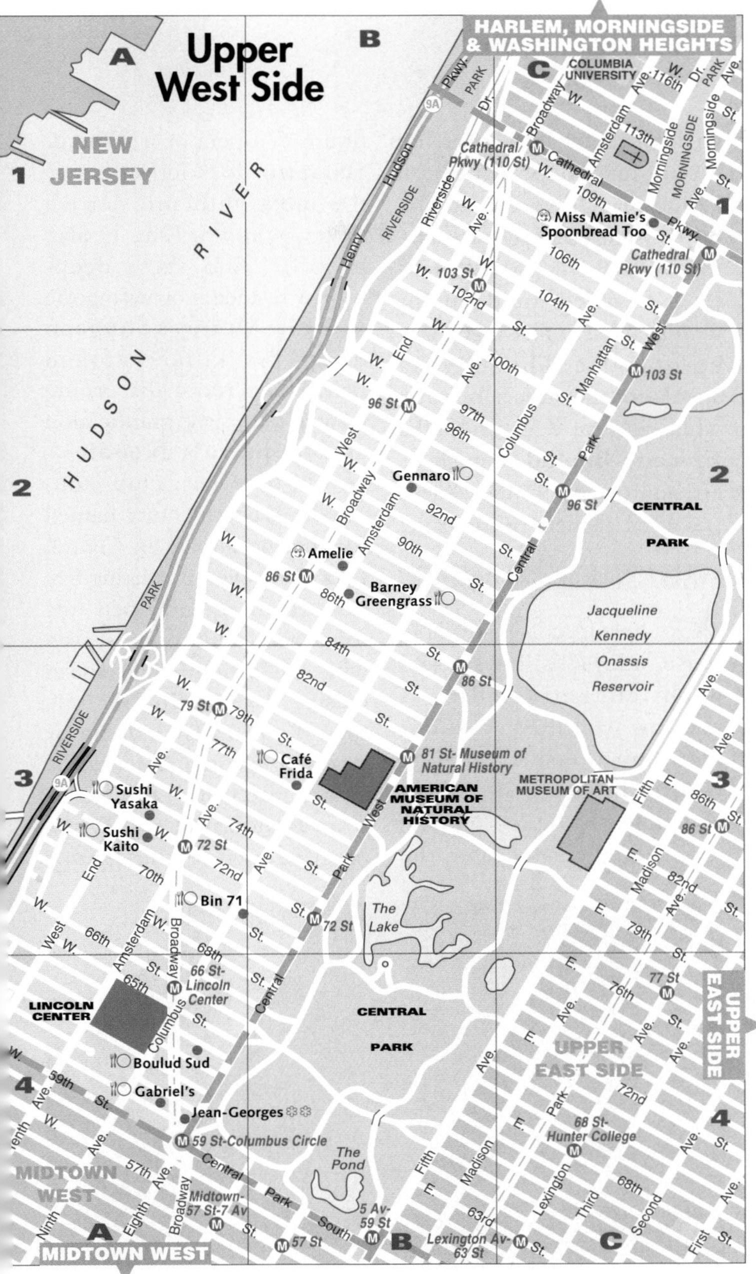
Upper West Side
HARLEM, MORNINGSIDE & WASHINGTON HEIGHTS
NEW JERSEY
HUDSON RIVER
COLUMBIA UNIVERSITY
Cathedral Pkwy (110 St)
Miss Mamie's Spoonbread Too
W. 103 St
96 St
103 St
Gennaro
Amelie
86 St
Barney Greengrass
CENTRAL PARK
Jacqueline Kennedy Onassis Reservoir
79 St
81 St-Museum of Natural History
AMERICAN MUSEUM OF NATURAL HISTORY
METROPOLITAN MUSEUM OF ART
Café Frida
Sushi Yasaka
Sushi Kaito
72 St
Bin 71
The Lake
66 St-Lincoln Center
LINCOLN CENTER
77 St
UPPER EAST SIDE
Boulud Sud
Gabriel's
Jean-Georges
59 St-Columbus Circle
The Pond
68 St-Hunter College
MIDTOWN WEST
Midtown-57 St-7 Av
57 St
5 Av-59 St
Lexington Av-63 St

an intellectual hub—cue the distinguished presence of Columbia University to the north—and coveted real estate mecca, with residential high-rises freckled amid quaint townhouses. In fact, legendary co-ops like The Dakota speak to the area's history, while agreeable eateries like **Épicerie Boulud** nourish its affluent tenants, hungry locals and Ivy Leaguers on the run.

ALL IN THE FAMILY

Acknowledged for strolling, these sidewalks are stacked with charming diners and pre-war brownstones featuring polished parquet floors, intricate moldings and bookish locals—arguing with equal gusto over the future of opera or if **Fine & Schapiro** does indeed serve the most authentic Jewish treats in town. One is also likely to find these deep-rooted residents browsing the shelves at **Murray's Sturgeon Shop** for killer smoked fish; while more discerning palates may seek gratification at **Cleopatra's Needle**—an old-time jazz club-cum-Middle Eastern eatery named for the monument in Central Park. However, if stirring live performances and open mic (on Sunday afternoons) served with a side of Mediterranean cuisine doesn't fit your bill, then keep it easy indoors by stocking up on a selection of simple yet tasty sandwiches from **Indie Food and Wine**. Nestled inside the Elinor

Bunin Munroe Film Center, this interesting café aims to entice the palates of Lincoln Center visitors by way of Italian sandwiches and salads, finished with American flair. Scholars on a budget will find familiar, old-time kitsch and cuisine at **The Cottage**, a Chinese-American standby preparing nostalgic fare late into the night for families and caffeinated locals.

Migrating from the Far East and back to the Med, prepare for an evening in with nonna by stocking up on sips and other specialties from **Salumeria Rosi Parmacotto**. Regardless of your choice to dine-in or take-out, this Italian stallion is a guaranteed good time. Wallet-watching residents may rest easy as the price is always right at **Celeste**—known for churning out a perfect pizza as well as a regal Sunday afternoon repast. And in keeping with the value-meal theme, "Recession Specials" are all the rage at legendary **Gray's Papaya**—the politically outspoken (check the window slogans!) and quintessential hot dog chain.

BRUNCH AND BAKE

This dominantly residential region also jumped on the bakery-brunch bandwagon long before its counterparts. Now these paths are rarely short on calorie-rich eats. From chocolates at **Mondel** and trove full of treasures at **Urbani Truffles**, to madeleines at **La Toulousaine**, the Upper West Side flaunts it all. In-the-know tenants get their sweet fix at **Levain**, where the addiction to chocolate chip cookies is only surpassed by their size.

MEDLEY OF MARKETS

This "spirited" sense extends to all aspects of life in the Upper West Side—particularly food. For foodies and home cooks, **Tucker Square Greenmarket** (anchored on West 66th and open on Thursdays, as well as Saturdays) is popular for its leafy greens and Mexican provisions—papalo anyone? Equally storied is the original **Fairway**, a culinary shrine to well-priced gourmet finds. Intrepid shoppers should also brave its famously cramped elevator to visit the exclusively organic second floor. Finally, no trip to this quarter is complete without a visit to **Zabar's**—home to all things "deli." Ogle their olives; grab some knishes to nosh on; then take the time to admire their line of exquisite kitchen supplies. Amidst all this culinary fun, don't forget that smaller purveyors still reside (and reign supreme) here. In fact, **Zingone Brothers**, once a fruit and vegetable stall, is now a famous, family owned-and-operated grocer that teems with conventional goodies—and treats you like a long-lost buddy.

AMELIE

French • Neighborhood

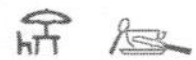

MAP: B2

From the French chefs, staff and owners, to that nation's culinary favorites (moules, but of course!), Amelie is the embodiment of that winsome neighborhood bistro of your dreams.

The postage stamp-sized restaurant radiates with warmth, so settle in with a glass of wine before perusing the menu—it's scattered with delicacies alongside as an ever-changing roster of specials. A perfect sphere of goat cheese rolled in crushed pistachios and drizzled with honey starts things off right. Then move on to the delicate, Southern France-inspired ravioli filled with comté and a blend of cheeses in a heady vegetable-based broth. Since prices are as palatable as the dishes, throw in truffle slices for a luxe accompaniment and you have a signature-in-the-making.

566 Amsterdam Ave. (bet. 87th & 88th Sts.)
86th St (Broadway)
(646) 422-7167 — **WEB:** www.ameliewinebar.com
Lunch Sat - Sun Dinner nightly **PRICE:** $$

BARNEY GREENGRASS

Deli • Delicatessen

MAP: B2

Bagels and bialys reign supreme in this culinary institution, set amid a culturally rich stretch dotted with synagogues and purveyors of authentic deli delights. Not all are created equal, though, and little details make all the difference inside this sturgeon king, lauded for its weathered décor featuring muraled walls, a storied past, and service that is as authentically NY as can be. It's the sort of spot families flock to for brunch—imagine a triple-decker (tongue, turkey and Swiss cheese) on rye, paired with a pickle, of course.

Whether you take-out or eat-in, items like chopped liver with caramelized onions and boiled egg are sure to sate. Finish with a black-and-white cookie, rugelach, or rice pudding, which are all local faves and fittingly so.

541 Amsterdam Ave. (bet. 86th & 87th Sts.)
86 St (Broadway)
(212) 724-4707 — **WEB:** www.barneygreengrass.com
Lunch Tue - Sun **PRICE:**

BIN 71

Italian • Wine bar

MAP: A3

This little enoteca has been a smash-hit since day one and spawned its own cluster of knockoffs, though none have quite the same talent for pairing tasty little bites with excellent wines by the glass. The smartly designed space offers a marble U-shaped bar that makes use of every square inch but stays comfortable, especially for solo diners.

The Italian-leaning menu's small portions encourage diners to try a number of different plates. Start with gazpacho made from late-summer corn, avocado and Jonah crab meat, or smoky tender whole grilled squid. Meatballs are a delicious surprise, seasoned with cumin and fennel, then simmered in a deep golden sauce of white wine, bay leaf and tangy lemon with nary a tomato in sight, but plenty of bread for sopping.

237 Columbus Ave. (bet. 70th & 71st Sts.)
72 St (Broadway)
(212) 362-5446 — **WEB:** www.bin71.com
Lunch & dinner Tue - Sun

PRICE: $$

BOULUD SUD

Mediterranean • Contemporary décor

MAP: A4

Still popular with theatergoers and neighborhood newcomers after many years, this spot is Chef Daniel Boulud's ode to Mediterranean cuisine—from Morocco to Italy to Turkey and back again. Packed and lively, the dining room is airy with vaulted ceilings, natural lighting and long striped banquettes. A semi-open kitchen allows a glimpse into the creation of deftly prepared delicacies.

The menu here is light yet dense with bright flavor, from the crudo du jour (perhaps cubes of hamachi with gently braised cauliflower, pignoli, white raisins, and herbs) to a Sicilian sardine escabeche swirled with olive oil, white raisins and pine nuts. Huge morsels of chicken tagine with couscous, wilted greens and preserved lemons make a hearty dish.

20 W. 64th St. (bet. Broadway & Central Park West)
66 St - Lincoln Center
(212) 595-1313 — **WEB:** www.bouludsud.com
Lunch & dinner daily

PRICE: $$$

CAFÉ FRIDA

Mexican • Neighborhood

MAP: B3

Festive and friendly with happy hour margaritas that flow like the Rio Grande, Café Frida is almost better than it needs to be, considering its high-traffic location across from the Museum of Natural History. Overall, it feels like a rustic and welcoming hacienda. The extensive tequila list complements the relatively economical fare, showcasing traditional moles.

Peruse the menu while delving into the guacamole served in a comal with crisp chips and fiery habanero sauce on the side. Don't miss the clear and warming sopa Azteca, a restorative consommé bobbing with chicken, cactus leaf and abundant vegetables as well as an array of accompaniments. Finally, tlacoyos spread with a creamy fava purée and slow-cooked pork carnitas are muy buenas.

368 Columbus Ave. (bet. 77th & 78th Sts.)
81 St - Museum of Natural History
(212) 712-2929 — **WEB:** www.cafefrida.com
Lunch & dinner daily **PRICE:** $$

GABRIEL'S

Italian • Mediterranean décor

MAP: A4

Gabriel's is a quiet stalwart that has managed to survive decades of the fickle local dining scene. This is all thanks to their great Italian-American cooking and the regulars who love it. Guests enter through a wide area outfitted with a dark wood bar, and are then led into the sunny-yellow dining room adorned with contemporary art.

The menu focuses on classic dishes as well as a few daily specials. Nothing here seems to be making a statement, yet the items are hugely popular. House-made pastas are prepared with great care, as are sauces like the umami-rich duck ragù with porcini, tomatoes, and the smart addition of black olives. Desserts like tiramisu are always satisfying, starring Marsala- and espresso-soaked ladyfingers with mascarpone-zabaglione.

11 W. 60th St. (bet. Broadway & Eighth Ave.)
59 St - Columbus Circle
(212) 956-4600 — **WEB:** www.gabrielsnyc.com
Lunch & dinner Mon - Sat **PRICE:** $$$

GENNARO 

Italian • Trattoria

MAP: B2

Despite its age, Gennaro hasn't lost its good looks or popularity—it still packs in hungry locals nightly who aren't deterred by its borderline gritty surrounds or no-reservations policy. Come early or risk waiting, which isn't so bad considering their bar, whose by-the-glass offerings are vast and very appealing with both familiar and unusual Italian choices.

The menu can be overwhelming considering its long list of pastas and daily specials, so trust your gut and you can't go wrong. Start with the polenta, served almost quattro stagione-style, with Gorgonzola, prosciutto, and sliced portobellos; before twirling your taste buds around chewy bucatini showered with pecorino and pepper. The tiramisu is a light, creamy, and fluffy slam dunk.

665 Amsterdam Ave. (bet. 92nd & 93rd Sts.)
96 St (Broadway)
(212) 665-5348 — **WEB:** www.gennaronyc.com
Dinner nightly

PRICE: $$

MISS MAMIE'S SPOONBREAD TOO

Southern • Simple

MAP: C1

Come to Miss Mamie's and plan to indulge, Southern style. This tiny institution sports a bright, clean dining room, and is furnished with comfortable wicker chairs, roomy tables, and lots of flower arrangements. But despite its somewhat sophisticated appearance, the kitchen still embraces such tried-and-true classics as fried chicken thighs with black-eyed peas and collard greens, Louisiana catfish, and a creamy red velvet cake for dessert. Grab a fresh-squeezed lemonade and dive into the sampler, stocked with deep-fried shrimp, fall-off-the-bone beef short ribs, more fried chicken, and probably too many sides of cornbread stuffing and hoppin' John.

And if on offer, devour a wedge of the decadent and classically Southern banana pudding.

366 W. 110th St./Cathedral Pkwy. (bet. Columbus & Manhattan Aves.)
Cathedral Pkwy/110 St (Central Park West)
(212) 865-6744 — **WEB:** www.spoonbreadinc.com
Lunch & dinner daily

PRICE:

JEAN-GEORGES ✿✿

Contemporary • Elegant

MAP: A4

The longevity of Chef Jean-Georges Vongerichten's flagship restaurant can be attributed to a combination of factors—a sumptuous dining room with a superior location, a discreet atmosphere, as well as its contemporary French cuisine.

Lunch is a superb option for those who don't want to break the bank. However, the best way to experience the talent of the kitchen here is to go for the prix-fixe dinner menu, where you might get a choice of seven or eight compositions per course. Classical French techniques underpin the cooking, although sometimes you'll come across subtle influences of a more global heritage, including yuzu with creamy sea urchin, or chipotle with shrimp. Desserts are more elaborate constructions and the ingredients come from the luxury end of the counter.

Like walking through Business Class on your way to First, you have to pass through the appealingly buzzy Nougatine to get to this restaurant. The low-slung chairs and large tables mean you need a certain confidence in your conversational delivery if you want to entertain the whole table. If you're here on a date, which many appear to be, you could find yourself sitting side-by-side—the new orthodoxy of dining à deux.

---

1 Central Park West (bet. 60th & 61st Sts.)

59 St - Columbus Circle

(212) 299-3900 — **WEB:** www.jean-georgesrestaurant.com

Lunch & dinner daily **PRICE: $$$$**

SUSHI KAITO

Japanese • Minimalist

MAP: A3

Diners seeking an authentic and appetizing omakase need to look no further than Sushi Kaito. This tiny and out-of-the-way spot is an absolute gem. Owner Yoko Hasegawa christened it "kaito," which means sea breeze, and the space with 12 seats does indeed feel like a fresh ocean breeze. This is classic-style omakase from start to finish, and with a few exceptions, it's largely focused on nigiri. Choose from the 12-course or the 16-course menu, featuring every type of fish from Spanish mackerel and barracuda, to a perfect slice of sea bream and Arctic char. All of the excellent quality product is treated with great care and accoutrements are minimal but enhance the flavors when employed.

Sake lovers should note that Sushi Kaito does not offer alcohol.

244 W. 72nd St. (bet. Broadway & West End Ave.)
72 St (Broadway)
(212) 799-1278 – **WEB:** www.sushikaito.net
Dinner Tue - Sun

PRICE: $$$

SUSHI YASAKA

Japanese • Family

MAP: A3

There are no decorative distractions at this efficient if spare sushi-ya located a few steps below street level. The simple space offers three rows of tables, unadorned white walls, a well-lit counter in the rear and is warmed-up by enthusiastic servers. Devoted customers know the draw here is not atmosphere, but the quality and excellent value omakase.

Fish can be surprisingly luscious, especially the salmon, which has a remarkably clean finish and great salty note. The medium fatty tuna needs nothing more than a kiss of soy sauce. A 12-course omakase might also include giant clam, uni, sea eel, fluke, smelt roe, and for dessert, tamago. The kanto soba is excellent too, with a rich soy-bonito broth brimming with scallions, seaweed and a fish cake.

251 W. 72nd St. (bet. Broadway & West End Ave.)
72 St (Broadway)
(212) 496-8466 – **WEB:** www.sushiyasaka.com
Lunch & dinner daily

PRICE: $$

THE BRONX

THE BRONX

The only borough attached to the island of Manhattan, the Bronx boasts such awe-inspiring sights as the Bronx Zoo, Hall of Fame for Great Americans, as well as Yankee Stadium. However, it is also revered as a hotbed of culinary treasures. For instance, The New York Botanical Garden is devoted to education and hosts many garden- and food-related classes. In fact, the Botanical Garden's Bronx Green-Up is an acclaimed program aimed at improving inner-city areas by offering them agricultural advice and practical training. Located along the west side, Belmont is a residential quarter marked by various ethnic and religious groups. Once an Italian hub, its population is now comprised of Hispanics (primarily Puerto Ricans), African-Americans, West Indians and Albanians. Much of the Bronx today consists of parkland, like Pelham Bay Park with its sandy Orchard Beach. And since a day at the beach is never complete without salty eats, you'll want to step into pizza paradise—**Louie & Ernie's**—for a seriously cheesy slice. Just as home cooks and haute chefs alike stock up on spices, herbs and seeds from the myriad specialty stores around the way, thirsty travelers may pop

into **Gun Hill Brewing Co.** for an impressive bevy and more. Beyond, City Island is a gem of a coastal community teeming with seafood spots. **The Black Whale** is a local fixture frequented for its classic-meets-contemporary cuisine and quenching cocktails. Savor their offerings, either inside the quirky dining room or out in the garden. When the sun beats down, stop by **Lickety Split** for a cooling scoop of sorbet or ice cream, or both! Belmont's most renowned street, Arthur Avenue, is home to Italian food paradise—**The Arthur Avenue Retail Market.** This enclosed oasis is a culinary emporium overrun with in-the-know shoppers as well as famed epicureans, who can be seen prowling for quality pasta, homemade sausages, extra virgin olive oil, notorious heroes, heirloom seeds and so much more. Nearby, some begin by diving into a ball of rich, gooey mozzarella at **Joe's Deli** (open on Sundays!), while others may grab them to go—along with pistachio-studded mortadella from **Teitel Brothers** or salumi from **Calabria Pork Store**.

Beyond this venerable marketplace, find early-risers ravenously tearing into freshly baked breads from either **Terranova** or **Addeo Bakers**—the choices are plenty. Come lunchtime, and you'll find a spectrum of Eastern European eats. At **Tony & Tina's Pizzeria**, skip the signatures and opt for Albanian or Kosovar burek (flaky rolls with fillings such as sweet pumpkin purée). South Bronxite singles meanwhile revel in Ecuadorian delights like bollon de verde at **Ricuras Panderia**. Then stroll southeast to arrive at **Gustiamo's** warehouse, which continues to flourish as a city-wide favorite for regional Italian specialties—think olive oils, homemade pastas and San Marzano tomatoes. A stone's throw away, the butchers at **Honeywell Meat Market** can be seen teaching rookies a thing or two about breaking down a side of beef, which will alway reign supreme. But over on Willis Avenue, Mott Haven's main drag, bright awnings designate a plethora of Puerto Rican diners and Mexican bodegas.

YANKEE STADIUM

Home to the "Sultans of swat" (aka the "Bronx Bombers"), **Yankee Stadium** is *the* spot for world-champion baseball. And what goes best with baseball? Big and bold bites, of course, all of which may be found at the stadium's own food court. **Lobel's**, the ultimate butcher, is one such tenant and crafts perfectly marbled steak sandwiches to order. **NYY Steakhouse** is another home run for steaks, while **Mighty Quinn's BBQ** keeps things real but delectable. Refined palates, however, will relish the farm-fresh produce from seasonal cart, **Farmers Market Presented by Melissa**.

COMFORT FOODS

Eastchester, Wakefield and Williamsbridge are home to diverse cultures, and ergo, each of their unique treats. Still, there are everyday vendors to be frequented here. Just as **Astor Prime Meats** presents premium grade meats for every type of holiday feast, **G & R Deli** pays homage to the

neighborhood's deep Italian roots by delivering authentic flavors in sausages and meat sauce sold by the quart. Then there's **Sal & Dom's** who stick with this line of duty by serving deliciously flaky sfogliatelle, while over on Grand Concourse, **Bate Nabaya** and **Papaye** cook up a buffet of pungent Ghanaian goodies for the West African community. Indulge in something sweet at **Kingston Tropical Bakery** or **Valencia Bakery**, yet another marvel among the Bronx's mighty Puerto Rican masses. It is also important to note that Asian food has officially arrived in the Bronx, with **Phnom Penh-Nha Trang Market** bagging a variety of Vietnamese ingredients necessary for a Southeast Asian dinner. **Sabrosura** proffers a blend of Spanish and Chinese inspiration, and even purists can't help but crave their yucca chips paired with sweet crabmeat. And over in the Castle Hill area of this vibrant borough, **Packsun Halal Chicken** packs 'em in with warm, welcoming service, as well as wonderfully wholesome meat feasts. Bringing it back to the basics though, the hamburger craze rages on uptown at **Bronx Alehouse**, pouring a litany of beers. Bronx beer you say? You bet—and there is an equally thrilling selection to be savored at **The Bronx Brewery** over on East 136th Street.

Hosts in-the-know keep the house party hoppin' and stoves turning by stocking up on pantry staples for late-night snacking from **Palm Tree Marketplace**, where they are also likely to find everything required for a Jamaican-themed dinner feast. **Hunts Point Food Distribution Center** is another epicurean wonder, vital to New York City's food services industry. This vast 329-acre complex of wholesalers, distributors and food-processing vendors is home to the **Hunts Point Meat Market** that sells every imaginable cut under the sun. Also housed within these grounds is the **Hunts Point Terminal Produce Market** supplying patrons with fantastic variety, as well as the famous **Fulton Fish Market**. This formidable network of stores caters to the city's most celebrated chefs, restaurateurs and wholesale suppliers. Of course, such mouthwatering cruising is bound to result in voracious cravings, all of which may be satisfied at **Sam's Soul Food** located on the Grand Concourse. It's a classic joint oozing with potent doses of Bronx flavor.

RIVERDALE

Riverdale may not be known for its culinary distinction, but its winning location at the northernmost tip of the city affords it incredible views, and as a result, lavish mansions. Its moneyed residents can be seen mingling with curious visitors over the aromatic offerings at **S&S Cheesecake**, or freshly baked babkas at the primped **Garden Gourmet** on Broadway. From here, those in need of more stirring sips may head to **Skyview Wines** boasting exceptional kosher varietals. Finish with style and flair at **Lloyd's Carrot Cake**, which has been doling out divine slices of red velvet or German chocolate cake to the community for over a quarter-century.

The Bronx

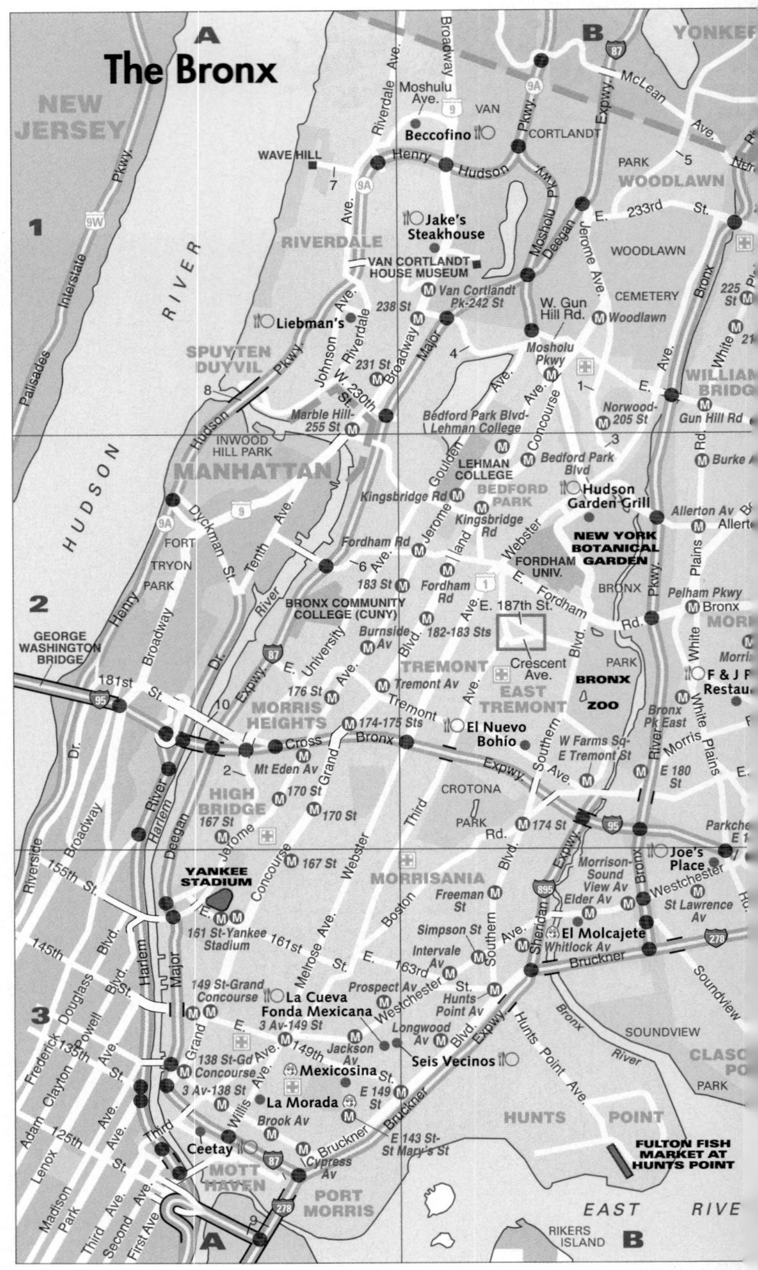

The Bronx
NEW JERSEY
HUDSON
RIVER
MANHATTAN
RIVERDALE
SPUYTEN DUYVIL
WAVE HILL
Beccofino
Jake's Steakhouse
VAN CORTLANDT HOUSE MUSEUM
Liebman's
VAN CORTLANDT PARK
WOODLAWN
WOODLAWN CEMETERY
INWOOD HILL PARK
LEHMAN COLLEGE
BEDFORD PARK
Hudson Garden Grill
NEW YORK BOTANICAL GARDEN
FORDHAM UNIV.
FORT TRYON PARK
BRONX COMMUNITY COLLEGE (CUNY)
GEORGE WASHINGTON BRIDGE
TREMONT
EAST TREMONT
BRONX PARK
BRONX ZOO
MORRIS HEIGHTS
El Nuevo Bohío
F & J Restau
HIGH BRIDGE
CROTONA PARK
Joe's Place
YANKEE STADIUM
MORRISANIA
El Molcajete
La Cueva Fonda Mexicana
Seis Vecinos
Mexicosina
La Morada
Ceetay
SOUNDVIEW PARK
HUNTS POINT
FULTON FISH MARKET AT HUNTS POINT
MOTT HAVEN
PORT MORRIS
EAST RIVER
RIKERS ISLAND

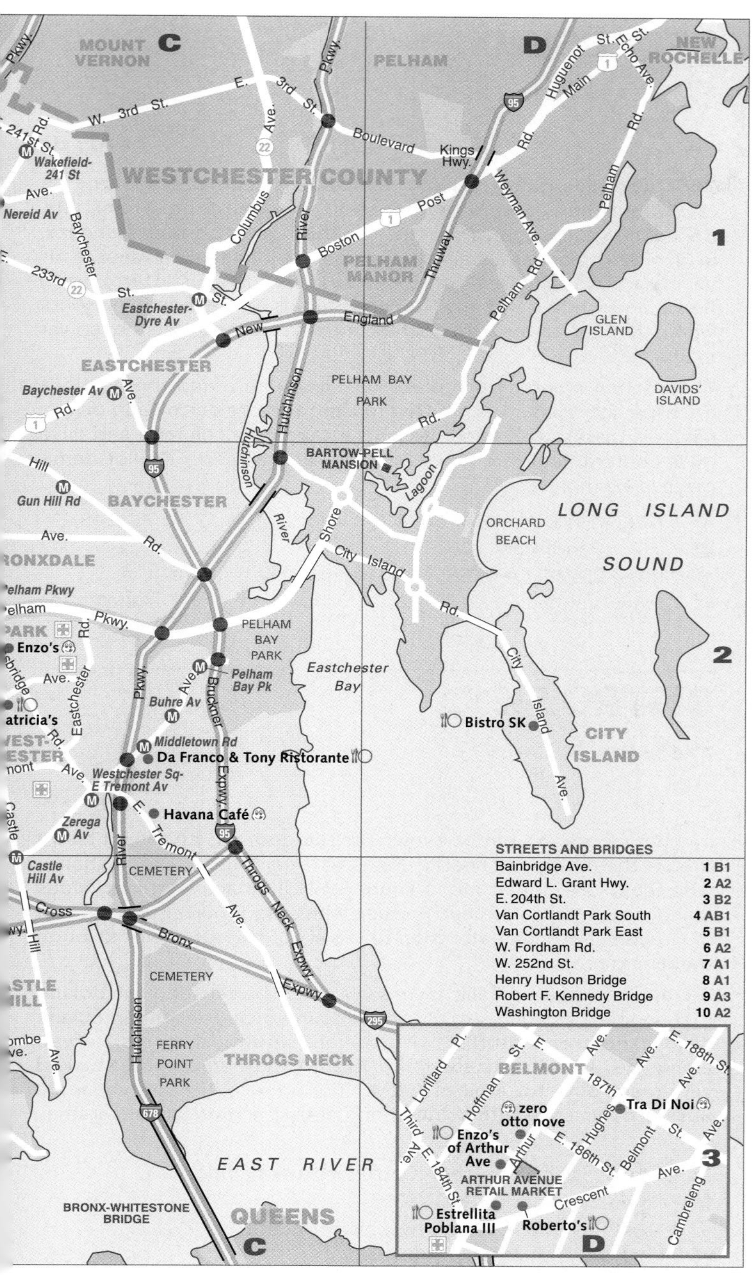
MOUNT VERNON
C
D
PELHAM
NEW ROCHELLE
WESTCHESTER COUNTY
PELHAM MANOR
GLEN ISLAND
DAVIDS' ISLAND
EASTCHESTER
PELHAM BAY PARK
BARTOW-PELL MANSION
BAYCHESTER
LONG ISLAND SOUND
ORCHARD BEACH
BRONXDALE
Eastchester Bay
CITY ISLAND
Bistro SK
Enzo's
Patricia's
Da Franco & Tony Ristorante
Havana Café
CEMETERY
THROGS NECK
FERRY POINT PARK
EAST RIVER
BRONX-WHITESTONE BRIDGE
QUEENS
Wakefield-241 St
Nereid Av
Eastchester-Dyre Av
Baychester Av
Gun Hill Rd
Pelham Bay Pk
Buhre Av
Middletown Rd
Westchester Sq-E Tremont Av
Zerega Av
Castle Hill Av
BELMONT
zero otto nove
Tra Di Noi
Enzo's of Arthur Ave
ARTHUR AVENUE RETAIL MARKET
Estrellita Poblana III
Roberto's
1
2
3
STREETS AND BRIDGES
Bainbridge Ave. 1 B1
Edward L. Grant Hwy. 2 A2
E. 204th St. 3 B2
Van Cortlandt Park South 4 AB1
Van Cortlandt Park East 5 B1
W. Fordham Rd. 6 A2
W. 252nd St. 7 A1
Henry Hudson Bridge 8 A1
Robert F. Kennedy Bridge 9 A3
Washington Bridge 10 A2

BECCOFINO

Italian • Family

MAP: B1

Poor little Riverdale—its leafy residential streets may be long on charm but they come up rather short on good food. Thankfully, Beccofino stands apart from the neighborhood's ho-hum standard. In fact, this American-leaning Italian spot has been a local favorite for years—and with good reason. Exposed brick walls, rustic terra-cotta floors and white deli paper-covered tables lend a homey setting, where the specials are handwritten and then tucked inside the regular menu.

The kitchen creates each plate with great care and the portions are especially generous. Stuffed mushrooms are earthy and divine; cavatelli tossed with sweet Italian sausage, broccoli rabe and olive oil is contentment in a bowl; and veal with a sherry-shallot demi-glace is exemplary.

5704 Mosholu Ave. (at Fieldston Rd.)

Van Cortlandt Park - 242 St

(718) 432-2604 — **WEB:** www.beccofinorestaurant.com

Dinner nightly

PRICE: $$

BISTRO SK

French • Family

MAP: D2

In a neighborhood better known for seafood, this charming bistro breaks the mold with hearty plates of French food. The husband-wife team lures locals into a snug, dimly lit space with marvelous mahogany-hued onion soup finished with brandy and a sultry mound of Gruyère. Particular attention to the art of service shines through the dining room.

A craving for classic Gallic dishes will surely be satisfied by cooking that is more solid than revelatory. Signatures include a tender roulade of chicken breast stuffed with spinach and mushrooms, served alongside haricot verts and fluffy, buttery mashed potatoes tucked with black olive for a bit of "wow!" For a finale, try the pineapple upside-down cake with a grilled ring of fruit and drizzle of caramel.

273 City Island Ave. (bet. Carroll & Hawkins Sts.)

Pelham Bay Park (& Bus BX29)

(718) 885-1670 — **WEB:** www.bistrosk.com

Lunch Sun Dinner Tue - Sun

PRICE: $$

CEETAY

Asian • Pub

MAP: A3

Its location near Hunts Point and the burgeoning South Bronx art community may have put it on the foodie trail, but Ceetay has become known for inventive Asian cooking at its best. The open kitchen offers diners a view of the race among cooks cutting, washing, and packing up an endless number of takeout orders. The tiny dining room features Mason jar fixtures, a handcrafted bar, and a wall papered with yellowing Asian newspapers.

Creative specials include a seared square of sesame-studded rice "bruschetta" topped with avocado purée, tuna tartare, and frizzled onions. But, don't miss such high-flying maki as the Kawasaki roll with a mishmash of crab, scallion, sweet glaze, and more. Traditional sushi here stands equally strong, with very nice maguro, ebi and uni.

129 Alexander Ave. (at Bruckner Blvd.)
3 Av - 138 St
(718) 618-7020 — **WEB:** www.ceetay.com
Lunch Mon - Fri Dinner nightly **PRICE:** $$

DA FRANCO & TONY RISTORANTE

Italian • Family

MAP: C2

There is so much to love here, where sharply dressed servers dish up equal parts warmth, hospitality and steaming bowls of scrumptious pasta. The menu leans heavily towards that nostalgic sort of red-sauce, Italian-American cooking that is again finding more and more respect, thanks to mouthwatering dishes like merluzzo marechiaro and veal scaloppini.

The interior is lovely, which is particularly important since you're in for a bit of a wait (everything is made fresh to order). But who would complain when fluffy knobs of potato gnocchi arrive tossed in basil pesto with plush Gorgonzola cheese and walnuts. Their chicken scarpariello is perfectly caramelized, deeply flavored and bathed in a sinfully rich wine broth, fragrant with rosemary.

2815 Middletown Rd. (bet. Hutchinson River Pkwy. East & Mulford Ave.)
Middletown Rd
(718) 684-2815 — **WEB:** www.dafrancoandtony.com
Lunch & dinner daily **PRICE:** $$

EL MOLCAJETE

Mexican • Simple

MAP: B3

This bright, cheerful Mexican gem can be found in the Soundview section of the Bronx, which was once upon a time lined with Italian flags, bakeries and butchers. Today, you'll find a global collection of restaurants, including south-of-the-border hot spots, pan-African grocery stores, Puerto Rican lechoneras and Dominican diners.

Breakfast at El Molcajete kicks off with delicious egg sandwiches, with a Mexican twist. Lunch brings mouthwatering tacos, tortas and cemitas—served with smoky red and spicy green sauces on the side. Don't miss the sumptuous gordita, a thick masa cake filled with luscious pork and then floated with cilantro, smooth crema and serrano peppers; or the tender cabeza de res (cow head) and gamey barbacoa (barbecue goat) tacos.

1506-1508 Westchester Ave. (bet. Elder & Wheeler Aves.)
Elder Av
(917) 688-1433 – **WEB:** N/A
Lunch & dinner daily **PRICE:**

EL NUEVO BOHÍO

Puerto Rican • Simple

MAP: B2

On a prominent corner, windows filled with lechòn lure passersby with mouthwatering visions of shiny-skinned roast pork. Beloved by the local Puerto Rican community, as well as a wave of newcomers, the front room is minimally adorned and filled with lines of to-go orders. Snag a seat in the back— where bright walls are flooded with photos—for friendly table service.

Begin with morcilla, a thick blood sausage with chili peppers, cilantro and garlic, before moving on to succulent pernil, pork shoulder, roasted to a luxuriously crisp exterior. Speaking of which, some 30 hogs are delivered here each week and during the holidays, you can also get an entire cooked pig to go. Close out with such complex sopas as cow's feet with yucca or asopado de camarones.

791 E. Tremont Ave. (at Mapes Ave.)
West Farms Sq - E Tremont Av
(718) 294-3905 – **WEB:** www.elnuevobohiorestaurant.com
Lunch & dinner daily **PRICE:**

ENZO'S 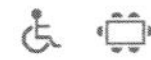

Italian • Family

MAP: C2

Not to be confused with an unrelated spot on Arthur Avenue, this rather polished and airy restaurant has its own distinct personality. Its loyal local following means that weekend waits are to be expected; and the warm aura heightened by spot-on service seems to welcome everyone like family.

Inspired by the Italian-American passion for gathering at the table, Enzo's offers the kind of cooking that revolves around long-simmered meat sauces and myriad interpretations of house-made pasta. Yet the kitchen knows just how to break a few rules, as seen in the spicy and creamy penne alla vodka. Other highlights include perfectly cooked chicken scarpariello made with dark, juicy morsels of bone-in meat married with a bit of garlic, wine and excellent olive oil.

1998 Williamsbridge Rd. (at Neill Ave.)
Morris Park
(718) 409-3828 — **WEB:** www.enzosbronxrestaurant.com
Lunch & dinner daily **PRICE: $$**

ENZO'S OF ARTHUR AVE

Italian • Trattoria

MAP: D3

Make your way past the front doors of this Bronx beau and enter into one of two wings—either a sprawling and rustic dining room or a welcoming bar that is jam-packed on weekends. You'd be hard-pressed to find a bad word at this longstanding hearty and saucy joint, nestled into thriving Arthur Avenue. Servers whiz by, delivering glistening clams oreganata and tender fish Livornese. Enzo's affable manager is usually a step behind, checking on your table like you're one of the family.

Begin with gnocchi in tegamino, with tomato, parmesan and a kiss of sage. Then dive into juicy pork chops drenched in white wine sauce and topped with spicy pickled cherry peppers. Tender chicken breast arrives stuffed with prosciutto, mozzarella and mushroom-cognac sauce.

2339 Arthur Ave. (bet. Crescent Ave. & 186th St.)
Fordham Rd (Grand Concourse)
(718) 733-4455 — **WEB:** N/A
Lunch & dinner daily **PRICE: $$**

ESTRELLITA POBLANA III

Mexican • Simple

MAP: D3

The Arthur Avenue area may be known as the artery of the Little Italy of the Bronx, but a Mexican restaurant shines here with its fluffy tamales loaded with tender, fragrant corn and so much more. The small interior is brightened with gold walls, a fuchsia ceiling and three stars set in the coffered ceiling. Exposed brick and a semi-open kitchen complete the comfortable scene.

Conversation is common between the pleasant servers and other diners. Pancita, a spicy tripe stew, is a real eye-opener with its abundance of toasted chilies. The bistec Estrellita is served with a fiery habanero sauce, topped with pico de gallo and flanked by a side of rice and beans. Flan is a lovely finish—though that generous steak may fulfill even the heartiest appetite.

2328 Arthur Ave. (bet. Crescent Ave. & 186th St.)
Fordham Rd (Grand Concourse)
(718) 220-7641 — **WEB:** www.estrellitapoblanaiii.com
Lunch & dinner daily **PRICE:** ⊜

F & J PINE RESTAURANT

Italian • Neighborhood

MAP: B2

This institution began as a simple storefront eatery in 1969. These days, Frankie & Johnnie's Tavern (as it is lovingly referred to) covers an entire city block, with a catering hall to boot. Locals, celebrities, Yankees and their fans love to roll in and pull up their sleeves in this large dining room, with a welcoming bar, pizza oven, back garden and brass tags listing luminaries like "Rocco the Jeweler."

The Bastone family has been critical to the Bronx food scene for over 50 years now, and it shows through cooking that is as solid as it gets. No one is reinventing the wheel, but gargantuan portions of beloved Italian-American classics like stuffed pork chops, delicious pizzette, tender stuffed artichokes and fresh seafood pastas more than hit the spot.

1913 Bronxdale Ave. (bet. Matthews & Muliner Aves.)
Bronx Park East
(718) 792-5956 — **WEB:** www.fjpine.com
Lunch & dinner daily **PRICE:** $$

HAVANA CAFÉ

Latin American • Family

MAP: C2

This bumping Latin café straddles a corner of the Schuylerville section, and when the weather permits, grab a seat in its palm tree-shaded sidewalk retreat. Inside, find a friendly bar, ceiling fans and tropical fronds. The partners behind this operation have deep roots in the Bronx, and they've hit upon a great formula here—so much so, they've opened a second spot nearby called Cabo. The classic Cuban-American black bean soup, frijoles negro, gets a zesty kick from lime-spiked crème fraîche. Then tender palomilla is topped with caramelized onions and paired with yucca fries; while coconut rice pudding empanadas are filled with dates for a sweet finale.

On Tuesday nights, follow the lively tunes emanating from around the way to dance the night away.

3151 E. Tremont Ave. (at LaSalle Ave.)

Westchester Sq - E Tremont (& Bus BX42)

(718) 518-1800 — **WEB:** www.bronxhavanacafe.com

Lunch & dinner daily

PRICE: $$

HUDSON GARDEN GRILL

American • Design

MAP: B2

There are many reasons why this is such an exciting partnership between The New York Botanical Garden and Chef Julian Alonzo, not the least of which is the idyllic setting. It is situated within sight of the landmarked Haupt Conservatory, open and airy, where huge arched windows overlook the manicured lawns.

This menu is polished, makes the most of locally sourced ingredients, and exceeds expectations with cooking that is as beautiful as the surroundings. Start with savory monkey bread served with honey butter in a cast-iron pan. Then move on to tender crab cakes with pickled cucumbers, sea beans and mustard seeds.

The only disappointment may be is that it keeps the same hours as the NYBT. But not to worry, as they are now open until 6:00 P.M. on weekends.

2900 Southern Blvd. (in New York Botanical Garden)

Bedford Pk Blvd

(646) 627-7711 — **WEB:** www.nybg.org/visit/hudson-garden-grill.php

Lunch Tue - Sun

PRICE: $$$

JAKE'S STEAKHOUSE

Steakhouse • Tavern

MAP: B1

While the city may be chock-a-block with steakhouses, it's hard to argue with this gem's deft cooking. Duck behind the limestone facade and you'll find a clubby, multi-level space with private nooks, a lively, well-stocked bar, flat-screens displaying the latest games and an upstairs wall of windows overlooking Van Cortlandt Park.

A true American steakhouse ought to have a substantial shrimp cocktail, and at Jake's this classic starter arrives fresh and delicious with the sweetness of plump shrimp offset by a tangy cocktail sauce. Any steak on the menu can be topped with Gorgonzola and a thatch of frizzled fried onions, though a succulent and well-marbled T-bone seared to rosy-pink perfection begs for little beyond a fork, knife and good conversation.

6031 Broadway (bet. Manhattan College Pkwy. & 251st St.)
Van Cortlandt Park - 242 St
(718) 581-0182 — **WEB:** www.jakessteakhouse.com
Lunch & dinner daily **PRICE: $$$**

JOE'S PLACE

Puerto Rican • Family

MAP: B3

From abuelas to niños, locals know to come to this "place" for solid Puerto Rican food. A glance at the wall of politicos and celebrities who have dined here proves how well-loved it truly is. The space is divided into two very different areas: a classic lunch counter also serving takeout and a proper dining room.

A wonderful Nuyorican accent can be heard at gathering family tables and tasted in classic dishes like mofongo al pilon de bistec (savory shredded beef over mashed plantains) or pernil con arroz y gandules (roasted pork with pigeon peas and rice). Prices become even more reasonable when you realize that dishes are big enough to be split three ways. Daily sopas are a highlight, but end meals with hot and flaky cheese-filled pastelitos.

1841 Westchester Ave. (at Thieriot Ave.)
Parkchester
(718) 918-2947 — **WEB:** www.joesplacebronx.com
Lunch & dinner daily **PRICE: $$**

LA CUEVA FONDA MEXICANA

Mexican • Simple

MAP: A3

When your food-crazed buddy tells you the only thing that matters is what's on the plate, you take them to La Cueva Fonda Mexicana. This tiny hole-in-the-wall Bronx hot spot is proof you don't need much to produce honest and authentic food. The décor is beyond simple—there are maybe a handful of tables—but these cooks take their responsibility quite seriously. The bustling open kitchen and intimate dining experience will make you feel like you're part of the family.

Guests feast on soft, homemade tortillas filled with heartwarming lengua, bright cilantro, jalapeños and a lick of spicy chipotle sauce; or brick-red caldo de res soup, simmering with tender beef. Don't miss the daily specials, or the excellent barbacoa, served only on weekends.

835 E. 152nd St. (bet. Union & Prospect Aves.)

E. 149th St

(347) 590-0570 – **WEB:** www.lacuevafondamexicanabx.com

Lunch & dinner daily **PRICE:**

LA MORADA

Mexican • Simple

MAP: A3

This sweet spot stands out for its authentic Oaxacan food, a rare delight even in this neighborhood. It's a homey, no frills sort of place that welcomes everyone, and the owner loves to chat about the traditions behind this region's cooking—or history and art as evidenced by the impromptu lending library that has emerged in the comfy back seating area.

This part of Mexico is known for its incredible moles, so sample a wonderfully complex red pumpkin seed version (pipián rojo de pepitas) with pork spare ribs. Another, the glossy mole Oaxaqueño, arrives fragrant with cloves, tomatillos, plantains, peanuts and chocolate, served over chicken. Don't miss the wildly fresh tamales either, filled with silky chicken, spices and covered with a rich tomatillo sauce.

308 Willis Ave. (bet. 140th & 141st Sts.)

3 Av - 138 St

(718) 292-0235 – **WEB:** www.lamoradanyc.com

Lunch & dinner Mon - Sat **PRICE:**

LIEBMAN'S

Deli • Delicatessen

MAP: A1

Some things never change (phew!) and thankfully this iconic kosher deli is still stuffing sandwiches and ladling matzo ball soup (reputed for its healing powers), just as it has for over 50 years. Residents wax poetic about the place: a true-blue deli with a neon sign in the front window, the grill slowly roasting hot dogs and meat-slicing machines churning out endless piles of pastrami.

Soulful classics include stuffed veal breast, potato latkes and tongue sandwiches with tangy pickles. Some order to go, but a hearty Reuben stacked with mounds of hot corned beef, sauerkraut and Russian dressing is more enjoyable when freshly plated and served in a comfortable booth. End with a perfect little rugelach filled with chocolate and ground nuts.

552 W. 235th St. (bet. Johnson & Oxford Aves.)
231 St
(718) 548-4534 – **WEB:** www.liebmansdeli.com
Lunch & dinner daily

PRICE: $$

MEXICOSINA

Mexican • Simple

MAP: A3

The light-filled interior of this Mexican powerhouse sitting on a quiet corner is a busy amalgam of rustic artifacts, wolf taxidermy and the Virgin Mother in all her glory with flowers and votives at her feet. And those huge jars of jamaica, horchata and the agua fresca del dia are just as tasty and refreshing as they are decorative.

If they have the tlayuda, order it. Its crunchy paper-thin base is smothered in a veritable fiesta of refried black beans, chicharrón, lettuce, queso Oaxaca, crema and much, much more. Other equally terrific specials have included chivo, a rich goat stew highlighting an intense habanero-spiked consommé or tender lamb barbacoa tacos. Cold accompanying salsas are so divine one could skip the chips and just eat them—with a spoon.

503 Jackson Ave. (at 147th St.)
E 149 St
(347) 498-1339 – **WEB:** www.mexicosina.com
Lunch & dinner daily

PRICE: $$

PATRICIA'S

Italian • Contemporary décor

MAP: C2

Much more than a neighborhood staple, Patricia's is an elegant restaurant committed to the convivial spirit of Southern Italy. Its seasonal fare is served in a gracious, brick-lined dining room among white tablecloths, chandeliers and the warmth of a wood-burning oven.

That brick oven churns out pleasing pizzas with lightly charred crusts, like the Regina simply adorned with buffalo mozzarella, torn basil and a drizzle of excellent olive oil. Spaghetti Frank Sinatra is a stain-making bowl of slippery pasta loaded with shrimp, clams, olives and capers in chunky tomato sauce.

A light touch is seen in the grilled vegetables, topped with paper-thin cremini mushrooms. Don't miss the flaky and gently poached baccalà alla Livornese in a sharp, tangy sauce.

1082 Morris Park Ave. (bet. Haight & Lurting Aves.)
Morris Park (& Bus BX8)
(718) 409-9069 – **WEB:** www.patriciasnyc.com
Lunch & dinner daily **PRICE:** $$

ROBERTO'S

Italian • Contemporary décor

MAP: D3

You can't miss this storied Italian-American favorite whose design falls somewhere between a cozy farmhouse and Mediterranean villa. In fact, Roberto's bright coral façade lets you know right away there's allegria to be had at this highly regarded respite.

This space is as ideal for big groups as it is for romantic evenings. Inside, you'll find a cozy, carved-wood bar and generously sized tables lit by candlelight. In addition to the regular menu (think wonderful, fun shapes of pasta al cartoccio as well as other classic entrées like grilled pork chop), it's always worth a look at the chef's delicious daily specials. Of course, save the best for last as evidenced by the sbriciolata crumb cake with amaretto, chunks of chocolate, ricotta and almonds.

603 Crescent Ave. (at Hughes Ave.)
Fordham Rd (Grand Concourse)
(718) 733-9503 – **WEB:** www.roberto089.com
Lunch & dinner Mon – Sat **PRICE:** $$

SEIS VECINOS

Latin American • Neighborhood

MAP: A3

The Bronx is immensely proud of its heritage, but that doesn't mean it resists change. In fact, this recruit fits in perfectly with the swiftly changing 'hood as it stands sentry at the base of a distinguished building on a prominent corner.

The interior is sunny and welcoming with a gracious staff to boot; the menu is melting pot Central America featuring papusas from El Salvador, baleadas from Honduras and enchiladas from Mexico. Go for a side of cheese—the cuajada is a soft curd variety offering a taste of Nicaragua. Tacos, like the enchilada with a spicy pork concoction, are simple but gratifying; while the heartier, fork-tender oxtail floating in an intense sauce with a hint of sweetness embodies the kitchen's complexity of flavors.

640 Prospect Ave. (at Kelly St.)
E. 149th St
(718) 684-8604 — **WEB:** www.seisvecinosnyc.com
Lunch & dinner daily **PRICE:** $$

TRA DI NOI

Italian • Trattoria

MAP: D3

Decked out with crimson walls and red-checkered tablecloths, this is the kind of place where diners feel like they're in on a delicious secret—and that's no coincidence, as Tra Di Noi is Italian for "between us."

Responsible for the success behind this tiny spot is Chef/owner Marco Coletta, who runs the front and back of house with the precision of an air traffic controller and the passion of an Italian direttore. This sincerity shines through in the cooking, from the ethereally light gnocchi di patate in a rich lamb ragù to the quickly pan-fried fillet of sole Francese nestled in a creamy lemon sauce with shrimp, parsley and white wine. Only a few desserts are on offer, and all are made in house. For a classic finale, go with the ricotta cheesecake.

622 E. 187th St. (bet. Belmont & Hughes Aves.)
Fordham Rd (Grand Concourse)
(718) 295-1784 — **WEB:** www.tradinoi.com
Lunch Tue - Fri Dinner Tue - Sun **PRICE:** $$

ZERO OTTO NOVE

Italian • Trattoria

MAP: D3

An icon in its own right, this beloved Italian is located across the way from yet another NY mainstay, namely the Arthur Avenue Retail Market. Brick and cement archways, high ceilings and a second-floor dining terrace strive to keep that oven—and its wares—within each table's line of vision.

The menu showcases Salerno-style cooking with pizzas, baked pastas and wood-fired entrées. In fact, any dish that is "al cartoccio" (in parchment) is sure to please. Open up this pouch to try the pitch-perfect al dente radiatori baked with porcini, cherry tomatoes, breadcrumbs and loads of deliciously spicy sausage. The ragù Salernitano is a gut-busting triumph of stewed braciole, sausage and tender meatballs. The Nutella calzone makes a sweet, rich finish.

2357 Arthur Ave. (at 186th St.)
Fordham Rd (Grand Concourse)
(718) 220-1027 – **WEB:** www.roberto089.com
Lunch Tue - Sat Dinner Tue - Sun **PRICE:** $$

Look for the symbol for a brilliant breakfast to start your day off right.

BROOKLYN

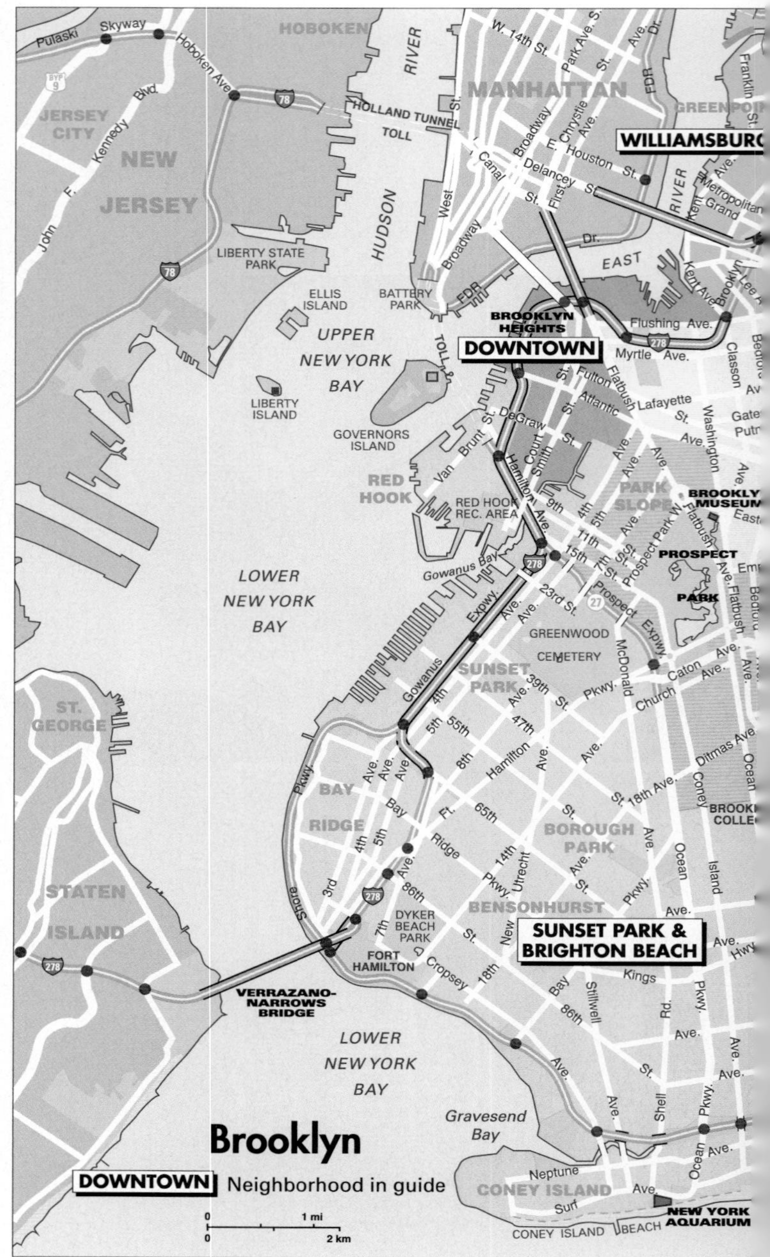

Brooklyn
DOWNTOWN Neighborhood in guide
WILLIAMSBURG
DOWNTOWN
SUNSET PARK & BRIGHTON BEACH
MANHATTAN
NEW JERSEY
JERSEY CITY
HOBOKEN
HUDSON RIVER
EAST RIVER
UPPER NEW YORK BAY
LOWER NEW YORK BAY
LIBERTY STATE PARK
ELLIS ISLAND
LIBERTY ISLAND
BATTERY PARK
GOVERNORS ISLAND
BROOKLYN HEIGHTS
RED HOOK
RED HOOK REC. AREA
PARK SLOPE
PROSPECT PARK
BROOKLYN MUSEUM
GREENWOOD CEMETERY
SUNSET PARK
BAY RIDGE
BOROUGH PARK
BENSONHURST
DYKER BEACH PARK
FORT HAMILTON
VERRAZANO-NARROWS BRIDGE
ST. GEORGE
STATEN ISLAND
Gravesend Bay
CONEY ISLAND
NEW YORK AQUARIUM
HOLLAND TUNNEL TOLL
Gowanus Bay
0 1 mi
0 2 km

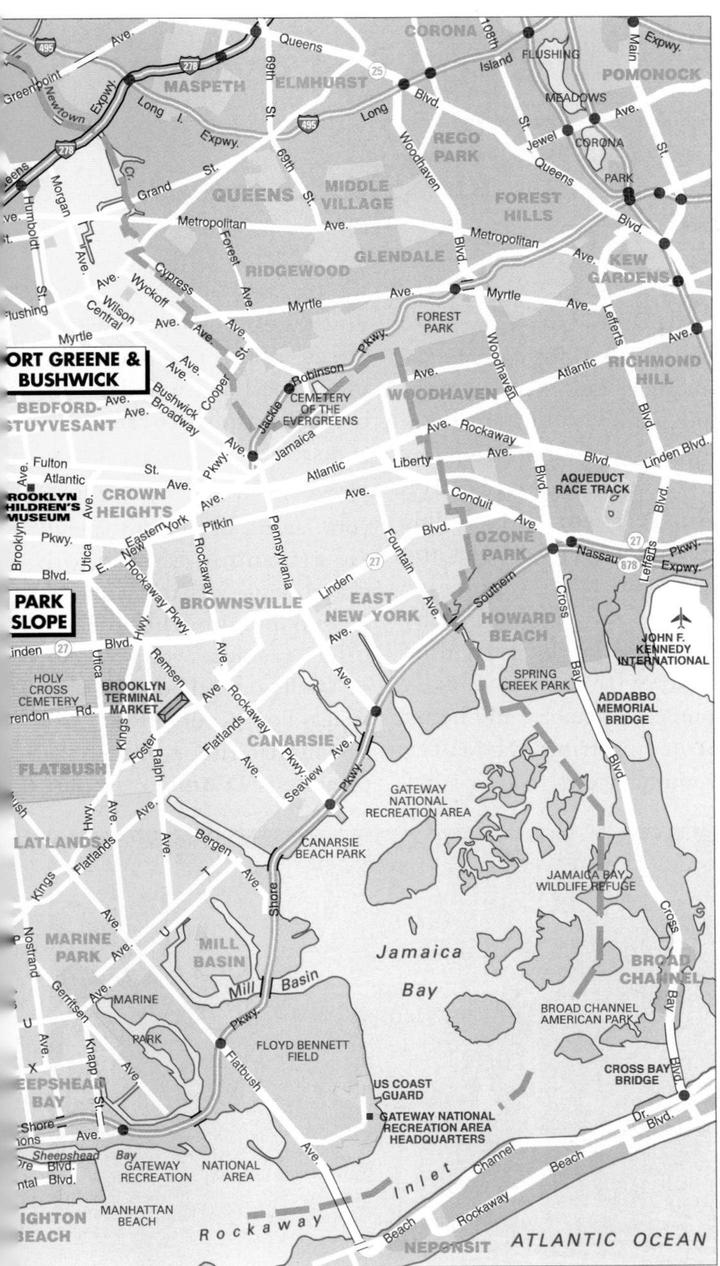
CORONA
FLUSHING MEADOWS CORONA PARK
POMONOCK
MASPETH
ELMHURST
REGO PARK
QUEENS
MIDDLE VILLAGE
FOREST HILLS
GLENDALE
RIDGEWOOD
KEW GARDENS
FOREST PARK
RICHMOND HILL
FORT GREENE & BUSHWICK
BEDFORD-STUYVESANT
CEMETERY OF THE EVERGREENS
WOODHAVEN
CROWN HEIGHTS
BROOKLYN CHILDREN'S MUSEUM
AQUEDUCT RACE TRACK
OZONE PARK
BROWNSVILLE
EAST NEW YORK
HOWARD BEACH
PARK SLOPE
JOHN F. KENNEDY INTERNATIONAL
SPRING CREEK PARK
HOLY CROSS CEMETERY
BROOKLYN TERMINAL MARKET
ADDABBO MEMORIAL BRIDGE
CANARSIE
FLATBUSH
GATEWAY NATIONAL RECREATION AREA
CANARSIE BEACH PARK
JAMAICA BAY WILDLIFE REFUGE
MARINE PARK
MILL BASIN
Jamaica Bay
BROAD CHANNEL
MARINE PARK
BROAD CHANNEL AMERICAN PARK
FLOYD BENNETT FIELD
CROSS BAY BRIDGE
US COAST GUARD
GATEWAY NATIONAL RECREATION AREA HEADQUARTERS
GATEWAY RECREATION NATIONAL AREA
MANHATTAN BEACH
Rockaway Inlet
NEPONSIT
ATLANTIC OCEAN
Queens Blvd.
Long Island Expwy.
Grand St.
Metropolitan Ave.
Myrtle Ave.
Woodhaven Blvd.
Atlantic Ave.
Jamaica Ave.
Liberty Ave.
Rockaway Blvd.
Conduit Ave.
Linden Blvd.
Pitkin Ave.
Eastern Pkwy.
Pennsylvania Ave.
Fountain Ave.
Nassau Expwy.
Southern Pkwy.
Cross Bay Blvd.
Rockaway Pkwy.
Flatlands Ave.
Seaview Ave.
Shore Pkwy.
Mill Basin
Flatbush Ave.
Kings Hwy.
Nostrand Ave.
Gerritsen Ave.
Knapp St.
Sheepshead Bay
Rockaway Beach Blvd.
Beach Channel Dr.

DOWNTOWN

BROOKLYN HEIGHTS · CARROLL GARDENS · COBBLE HILL

The Brooklyn Navy Yard may be a hub for commercial business and houses over 200 vendors, but its most impressive tenant remains the expansive **Brooklyn Grange Farm**. This leading green-roof consultant and urban farm is responsible for promoting healthy communities by providing them with fresh, locally sourced vegetables and herbs. After admiring DUMBO's stunning views, take a stroll down cobblestoned Water Street. Then make like every proud local and walk straight into **Jacques Torres** for a taste of chocolate bliss. However, if savory is more your speed, be sure to spend an afternoon in Carroll Gardens—a historically Italian neighborhood that offers residents a spectrum of family-owned butchers and bakers along Court Street. Also set amidst this commercial paradise is **D'Amico**, an old-

time haunt dealing in specialty roasted coffees and teas. Step inside for a rewarding whiff, before heading over to **Caputo's Fine Foods** for more substantial sustenance—including salumi-packed sandwiches, heartwarming lard bread and fresh mozz. Folks may also favor **G. Esposito & Sons** for sausages, sopressata, arancini and other such Italian-American fun. Tired travelers can then rest their weary heels at **Ferdinando's Focacceria**, an age-old establishment famous for cooking up the classics, which taste as if they were transported straight from nonna's kitchen in Palermo and on to your plate. But, for that truly perfect finale, stop by **Court Pastry** for such exceptional sweets as cannoli, marzipan cookies and Italian ice. As Court Street blends into family-friendly Cobble Hill, find **Staubitz Market**—the most sociable butcher in town—that blends the best of the old and the new by way of its top-quality chops, cheeses and charcuterie. Need a change in mood (and food)? Then make sure to shift "hills" from Cobble to Boerum in order to feast on Middle Eastern hits at **Sahadi's** or **Damascus Bakery**—each lauded for outrageously good pitas, spreads and pastries.

BROOKLYN DOWNTOWN
MANHATTAN
SOUTH ST. SEAPORT
The River Café
Gran Eléctrica
The Osprey
Atrium DUMBO
Celestine
MAIN ST. PARK
DUMBO
BROOKLYN BRIDGE PARK
Jack the Horse
High St
Clark St
CADMAN PLAZA
DOWNTOWN
BROOKLYN HEIGHTS
Court St
Court St-Borough Hall
Jay St-Metro Tech
EAST RIVER
NEW YORK HARBOR
COBBLE HILL
Sottocasa
La Vara
Mile End
Bergen St
Hoyt/Schermerhorn
BOERUM HILL
Battersby
CARROLL GARDENS
CARROLL PARK
Carroll St
Frankies 457 Spuntino
Ugly Baby
Prime Meats
Buttermilk Channel
RED HOOK
SUNSET PARK & BRIGHTON BEACH
COFFEY PARK
Smith-9 St
GOWANUS
WASHINGTON PARK
RED HOOK PLAYGROUND
GREENE PLAYGROUND

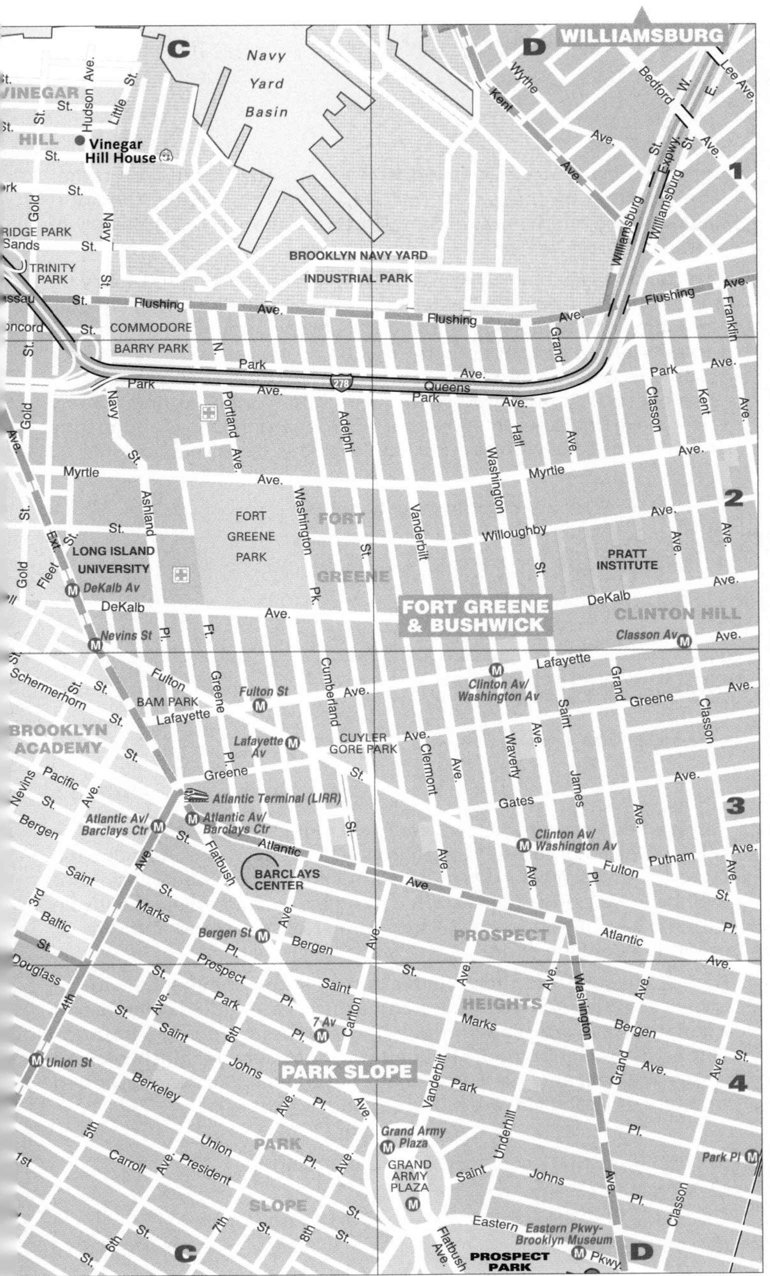
WILLIAMSBURG
C
D
Navy Yard Basin
VINEGAR HILL
Vinegar Hill House
BROOKLYN NAVY YARD INDUSTRIAL PARK
TRINITY PARK
COMMODORE BARRY PARK
Flushing Ave.
Park Ave.
Queens
278
Myrtle Ave.
Willoughby
DeKalb Ave.
FORT GREENE PARK
LONG ISLAND UNIVERSITY
DeKalb Av
Nevins St
FORT GREENE
FORT GREENE & BUSHWICK
PRATT INSTITUTE
CLINTON HILL
Classon Av
Lafayette
Clinton Av/ Washington Av
Fulton St
BAM PARK
BROOKLYN ACADEMY
Lafayette Av
CUYLER GORE PARK
Atlantic Terminal (LIRR)
Atlantic Av/ Barclays Ctr
BARCLAYS CENTER
Atlantic Ave.
Gates
Fulton
Putnam
PROSPECT HEIGHTS
Bergen St
Union St
7 Av
PARK SLOPE
Grand Army Plaza
GRAND ARMY PLAZA
Park Pl
Eastern Pkwy- Brooklyn Museum
PROSPECT PARK
1
2
3
4

ATRIUM DUMBO

Contemporary • Chic

MAP: B1

Set along Main Street, this industrial-chic retreat flaunts a rather iconic setting by the waterfront. Dark wood dominates the light-filled interior, amid metal accents and walls that sprout greenery to soften the room.

The cooking may have a farm-to-table focus, but a contemporary tilt is clear in everything that emerges from this bustling open kitchen. Heirloom carrots make for a beautiful composition here as they are served warm and topped with freekeh as well as black and white sesame seeds for a pop of color and great texture. Then shatteringly crisp fillets of Atlantic cod served with potato wedges and creamy tartar make Chef Laurent Kalkotour's European influences abundantly clear. Carrot cake with passion fruit sorbet is deservedly popular.

15 Main St. (bet. Plymouth & Water Sts.)
York St
(718) 858-1095 — **WEB:** www.atriumdumbo.com
Lunch & dinner daily **PRICE: $$$**

BATTERSBY

Contemporary • Neighborhood

MAP: B3

Yes, it's been open for a few years now, but intimate little Battersby still feels like a brand-new restaurant. Courtesy of Co-chefs Joseph Ogrodnek and Walker Stern, this kitchen may be wee in size, but their heartwarming breads crafted in-house and ingredients that spin with the season reflect the owners' ambitious, talented and forever grounded cooking style.

A meal chosen from their à la carte menu may commence with an endive salad perked up by cured tuna mojama, candied walnuts and a generous shaving of aged cheddar. Then dive in to heartier portions of roasted Berkshire pork enriched with summer succotash, pickled chilies and delicious jus. House-made ice creams, like peach studded with bits of fresh fruit, are a perfect parting gift.

255 Smith St. (bet. Degraw & Douglass Sts.)
Bergen St (Smith St.)
(718) 852-8321 — **WEB:** www.battersbybrooklyn.com
Dinner Tue - Sat **PRICE: $$$**

BUTTERMILK CHANNEL

American • Family

MAP: A4

Buttermilk Channel is the sort of joint we'd all like to have at the end of our street. It's warm and relaxed, run with care and attention, offers an appealing menu for all occasions—and has prices that encourage regular attendance. The name may refer to the tidal strait but also evokes feelings of comfort and cheer in a place that's already cute and where the close-set tables and large bar both add to the animated atmosphere.

The kitchen seeks out worthy suppliers and with no little skill imbues each creation with that little extra something, be it the cod with Littleneck clams, fresh linguini tossed with beets or indeed the buttermilk-fried chicken. This care is even evident at weekend brunches in standouts like the short rib hash.

524 Court St. (at Huntington St.)
Smith - 9 Sts
(718) 852-8490 — **WEB:** www.buttermilkchannelnyc.com
Lunch & dinner daily **PRICE:** $$

CELESTINE

Mediterranean • Intimate

MAP: B1

If you're lucky enough to call One John Street home, this area gem could very well serve as your personal kitchen—thanks to its location at the base of this residential building. The rest of us can simply dream about living on the water as we take in the magnificent views from the restaurant's soaring windows.

Celestine comes from a team of top restaurateurs who have some of Brooklyn's biggest hits under their belts. The small plates menu spotlights dishes from the Eastern Mediterranean (a less talked about collection of countries from Greece to North Africa); and fragrant spice blends season every item. Kabocha squash skordalia, for instance, veers away from tradition with successful results, while short rib manti are the ultimate in comfort food.

1 John St. (bet. Adams & Pearl Sts.)
York St
(718) 522-5356 — **WEB:** www.celestinebk.com
Lunch & dinner daily **PRICE:** $$

FRANKIES 457 SPUNTINO

Italian • Trattoria

MAP: B4

Frank Castronovo and Frank Falcinelli (collectively known as the Franks) have built a small empire for themselves based on delicious, seasonal Italian fare served in rustic little haunts. Frankies 457 Spuntino, a charming, brick-lined space with bare wood tables and a quiet, shady backyard strung with twinkling bistro lights, is a classic example of their easy Brooklyn style.

Seem familiar by now? Well, these guys wrote the book. Service is laid-back and unpretentious, perhaps because they know the food does the talking here: a wildly fresh fennel, celery root and parsley salad arrives with aged pecorino and a delicate lemon vinaigrette; while a tender tangle of linguini is laced with a tomato broth studded with fava beans and garlic.

457 Court St. (bet. 4th Pl. & Luquer St.)
Smith - 9 Sts
(718) 403-0033 — **WEB:** www.frankies457.com
Lunch & dinner daily

PRICE: $$

GRAN ELÉCTRICA

Mexican • Chic

MAP: B1

Looking to market ingredients and a pan-regional approach to Mexican cuisine, this stylish yet comfortable restaurant impresses with its lovely décor and lively vibe. Servers are engaged and enthusiastic about the menu's pleasures. An ideal visit starts with a margarita at the bar and moves to the garden as strings of lights flicker to life.

Mexico and Brooklyn are in balance on a menu that includes small plates such as memelitas con huitlacoche, filled with savory sautéed mushrooms and topped with creamy avocado. Flavors are bright in the deliciously untraditional poblano chile relleno stuffed with Havarti, roasted tomato-jalapeño salsa and tortillas. Carnitas tacos are tucked with chunks of crispy roasted Berkshire pork that simply bursts with flavor.

5 Front St. (bet. Dock & Old Fulton Sts.)
High St
(718) 852-2700 — **WEB:** www.granelectrica.com
Lunch Sat - Sun Dinner nightly

PRICE: $$

JACK THE HORSE

American • Tavern

MAP: B1

A Brooklyn Heights favorite, this sleepy American tavern is a consistent spot in a neighborhood that lacks a variety of serious eats. However, exposed brick walls covered with old-fashioned clocks set a cozy tone, and have regulars returning for the well-stocked bar, complete with myriad bitters.

Slurp a few bivalves at the Oyster Room next door before settling in to a table, or if thirst beckons, sip an Old-Fashioned with barrel strength Bourbon while perusing the menu. Some locals head straight for the burger—focaccia layered with Gruyère, caramelized Bourbon onions and a juicy beef patty. Though ricotta and butternut squash ravioli, tossed in sweet brown butter and topped with crumbled smoky bacon, is a fine alternative.

66 Hicks St. (at Cranberry St.)
High St
(718) 852-5084 – **WEB:** www.jackthehorse.com
Lunch Sun Dinner nightly

PRICE: $$

LA VARA

Spanish • Cozy

MAP: B3

Chef Alex Raij knows her tapas and helped kick-start the craze in Manhattan when she opened beloved Tía Pol years ago, before moving on to the equally popular El Quinto Pino. In 2012, the chef brought her cherished style to Brooklyn via La Vara, which she co-owns with husband, Eder Montero.

Billing itself as "cocina casera" or "home cooking," this kitchen has been a hit since day one, elevating its humble cuisine to such impressive levels that it's proved well worth the cab trip for non-Brooklynites. Product quality is excellent, and the playful spirit behind dishes is the definition of creative cooking. Menu highlights have featured coins of toothsome pulpo set over a crunchy parsley salad; while crispy suckling pig gives way to confit-tender meat.

268 Clinton St. (at Verandah Pl.)
Bergen St (Smith St.)
(718) 422-0065 – **WEB:** www.lavarany.com
Lunch Sat - Sun Dinner nightly

PRICE: $$

MILE END

Deli • Simple

MAP: B3

Boerum Hill's most bodacious deli serves up killer smoked meat among other treats. The tiny space gets lots of traffic, and those who can't find a seat along the counter or trio of communal tables can feast at home with takeout procured from the sidewalk window.

Now for the food: a cured and charred brisket sandwich, stacked onto soft rye bread and smeared with mustard, is the stuff that dreams are made of. The smoked mackerel sandwich heaped with fennel slaw, avocado and chunky tartar sauce is an eclectic take on the deli theme, which also reveals poutine and a Middle East-inspired falafel platter. Don't overlook the hand-rolled, wood-fired Montreal-style bagels from Black Seed Bagel shop.

97A Hoyt St. (bet. Atlantic Ave. & Pacific St.)
Hoyt - Schermerhorn
(718) 852-7510 — **WEB:** www.mileenddeli.com
Lunch & dinner daily

PRICE:

THE OSPREY

Contemporary • Chic

MAP: B1

The ultra-stylish 1 Hotel Brooklyn Bridge needed an equally hip restaurant to match, and The Osprey fits the bill. Considering its prime location and singular views (don't miss that incredible Manhattan skyline from the rooftop bar), they easily could have mailed it in. But no, this culinary gem was intent on making its own name—and they more than achieve that goal by offering excellent food that tastes as good as it looks.

The menu is varied and, as the flight pattern of the namesake bird suggests, apt to wander. There are nibbles, vegetarian-centric dishes and heartier rotisserie meats. Duck croquettes are paired with a creamy sauce spiked with piquillo peppers, and may be tailed by a simple branzino enriched with black olive tapenade and Puy lentils.

60 Furman St. (in the 1 Hotel Brooklyn Bridge)
High St
(347) 696-2505 — **WEB:** www.theospreybk.com
Lunch & dinner daily

PRICE: $$$

PRIME MEATS

European • Tavern

MAP: B4

Prime Meats stands tall and proud as a local gem for German-leaning eats set to American beats. The booths in front are bright and snug, while bentwood chairs and net curtains tied into a knot add to that brasserie feel. A warm vibe and cheery servers complete the picture.

Hand-crafted sausages, burgers and excellent steak frites are all the rage here. Nibble away on homemade pretzels while perusing the menu, which may traipse from Germany to France in a heartbeat, but always showcases a gutsy edge. Bold flavors shine through in a creamy roasted squash soup; jagerwurst, a lightly charred and delicately smoky sausage with red cabbage casserole; or Jen's German potato salad tossing waxy slices, chopped herbs and thick bacon in a pickled dressing.

465 Court St. (at Luquer St.)
Smith - 9 Sts
(718) 254-0327 — **WEB:** www.frankspm.com
Lunch & dinner daily

PRICE: $$

SOTTOCASA

Pizza • Neighborhood

MAP: B3

Located just below street level on frenetic Atlantic Avenue, a nondescript façade holds a quiet den of serious Neapolitan pizza magic. Enter and you'll find a simple, narrow, wood-paneled room with whitewashed brick walls; a little bar showcasing a handful of wines; an enormous, two-ton clay oven (imported directly from Naples); and a little patio out back for alfresco dining.

The mood is decidedly relaxed, and while there are delicious salads, antipasti and desserts to be tried at Sottocasa, the name of the game here is undoubtedly their wickedly good pizza, served folded, bianche or rosse (with—hurrah!—a gluten-free option as well). Regulars adore the Diavola pie, which comes laced with excellent mozzarella, fresh basil, black olives and hot sopressata.

298 Atlantic Ave. (bet. Hoyt & Smith Sts.)
Hoyt - Schermerhorn
(718) 852-8758 — **WEB:** www.sottocasanyc.com
Lunch Sat - Sun Dinner nightly

PRICE: $$

THE RIVER CAFÉ

Contemporary • Romantic

MAP: B1

Some things in life are worth dressing up for, and a visit to the illustrious River Café is certainly one of them. It enjoys, without question, one of the greatest settings of any restaurant, lying as it does in the shadow of the Brooklyn Bridge. In fact, the cityscape views are so spectacular, the ordering of a Manhattan as your pre-prandial cocktail seems the only obvious choice.

The entire place also oozes romance. A regiment of experienced, white-jacketed waitstaff keeps the whole operation ticking along like the well-oiled machine it is—and they can probably spot an impending marriage proposal even before the potential groom has left his seat.

However, don't come thinking that the food here will be playing second fiddle to the stellar views. In fact, it provides the perfect match for the setting. The ingredients are top-notch and the kitchen team has an inherent understanding of what goes with what—imagine succulent pork belly with scallops for example, or even glistening duck breast with sweet potato spätzle. It also knows that good cooking is not about showing how clever it is but about creating dishes that are at once balanced, easy to eat and eminently satisfying.

---

1 Water St. (bet. Furman & Old Fulton Sts.)

High St

(718) 522-5200 — **WEB:** www.therivercafe.com

Lunch Sat - Sun Dinner nightly

PRICE: $$$$

UGLY BABY

Thai • Colorful

MAP: B4

This wildly successful restaurant delivers excellent and unique cooking made with fresh aromatics and heat levels that honor the menu's promise of authentic "Thai style" spicing. The décor is a messy but eye-catching mix of streaked walls dripping with colorful dried paint and simple wooden furniture.

The menu spans the country's cooking from north to south, and offers many dishes rarely found in local restaurants. Be sure to try the tum kanoon (young jackfruit) pounded with fragrant curry paste, served with pork belly, shallots and deep-fried roselle. Kang hoh, chunks of tender pork shoulder with mung bean noodles and Chinese long beans, may be made with an intensely hot red curry, but still allows for every distinct flavor to come through.

407 Smith St. (bet. 4th & 5th Sts.)
Carroll St
(347) 689-3075 – **WEB:** www.uglybabynyc.com
Lunch Sat - Sun Dinner nightly **PRICE:** $$

VINEGAR HILL HOUSE

American • Tavern

MAP: C1

This local standout is situated in a waterfront neighborhood that feels not only charming but utterly untouched by time. The original carriage house was a butcher shop before becoming Vinegar Hill House—a lineage that seems apropos of such steady and perfectly delicious cooking.

From the kitchen, diners may expect such rustic and enchanting wood-fired items as a wintry fennel salad dressed in lemony olive oil and arranged with fronds over a swipe of burnt onion crème (think of the best onion dip you've ever had). Then, dig into a roasted half chicken with copious jus and a splash of snappy sherry vinegar served in a cast-iron skillet. Dark and impossibly moist chocolate Guinness cake is outrageously rich, beneath a thick layer of cream cheese frosting.

72 Hudson Ave. (near Water St.)
York St
(718) 522-1018 – **WEB:** www.vinegarhillhouse.com
Lunch Sat - Sun Dinner nightly **PRICE:** $$

FORT GREENE & BUSHWICK

BEDFORD STUYVESANT · CLINTON HILL · CROWN HEIGHTS

Brooklyn is particularly big on international cuisines, and its every nook overflows with enticing eats. Following suit, Fort Greene—set in the northwest corner and right across from Lower Manhattan—is famous for its West Indian and African communities (and cooking). **Bati** is one example of a traditional retreat for Ethiopian home food with a focus on vegetarian options. But, if good old-fashioned island cooking is what fits your mood, then get in line at **Gloria's Caribbean** for excellent roti, oxtail, jerk chicken and much, much more. Others may prefer to simply imbibe the vibe and feel the love at the annual West Indian Day parade—a veritable riot of color, fun and flavor. Like the hordes of ravenous locals, tired tourists should follow the culinary trail further east to Bedford-Stuyvesant.

Here in Bed-Stuy (as residents commonly refer to it), carb-junkies gather at **Clementine Bakery** for its nostalgic scene and addictive offerings, while home cooks looking to plan a Southern-themed evening should stock up on wares from **Carolina Country Store**. Bringing crave-worthy signatures straight from the namesake states, this food truck sensation is every carnivore's fantasy. Meanwhile, Mexico makes its presence known at old-time **Tortilleria Mexicana Los Hermanos**, a bona fide factory turning out some terrific tortillas in Bushwick. Not far behind, **Cesar's Empanada Truck** is mobbed for its cheesy renditions of the eponymous original. And if all's well that ends well, then be sure to seal the dessert deal over the 200-plus flavors found at **Dun-Well Doughnuts**. On the late night, famished revelers gather at **Berg'n** in Crown Heights. This boisterous beer hall pouring myriad drafts is also known to pop bottles of local brew that pair perfectly with a burger or two from **Landhaus**.

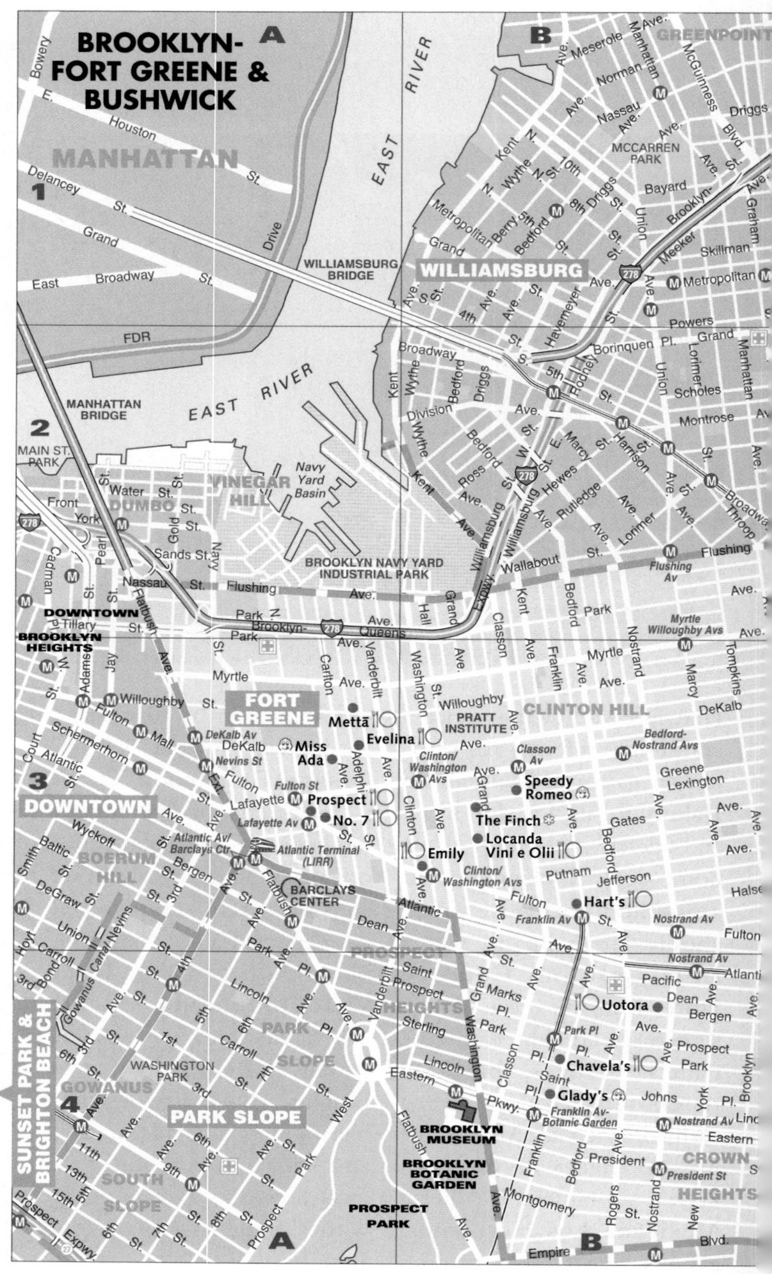

BROOKLYN-
FORT GREENE &
BUSHWICK
A
B
1
2
3
4
MANHATTAN
EAST RIVER
WILLIAMSBURG BRIDGE
MANHATTAN BRIDGE
MAIN ST. PARK
DUMBO
VINEGAR HILL
Navy Yard Basin
BROOKLYN NAVY YARD INDUSTRIAL PARK
GREENPOINT
MCCARREN PARK
WILLIAMSBURG
DOWNTOWN BROOKLYN
BROOKLYN HEIGHTS
FORT GREENE
CLINTON HILL
PRATT INSTITUTE
DOWNTOWN
BOERUM HILL
Atlantic Terminal (LIRR)
BARCLAYS CENTER
PROSPECT HEIGHTS
PARK SLOPE
WASHINGTON PARK
GOWANUS
SOUTH SLOPE
BROOKLYN MUSEUM
BROOKLYN BOTANIC GARDEN
PROSPECT PARK
CROWN HEIGHTS
SUNSET PARK & BRIGHTON BEACH
Mettā
Evelina
Miss Ada
Prospect
No. 7
Speedy Romeo
The Finch
Locanda Vini e Olii
Emily
Hart's
Uotora
Chavela's
Glady's
DeKalb Av
Nevins St
Fulton St
Lafayette Av
Atlantic Av/ Barclays Ctr
Clinton/ Washington Avs
Classon Av
Bedford-Nostrand Avs
Myrtle Willoughby Avs
Flushing Av
Franklin Av
Nostrand Av
Park Pl
Franklin Av- Botanic Garden
President St

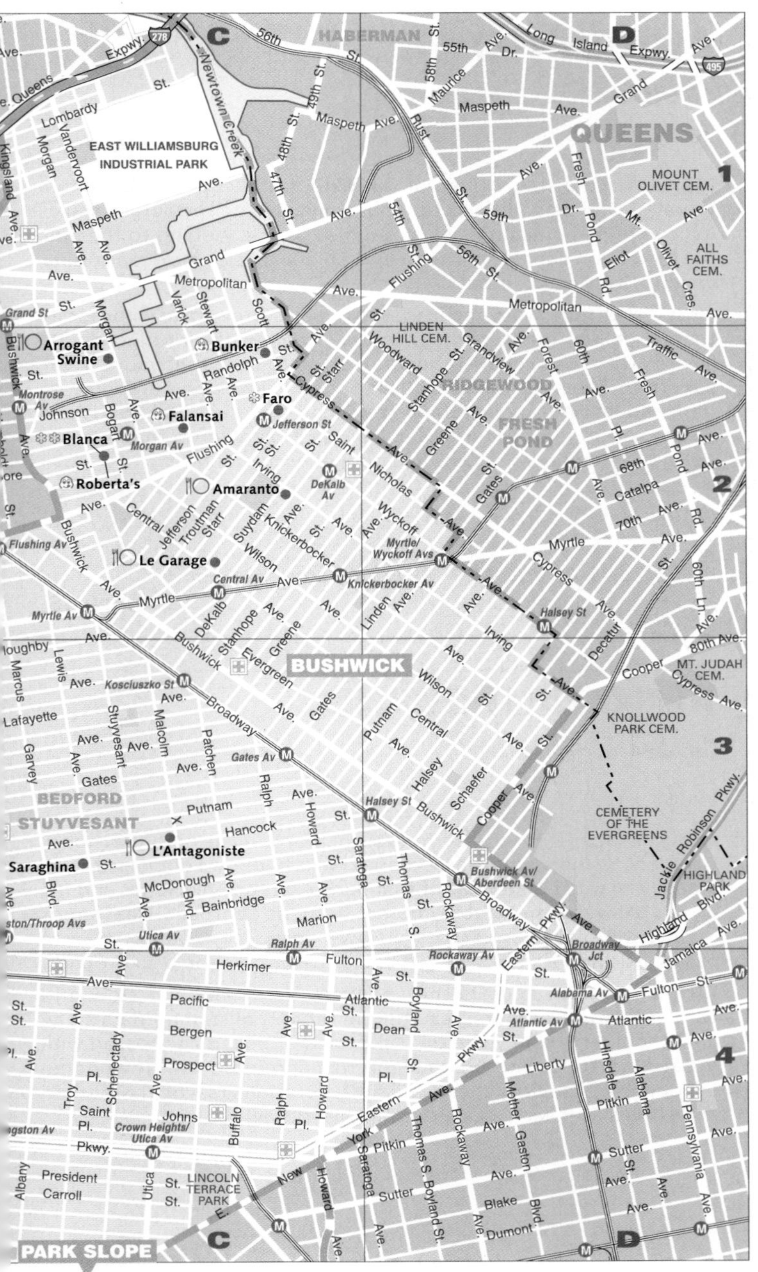
C
D
HABERMAN
QUEENS
EAST WILLIAMSBURG INDUSTRIAL PARK
Newtown Creek
Queens Expwy.
Long Island Expwy.
278
495
MOUNT OLIVET CEM.
ALL FAITHS CEM.
LINDEN HILL CEM.
RIDGEWOOD
FRESH POND
BUSHWICK
BEDFORD STUYVESANT
MT. JUDAH CEM.
KNOLLWOOD PARK CEM.
CEMETERY OF THE EVERGREENS
HIGHLAND PARK
LINCOLN TERRACE PARK
PARK SLOPE
1
2
3
4
Arrogant Swine
Bunker
Faro
Falansai
Blanca
Roberta's
Amaranto
Le Garage
L'Antagoniste
Saraghina
Grand St
Montrose Av
Morgan Av
Jefferson St
DeKalb Av
Flushing Av
Central Av
Knickerbocker Av
Myrtle/Wyckoff Avs
Myrtle Av
Halsey St
Kosciuszko St
Gates Av
Bushwick Av/Aberdeen St
Broadway Jct
Alabama Av
Atlantic Av
Rockaway Av
Ralph Av
Utica Av
Crown Heights/Utica Av
Kingston/Throop Avs
Kingston Av
Metropolitan Ave.
Grand Ave.
Maspeth Ave.
Flushing Ave.
Bushwick Ave.
Myrtle Ave.
Cypress Ave.
Wyckoff Ave.
Knickerbocker Ave.
Irving Ave.
Wilson Ave.
Central Ave.
Evergreen Ave.
Broadway
Jackie Robinson Pkwy.
Eastern Pkwy.
Atlantic Ave.
Fulton St.
Jamaica Ave.
Highland Blvd.
New York Ave.
Pitkin Ave.
Sutter Ave.
Liberty Ave.
Herkimer St.
Pacific St.
Bergen St.
Dean St.
Prospect Pl.
Saint Johns Pl.
President St.
Carroll St.
Fresh Pond Rd.
Eliot Ave.
Mt. Olivet Cres.
Traffic Ave.

AMARANTO

Mexican • Simple

MAP: C2

Named for the staple grain of the Aztecs and emblazoned with a mural of Quetzalcoatl, this tidy but truly caliente restaurant makes its love of its homeland clear from first glance. Adding to the lure, the father-son duo delivers their own unique take on Mexican cuisine, which is irresistible at best.

Most dishes here, from enchiladas to tamales, are sure to incorporate their excellent masa. Memelitas may begin with griddled dough layered with crispy chorizo, vegetables, pinto beans and more. Then, superb tortillas are folded with shredded chicken and draped with dark and luscious mole poblano enriched with cacao, almonds and spices. A range of other moles include pipian verde that dresses deliciously tender short ribs in a pool of nutty richness.

887 Hart St. (at Irving Ave.)
DeKalb Av
(718) 576-6001 — **WEB:** www.amarantobklyn.com
Lunch & dinner daily

PRICE: $$

ARROGANT SWINE

Barbecue • Simple

MAP: C2

A boon to this otherwise industrial warehouse neighborhood, Arrogant Swine's whitewashed brick walls and rows of picnic tables steadily fill with hungry patrons. Striking exterior wall murals and the aroma of sweet smoke both impress from the approach. Heat lamps extend the season for savoring slow-cooked pork outdoors, with rock music and a smoke-fueled barbecue buzz in the background.

Whole hog barbecue is the specialty here—smoked slow and whole over live embers, resulting in tender, glistening meat. The loin, shoulder and jowl are then chopped or pulled and tossed with a Carolina-style vinegar sauce. Sides complete the downhome experience, especially their traditional cornpone (savory cornbread in an iron skillet with bacon drippings and slaw).

173 Morgan Ave. (bet. Meserole & Scholes Sts.)
Morgan Av
(347) 328-5595 — **WEB:** www.arrogantswine.com
Lunch & dinner Tues - Sun

PRICE: ⊜

BLANCA ✿✿

Contemporary • Minimalist

MAP: C2

This gleaming kitchen for serious eaters is located deep within the compound that helped elevate this industrial quadrant of Bushwick into a perch for haute cuisine. It takes a bit of a luck to score a seat at Blanca, as seating is limited and very much in demand, but you'll feel blessed indeed once you settle in. Here, products and dishes take inspiration from around the world, while warm, fluid service keeps the mood friendly among the small group.

Blanca serves a carefully conceived multi-course tasting that promises immense creativity and an artist's ability to weave an unforgettable experience. This is dinner theater, with all eyes fixed on Chef Carlo Mirarchi quietly turning out plates of perfection. The execution, even in simple dishes, is par excellence.

Menus aren't presented until the end of the meal, but list dishes like sunflower seed "milk" topped with Pink Lady apple cubes and a mouth-coating grating of foie gras, tied together with chili and salt flakes. Fantastic pastas include tightly wound strands of cavatappi tossed in a spicy, creamy sauce made ultra-rich with the addition of Hokkaido uni. Makrut lime makes coconut ice and cashew ice cream refreshing and quite delicious.

---

261 Moore St. (bet. Bogart & White Sts.)
Morgan Av
(347) 799-2807 — **WEB:** www.blancanyc.com
Dinner Wed - Sat

PRICE: $$$$

BUNKER

Vietnamese • Colorful

MAP: C2

Chef Jimmy Tu could cook his killer Vietnamese street food out of a box, and the masses would still line up. But lucky for us, he and partner/brother Jacky Tu have found bigger and better digs to park their beloved Bunker. Tucked into an industrial Bushwick block, this fun and fresh space features colorful cinder block walls, a bamboo wood bar lined with Crayola-bright metal stools and ample seating for their fans.

And oh, is that fandom deserved. Think caramelized wild shrimp with heritage pork and basil; or fragrant grass-fed oxtail stew. Don't miss the bánh xèo either, which is a crispy, turmeric-laced Vietnamese crêpe tucked with heritage bacon and wild prawns, served over crunchy bean sprouts and paired with Thai basil, red lettuce and mint.

99 Scott Ave. (at Randolph St.)
Jefferson St
(718) 386-4282 – **WEB:** www.bunkernyc.com
Lunch & dinner Tue - Sun

PRICE: $$

CHAVELA'S

Mexican • Neighborhood

MAP: B4

Look for the light blue dome and wrought-iron doors to enter Chavela's and find an absolute riot of color inside. From the bar's Mexican tiles to the wall of ceramic butterflies, it is a study in artistic sensibilities. Mexico City native, Chef Arturo Leonar, is the man behind this menu and his guacamole—traditional or creative with smoked trout, pico de gallo and morita chile salsa—is just as pleasing. Taquitos de cangrego are perfectly balanced with sweet crabmeat and spicy salsa verde; while a tender pork short rib stew named costilla en salsa verde is studded with nopales and served with a mountain of yellow rice and refried black beans for a hearty finale.

Brunchers rejoice, as the kitchen does its best work during this most popular meal of the week.

736 Franklin Ave. (at Sterling Pl.)
Franklin St
(718) 622-3100 – **WEB:** www.chavelasnyc.com
Lunch & dinner daily

PRICE: ⚭

EMILY

Pizza • Neighborhood

MAP: B3

This charming Fort Greene trattoria arrives courtesy of Matt Hyland—a graduate of the Institute of Culinary Education and a former partner at Sottocasa. Named for his wife, this is a cozy, intimate reprieve from bustling Fulton Street, with a simple décor and small back bar where you can catch a glimpse of the kitchen's wood-fired pizza oven. The rustic tables bustle with young families from the neighborhood.

Whet your appetite with Asian-inspired small plates like sticky-spicy Korean-style wings or tender Sichuan pork ribs before ordering one of the lip-smacking pizzas listed as reds, pinks (vodka sauce) and greens (tomatillo sauce). Or, head straight for the epic grass-fed, dry-aged burger with caramelized onions and Grafton cheddar.

919 Fulton St. (bet. Clinton & Waverly Aves.)
Clinton - Washington Avs
(347) 844-9588 — **WEB:** www.pizzalovesemily.com
Lunch Sat - Sun Dinner nightly **PRICE:** $$

EVELINA

Italian • Trattoria

MAP: A3

As if this hipster nest needed another reminder that there is really great Italian food in this neighborhood, the "team" behind Emporio, Aurora and Baker & Co. swoops in to make the day even more delicious in Fort Greene. Of course, thanks is in large part due to the kitchen as it ensures that the menu focuses on authentic items. The convivial room is tight but no one seems to notice once the food arrives. Italian-speaking servers pamper guests with such effortless hospitality, making everyone feel special.

Highlights unveil charred trumpet mushrooms with ricotta and black garlic, as well as risotto that is an ideal rendition of cacio e pepe with the addition of shrimp for a bit of ocean flavor. Finish with a lineup of simple desserts, including biscotti.

211 DeKalb Ave. (at Adelphi St.)
Clinton - Washington Avs
(929) 298-0209 — **WEB:** www.evelinabk.com
Lunch Sat - Sun Dinner nightly **PRICE:** $$

FALANSAI

Vietnamese • Simple

MAP: C2

Just say yes should someone invite you to sample the amazing food at Falansai. Bay Area food enthusiasts might recognize Chef/owner Henry Trieu from his days cooking at the popular Slanted Door; here at Falansai, a pretty little nook that feels miles from the gritty streets surrounding it, Trieu elevates the already complex Vietnamese cuisine to the next level. The results will knock your socks off—honestly, you might never look at a bánh mì the same way again.

Don't miss the tender shrimp fritters, enveloped by mashed cassava and chilies; fresh papaya salad laced with mint leaves, sweet poached shrimp, and crushed toasted peanuts; or a surprisingly complex and special coconut curry bobbing with sweet kabocha squash, Thai eggplant and tender carrots.

112 Harrison Pl. (at Porter Ave.)
Morgan Av
(347) 599-1190 — **WEB:** www.falansai.com
Lunch Tue - Fri Dinner Tue - Sun

PRICE: $$

GLADY'S

Caribbean • Simple

MAP: B4

Ready to live the Caribbean dream? All it takes is a few sips of a rum cocktail at Chef/owner Michael Jacober's festive café. This turquoise-tinted destination is where locals come together for happy hour libations (the comprehensive list features bottles from Jamaica, Trinidad and Barbados) as well as for flavor-packed dishes at budget prices.

The kitchen is liberal with Jamaica's signature jerk seasoning, a magical blend of allspice, Scotch bonnet pepper and citrus that's applied to chicken, pork, seitan and even whole lobsters. The latter are kept fresh in a tank and a thrown onto a pimento wood-fired grill. Save room for the succulent bowl of curry goat with chunks of potatoes and carrots, best enjoyed with a side of coconut-scented rice and peas.

788 Franklin Ave. (at Lincoln Pl.)
Franklin Av
(718) 622-0249 — **WEB:** www.gladysnyc.com
Lunch & dinner daily

PRICE: $$

FARO ✿

American • Chic

♿ **MAP:** C2

Earth, Wheat, Fire is their motto and it is a perfect encapsulation of this concise menu, which is designed around seasonal vegetables and excellent house-made pastas. Faro is the kind of restaurant that one wants to return to—time and again.

The dining room is enveloped in glossy white, furnished with an exposed kitchen at the rear and a wood-fired oven that features prominently throughout their cooking. The overall vibe may be sophisticated and upscale, but it is also undeniably luring and ever so comfortable.

The scent of wood smoke in the air may be the ultimate amuse-bouche and an accurate prelude to the savory courses that are to follow. Here, even the most dedicated pasta master will likely be new to the squid-ink frascatelli (similar in appearance to a semolina spaetzle tinted black), which is served with exceptionally tender octopus and spicy 'nduja. Famished diners may also tuck into judiciously dressed agnolotti stuffed with ember-roasted sweet potato, followed by duck breast with rutabaga rosti, apple and crème fraîche. The chocolate dessert is a rustic delight, combining lush mousse in a dark and crumbly shortbread shell, topped with Nutella ice cream and hot fudge.

---

436 Jefferson St. (bet. St Nicholas & Wyckoff Aves.)

Jefferson St

(718) 381-8201 – **WEB:** www.farobk.com

Dinner nightly **PRICE:** $$

THE FINCH ✿

American • Chic

MAP: B3

If you've ever had Brooklyn envy, buckle your seatbelt. Tucked among rows of brownstones straight off the set of a movie, The Finch's charming location pulls at your heartstrings long before Chef Gabe McMackin's outrageously good food warms your soul.

Duck behind the bright blue façade, and things get even better: a warm staff welcomes you to a charming, rustic décor replete with wood-beamed ceilings and farmhouse chairs. At the heart of this expansive space, which sprawls out into a series of cozy nooks, is an open kitchen where the chef extraordinaire guides his team to excellence before an audience of diners seated at a Carrara marble counter.

Modern yet comforting, McMackin's dishes mix skill and personality. The food is well-executed, satisfying and carefully sourced—from tender shishito peppers, blistered to perfection, with a squirt of lemon and crunchy sea salt, to shaved lamb tongue with fennel, green olives, orange and chili. Tender green leaves of Swiss chard are pressed between thin sheets of pasta, topped with pine nuts and baked with a savory parmesan breadcrumb crust in what may be the most delicious, soul-satisfying, impossible-not-to-finish vegetable lasagna ever.

---

212 Greene Ave. (bet. Cambridge Pl. & Grand Ave.)

Classon Av

(718) 218-4444 — **WEB:** www.thefinchnyc.com

Lunch Sun Dinner nightly **PRICE:** $$$

HART'S

Contemporary • Cozy

MAP: B3

Tucked behind the elevated Franklin Avenue subway stairs, this intimate little Mediterranean venue has been causing quite a stir. A pretty slate-blue façade directs you to a small space containing whitewashed brick walls, blonde wood tables and a skylight. A handful of seats at the low marble counter face a wall of shelved liquor bottles and offer a view into the mini kitchen.

However, there is nothing mini about Chef Nick Perkins' culinary skills. In fact, he is the master of working magic out of a small kitchen. An heirloom tomato salad, laced with olive oil and crushed dried red chili, is paired with escabeche-style mussels; while a generous portion of golden pork Milanese is plated with sliced cucumber and shaved fennel for a bit of fun and flair.

506 Franklin Ave. (bet. Fulton St. & Jefferson Ave.)
Franklin Av
(718) 636-6228 — **WEB:** www.hartsbrooklyn.com
Lunch Sat - Sun Dinner Tue - Sun **PRICE:** $$

L'ANTAGONISTE

French • Bistro

MAP: C3

From the razor-sharp service staff and its charming décor (think elegantly set wood tables and banquettes), to the killer but notably traditional French menu, everything about this buzzing hangout in burgeoning Bed-Stuy is bang-on. The fact that it is surrounded by bodegas and a fast food joint simply adds to the overall intrigue.

Owner Amadeus Broger is the master of operations here and appears to have just one, single formula in mind—and that is to churn out serious food in a fun and convivial setting. Don't miss the soufflé au fromage, rendered light and frothy with nutty Comté; the tournedos Rossini, tender filet mignon over a potato pancake, topped with foie gras medallions and finished with Madeira; or the perfectly executed duck a l'orange.

238 Malcom X Blvd. (at Hancock St.)
Utica Av
(917) 966-5300 — **WEB:** www.lantagoniste.com
Lunch Sat - Sun Dinner nightly **PRICE:** $$$

LE GARAGE

French • Contemporary décor

MAP: C2

As the name implies, this chic Bushwick address once housed a garage. Nowadays, you'll find a bright and cheerful space boasting whitewashed brick walls, sleek blonde wood and sunny-yellow accents. The walls are hung with old black-and-white photographs of co-owner Catherine Allswang's previous restaurants in Paris. Now, with Le Garage, she partners with her daughter Rachel to bring a contemporary French menu to Brooklyn.

Classic dishes like leeks vinaigrette are cooked to silky perfection, and served chilled with finely diced hard-boiled egg. However, their heartier options are just as impressive: imagine the likes of slow-cooked pork cheek dressed with savory pan juices, pink grapefruit segments, braised radicchio and peppery watercress.

157 Suydam St. (bet. Central & Wilson Aves.)
Central Av
(347) 295-1700 – **WEB:** www.legaragebrooklyn.com
Lunch Sat - Sun Dinner Tue - Sun **PRICE:** $$

LOCANDA VINI E OLII

Italian • Trattoria

MAP: B3

While regulars at this beloved Clinton Hill jewel know just where to go, the uninitiated may be surprised to find it tucked underneath a sign that reads Lewis Drug Store. Old-school without feeling hyper-designed, the ambience at this re-purposed apothecary is truly special. Envision lace-covered windows, a penny-tile floor and ladder-fronted shelves filled with vintage glassware and cookbooks.

Tuscany influences the cooking here, where the diverse list of antipasti includes tripe alla Fiorentina, and the pasta is expertly prepared, like a luscious tangle of chitarra con le sarde. Salads follow entrées on the menu, but no one will raise an eyebrow if you order the baby spinach with roasted beets and pecorino before the charred poussin al mattone.

129 Gates Ave. (at Cambridge Pl.)
Clinton - Washington Avs
(718) 622-9202 – **WEB:** www.locandany.com
Dinner nightly **PRICE:** $$

METTĀ

Contemporary • Rustic

MAP: A3

This kitchen has made its mark with distinguishing open-fire cooking, searing its way through hot-off-the-grill food. Occupants inside the snugly arranged room may start with a cool bluefish tonnato, served as a dip with radishes and other market vegetables, as if in preparation for the smoky flavors that are to come. Then, grilled steaks make their arrival with chimichurri and wilted greens to combat the richness of the meat. Pair them with bronzed carrots, enriched with an herbaceous oil and farmers cheese, for a fine balance. Finish on a high note with lovage ice cream accompanied by parsnip cake.

Set on a quiet corner of Fort Greene, this fire-hot spot centers around a big-as-life kitchen that can be observed by every one of its pretty patrons.

197 Adelphi St. (at Willoughby Ave.)
Fulton St
(718) 233-9134 — **WEB:** www.mettabk.com
Dinner Tue - Sun **PRICE:** $$

MISS ADA

Middle Eastern • Chic

MAP: A3

Middle Eastern eateries are popping up faster than you can say labneh, but Miss Ada stands apart from the pack. This Fort Greene charmer delivers a one-two punch of good looks and great food. Rustic chic meets urban cool in the dining room, but wait, what's that out back? It's only the most darling backyard patio and garden beseeching you to plant yourself and stay a while.

Chef Tomer Blechman puts his own stamp on the ancient cuisine of the Middle East with hit after delicious hit. Even items that seem basic—creamy, smooth hummus and the fluffy cloud-like pita—are elevated here. Smoky octopus, so tender and fragrant, is ramped up with grassy Castelvetrano olives, while hanger steak bathed in a charred onion tahini will have you begging for more.

184 DeKalb Ave. (bet. Carlton Ave. & Cumberland St.)
Clinton - Washington Avs
(917) 909-1023 — **WEB:** www.missadanyc.com
Lunch Sun Dinner Tue - Sun **PRICE:** $$

NO. 7

American • Neighborhood

MAP: A3

With its worn-in good looks, it's no surprise that No. 7 is this neighborhood's favorite hangout—a place where a cool crowd sips at the lively bar and sink into the dining room's sumptuous, horseshoe-shaped banquette. Add to that a menu so intriguingly original, it started a movement (the brand now includes kiosks serving sandwiches and veggie burgers), and you've got a recipe for success.

A delicious alchemy is at work in this open kitchen creating the likes of braised pork shoulder-stuffed cabbage paired with grilled stone fruit panzanella. Starters and dessert here are every bit as fun as the main event. The proof is in the perfectly ripe avocado topped with smoked trout, tobiko and jalapeño oil, followed by the decadent brandy Alexander tiramisu.

7 Greene Ave. (bet. Cumberland & Fulton Sts.)

Lafayette Av

(718) 522-6370 — **WEB:** www.no7restaurant.com

Lunch Sat - Sun Dinner Tue - Sun **PRICE:** $$

PROSPECT

American • Neighborhood

MAP: A3

This Fort Greene standout offers delicious cooking and just so happens to be pretty cool, too. The beverage menu features riffs on the Negroni cocktail—one for instance substitutes reposado tequila for gin. Walls are lined with reclaimed planks of the Coney Island boardwalk, and genuinely hospitable service tames the packed house.

Quality trumps quantity in the streamlined selection of product-driven creations. A neatly arranged row of silver dollar-sized kimchi pancakes, topped with tender strands of pulled pork make an enticing starter; while toothsome and tender house-made gnocchi is plated with snap peas, sautéed wild mushrooms and sweet peas for a springtime treat. Finish with a contemporary take on banana cake enhanced with coconut cream foam.

773 Fulton St. (bet. Oxford & Portland Aves.)

Lafayette Av

(718) 596-6826 — **WEB:** www.prospectbk.com

Dinner Mon - Sat **PRICE:** $$

ROBERTA'S

Contemporary • Trendy

MAP: C2

Entering through this (now) iconic red door is like a trip through the looking glass and into Bushwick's foodie wonderland. The city's love affair with Roberta's seems stronger each year, and for good reason. Everything from the industrial space to the underground bohemian vibe epitomizes Brooklyn-chic. Takeaway is always an option, so when the wait for a table is too long, snag a porchetta sandwich to-go.

Queens native Carlo Mirarchi is the master craftsman here, turning out a range of crowning, creatively named pizzas. Speckenwolf sings with dried oregano, house-made mozzarella, thinly sliced speck and roasted cremini mushrooms, while Crispy Glover oozes with creamy Taleggio, ribbons of porky guanciale. shaved garlic, red onion and spicy chili oil.

261 Moore St. (bet. Bogart & White Sts.)

Morgan Av

(718) 417-1118 – **WEB:** www.robertaspizza.com

Lunch & dinner daily — **PRICE: $$**

SARAGHINA

Italian • Rustic

MAP: C3

If you build it, they will come: and sure enough, from the moment Saraghina opened its doors to a just-burgeoning Bed-Stuy, diners have flooded this cool, multi-room restaurant decorated with garage-sale knickknacks, old butcher signs and marmalade jars. It's downright adorable. But, the delicious food is what fills these seats.

Still best known for their irresistible pizzas, blistered to puffy perfection, the menu offers all kinds of heavenly dishes not to miss, like the fried calamari and shrimp, served with tangy lemon and aïoli; or a wood fire-roasted side of cauliflower mixed with creamy mascarpone, tart labneh and Marcona almonds.

Just around the corner, at 433 Halsey, a sister bakery serves up fresh pastries and a mean espresso all day.

435 Halsey St. (at Lewis Ave.)

Utica Av

(718) 574-0010 – **WEB:** www.saraghina.com

Lunch & dinner daily — **PRICE: $$**

SPEEDY ROMEO

American • Pizzeria

MAP: B3

Named for a racehorse and just as focused and quick, Speedy Romeo is in for a successful run. Part tavern, part roadside grill, its kitschy décor and modern touches transform this former automotive shop into a surprisingly attractive spot.

The owner benefited from years at Jean-Georges' empire, and that intelligence and experience is conveyed through the smart accents and whimsical menu that begins with Italian ingredients. Look to the wood-burning oven for smoky, meaty artichoke halves topped with lemon aïoli, sourdough crumbs, mint and peppery arugula. Take a chance on the non-traditional but utterly fantastic pizza combinations, such as the St. Louis, layering a proper crust with meats, pickled chillies and Midwestern Provel cheese.

376 Classon Ave. (at Greene Ave.)
Classon Av
(718) 230-0061 – **WEB:** www.speedyromeo.com
Lunch & dinner daily **PRICE:** $$

UOTORA

Japanese • Minimalist

MAP: B4

Lucky are those who call Crown Heights home, for Uotora is the kind of cozy and excellent sushiya we all want to call our local spot. The sparsely decorated room, lined with minimalist blonde wood, sets a serene backdrop for the real star of the show: wildly pristine fish, flown in directly from Japan.

Accordingly, their à la carte offers a few cooked items as well as a delicious lineup of plates, but the highlight is surely the sushi and sashimi, featuring fish aged in-house and prepared Edomae-style. These methods may be trending right now, but take true chops to master—and the itamae here (who hail from the esteemed Sushi of Gari) absolutely nail them. Throw in affordable prices along with a welcoming staff, and you have a hit worth a cab from the city.

1075 Bergen St. (bet. Rogers & Nostrand Aves.)
Nostrand Av
(718) 513-0724 – **WEB:** www.uotorany.com
Dinner Tue - Sun **PRICE:** $$

PARK SLOPE

DITMAS PARK · PROPSECT HEIGHTS

Bordering Prospect Park, historic Park Slope brags of fancy trattorias and chic cafés perpetually crammed with stroller-rolling parents. Set in the heart of the 'hood, **The Park Slope Food Coop** is a veteran member-operated and owned purveyor of locally farmed produce, grass-fed meat and free-range poultry. Lauded as the largest of its kind in the country, membership is offered to anyone willing to pay a small fee and work a shift of less than three hours each month. The like-minded **Grand Army Plaza Greenmarket**, held every Saturday at Prospect Park, is a shopping haven among area residents craving organic, farm-fresh produce as well as cooking programs and demonstrations to boot. Close at hand on Flatbush Avenue, **Bklyn Larder** is an artisanal provisions store that sells every imaginable type of cheese, meat, snack, beverage and sweet. In Kensington, the **Carnival Fresh Market** is open 24-hours a day and stocks a dizzying array of items—from Pakistan and the Middle East all the way to

Mexico and Russia—thereby catering to its melting-pot community. Over in Windsor Terrace, **Brancaccio's Food Shop** is a serious dine-in and take-out destination that keeps the crowds returning for more Italian-American eats (think caponata and meatballs) or even breakfast specials highlighting eggs, potatoes, cheese and meats. Ramen is yet another wildly popular comfort food in this Brooklyn nook, so during those cold and wintry days, head to **Chuko's** in Prospect Heights for an impressive selection, complete with vegetarian options that are bound to stun. The juicy dumplings at **East Wind Snack Shop** are just right for chasing away those afternoon hunger pangs; and pies are all the rage at **Four & Twenty Blackbirds**. Of course, white chocolate-coconut rolls and other Caribbean treats will always remain front and center at **Allan's Bakery.** Finally, go big or go home with a bold cup of tea (or coffee) at **Qathra Cafe**.

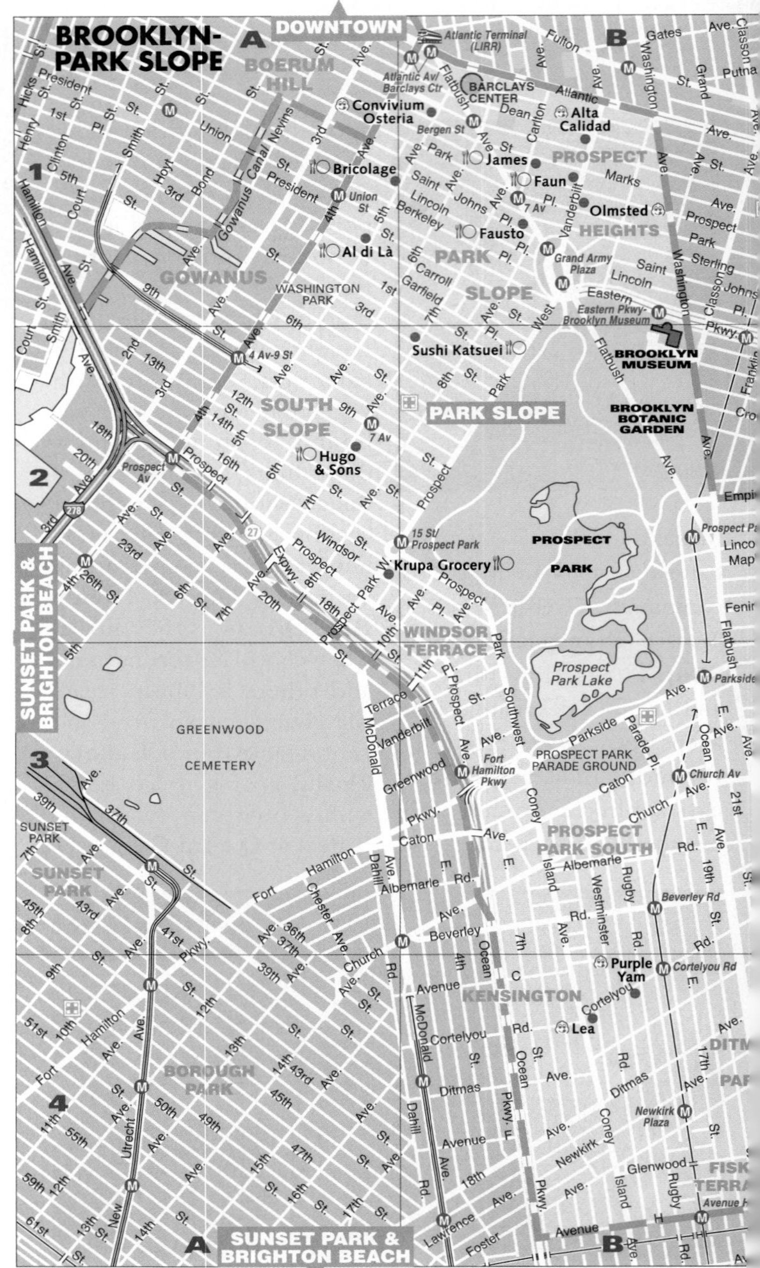
BROOKLYN-PARK SLOPE
DOWNTOWN
SUNSET PARK & BRIGHTON BEACH
BOERUM HILL
GOWANUS
PARK SLOPE
SOUTH SLOPE
PROSPECT HEIGHTS
WINDSOR TERRACE
PROSPECT PARK SOUTH
KENSINGTON
SUNSET PARK
BOROUGH PARK
WASHINGTON PARK
GREENWOOD CEMETERY
PROSPECT PARK
Prospect Park Lake
PROSPECT PARK PARADE GROUND
BROOKLYN MUSEUM
BROOKLYN BOTANIC GARDEN
BARCLAYS CENTER
Atlantic Terminal (LIRR)
Convivium Osteria
Alta Calidad
Bricolage
James
Faun
Olmsted
Fausto
Al di Là
Sushi Katsuei
Hugo & Sons
Krupa Grocery
Purple Yam
Lea

FORT GREENE & BUSHWICK
SUNSET PARK & BRIGHTON BEACH
BEDFORD STUYVESANT
CROWN HEIGHTS
WINGATE
EAST FLATBUSH
BROWNSVILLE
REMSEN VILLAGE
FARRAGUT
FLATLANDS
HOLY CROSS CEMETERY
LINCOLN TERRACE PARK
WINGATE PARK
PAERDEGAT PARK
BROOKLYN COLLEGE
Paerdegat Basin
Sterling St
Winthrop St
Church Av
Beverley Rd
Newkirk Av
Flatbush Av/ Brooklyn College

AL DI LÀ

Italian • Neighborhood

MAP: A1

When Al di Là opened nearly twenty years ago, it was a forward-thinking husband-and-wife operation serving rustic food to a gentrifying neighborhood. Today, it is every local's favorite spot for soul-satisfying pastas. This is a kitchen that is cherished by that special, old-school sort of diner—who may be found lunching on a duo of insalata di farro tossed with roasted beets, red onion, spinach, goat cheese and toasted pistachios paired with a daily panino of pork belly with pickles, horseradish mayo and salsa verde. Tables are laden with hearty and chewy ricotta cavatelli with smoky and enticingly charred cauliflower, anchovies, chili and tomato sauce finished with grated pecorino.

The room may show wear, but consider that part of its charm.

248 Fifth Ave. (at Carroll St.)
Union St
(718) 783-4565 — **WEB:** www.aldilatrattoria.com
Lunch & dinner daily **PRICE:** $$

ALTA CALIDAD

Mexican • Contemporary décor

MAP: B1

What's in a name? Well, at Akhtar Nawab's contemporary Mexican restaurant, it's "high quality." Literally.

This supremely talented chef takes thoroughly Mexican dishes and shakes them up just enough for a satisfying surprise. His creativity is boundless but never veers out of focus. Case in point? Crispy skate tacos smothered with smoky salsa and pickled ramps or the pumpkin blossom quesadilla. Other standouts include the oh-so-tender lamb ribs, shellacked in Coca-Cola for that glorious hint of caramel, as well as the meaty fluke ceviche enhanced by habanero and mandarin. Like Nawab's creativity at the burner, the menu is seemingly limitless, offering an array of plates you'll want to sample. Bring a friend, or three, to justify ordering more treats.

552 Vanderbilt Ave. (at Dean St.)
Bergen St (Flatbush Ave.)
(718) 622-1111 — **WEB:** www.altacalidadbk.com
Lunch Thu – Sun Dinner nightly **PRICE:** $$

BRICOLAGE

Vietnamese • Simple

MAP: A1

This Vietnamese gem is overseen and owned by husband-and-wife team, Edward and Lien Lin, who are alums of SF's popular Slanted Door. Tucked into a simple wood-and-exposed-brick space in family-friendly Park Slope, this open kitchen bustles with energy as diners huddle in lively conversation. Bricolage bills itself as a gastropub (and the creative cocktails are certainly fantastic), but make no mistake—this is modern, next-level bar food.

Crispy, golden imperial rolls are routinely churned out of the kitchen and arrive stuffed with glass noodles, crunchy cabbage, earthy mushrooms and minced pork. Then look forward to "Unshaking Beef," laced in a sweet and salty marinade, seared to tender, juicy perfection and served alongside a peppery watercress salad.

162 Fifth Ave. (bet. Degraw & Douglass Sts.)
Union St
(718) 230-1835 — **WEB:** www.bricolage.nyc
Lunch & dinner daily

PRICE: $$

CONVIVIUM OSTERIA

Italian • Rustic

MAP: B1

Brought to you by Chef/owners Carlo and Michelle Pulixi, this cozy Italian storefront has been known to stop passersby in their tracks. At a time when fast-casual expansions are dominating the culinary landscape, this osteria—laden with gleaming copper pots and rustic clay urns to reflect the chef's Sardinian home—is a refreshing find.

The menu is built around carefully sourced meats and produce that are deftly prepared and presented. Try the braised artichoke, delicately dressed with olive oil, garlic and herbs. Then, rabbit imbued with prosciutto, rosemary and olives, is an uncommonly good pleasure that is set over crostini di polenta. The cooking is streamlined and authentic, but pay equal attention to their delicious daily specials.

68 Fifth Ave. (bet. Bergen St. & St Marks Ave.)
Bergen St (Flatbush Ave.)
(718) 857-1833 — **WEB:** www.convivium-osteria.com
Dinner nightly

PRICE: $$

FAUN

Contemporary • Cozy

MAP: B1

Chef Brian Leth has been at the helm of this delicious restaurant for a while now. Donning a pale palette with marble surfaces and an open kitchen, Faun is warm, intimate and tranquil, complete with a long bar for socializing and the kind of charming backyard diners clamor for on warm days.

The kitchen turns out a wonderful, well-priced prix-fixe, where for $60 a pop, diners can dig into three ample courses. Begin with crisp marrow «arancini» poised atop a fava bean pureé and coddled with trout roe. Homemade pastas like the cresta di gallo nero may look dark but sports a light and saline tomato sauce studded with seafood and capers. For dessert, a soft vanilla bean-panna cotta is served with a crunchy pumpkin-seed cracker for perfect symmetry and flavor.

606 Vanderbilt Ave. (bet. Prospect Pl. & St. Marks Ave.)
Bergen St (Flatbush Ave.)
(718) 576-6120 — **WEB:** www.faun.nyc
Dinner Tue - Sun

PRICE: $$

FAUSTO

Italian • Contemporary décor

MAP: B1

Having dispensed with its previous incarnation, this attractive spot has remerged as a sleek and upscale restaurant. Fausto may serve consistently delicious Italian-influenced food, but its overall ethos is guided by restaurateur (and sommelier), Joe Campanale.

The kitchen showcases a distinctive take on Southern regional fare that ensures each bowl of pasta is a showstopper. Find evidence of this in the whole-wheat bigoli al torchio, twirled with duck ragù and Piave Vecchio. But regardless of what you eat, be sure to start your meal with roasted heirloom vegetables set atop goat cheese with pistachios and a drizzle of honey. Forge ahead with impressive fish and seafood items, before closing out on a superb cheese course in lieu of dessert.

348 Flatbush Ave. (bet. Eighth Ave. & Sterling Pl.)
Grand Army Plaza
(917) 909-1427 — **WEB:** www.faustobrooklyn.com
Dinner nightly

PRICE: $$$

HUGO & SONS

Italian • Neighborhood

MAP: A2

Hugo & Sons may contain every requisite detail that conjures the look of rustic Italian hospitality straight from the heart of Park Slope, thanks to exposed brick, penny-tiled floors and wood planters. Yet this is a special little family-focused place, where the skilled chef/owner, Andrea Taormina, is attentive and hands-on.

The simple and uncomplicated cooking highlights the best of each ingredient. Crispy Brussels sprouts are true to their name, with loose and lightly charred outer layers, tender and moist within, finished with a zing of lemon zest, parsley, and aïoli. Heartier courses are thoroughly delicious, especially the pork braciole lined with breadcrumbs, pine nuts, raisins and hard-cooked egg, then seared and served in a chunky tomato sauce.

367 Seventh Ave. (at 11th St.)
7 Av (9th St.)
(718) 499-0020 — **WEB:** www.hugoandsons.com
Lunch Sat - Sun Dinner nightly **PRICE:** $$

JAMES

American • Bistro

MAP: B1

This romantic restaurant holds a nostalgic sort of charm, as though it's been a fixture on the corner for a hundred years. It hasn't, of course, but its design incorporating the likes of a pressed-tin ceiling, silver bowls filled with bright citrus, whitewashed exposed brick walls and tufted leather banquettes lend it an old-school sort of sophistication.

Executive Chef Bryan Calvert pulls most of the herbs, that are featured on plates set right before you, from the rooftop garden. Dishes wander from sautéed Carolina shrimp laid over creamy "polenta" to crispy honey-glazed pork belly—all of them divine. Carnivores will relish their popular burger night, which the restaurant presents every Monday, with an expanded burger menu and happy hour prices all night.

605 Carlton Ave. (at St. Marks Ave.)
7 Av (Flatbush Ave.)
(718) 942-4255 — **WEB:** www.jamesrestaurantny.com
Lunch Sat - Sun Dinner nightly **PRICE:** $$

KRUPA GROCERY

American • Neighborhood

MAP: A2

Since its arrival on the scene, Krupa Grocery has been a hit, and thereby, earned a steady roster of regulars. Owner Peter Cooke's cooking is so simple and perfectly calibrated, that it's hard to miss. Get things started with country toast, served alongside delicious spreads like smashed pea and fava bean with pecorino, tarragon vinaigrette and pea leaves; or whipped lardo with radish, caper salad and parsley. For dinner, try buttermilk-fried skate set over cracked hominy with basil seeds and salsa verde. Brunch is also a slam dunk here and is alone worth the visit.

Designed with a long industrial bar that's ideal for solo eating or lingering couples, the interior is effortlessly cool, but the place to be come summer is undoubtedly the gorgeous backyard.

231 Prospect Park West (bet. 16th St. & Windsor Pl.)
15 St - Prospect Park
(718) 709-7098 – **WEB:** www.krupagrocery.com
Lunch Wed - Mon Dinner nightly **PRICE:** $$

LEA

Italian • Neighborhood

MAP: B4

You'll fall hard and fast for Lea, an inviting spot with solid Italian-leaning food. Sidewalk seats are charming but come inside to properly admire the beauty of this airy space dominated by a wood-burning oven. It's imported from Naples, of course, and that shows in their signature delicately crisp pizzas.

The Kingpin topped with hand-crushed tomatoes, fior di latte and prosciutto, for instance, will have carb fans addicted. Then, ribbons of pappardelle are tossed with Swiss chard, green olives and raisins for a deliciously balanced creation. Desserts too earn their rightful place here, as evidenced by the cheesecake. Drizzled with honey and sprinkled with pistachio, Lea's slice is uniquely Italian, especially when paired with a Sicilian frappato.

1022 Cortelyou Rd. (at Stratford Rd.)
Cortelyou Rd
(718) 928-7100 – **WEB:** www.leabrooklyn.com
Lunch & dinner daily **PRICE:** $$

OLMSTED

Contemporary • Trendy

MAP: B1

Olmsted hasn't lost any of its luster, with Brooklynites continuing to pack its ever-hip and happening space. Reservations are a challenge, but those lucky enough to nab a seat are treated to Chef Greg Baxtrom's concise and thoughtfully conceived menu of starters and entrées.

Forget farm to table; this kitchen is backyard to table thanks to a blooming and expanded vegetable and herb garden. Creativity is abundant, as seen in snap pea sushi, which subs out rice for raw peas; and lobster thermidor with meaty crackers alongside a frothy lobster-Gruyère dip. While the carte changes often, a few constants remain, like the Thai green papaya salad tweaked with shaved asparagus, or a carrot crêpe draped over clams and plated on an orange dish—natch.

659 Vanderbilt Ave. (bet. Park & Prospect Pls.)
Grand Army Plaza
(718) 552-2610 – **WEB:** www.olmstednyc.com
Dinner nightly

PRICE: $$

PURPLE YAM

Asian • Simple

MAP: B4

Owners Amy Besa and Romy Dorotan mix and match Southeast Asian dishes in such an appealing way at this neighborhood café, you'll have trouble figuring out what not to order. So follow the lead from the crowd—a smart, urbane mix of neighborhood types and savvy gourmands—and try a little bit of everything by sharing. Begin with pa jun, a delicious Korean scallion-and-shrimp pancake, and then move on to tender oxtail kare-kare, braised in peanut sauce and loaded with adobo, root vegetables and fermented fish paste. Other hits include the deliciously tangy and garlicky chicken adobo served with a refreshing green mango salad. Save room for dessert, with alluring selections ranging from champorrado to housemade ice creams, sorbets and even infused shochu.

1314 Cortelyou Rd. (bet. Argyle & Rugby Rds.)
Cortelyou Rd
(718) 940-8188 – **WEB:** www.purpleyamnyc.com
Lunch Sat - Sun Dinner nightly

PRICE: $$

SUSHI KATSUEI

Japanese • Minimalist

MAP: B2

Sushi Katsuei does Park Slope proud flaunting some of the borough's best sushi, expertly seasoned and sliced. Humming with locals, families and their kids in tow, the mood here is always upbeat and warm. While the counter appears to be reserved for their regular diners, tables are attended to by a cadre of informed servers. The chefs know their stuff as they showcase quality fish, but the menu is equally well-suited to those who just want a spicy tuna roll or a cooked dish. Most stray from the pedestrian and surrender to the omakase, where you will be rewarded with a parade of elevated sushi and sashimi. Tempura dishes are just as enticing, especially the naturally sweet roasted pumpkin.

Prices are fantastic for such high quality food.

210 Seventh Ave. (at 3rd St.)
7 Av (9th St.)
(718) 788-5338 – **WEB:** www.sushikatsuei.com
Lunch Sat - Sun Dinner nightly **PRICE:** $$

SUNSET PARK & BRIGHTON BEACH

BAY RIDGE · RED HOOK

Red Hook rests on Brooklyn's waterfront, where diligent locals and responsible residents have transformed the area's aged piers and deserted warehouses into cool breweries, bakeries and bistros. Following this lead, the **Red Hook Lobster Pound** is a popular hangout for seafood fans, but if sugar is what you favor, then **Baked** is best, perhaps followed by **Steve's Authentic Key Lime Pie**. Close the deal at **Cacao Prieto**, widely cherished for its family farm-sourced chocolates and spirits. Just as **Red Hook Village Farmer's Market** (open on Saturdays) brings pristine produce from its Community Farm to the locality, trucks and tents in **Red Hook Ball Fields** cater to natives in the know with delicious Central American and Caribbean cuisine. Dining destinations in their own right, these diners-on-wheels may only be parked on weekends from May through October, but promise to leave an impression that lasts year-round. Meanwhile, carnivores on a mission venture out east to Gowanus where **Fletcher's Brooklyn Barbecue** proffers tons of variety and quality. Not far behind, Bensonhurst best-seller—**Bari Pork Store**—sticks to perfecting the pig. Foodies can also be found scouring the shelves of **G & S Salumeria and Pork Store** for delicious cold cuts to be stuffed into hearty sandwiches. However, even flesh fiends need a break, perhaps at **Four**

& Twenty Blackbirds, which is a bakeshop flaunting the best black bottom oatmeal pie in town. Others may head toward **Raaka Chocolate** showcasing beans in all their glory, while also ensuring a healthy relationship with the environment. Pair these sweets with cherries from **Dell's Maraschino** and know you're in for a tantalizing treat.

An afternoon in Sunset Park is a must—especially for mouthwatering Mexican flavors. Some take their tacos to this nabe's namesake park for one-of-a-kind views of the Manhattan skyline. Others cool off with an original ice pop (paleta) at **Sley Deli**—an authentic grocer booming with business in Borough Park. Of course, die-hard butter cookie fans can't imagine going a day without a whiff from **St. Anthony's Bakery**. Across from Maimonides Medical Center, **Fei Long Market** is a giant emporium flooded with Asian gourmands in search of dried squid, eel and other such exotic things. Slightly south, where Mexico meets China, sidewalks teem with vendors steaming tofu and fishmongers purveying wonderfully offbeat eats—bullfrog anyone? More mainstream but equally popular is **Ba Xuyên**, a modest storefront revered for its deliciously crusty bánh mì. Moving from the Far East to a flock of kosher restaurants, **Di Fara** is a favored pizzeria with a mini offshoot (**MD Kitchen**) in Midwood. **Totonno's Pizza** is another sought-after haunt for Neapolitan-style pies; and **Joe's of Avenue U** is divine for crispy chickpea panelle. Brighton Beach is at the southernmost tip of Brooklyn, and best known for its borscht and blintzes. This dominantly Russian quarter cradles a number of restaurants that churn out staples for its patrons packed within. But for a true alfresco snack to tote, **Gold Label International Food** remains unrivaled. Speaking of the outdoors, if a stroll along the Coney Island boardwalk doesn't trigger a sense of nostalgia for summers by the beach, an all-beef hot dog from the original **Nathan's Famous** stand offers a slice of Americana that everyone is bound to love. Couple these goodies with juicy kielbasa from **Jubilat Provisions** for a true-blue meat feast. Customs, traditions and cuisine all come alive in culinary bastion, **Moldova**; while the wistful scene at **Octopus Garden** is never-ending—with Italian regulars stocking up on goods for the Christmas Feast of the Seven Fishes. Also settled within this Eastern European enclave is **Mansoura**, a Syrian institution proudly preparing savories and pastries. **Le Sajj** dishes up Lebanese food with live tunes (on Saturdays); and across the way, local sensation **Lindenwood Diner** is beloved for its liberally spiced Caribbean-Latin cuisine. Of course, while there is no confusing the Chesapeake with Sheepshead Bay, **Randazzo's Clam Bar** promises to provide diners with a superior seafood experience. However, just in case you forget that beef is always king here, there are big, bold flavors to be had at **Brennan & Carr**—where the menu doesn't change, but New Yorkers love it all the same.

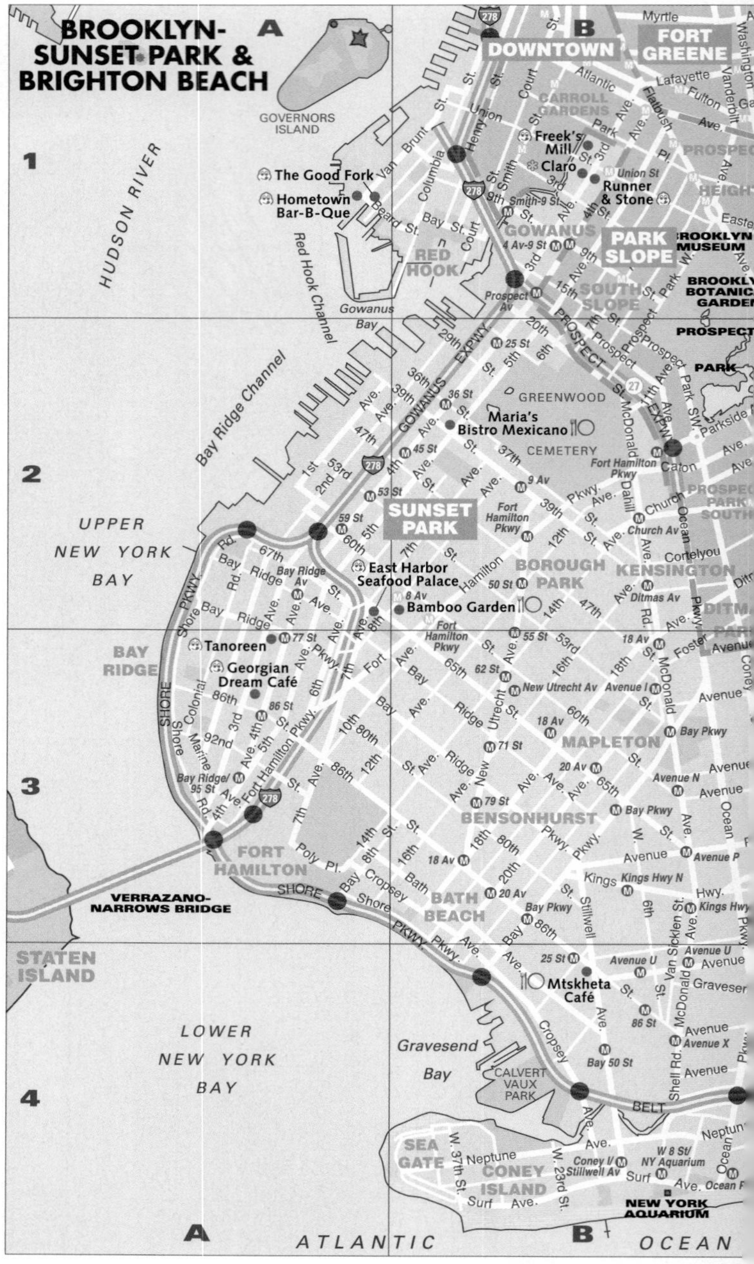

BROOKLYN-SUNSET PARK & BRIGHTON BEACH
GOVERNORS ISLAND
HUDSON RIVER
DOWNTOWN
FORT GREENE
CARROLL GARDENS
The Good Fork
Hometown Bar-B-Que
Freek's Mill
Claro
Runner & Stone
GOWANUS
RED HOOK
PARK SLOPE
SOUTH SLOPE
BROOKLYN MUSEUM
BROOKLYN BOTANIC GARDEN
PROSPECT PARK
Gowanus Bay
Red Hook Channel
Bay Ridge Channel
GREENWOOD CEMETERY
Maria's Bistro Mexicano
SUNSET PARK
UPPER NEW YORK BAY
East Harbor Seafood Palace
Bamboo Garden
BOROUGH PARK
KENSINGTON
BAY RIDGE
Tanoreen
Georgian Dream Café
MAPLETON
BENSONHURST
FORT HAMILTON
VERRAZANO-NARROWS BRIDGE
BATH BEACH
STATEN ISLAND
Mtskheta Café
LOWER NEW YORK BAY
Gravesend Bay
CALVERT VAUX PARK
SEA GATE
CONEY ISLAND
NEW YORK AQUARIUM
ATLANTIC OCEAN

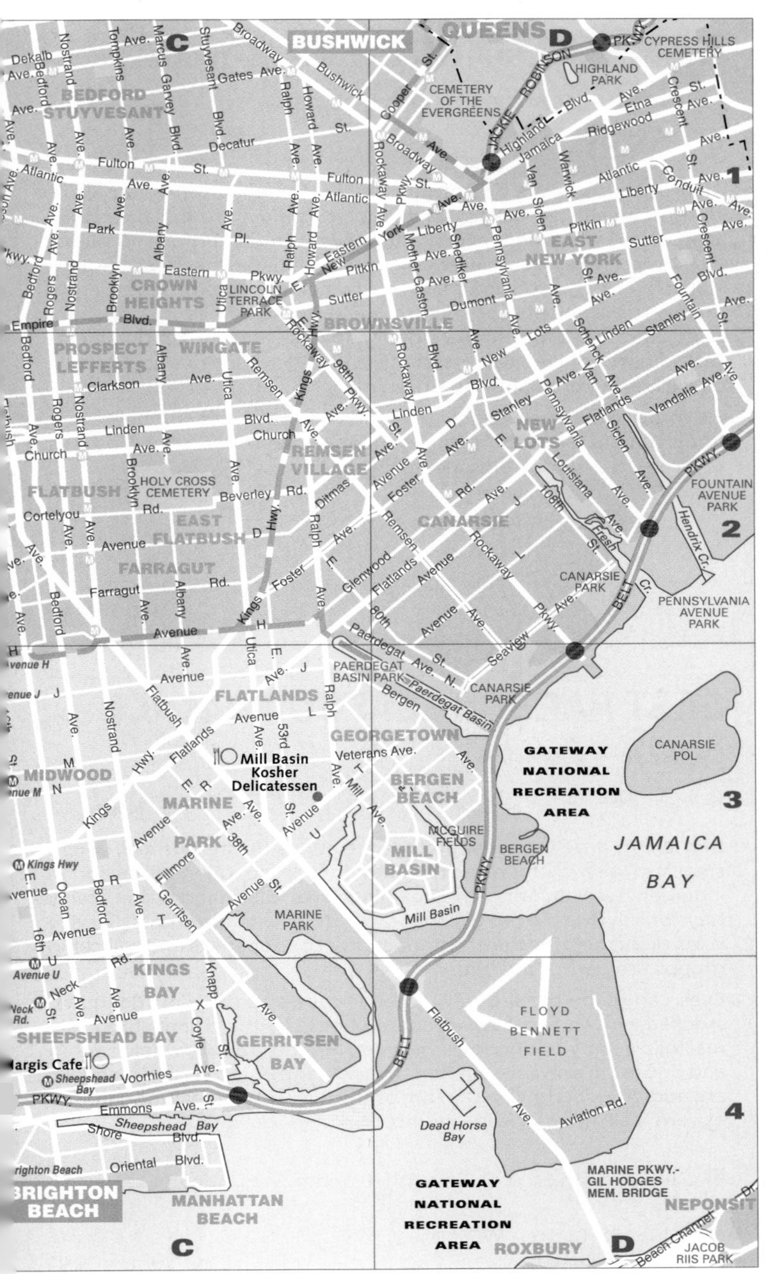
QUEENS
BUSHWICK
BEDFORD STUYVESANT
CYPRESS HILLS CEMETERY
HIGHLAND PARK
CEMETERY OF THE EVERGREENS
EAST NEW YORK
CROWN HEIGHTS
LINCOLN TERRACE PARK
BROWNSVILLE
PROSPECT LEFFERTS
WINGATE
REMSEN VILLAGE
NEW LOTS
FLATBUSH
HOLY CROSS CEMETERY
EAST FLATBUSH
FARRAGUT
CANARSIE
FOUNTAIN AVENUE PARK
CANARSIE PARK
PENNSYLVANIA AVENUE PARK
PAERDEGAT BASIN PARK
FLATLANDS
GEORGETOWN
Mill Basin Kosher Delicatessen
MIDWOOD
MARINE PARK
BERGEN BEACH
MCGUIRE FIELDS
MILL BASIN
GATEWAY NATIONAL RECREATION AREA
CANARSIE POL
JAMAICA BAY
KINGS BAY
SHEEPSHEAD BAY
GERRITSEN BAY
FLOYD BENNETT FIELD
Dead Horse Bay
BRIGHTON BEACH
MANHATTAN BEACH
MARINE PKWY.-GIL HODGES MEM. BRIDGE
NEPONSIT
ROXBURY
JACOB RIIS PARK

BAMBOO GARDEN

Chinese • Family

MAP: B2

Just because this is one of Sunset Park's most cherished parlors doesn't mean she looks tired. In fact, this dining room is as dolled up as ever, with chandeliers, a floral-patterned carpet and plenty of mirrors. Take a seat and within seconds that dim sum cart will be rolled over. Go ahead and try to refuse the goods from these friendly ladies. They win out every time, guiding you to try pillowy pork buns filled with sweet and smoky pork or spinach and shrimp dumplings bursting with chives. Other standouts include crispy rice noodle rolls, as well as the pork and shrimp siu mai.

Be forewarned however, as weekends get busy and competitive as items run out. Spot something you like? Snag it now or risk losing it forever—to a worthy opponent...er...diner.

6409 Eighth Ave. (at 64th St.)

8 Av

(718) 238-1122 – **WEB:** N/A

Lunch & dinner daily

PRICE:

EAST HARBOR SEAFOOD PALACE

Chinese • Family

MAP: A2

Dim sum is a well-orchestrated dance at this boisterous hall, where small crowds wait for a spot at one of the large round tables for an indulgent weekend brunch. Steaming carts roll by and waiters ferry trays briskly into the red dining room with shiny gold accents. Service is quick but helpful; the constant clatter of chopsticks and rollicking groups are part of the fun.

Eyes can guide the ordering when it comes to the dim sum carts, stocked with authentically prepared bites. Try the plump shrimp siu mai followed by rice noodles wrapped around crunchy whole shrimp and doused in a sweet-salty soy sauce. Snappy, stir-fried green beans are addictively crunchy. Don't miss the Singapore mei fun, a mound of vermicelli noodles with shrimp, pork and scallions.

714-726 65th St. (bet. Seventh & Eighth Aves.)

8 Av

(718) 765-0098 – **WEB:** N/A

Lunch & dinner daily

PRICE: $$

CLARO ✿

Mexican • Cozy

MAP: B1

Oaxaca by way of Gowanus? When it's this seriously delicious, you bet. Arriving courtesy of Chef/co-owners Chad Shaner and T.J. Steele along with partner, J.T. Stewart, this Mexican charmer is an instant hit. Locals are particularly quick to head to the restaurant's breezy backyard, where groups take to the clever mezcal-focused cocktail list. Of course, as word of the delicious food gets out, even more fans will follow.

The interior is small and stars a wood-fired oven, bar up front, smattering of tables, as well as a garden complete with its own kitchen. Service is bright, friendly and accessible, but the real draw is their excellent Oaxacan dishes, rendered true to their classical roots in some and then spun with creative riffs in others.

The barbacoa is a point of pride and the kitchen only cooks so much of it daily, so plan to get here early if you intend to feast on this popular item. Savory barbacoa tacos are then laced with spicy green salsa and paired with a bowl of soulful consommé. Other high points include tender seared octopus with bacon and pickled chilies piled on to crispy tortillas. Don't forget about the black beans though, which boast that perfect combo of smoke and heat.

---

284 Third Ave. (bet. Carroll & President Sts.)

Union St

(347) 721-3126 — **WEB:** www.clarobk.com

Lunch Sat - Sun Dinner nightly

PRICE: $$

FREEK'S MILL

American • Brasserie

MAP: B1

Walking down the quiet and industrial Nevins Street, you'd never expect to find a restaurant as energetic and inviting as Freek's Mill. Inside, you'll find a cozy, intimate space with exposed brick walls, filament light bulbs and a wood-burning oven in the back of the dining room—it's that Brooklyn feel we've come to know and love, and this contemporary American small plates spot does it just so.

The cuisine is seasonal, light and fresh, with each plate delivering something unique and unexpected. For a dish with full throttle flavor, opt for the kale and ricotta agnolotti with cubes of bacon and brunoised apple. Then prepare to dig in to the most heartbreakingly tender pork jowl with an appealingly gelatinous texture and a kick of heat.

285 Nevins St. (at Sackett St.)
Union St
(718) 852-3000 — **WEB:** www.freeksmill.com
Lunch Sat - Sun Dinner Tue - Sun

PRICE: $$

GEORGIAN DREAM CAFÉ

Central Asian • Simple

MAP: A3

Gut-busting breads, heartwarming soups and juicy kebabs—this is the stuff of dreams—and after just one meal at this dreamy café, you'll be counting the days until your return. The interior has been designed to mimic a quaint village, right down to the ersatz-style street lights and balconies. It also oozes comfort before you've even taken your first bite of a soft dumpling.

Begin with the assorted pkhali, three salads composed of chopped green beans, spinach, walnuts and leeks, all spiced to the hilt. Winter's chill doesn't have a chance after you've devoured the chakapuli soup, but really, nothing says Georgian food quite like the khachapuri acharuli, a classic baked bread cradling a buttery, cheesy center that is as delectable as it sounds.

8309 Third Ave. (at 83rd St.)
86 St
(718) 333-5363 — **WEB:** www.georgiandreamrestaurant.com
Lunch & dinner daily

PRICE:

THE GOOD FORK

Contemporary • Neighborhood

MAP: A1

The Good Fork is the perfect neighborhood restaurant with a serious local following. Located on food-centric Van Brunt Street near the Red Hook Waterfront, this inviting spot swaps New York pretense for pure passion—it's the dream of a married couple who built the restaurant from scratch, literally. Co-owner Ben Schneider crafted the space, while his classically trained wife, Chef Sohui Kim, helms the kitchen.

Her cuisine emphasizes Korean and other global flavors, as well as a commitment to locality. Homemade dumplings are filled with nicely seasoned pork, crisped and served with a black vinegar dipping sauce. Scallion pancakes are a staple with their umami wonder, while true happiness is a warm bowl of the plump coconut milk-scented mussels.

391 Van Brunt St. (bet. Coffey & Van Dyke Sts.)
Smith - 9 Sts (& Bus B61)
(718) 643-6636 — **WEB:** www.goodfork.com
Lunch Sat - Sun Dinner Tue - Sun

PRICE: $$

HOMETOWN BAR-B-QUE

Barbecue • Rustic

MAP: A1

The trek to Red Hook is worth it once you get a taste of this Texas 'cue. Pitmaster Bill Durney is doing the Longhorn State proud with his smoked brisket that will rock your world. Some dishes, like the Korean sticky ribs, are laced with worldly influences, while old-time classics like banana pudding are done just right.

Sausages snap and explode with juice and chili-spiced bite (each is sold by the plump quarter-pound link), and then there is the lamb belly. Piled high and dripping with glistening fat, it is equal parts intensely smoky and distinctly gamey.

The warehouse-like space is clad in repurposed wood and furnished with communal picnic tables that lend an intimate and friendly vibe. Water Taxi is the easiest way here from Manhattan.

454 Van Brunt St. (entrance on Reed St.)
Smith - 9 Sts (& Bus B61)
(347) 294-4644 — **WEB:** www.hometownbarbque.com
Lunch & dinner Tue - Sun

PRICE: $$

MARIA'S BISTRO MEXICANO

Mexican • Colorful

MAP: B2

In a vibrant pocket of Brooklyn, locals flock to this timeworn façade for generous portions of fresh and well-priced Mexican cuisine. Complete with a backyard, the décor of this quirky neighborhood staple is distinctly authentic, from its bright woven textiles and vibrant pink walls, to lava rock molcajetes that top each table.

Start your meal with a delicious and filling chorizo taco topped with onion, tomato, and cilantro. Crepas de elote are stuffed with bits of tender onion, juicy corn and poblano peppers. The chile poblano is a house specialty that satisfies with its one-two punch: one is plumped with a savory combination of cheeses, while another is stuffed with a beguiling mixture of chicken, almonds, diced plantain and crunchy apple.

886 Fifth Ave. (bet. 38th & 39th Sts.)
36 St
(718) 438-1608 — **WEB:** N/A
Lunch & dinner daily

PRICE: $$

MILL BASIN KOSHER DELICATESSEN

Deli • Family

MAP: C3

This middle-aged Brooklyn treasure is as old-school as it gets, and though it's a bit of a trek to Mill Basin, anyone looking for a true-blue Jewish deli won't think twice. Part deli counter, part artsy dining room and part party hall, Mark Schachner's beloved spot serves up all the classics—from beef tongue sandwiches to gefilte fish.

The wildly overstuffed sandwiches (all served with homemade pickles and coleslaw) are a home run, as in soft rye bread with pastrami, which is steamed not once but twice, leaving the meat juicy yet hardly fatty. Then dive into a heap of thin latke chips that are fried until golden-brown, crunchy on the outside, tender and chewy on the inside. Garnished with a mound of shiny caramelized onions, this is a sweet treat indeed.

5823 Avenue T (bet. 58th & 59th Sts.)
(718) 241-4910 — **WEB:** www.millbasindeli.com
Lunch & dinner daily

PRICE: $$

MTSKHETA CAFÉ

Central Asian • Simple

MAP: B4

Bordering Bath Beach, Mtskheta Café pumps out Georgian classics in a green-hued, faux-brick dining room, complete with paper napkins, a campy jungle mural and TV looping foreign music videos. While the décor may be lacking, the service and food excel, setting this impossible-to-pronounce restaurant apart from the nearby bodegas and elevated subway tracks.

Whether or not you can deduce what's on the Cyrillic-scripted menu, friendly servers stand by, directing guests to native dishes like badrijani, an almost overwhelming helping of eggplant stuffed with walnut purée. But oh that fried khinkali, a homestyle dish composed of browned dumplings filled with broth and a beef meatball. Once dipped into sour cream, it's worth every second of the 30-minute wait.

2568 86th St. (bet. Bay 41st St. & Stillwell Ave.)
25 Av
(718) 676-1868 — **WEB:** N/A
Lunch & dinner Thu - Tue

PRICE: ⊜

NARGIS CAFE

Central Asian • Family

MAP: C4

This industrial strip is ground zero for Central Asian hot spots, where Nargis Cafe endures as a real treat. Composed of a front bar area and larger, brighter dining room, the entire space is brought together with marvelous Persian rugs and exotic pierced-metal sconces.

Nargis hits a strong stride among the locals for its convivial vibe and unique repertoire of dishes that may include a bojon salad of smoky eggplant tossed with garlic, peppers, carrots and cucumber. Kebabs are taken seriously here, so try the succulent lamb with chopped onion and dill. Uzbek plov studded with chickpeas, lamb and raisins is simple but imperative. For dessert, the honey-sweet chak-chak is fried but surprisingly light and exquisitely indulgent.

2818 Coney Island Ave. (bet. Kathleen Pl. & Avenue Z)
Sheepshead Bay
(718) 872-7888 — **WEB:** www.nargiscafe.com
Lunch & dinner daily

PRICE: $$

RUNNER & STONE

Contemporary • Neighborhood

MAP: B1

This ambitious operation has a clear sense of purpose. Its name refers to the two stones used to grind grain; the location is just blocks from where the city's first tidewater grist mill once stood; and a Per Se alum heads the bakery. Inside, the theme continues with walls constructed of concrete blocks shaped like flour sacks.

Lunchtime sandwiches showcase house-baked breads, like whole wheat pain au lait grilled with cheddar and pickled peppers; or falafel-inspired broccoli fritters in a warm pita with harissa and walnut-yogurt sauce. Come dinner, the homemade pastas or fish of the day, like seared local porgy with olive romesco, impress. Desserts however are the real showstoppers, as evidenced by a bronzed raspberry cobbler with creamy corn ice cream.

285 Third Ave. (bet. Carroll & President Sts.)
Union St
(718) 576-3360 — **WEB:** www.runnerandstone.com
Lunch & dinner daily **PRICE:** $$

TANOREEN

Middle Eastern • Mediterranean décor

MAP: A3

This warm Middle Eastern restaurant is tucked into an unassuming Bay Ridge corner and run by Chef/owner Rawia Bishara and her daughter.

Meals graciously commence with pickled vegetables and za'atar-dusted flatbread and are followed by a tableful of unique plates brimming with flavors and colors. Turkish salad is actually a bright red tomato spread, shot with harissa and dressed with bits of diced cucumber and a drizzle of excellent olive oil. Appetizers are numerous (grape leaves are a lively sure thing), but don't miss the mansaf, a homey dish consisting of braised lamb doused in creamy yogurt and served over a mound of fluffy rice. Like so many of the other dishes, it's massive, so come hungry or armed with friends.

7523 Third Ave. (at 76th St.)
77 St
(718) 748-5600 — **WEB:** www.tanoreen.com
Lunch & dinner Tue - Sun **PRICE:** $$

WILLIAMSBURG

GREENPOINT

Williamsburg—traditionally an Italian, Hispanic and Hasidic hub—is now a mecca for hipsters and artists. Here in Billyburg, creative culinary endeavors abound and include several, small-scale stores preparing terrific eats—imagine the artisan chocolate line crafted at **Mast Brothers** and you'll start to get the picture. Bring an appetite or posse of friends to **Smorgasburg**, where sharing is crucial for a true gustatory experience. This open-air market is held on the waterfront from spring through fall and headlines everything from beef sliders and brisket, to bulgogi and chana masala. Less interested in eating and more so in cooking? Sign up for a class at **Brooklyn Kitchen**, where home cooks can keep up with haute chefs by learning how to pickle, bake and ferment... even kombucha! Have an artisanal business idea? **FoodWorks** inside the former Pfizer building is a culinary-centric incubator. Just as **Pies 'n' Thighs** soothes the soul with down-home goodness, there's no going wrong with a cup of joe from **Toby's Estate** or **Blue Bottle Coffee Co.** on Berry Street. If you're craving a different type of

pick-me-up, **Bedford Cheese Shop** makes an ideal stop for a wedge or two among those on the run. Early birds can also be found here devouring breakfast or lunch from their café-style menu, while happy-hour snackers will definitely savor those wine and meat boards to boot. Inspired by the art of butchery, **Marlow & Daughters** is adored for regionally sourced meat, house-made sausages and dry goods. Speaking of which, locals who live and breathe by meat and cheese make routine trips to **Best Pizza**, a destination that delivers on what its moniker proclaims. In keeping with the vibe of this neighborhood, their interior is disheveled by design, but that doesn't keep patrons from coming in for a slice of "white." Tried and true **Fette Sau** brings rudimentary comfort with roadhouse-style barbecue to residents; just as the falafel at Palestinian-owned **Oasis** has been winning over hearts for sometime now. In Greenpoint, bakeries offer stacks of traditional Polish pastries; but for a change of pace head to **Ovenly**, just steps away from WNYC Transmitter Park, for a slice of pitch-dark Brooklyn blackout cake.

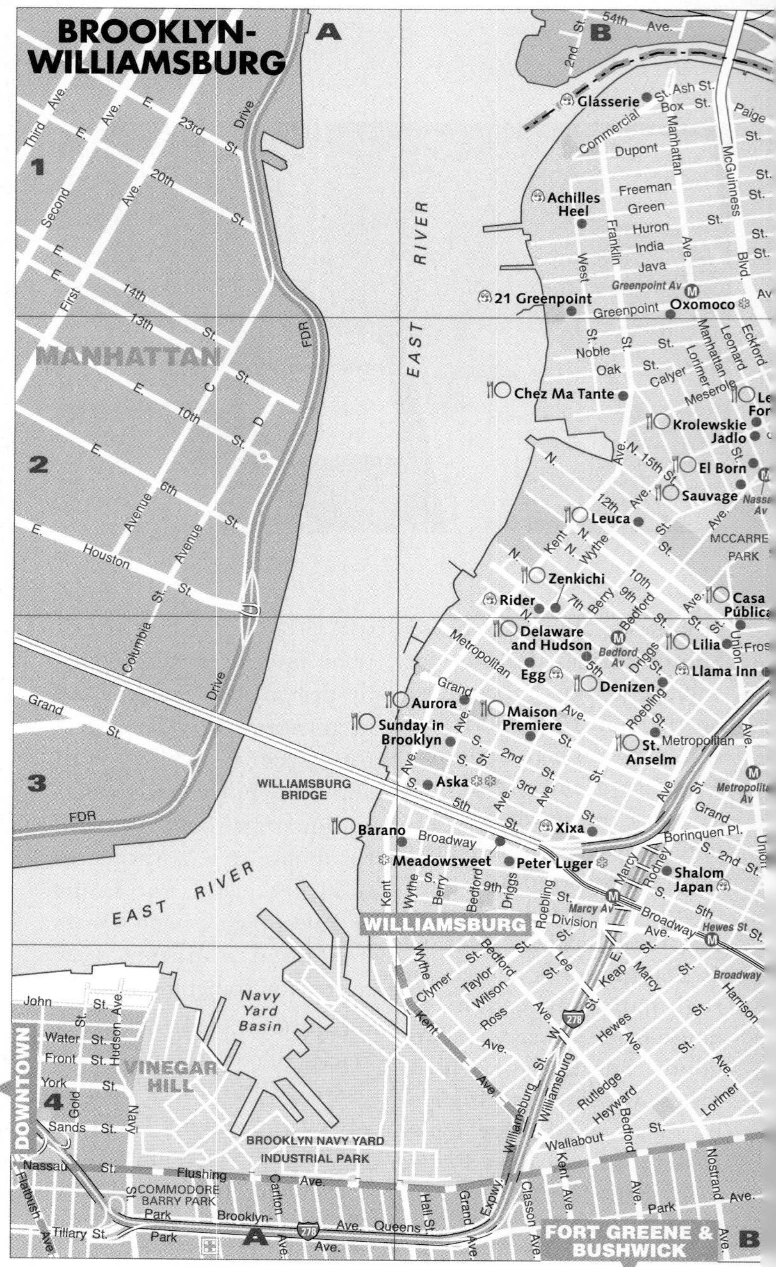
BROOKLYN-
WILLIAMSBURG
MANHATTAN
EAST RIVER
WILLIAMSBURG BRIDGE
Glasserie
Achilles Heel
21 Greenpoint
Oxomoco
Chez Ma Tante
Krolewskie Jadlo
El Born
Sauvage
Leuca
Zenkichi
Rider
Casa Pública
Delaware and Hudson
Lilia
Llama Inn
Egg
Denizen
Aurora
Maison Premiere
Sunday in Brooklyn
St. Anselm
Aska
Xixa
Barano
Meadowsweet
Peter Luger
Shalom Japan
WILLIAMSBURG
Navy Yard Basin
VINEGAR HILL
BROOKLYN NAVY YARD INDUSTRIAL PARK
COMMODORE BARRY PARK
DOWNTOWN
FORT GREENE & BUSHWICK
MCCARREN PARK

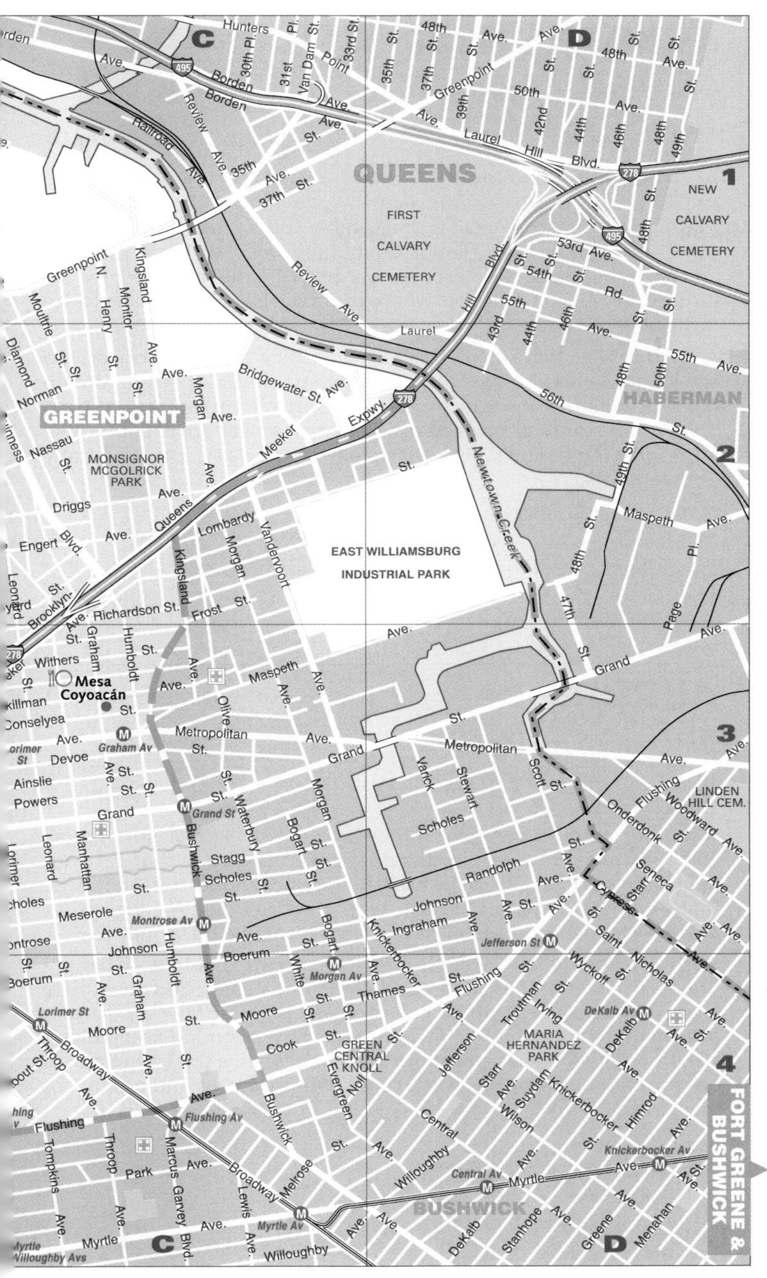

ACHILLES HEEL

Gastropub • Tavern

MAP: B1

Ace restaurateur Andrew Tarlow (of Diner, Marlow & Sons, The Reynard and more) brings next-level bar food to a tavern in Greenpoint—and the result is predictably spectacular. Located near the East River, Achilles Heel is beautifully worn, with big windows and an authentic dockside tavern warmth. But, the real treasures are turned out of its tiny kitchen, where the menu is succinct but surprise dishes are common.

A crisp three-bean salad is paired with thick aïoli and soft-crumb sourdough; while lobster mushrooms are pooled in a perfect tomato dashi. Regulars know not to miss their array of fresh bread (from She Wolf Bakery); briny oysters aplenty; as well as an inventive take on open-face sandwiches—especially that sweet corn and baby eggplant toast.

180 West St. (at Green St.)
Greenpoint Av
(347) 987-3666 — **WEB:** www.achillesheelnyc.com
Lunch Sat - Sun Dinner nightly **PRICE:** $$

AURORA

Italian • Trattoria

MAP: B3

A waning sun over the twinkling East River; a chilled glass of Italian white in an ivy-covered garden: these are the details that set your heart in motion at this beloved little neighborhood trattoria. And, that's long before you sink your teeth into their homemade dishes laced with pristine seasonal ingredients. La vita é bella, indeed.

Aurora takes Italian cooking back to its rustic roots with simply dressed market greens; impeccably executed pastas; and beautifully seasoned meats and whole fish. A lovely plate of fave e pecorino arrives bursting with fresh fava beans, sharp pecorino and springy additions like fennel, pea shoots and mint; while a thick tangle of al dente spaghetti is paired with plump shrimp, chilies and a touch of mullet roe.

70 Grand St. (at Wythe Ave.)
Bedford Av
(718) 388-5100 — **WEB:** www.aurorabk.com
Lunch & dinner daily **PRICE:** $$

ASKA ✿✿

Scandinavian • Chic

MAP: B3

A dramatic space in a former warehouse is made even more theatrical by clever lighting: the darkness of the dining room is juxtaposed with the brightness of the open kitchen, which sits on one side of the room like a stage. Tablecloths are black; the uniforms of the waitstaff are black, but your eyes are drawn inexorably towards the white-jacketed chefs as they go about their work with quiet efficiency.

Eating here may be a serious business, but happily the place isn't blighted by a monastic atmosphere—a contented buzz fills the room, helped along by the chefs who deliver the dishes themselves and describe them with contagious enthusiasm.

Expect around 19 courses—that may seem daunting but each one, whether a squid tart or meltingly soft dry-aged ribeye, is small and exquisitely formed. Swedish chef Fredrik Berselius and his team use a myriad of techniques from fermenting and pickling to curing, smoking and preserving. This is new Nordic cuisine that celebrates man's relationship with nature and the changing seasons. It's clever without being self-congratulatory, original without being gimmicky and complex without being complicated—a kitchen shimmering with intelligence.

---

47 S. 5th St. (bet. Kent & Wythe Aves.)

Marcy Av

(929) 337-6792 — **WEB:** www.askanyc.com

Dinner Tue - Sat

PRICE: $$$$

BARANO

Italian • Contemporary décor

MAP: B3

Barano welcomes diners to the rather unknown specialties of the Italian island of Ischia. This stylish dining room sits at the foot of a residential development, just a stone's throw from the East River and Williamsburg Bridge.

Start with an array of sfizzi like wood-fired olives with fennel seeds, celery and lemon. The pasta is always a strong point on the menu, so definitely go for the "tasting" that might feature the fusilli lunghi with white Bolognese; maccheroni alla pummarola with tomatoes and chili; or even bucatini with rabbit ragù. Then, lamb ribs are slowly roasted until fork-tender, in the wood-burning oven right in full view of the dining room before arriving at your table. Lovely, well-rounded desserts include affogato and cannoli.

26 Broadway (bet. Kent & Wythe Aves.)
Marcy Av
(347) 987-4500 – **WEB:** www.baranobk.com
Lunch Sun Dinner nightly **PRICE:** $$$

CASA PÚBLICA

Mexican • Contemporary décor

MAP: B3

This breezy Williamsburg restaurant will transport you to sunny Mexico in a flash. Tucked into a multi-room space boasting floor-to-ceiling windows, an ample bar and gorgeous imported floor tiles, Casa Pública is like a modern-day hacienda filled with well-crafted small plates and dreamy cocktails. Here, tequila is a food group of its own.

Everything on Casa Pública's menu is executed with care, but this kitchen is so talented you should try venturing outside your comfort zone. Aguachile ceviche arrives wildly fresh, chockablock with tender sea scallops, serrano chilies and crunchy jicama. For dinner, try the carne encebollada, a sizzling platter of Creekstone ribeye topped with sweet, melted ramps, meco chilies and smoky bone marrow.

594 Union Ave. (at Richardson St.)
Bedford Av
(718) 388-3555 – **WEB:** www.casapublicabk.com
Lunch Sat - Sun Dinner nightly **PRICE:** $$$

CHEZ MA TANTE

Gastropub • Trendy

MAP: B2

Named for Montreal's beloved hot dog shack, you will find this ultra-popular spot located on a windswept corner of Greenpoint. Aidan O'Neal and veteran NY'er Jake Leiber have made a name for themselves at this intimate little gem, which sports a meat-centric mentality along with a modern French-Canadian sensibility—potted meats anyone? Porky dishes and pâtés are part and parcel of this dining experience, so don't leave without tucking in to the pig's head terrine. Lighter appetites can balance out such heavy leaning dishes with a roasted half-chicken accompanied by charred onions and set atop a bed of nutty and vibrant romesco.

Desserts—including the chocolate flourless cake—are equally popular. But, it is brunch that warrants a queue of famished locals.

92 Calyer St. (at Franklin St.)
Greenpoint Av
(718) 389-3606 — **WEB:** www.chezmatantenyc.com
Lunch Sat - Sun Dinner nightly **PRICE:** $$$

DELAWARE AND HUDSON

American • Neighborhood

MAP: B3

This is a true-blue local spot, filled with creaky wood tables, a bare warehouse floor and high ceilings to balance the small and narrow but polished space. The kitchen prepares a single fixed menu of farm-to-table fare that focuses on the Mid-Atlantic region. Service is friendly and talkative, enhancing the casual ambience.

Meals begin with a flurry of small bites, the best of which is the made-to-order pretzel roll. It is fluffy, soft and has its own cult following. Following this, sample larger dishes such as buttery noodles with English peas and ham, or tender and juicy braised rabbit thigh with honey, vinegar and thyme. An assortment of desserts may feature the likes of chocolate torte, strawberry macarons or peanut butter-chocolate truffles.

135 N. 5th St. (bet. Bedford Ave. & Berry St.)
Bedford Av
(718) 218-8191 — **WEB:** www.delawareandhudson.com
Lunch & dinner Tue - Sun **PRICE:** $$$

DENIZEN

American • Cozy

MAP: B3

Exceptionally good, next-level cheese is the star of this Williamsburg gem, whether it's a spruce-wrapped Harbison from Jasper Hill in Vermont, or French goat milk blue from La Ferme de La Tremblaye. But the menu doesn't stop at fromage—and Denizen's sophisticated small plates are delicious enough to merit a proper dinner.

French onion toast is topped with braised oxtail ragout and soft ribbons of Timberdoodle; butter-poached tilefish bobs in a 'nduja broth over braised sunchokes and cabbage; and burrata plated with broccoli pesto, white anchovies and sunflower oil is served with crisp rye toast. The modern, tavern-like space is small, so you can expect a wait—but that's not necessarily a bad thing with such an impressive wine list to peruse.

88 Roebling St. (at N. 7th St.)
Bedford Av
(929) 337-6412 — **WEB:** www.denizenbrooklyn.com
Lunch Sat - Sun Dinner nightly

PRICE: $$

EGG

American • Simple

MAP: B3

Breakfast is served all day at this popular Williamsburg spot, which has an outpost in Tokyo. The setting is industrial but inviting—flushed with light bouncing off concrete floors, plain wood tables and light-colored brick walls.

The star of the show is the fantastic buttermilk biscuits, fresh-baked beauties that are split and smothered with pork sausage-studded sawmill gravy. These may then be stacked with country ham, house-made fig jam and Vermont cheddar cheese; or simply accompanied by molasses, honey or jelly. A plump fried oyster sandwich appears laced with a mustard-pickled okra remoulade. Much of the produce is sourced locally—a good part of it provided by Goatfell Farm (located on the northern edge of the Catskills mountain range).

109 N. Third St. (bet. Berry St. & Wythe Ave.)
Bedford Av
(718) 302-5151 — **WEB:** www.eggrestaurant.com
Lunch daily

PRICE:

EL BORN

Spanish • Neighborhood

MAP: B2

Named for a trendy neighborhood in Barcelona, this Greenpoint tapas den has a decidedly urban feel. Make your way inside to discover a glossy space, featuring a neon squiggle suspended from the ceiling, red Shaker-style chairs, as well as a long bar with twelve contemporary (but comfy!) stools for perching.

Over in the kitchen, the chefs slide effortlessly between Andalusia, Catalonia and Castilla-La Mancha, giving each of their dishes a dusting of contemporary flair. Warm goat cheese croquetas are served with apple compote; while shaved summer squash straddles sweet-salty perfection with jamon Ibérico, blueberries and padrón pepper vinaigrette. For a flavor-packed finale, go for stone-grilled octopus seasoned with olive oil, thyme and paprika.

651 Manhattan Ave. (bet. Nassau & Norman Aves.)
Nassau Av
(347) 844-9295 – **WEB:** www.elbornnyc.com
Lunch Sat - Sun Dinner nightly

PRICE: $$

GLASSERIE

Middle Eastern • Rustic

MAP: B1

Housed in an old glass factory, the beautiful Glasserie is colorful, rustic and industrial, with many original details, including a welcoming bar and small door that peeks into the bustling kitchen. Add to this lovely setting a straight-up delicious Middle Eastern menu from a wildly talented kitchen, and you begin to understand why the crowds are flocking to this hot spot.

Manning the kitchen is Jeff Kouba, a talented chef who favors organic and locally sourced ingredients. Highlights may include the table-shared mezze feast—served with ten or so incredible small dishes—or the rabbit taco, spiked with harissa and folded into a thin kohlrabi "taco" with herbs and radish. The silky chicken liver mousse, served with arak, is a crowd-pleaser and fittingly so.

95 Commercial St. (bet. Box St. & Manhattan Ave.)
Greenpoint Av
(718) 389-0640 – **WEB:** www.glasserienyc.com
Lunch Sat - Sun Dinner nightly

PRICE: $$

KROLEWSKIE JADLO

Polish • Rustic

MAP: B2

Krolewskie Jadlo (or «King's feast» in Polish) sits in a Greenpoint enclave still known for its vibrant Polish population. Although the size of this community has decreased through the years, the area still thrives with a distinct and authentic Eastern European soul. The room is pleasant and routinely packed with crowds of friends and families speaking in their native Polish.

Groups take advantage of shared platters, like the koryto for four, which is a delicious and inexpensive way to sample some of the restaurant's most popular items. The Polish plate brings all one could hope for in hearty old-world cooking, from pan-fried potato pierogies to links of smoky kielbasa. But this kitchen is also known for its desserts, so plan to end with a sweet treat.

694 Manhattan Ave. (bet. Nassau & Norman Aves.)
Nassau Av
(718) 383-8993 – **WEB:** www.krolewskiejadlo.com
Lunch & dinner daily **PRICE:** $$

LE FOND

French • Bistro

MAP: B2

Chef-owner Jake Eberle's cute corner restaurant shows us that not every dish needs reimagining and not every recipe requires reinterpretation. He's a French-trained chef whose cooking is crisp, clean and comfortingly classic—and his well-balanced menu includes words like "roulade" and "blancmange" that here seem curiously reassuring. That's not to say his food doesn't pack a punch: the rich, meaty cassoulet could keep an army on the march for days.

Globe lights hang from the ceiling to illuminate a sea-blue room with bespoke wooden furniture. The acoustics can be bouncy and those lacking the necessary padding will find the seating a little numbing. But, there is honest toil and earnest endeavor happening here and it deserves every ounce of support.

105 Norman Ave. (at Leonard St.)
Nassau Av
(718) 389-6859 – **WEB:** www.lefondbk.com
Lunch Sun Dinner Tue - Sun **PRICE:** $$

LEUCA

Italian • Mediterranean décor

MAP: B2

This well-curated addition to the local scene arrives courtesy of NoHo Hospitality Group with the talented Andrew Carmellini at the helm of the kitchen. Named for the charming maritime town in the southernmost region of Puglia, Italy, Leuca is tucked into the wildly popular William Vale Hotel and boasts striking views of the Manhattan skyline. The space features a bright and lovely dining room with yellow leather chairs and marble-topped tables, as well as a second elegant nook fitted out with wood paneling and oversized black-and-white photographs.

Dinner might unveil tender lemon chicken for two, fragrant with spices and strung with blistered peppers; or a delicious tangle of spaghetti and sea urchin topped with succulent crab and spicy chili flakes.

111 N. 12 th St. (bet. Berry St. & Wythe Ave.)
Nassau Av
(718) 581-5900 – **WEB:** www.leuca.com
Lunch Mon - Fri Dinner nightly **PRICE:** $$$

LILIA

Italian • Contemporary décor

MAP: B3

Tucked amongst the mish-mash of shiny new condos and the roar of the BQE that make up this part of Williamsburg, sleek Lilia occupies an old corner auto shop. The transformation was dramatic, replete with large iron casement windows, unique tiling and contemplation-worthy artwork.

Most of the dishes at Lilia ooze authenticity, made all the better by a warm, knowledgeable service staff who are happy to elaborate on details. But, look out for those pastas whipped up by Chef Missy Robbins as they could bring even the savviest of diners to their knees. Dinner might begin with cured sardines laid over a thick slice of sourdough, dotted with dill and capers; or chewy rigatoni in a chunky tomato sauce alla "diavola" humming with chili pepper and salty pecorino.

567 Union Ave. (at N. 10th St.)
Lorimer St - Metropolitan Av
(718) 576-3095 – **WEB:** www.lilianewyork.com
Dinner nightly **PRICE:** $$$

LLAMA INN

Peruvian • Contemporary décor

MAP: B3

Upbeat, modern and cool, Llama Inn pays respect to all styles of Peruvian cooking, but with the technical flair of Chef Erik Ramirez who has trained in New York's top restaurants. The result is a fresh, fun and spontaneous cuisine that aims to elevate Peruvian food.

Fish courses are notable, and nowhere is that more clear than in the fresh and expertly cut raw sea bream tiradito with persimmon, ginger, yuzu and nutty poppy seeds. Fluke ceviche is just as memorable, served in a bit of dashi with lime, onion, cilantro, aji and wonderfully spicy leche de tigre. Then move on to devour decadent little skewers of pork belly brushed with Chinese fivespice, soy, garlic and barbecue sauce. Excellent desserts include airy coffee mousse with chocolate and lucuma.

50 Withers St. (bet. Lorimer & Union Sts.)
Lorimer St - Metropolitan Av
(718) 387-3434 — **WEB:** www.llamainnnyc.com
Lunch Sat - Sun Dinner nightly **PRICE: $$**

MAISON PREMIERE

Seafood • Trendy

MAP: B3

This ultra-retro tavern may feel dark and old-timey, like a watering hole where the Founding Fathers would have stopped for fortification before fending off the British. But, the massive, U-shaped bar is particularly coveted, so arrive early or prepare to wait for your absinthe drip.

To accompany the stellar sips, a vast selection of oysters, clams and group-friendly seafood plateaux seem to pop up on every table. The kitchen's talent is equally clear in such preparations as luscious sea urchin served in a chilled shellfish consommé with fragrant lemongrass and thin slices of sweet grapes. Heartier appetites will delight in a thick, juicy pork Porterhouse, glazed with jus, served alongside braised kale, roasted beets and finished with zippy horseradish cream.

298 Bedford Ave. (bet. S. 1st & Grand Sts.)
Bedford Av
(347) 335-0446 — **WEB:** www.maisonpremiere.com
Lunch & dinner daily **PRICE: $$$**

MESA COYOACÁN

Mexican • Bistro

MAP: C3

Mexico City native, Chef Ivan Garcia is at the helm of this Brooklyn hot spot, where wolfish appetites are sated with richly flavored cooking. Fronted by windows that open up on to bustling Graham Avenue, the long space is outfitted with patterned wallpaper, snug banquettes and communal tables.

The kitchen's spirited presentations are simply a joy. Partake in tacos featuring hand-crafted tortillas, like the suadero for instance, stuffed with beef brisket and avocado salsa; or torta tinga de pollo, packed with shredded chipotle-braised chicken, mashed black beans, pickled jalapeños and a toasted roll to sop up that delish sauce. Reposado and diced mango enhance the pastel tres leches—and to keep the tequila flowing, hit up nearby Zona Rosa.

372 Graham Ave. (bet. Conselyea St. & Skillman Ave.)
Graham Av
(718) 782-8171 – **WEB:** www.mesacoyoacan.com
Lunch Wed - Sun Dinner nightly — **PRICE:** $$

RIDER

Contemporary • Design

MAP: B2

Some may think this hip, bi-level eatery is an offshoot of the Brooklyn performance space National Sawdust, but in fact Rider vies for top billing. Downstairs, you'll find an industrial vibe outfitted with concrete flooring, exposed brick walls and comfy banquettes; upstairs it's polished, low-lit and moodier.

Patrick Connolly has put together an exciting menu designed for sharing, with a refreshing focus on vegetables. The execution and flavors transcend the trendiness of the space, offering unfussy, timeless dishes that may be considered small plates, but are generously portioned. Try gemelli bathed in mushroom ragù with crisp breadcrumbs, or grilled mortadella on sourdough with ricotta, toasted sunflower seeds and a nasturtium "pesto."

80 N. 6th St. (at Wythe Ave.)
Bedford Av
(347) 452-4905 – **WEB:** www.riderbklyn.com
Lunch Sat - Sun Dinner Tue - Sun — **PRICE:** $$

MEADOWSWEET

Mediterranean • Bistro

MAP: B3

Tucked next to the steely skeleton of the Williamsburg Bridge, Meadowsweet cuts a stylish industrial figure with its glass-fronted façade, whitewashed brick walls and original mosaic-tiled floors. Leather banquettes line the wall, and pendant bulbs illuminate one of several beautiful oil paintings of a meadow. Inside, the restaurant jumps with Williamsburg's finest—along with more than a few bridge-hoppers from Manhattan and beyond. And that's on a slow night.

The fuss is quite merited. Despite ample competition in this section of town, Chef/owner Polo Dobkin and wife, Stephanie Lempert, manage to elevate the kitchen's dishes into next-level territory, and they do so in a lovely, urbane setting with loads of charm and friendly service.

The inventive American menu gets a lift from Mediterranean accents: fried artichokes served with a tangle of bitter-spicy arugula in a creamy vinaigrette are positively addictive. Crisped black bass with a parsley root velouté sings with a side of green apple cabbage, which is flecked with chunks of smoky bacon. There's an impressive list of cocktails and wine; not to mention a globetrotting beer selection ranging from Austrian lagers to Japanese ales.

---

149 Broadway (bet. Bedford & Driggs Aves.)

Marcy Av

(718) 384-0673 — **WEB:** www.meadowsweetnyc.com

Lunch Thu - Sun Dinner Wed - Mon **PRICE: $$$**

OXOMOCO ✿

Mexican • Trendy

MAP: B1

Don't let the sunny, easygoing vibe at Oxomoco fool you. This is a serious restaurant, capable of great magic when cooking in its wood-fired oven. The attractive interior feels like a resort, with a long bar, giant skylight to maximize the natural light of such a narrow space, and outdoor patio. The room is lively and packed but always conducive to conversations.

Tacos may be the main draw, especially when their near-perfect tortillas are piled with superb lamb barbacoa or soft-shell crab. However, this kitchen doesn't stick to one dish or even area of Mexico. Instead, it reaches widely across myriad regions, always balancing abundance with fresh and vibrant flavors. The menu entices with its tempting large and small items, including tropical hamachi agua chile or the tlayuda crafted from smoky corn on a crisp shell. Other highlights include the brined, fried and smoked "giant chicken."

Apprized diners know never to pass up on such ace plates as the clever and totally original hoja santa curd, accompanied by roasted strawberries, raspberry granita and finished with spicy olive oil. The three-tiered tres leches cake is a savory and none-too-sweet delicacy, enriched with grilled peaches.

---

128 Greenpoint Ave. (bet. Manhattan & Franklin Aves.)

Greenpoint Av

(646) 688-4180 – **WEB:** www.oxomoconyc.com

Dinner nightly **PRICE: $$$**

PETER LUGER ✿

Steakhouse • Vintage

MAP: B3

More than just an icon of the New York dining scene—Peter Luger is an idolized classic. Run on wheels by a team of gloriously forthright waiters, this munificent paean to beef doesn't just serve legendary steaks, it provides a side helping of history too. The wood paneling and beer-hall tables tell of family gatherings, friends united, deal making, success celebrated and stories swapped. It's evocative and unforgettable. It's also unapologetically old-school—computerization and credit cards remain fanciful futuristic concepts, so you'll need to come with a few Benjamins tucked into your wallet.

Start with a thick slice of bacon to get your taste buds up to speed before the steak arrives. These slabs of finely marbled Porterhouse are dry-aged in-house for around 28 days, which means there's tenderloin on one side of the bone and strip steak on the other. They are then broiled to perfection, sliced before being brought to the table, and served with their own sauce as well as a host of sides, which range from their version of German fried potatoes to creamed spinach.

If you can still feel a pulse, go ahead and order dessert, if only to get a mound of their famous schlag made in back.

---

178 Broadway (at Driggs Ave.)

Marcy Av

(718) 387-7400 — **WEB:** www.peterluger.com

Lunch & dinner daily

PRICE: $$$$

SAUVAGE

Contemporary • Brasserie

MAP: B2

Sauvage means "wild and natural" in French, and that's a perfectly apt description for this handsome restaurant with a thoughtful list of naturalist wines. Select one of the organic, biodynamic offerings; then sit back, relax and take in the leather booths, walnut bar, hand-blown glass chandeliers and tropical plants.

But enough about drinks and décor, because the kitchen happens to be whipping up dishes that absolutely thrill. Highlights include roasted cauliflower served with anchovy and peppercorn; or even Japanese potatoes dressed with beef fat-vinaigrette. Pooled in a vinegar swirl, crispy sweetbreads are delivered with mushrooms and watercress. Pan-seared rabbit with turnip purée and a mustard seed-honey "broth" makes for a hearty and fragrant finale.

905 Lorimer St. (at Nassau Ave.)
Nassau Av
(718) 486-6816 – **WEB:** www.sauvageny.com
Lunch & dinner daily **PRICE:** $$$

SHALOM JAPAN

Fusion • Contemporary décor

MAP: B3

The curious moniker of this sweet spot refers to the backgrounds of its husband-and-wife team, Chefs Aaron Israel and Sawako Okochi. Each has an impressive resume, and together the result is a unique labor of love.

Nightly specials are displayed via a wall-mounted blackboard with small plates progressing to a handful of entrées. Monkfish hot pot features ankimo-enriched miso broth, ground shrimp balls, glass noodles and a heap of fragrant herbs. The house-baked sake kasu challah with raisin butter is a highly recommended start. But, it may also turn up as toro toast smeared with scallion, wasabi cream cheese and topped with finely chopped, smoked lean tuna belly. Still craving more? Experience it once again in the warm chocolate bread pudding.

301 S. 4th St. (at Rodney St.)
Marcy Av
(718) 388-4012 – **WEB:** www.shalomjapannyc.com
Lunch Sat - Sun Dinner nightly **PRICE:** $$

ST. ANSELM

American • Tavern

MAP: B3

Step through the heavy wood-framed glass door and let the smell of charred meat and grassy notes from chimichurri greet you. The low ceiling is shingled with distressed wood to lend a rustic note to the room. Its open floor plan accentuates the bright flames from the sizzling grill, visible through the kitchen.

Settle down at the bar to sample offbeat wines and cocktails. A genuine sense of contentedness fills the packed room, as guests enjoy small plates of monster prawns, grilled quickly in their steaming shells, finished with garlic, parsley and a hint of spice. Sweet tea-brined young chicken served with head and feet intact may seem like it isn't for everyone, but it should be. Perfectly moist and whole-roasted, it is a pure, hands-on pleasure.

355 Metropolitan Ave. (bet. Havemeyer & Roebling Sts.)
Bedford Av
(718) 384-5054 — **WEB:** N/A
Lunch Sat - Sun Dinner nightly **PRICE:** $$

SUNDAY IN BROOKLYN

American • Trendy

MAP: B3

With all due respect to Monday through Saturday, the best day may be "Sunday in Brooklyn". That is if grooving to old-school hip hop with a well-made cocktail in one hand and freshly baked sourdough slathered with beer butter in another is your kind of thing. This café is free of that formulaic hipster décor and instead flaunts a rustic villa-meets-ski cabin look.

Those warm, gooey sticky buns are sinfully delicious and no one skips the breads. The kitchen also deserves praise for brunch, which is on everyone's mind. However, it's far from the only game here, where the chef curries favor with diners all day long. A budget-friendly Dark and Stormy can be a fine tonic against inclement weather. Don't miss the market for goodies like smoked fish and irresistible pastries.

348 Wythe Ave. (at S. 2nd St.)
Bedford Av
(347) 222-6722 — **WEB:** www.sundayinbrooklyn.com
Lunch & dinner daily **PRICE:** $$$

21 GREENPOINT

American • Rustic

MAP: B1

A big and bright red wood-burning oven is not merely a visual centerpiece at 21 Greenpoint, it is also the soul of their thoroughly pleasing American fare. Similarly, the space oozes with that appealingly familiar feel, featuring plank floors, mosaics and disheveled walls. This is where those breads and pizze are baked, just as meats and root vegetables are roasted.

It's hard to achieve this level of delicious, well-sourced cooking in hipster Williamsburg, but the menu excels in this regard. It also changes daily and is notably accommodating to both vegans and vegetarians. When offered, don't miss their multi-course Sunday night prix-fixe, which may include a frittata, peppery pork shoulder soup with foraged mushrooms and much, much more.

21 Greenpoint Ave. (bet. the East River & West St.)
Greenpoint Av
(718) 383-8833 — **WEB:** www.21greenpoint.com
Lunch Sat - Sun Dinner Tue - Sun **PRICE:** $$

XIXA

Mexican • Contemporary décor

MAP: B3

Thanks to the trademark style of Chef Jason Marcus, this lovely Mexican favorite draws those chill, relaxed Williamsburg crowds into its slender space. Everything seems to glow beneath etched brass ceiling pendants, as servers carefully place course after well-paced course on those tiny tables.

A delicious alchemy is at work here, as evidenced by the remarkably delicate corn flan tamal, topped with buttery roasted corn, set over garlic-poblano cream and tucked with pickled trumpet mushrooms. Tacos are also absolute standouts, thanks to soft, warm tortillas folded with roasted bone marrow, chorizo marmalade and charred lime. Like the menu, the beverage listing is loads of fun, with wines whimsically arranged under headings of iconic women.

241 S. 4th St. (bet. Havemeyer & Roebling Sts.)
Marcy Av
(718) 388-8860 — **WEB:** www.xixany.com
Dinner Wed - Sun **PRICE:** $$

ZENKICHI

Japanese • Intimate

MAP: B2

From its mysterious entry to its dedicated staff who fuss over every detail, Zenkichi reminds even the most jaded diner why going out to eat can be pure magic. The atmosphere is relaxed but focused, and the omakase is surprisingly well-priced for this neighborhood. Secluded booths offer a sexy vibe for date night, where couples can ring a bell for service. And Akariba, a cool little cash-only bar downstairs, serves up such treats as oysters and sake.

In addition to the à la carte and dessert menus, this kitchen also offers a seasonal omakase provided two or more diners partake. But unlike the typical parade, there's something here for everyone, and the pre-determined dishes may unveil saikyo miso cod or a heap of summer vegetables in tosazu gelée.

77 N. 6th St. (at Wythe Ave.)
Bedford Av
(718) 388-8985 – **WEB:** www.zenkichi.com
Dinner nightly

PRICE: $$

Look for our symbol spotlighting restaurants with a serious cocktail list.

QUEENS

QUEENS

Nearly as large as Manhattan, the Bronx and Staten Island combined, Queens covers over 100 square miles of land on the western end of Long Island. Reputedly the most ethnically varied district in the world, its diversified nature is reflected in the numerous immigrants who arrive here each year for its affordable housing, strong sense of community and cultural explosion. Such a unique convergence of cultures results in this stately borough's predominantly global and very distinctive flavor. Ergo, its vibrant streets prosper with amazing and affordable international eats.

GLOBE-TROTTING

Begin your around-the-world feast in Astoria, a charming quarter of old-world brick row houses and Mediterranean groceries. Discover grilled octopus bookended by baklava at one of the many terrific Greek joints. Then, prolong your culinary spree over juicy kebabs at **Little Egypt** on Steinway Street; or chow on equally hearty Czech tlačenka at the popular **Bohemian**

Hall & Beer Garden. On lazy days, brew buffs can be found at Astoria's hottest beer havens—**Sweet Afton**—for an intimate setting with a serious selection, or equally sublime **Studio Square** for the ultimate alfresco experience. Showcasing similarly exquisite beverages alongside beautiful baked goods, **Leli's Bakery** may be a relatively young member of this area's dining scene, but hooks its troops with age-old roots—their commercial kitchen in the Bronx has been supplying fine-dining establishments with a wealth of sweetness since time immemorial. Founded in 1937, **La Guli** is an Italian pasticceria whose expert talent has been feeding families with rich, creamy cakes and cookies. And staying true to tradition, **The Lemon Ice King of Corona**, brought to you by the Benfaremo family, is a nostalgic ode to Italian ice complete with sugar-free selections for health-embattled hordes. But, for an unapologetically potent treat, **To Laiko** is the nabe's favorite for a delicious frappe.

Sojourning south and then to the east, **La Boulangerie** brings a slice of France to Forest Hills by way of fresh-baked loaves of white bread and crusty baguettes. Of course, cheese couples best with bread, and the choices are abundant at **Leo's Latticini Mama's** in Corona. **M. Wells Dinette**, which is housed inside MoMA PS 1, delivers insanely inventive items to curious visitors and the lucky locals of Long Island City. Proudly proffering an imaginative blend of diner signatures, Quebecois favorites and "are you serious!?" combos, this sequel to the original outstanding diner continues to charm crowds by simply doing their thing. While biding time here, feel the sass and spirit at MoMA PS

1's "Warm Up"—one of the city's greatest summer soirées, featuring a DJ, turntables and all that jazz.

Looking for something sweet to combat the heat? Look out for the **Doughnut Plant** nestled in the historic Falchi Building and boasting an outré selection, crafted from the best ingredients in town—tres leches doughnuts anyone? And what goes best with dessert? Coffee, of course, with a crowning range of roasted beans available at **Vassilaros and Sons**. Enhancing this quarter's global repute is **Güllüoglu**, a Turkish bakery and café whose elegant space and tasty bites bring Istanbul to life. But if South Asian flavors are a particular fave, then **Bundu Khan** is worth a trip for every type of grilled delight. Close out this range of global eats at cozy **Norma's Corner Shoppe**—a hot spot for homey, comfort cuisine.

ASIA MEETS THE AMERICAS

Flushing still reigns as Queens' most vibrant Asian haven and NY'ers are always dropping in for dim sum, Henan specialties or a bowl of pho like you'd find streetside in Saigon. Food vendors at Flushing's mini-malls offer foods from far flung corners of China that are light on the pockets but big on flavor. Of both local note and citywide acclaim, **New World Mall Food Court** is a clean, airy space serving excellent Asian goodies. You'll find everything at these inviting stalls—from hand-pulled noodles (at **Lang Zhou**) to Taiwanese shaved ice for the end of the night. On Saturdays, when the weather warms and the sun sets, grazers and shoppers flock to the **Queens International Night Market** at the New York Hall of Science in Flushing Meadows Corona Park. Their tempting array of inexpensive Asian and Latin American snacks further celebrates the rich diversity of this borough's communities. However, the offerings don't stop here. Over on Main Street, vegans feel the TLC at **Bodai Vegetarian** where such kosher-friendly dishes as vegetarian duck and seaweed-sesame rolls keep the crowds returning for more. These same health food fans as well as foodies from all walks may then trek east to arrive at **Queens County Farm Museum**, considered one of the largest working farms in the city that highlights sustainable farming, farm-to-table meals, livestock, a greenhouse and educational programs. From Flushing to Floral Park, **Real Usha Sweets & Snacks** cooks India's favorite street foods that also make for great dinner party treats. **Singh's Roti Shop and Bar** prepares West Indian delicacies like curry chicken, saltfish and aloo pie to gratify its contiguous community. But shifting gears from South to Central Asia, as many as 40,000 immigrants traveled to New York after the fall of the Soviet Union. They staked their claim in Forest Hills, and **King David Kosher Restaurant** remains a paragon among these elders and their families for Bukharian specialties.

Energy and variety personify Elmhurst, the thriving hearth of settlers from Latin America, China and Southeast Asia. The Royal Kathin, a celebration that occurs at the end of Thailand's rainy season, pays homage to the Buddhist monks. While Elmhurst's adaptation of this festival may lack the floods, it proffers many authentic Thai bites. Whitney Avenue is home to a booming restaurant row and small Southeast Asian storefronts. Indulge a gado gado craving at **Upi Jaya** or get your spicy laksa

on at **Taste Good**. If such pungent flavors don't fit the bill, then relocate from Asia to America at **Kesso Foods** for creamy Greek yogurt.

Cannelle Patisserie's French pastries keep sweet fiends alive, just as South Asians are front and center in Jackson Heights—take in the bhangra beats blaring from cars rolling along 74th Street. This dynamic commercial stretch is dotted with numerous Indian markets, Bengali sweet shops and Himalayan-style eateries serving all types of tandoori specialties, spicy curries and steaming-hot Tibetan momos. In keeping with the fact that Latin Americans also make up a large part of the demographic here, Roosevelt Avenue also swarms with taquerias, aromatic Colombian coffee shops and delightful little Argentinean spots that are bound to sate this vast range of assorted tastes.

WANDERING THROUGH WOODSIDE

Take this thriving thoroughfare all the way west to Woodside, where Irish bars mingle with numerous Thai restaurants to produce a bunch of cultural fun. Once home to an enormous Irish population, Woodside now shares its blocks with large Thai and Filipino communities—even if there are kelly-green awnings of decades-old pubs as well as clover-covered doors (which advertise in Gaelic) that dominate these streets. Set alongside **Donovan's Pub**, an age-old Irish respite that grills up some of the best burgers in town, is **Little Manila**. This eight-block stretch of Roosevelt Avenue is excellent for stocking up on Filipino food and groceries galore. Otherwise, simply join the line outside **Jollibee**, a fast-food chain serving up flavors from back home. If Filipino cooking sounds far too funky for your liking, rest easy as **Piemonte Ravioli** carries every choice of fresh, house-made pasta for an Italian cena con la famiglia. Finally, of course, down south in Sunnyside, one can also eat their way through Romania, Turkey, Mexico, Korea, China and more.

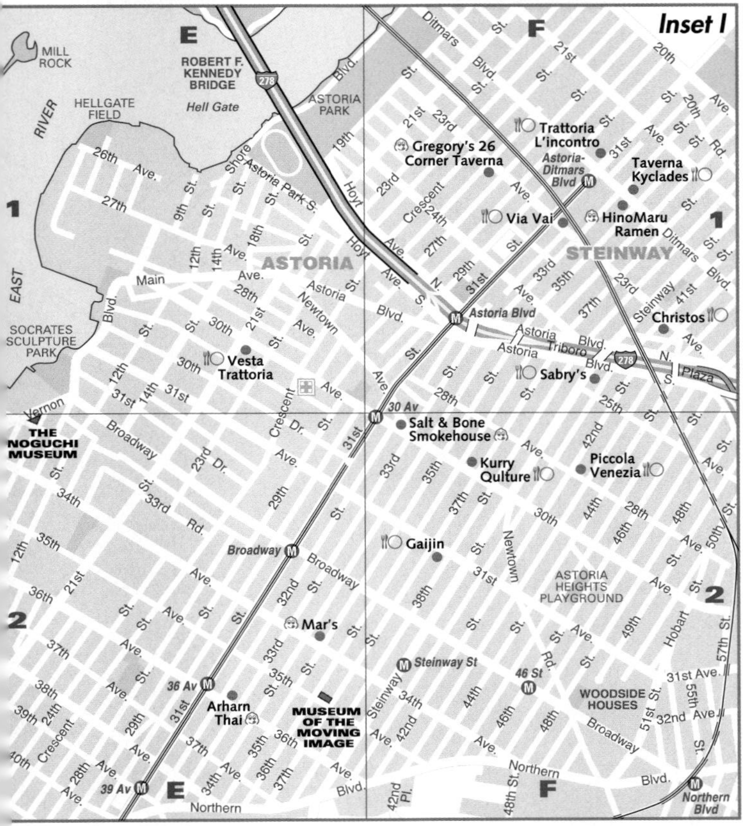

Inset I
E
F
1
2
MILL ROCK
ROBERT F. KENNEDY BRIDGE
Hell Gate
HELLGATE FIELD
EAST RIVER
ASTORIA PARK
SOCRATES SCULPTURE PARK
THE NOGUCHI MUSEUM
ASTORIA
STEINWAY
ASTORIA HEIGHTS PLAYGROUND
WOODSIDE HOUSES
MUSEUM OF THE MOVING IMAGE
Trattoria L'incontro
Gregory's 26 Corner Taverna
Taverna Kyclades
Via Vai
HinoMaru Ramen
Christos
Vesta Trattoria
Sabry's
Salt & Bone Smokehouse
Kurry Qulture
Piccola Venezia
Gaijin
Mar's
Arharn Thai
Astoria-Ditmars Blvd
Astoria Blvd
30 Av
Broadway
36 Av
39 Av
Steinway St
46 St
Northern Blvd
Ditmars Blvd.
Shore Blvd.
Astoria Park S.
Hoyt Ave.
Crescent St.
Main Ave.
Vernon Blvd.
Broadway
Newtown Ave.
Astoria Blvd.
Triboro Plaza
Steinway St.
Hobart St.
Northern Blvd.

Inset II
E
F
3
WOODSIDE
ELMHURST
BIG BUSH PARK
NEW CALVARY CEMETERY
NATHAN WEIDENBAUM PARK
Urubamba
Kitchen 79
Casa del Chef Bistro
Himalayan Yak
Ayada
Paet Rio
Sweet Yummy House
Tito
d's Grill
Taiwanese Gourmet
Jackson Hts-Roosevelt Av
82 St-Jackson Hts
90 St-Elmhurst Av
Woodside-61 St
Elmhurst Av
Grand Av-Newtown
Barnett Ave.
Roosevelt Ave.
Queens Blvd.
Broadway
Woodside Ave.
Brooklyn Queens Expwy.
Hampton St.
Judge St.
Baxter Ave.
Britton Ave.
Elmhurst Ave.
Kneeland Ave.
Codwise Pl.
Grand Ave.

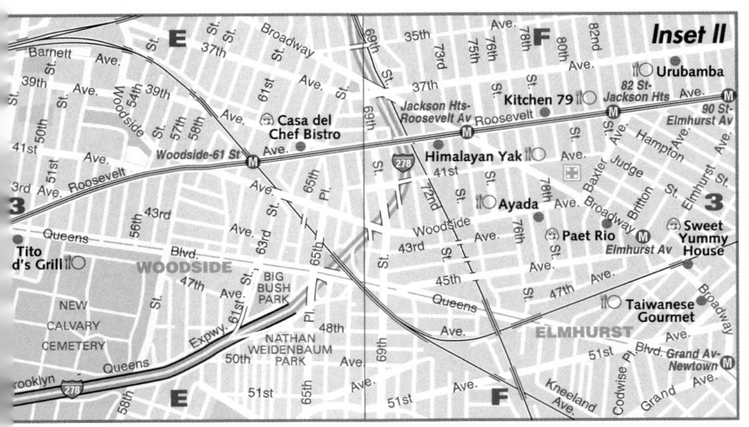

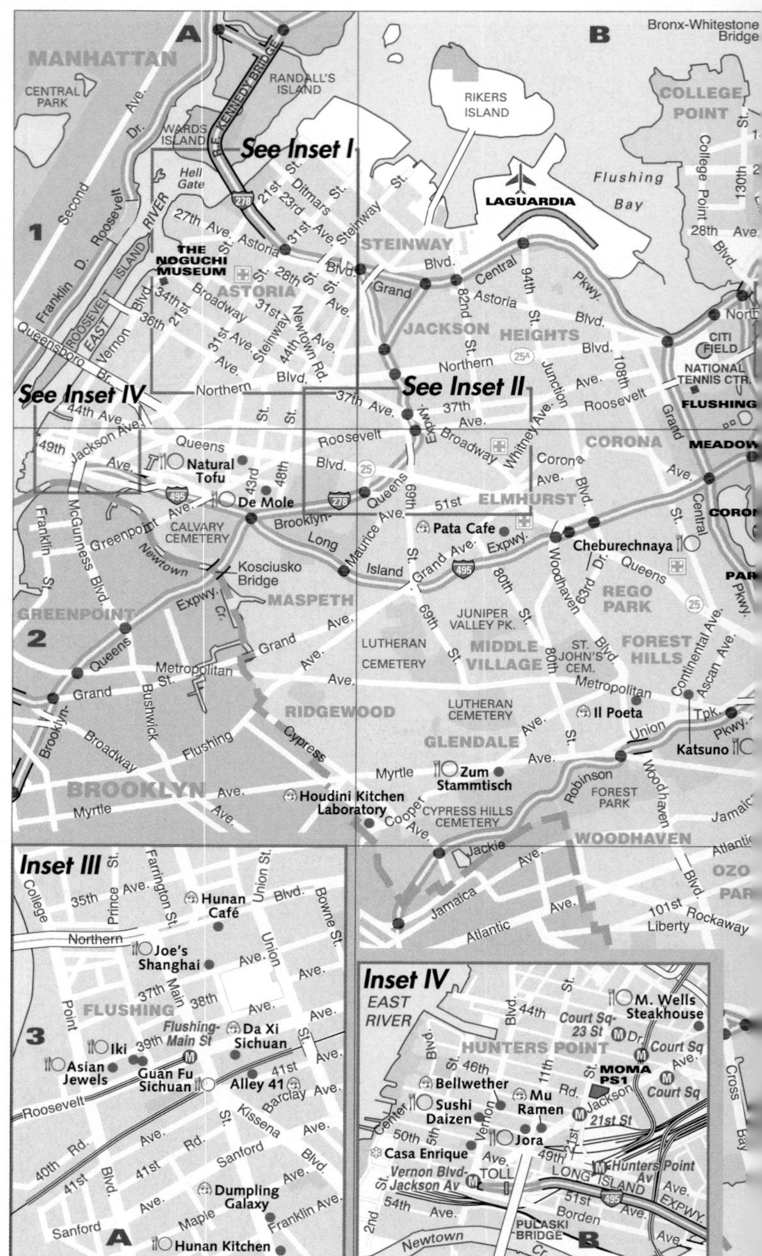

MANHATTAN
RANDALL'S ISLAND
RIKERS ISLAND
Bronx-Whitestone Bridge
COLLEGE POINT
See Inset I
See Inset II
See Inset IV
LAGUARDIA
Flushing Bay
THE NOGUCHI MUSEUM
ASTORIA
STEINWAY
JACKSON HEIGHTS
CITI FIELD
NATIONAL TENNIS CTR.
FLUSHING
CORONA
ELMHURST
Natural Tofu
De Mole
Pata Cafe
Cheburechnaya
CALVARY CEMETERY
Kosciusko Bridge
MASPETH
GREENPOINT
REGO PARK
FOREST HILLS
JUNIPER VALLEY PK.
MIDDLE VILLAGE
LUTHERAN CEMETERY
ST. JOHN'S CEM.
RIDGEWOOD
GLENDALE
Il Poeta
Katsuno
Zum Stammtisch
BROOKLYN
Houdini Kitchen Laboratory
CYPRESS HILLS CEMETERY
FOREST PARK
WOODHAVEN
Inset III
Hunan Café
Joe's Shanghai
FLUSHING
Flushing-Main St
Da Xi Sichuan
Iki
Asian Jewels
Guan Fu Sichuan
Alley 41
Dumpling Galaxy
Hunan Kitchen
Inset IV
EAST RIVER
M. Wells Steakhouse
Court Sq-23 St
Court Sq
HUNTERS POINT
MOMA PS1
Bellwether
Mu Ramen
Sushi Daizen
Jora
Casa Enrique
Vernon Blvd-Jackson Av
Hunters Point Av
21st St
PULASKI BRIDGE

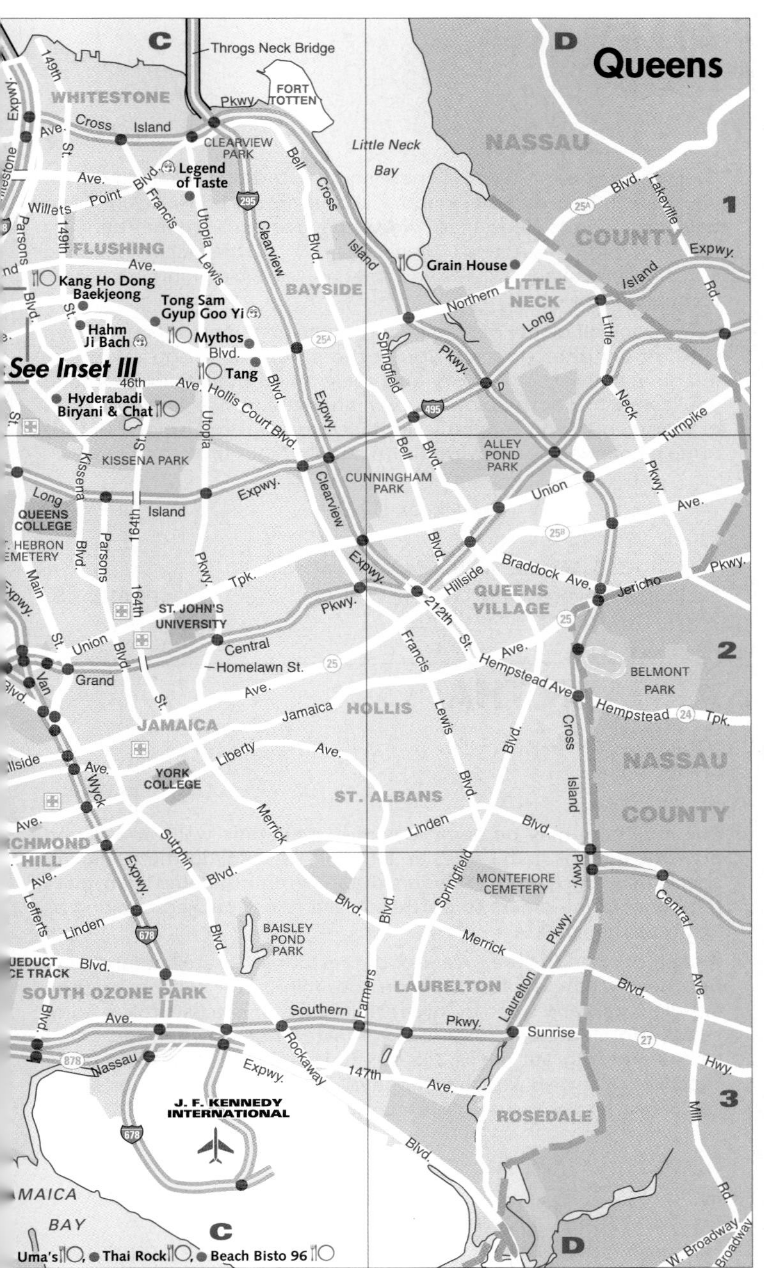
Queens
C
D
Throgs Neck Bridge
FORT TOTTEN
WHITESTONE
Little Neck Bay
NASSAU COUNTY
CLEARVIEW PARK
Legend of Taste
FLUSHING
Kang Ho Dong Baekjeong
Tong Sam Gyup Goo Yi
Hahm Ji Bach
Mythos
Tang
Grain House
BAYSIDE
LITTLE NECK
See Inset III
Hyderabadi Biryani & Chat
KISSENA PARK
QUEENS COLLEGE
CUNNINGHAM PARK
ALLEY POND PARK
ST. JOHN'S UNIVERSITY
QUEENS VILLAGE
BELMONT PARK
JAMAICA
HOLLIS
YORK COLLEGE
ST. ALBANS
MONTEFIORE CEMETERY
BAISLEY POND PARK
SOUTH OZONE PARK
LAURELTON
ROSEDALE
J. F. KENNEDY INTERNATIONAL
JAMAICA BAY
1
2
3
Uma's, Thai Rock, Beach Bisto 96

ALLEY 41

Chinese • Chic

MAP: A3

Everything about Alley 41 is unexpected—starting with the moment you walk in to a very sleek and stylish room carefully designed to balance concrete slabs, black wood chairs and glass panes beneath the spotlights. The setting is highly stylized, and the Sichuan cooking is just as appealing. Dishes can sometimes arrive at lightning speed, sometimes not.

Leave yourself plenty of time to peruse the mammoth menu, decked with glossy photos to get you in the mood for serious slurping. Imagine an intensely savory and spicy mung bean jello salad and you'll start to get the picture. Even anodyne dishes like mapo tofu or braised beef and vegetable vermicelli are wickedly spicy, but they bring a complex heat, layered with a funky, sour broth and chilies.

136-45 41st Ave. (bet. Main & Union Sts.)
Main St
(718) 353-3608 — **WEB:** www.alley41.com
Lunch & dinner daily **PRICE:** $$

ARHARN THAI

Thai • Simple

MAP: E2

The look here may be demure with its pale pink walls and gilded artwork, but this gem serves up a bounty of bold, northern-leaning specialties. And though tables are draped in embroidered linen, glass tops encourage diners to partake in the flavor-packed cooking as lustily as they please.

A shelf of snacks is the extent of the restaurant's retail component, but these will be the last thing on your mind after consuming their excellent gai yang sided by sweet chili sauce; or nua nam tok, a warm salad of grilled steak tossed with roasted rice powder, red onion slivers and fragrant herbs. Pla duk fu is very Thai and pairs puffy fried bits of catfish with lime, papaya, peanuts and raw onions for a can't-miss hit packed with superb crunch and flavor.

32-05 36th Ave. (bet. 32nd & 33rd Sts.)
36 Av
(718) 728-5563 — **WEB:** www.thaiastoria.com
Lunch & dinner daily **PRICE:**

ASIAN JEWELS ‖○

Seafood • Family

MAP: A3

Arguably the best dim sum in Flushing, this spectacular gem is an absolute must for anyone seeking serious seafood and very authentic Cantonese cooking. A longtime resident of 39th Avenue, the expansive dining room is outfitted with round, banquet-style tables, bamboo plants and ornate chandeliers.

Let the feasting begin with memorable crab-and-pork soup dumplings, before moving on to the thrill-inducing dim sum carts. Taste the likes of steamed rice rolls with honey-roast pork; spareribs with rice starch and black beans; chicken and ham wrapped in yuba; and poached jellyfish with scallions and sesame. The signature Dungeness crab—steamed and stir-fried with ginger and green onions, served with Japanese eggplant and garlic—is simply outstanding.

133-30 39th Ave. (bet. College Point Blvd. & Prince St.)
Flushing - Main St
(718) 359-8600 — **WEB:** www.asianjewelsseafood.com
Lunch & dinner daily **PRICE:** $$

AYADA ‖○

Thai • Colorful

MAP: F3

A bright green sign leads the way to little Ayada, where the décor's a bit plain and the food is anything but. Inside the popular Thai restaurant, guests are greeted with a smattering of tables; a simple, but homey setting; and a warm, family-focused staff to walk them through the menu.

And what a menu it is, with dishes like the crispy catfish salad, paired with green mango and laced with a perfectly balanced lime dressing; a whole, deep-fried snapper, served with more of that tropical fruit and tamarind sauce; a bowl of chewy drunken noodles sporting crisp green beans and tender chicken in a fragrant chili-garlic sauce; or fresh ripe mango and sticky rice, steamed to pearly, translucent perfection and carrying flavors of sweetened coconut milk.

77-08 Woodside Ave. (bet. 77th & 78th Sts.)
Elmhurst Av
(718) 424-0844 — **WEB:** N/A
Lunch & dinner daily **PRICE:** $$

BEACH BISTRO 96

Brazilian • Cozy

MAP: C3

Helmed by Brazilian-born chef Carlos Varella and his wife, former model Andressa Junqueira, this tiny orange shack perched on the edge of the Atlantic feels more like Bahia than Rockaway Beach. Once an outer borough no-man's land in steady state of decline, this seaside Queens nabe—now a summertime destination for surfers and hipsters alike—is finally having its day in the sun.

Beach Bistro 96 is basking in that glow with a decidedly laid-back vibe, walls lined in banana leaf print paper, and pristine, simple food that celebrates Brazil in all of its delicious glory. Don't head back to the surf without sampling the feijoada, a stew-like specialty bursting with pork and black beans; or the pasteis, golden-fried empanadas filled with ground beef.

95-19 Rockaway Beach Blvd. (at Beach 96 St.)
Beach 98 St
(718) 474-6000 — **WEB:** www.beachbistro96.com
Lunch & dinner Wed - Sun **PRICE:**

BELLWETHER

Contemporary • Trendy

MAP: B3

Black floors, stark white tables and white chairs. Bellwether is simple-chic, though don't let that fool you as its kitchen is seriously ambitious, turning out a seasonal, all-out menu that swings in different directions and is packed with creativity.

Griddled halloumi with raw sugar snap peas bathed in a wild garlic vinaigrette is a standout starter, while grilled blowfish tails are smoky and tender, coated with black sesame- and herbed-citrus breadcrumbs. A smear of black garlic aïoli adds extra oomph. But the do-not-miss dish? Braised Colorado lamb neck. Brined for three days, the fork-tender meat is then enhanced with sumac gravy, butter bean hummus and a garlicky sauce to form a hearty dish that could feed at least three hungry souls.

47-25 Vernon Blvd. (bet. 47 Ave. & 47 Rd.)
Vernon Blvd - Jackson Av
(718) 392-3257 — **WEB:** www.bellwethernyc.com
Dinner Tue - Sat **PRICE:** $$

CASA DEL CHEF BISTRO

Contemporary • Cozy

MAP: E3

Woodside may not be the obvious choice for a chef who's cooked at the esteemed Blue Hill, but for Alfonso Zhicay and his family, it was the only choice. Community drives them (it's why Zhicay spends his days cooking at a local charter school), but pristine ingredients (most of which are sourced from the Jackson Heights farmer's market) and serious technique define his kitchen.

His craftsmanship, likely honed under Dan Barber, is evident in such creative and well-executed dishes as the vegetable terrine, which hints at foie gras with its richness, and is accented by cocoa nibs as well as crunchy pink peppercorns for brightness and bitterness. Black bass is then perfectly seared and well paired with pumpkin pesto, adding a bit of nutty sweetness.

39-06 64th St. (bet. 39th & Roosevelt Aves.)
69 St
(718) 457-9000 — **WEB:** www.casadelchefny.com
Dinner nightly

PRICE: $$

CHEBURECHNAYA

Central Asian • Simple

MAP: B2

This may be a kosher spot with no bagel in sight, but one look at its counter loaded with layers of bowl-shaped noni toki bread and you quickly realize that a meal here is a dining adventure. Specializing in Bukharian (Central Asian) cuisine, longstanding Cheburechnaya has been a neighborhood pioneer.

The focused menu is more engrossing than the décor, and it's easy to want every cumin- and paprika-laced item on it. Bring your own vodka and start with the house specialty, chebureki, an empanada-like deep-fried wrap stuffed with either hand-cut lamb seasoned with cumin, chili, cilantro and paprika; or fennel-sparked cabbage. It may serve as the perfect complement to smoky lamb fat, tender quail, veal heart and seared beef sweetbread kebabs.

92-09 63rd Dr. (at Austin St.)
63 Dr - Rego Park
(718) 897-9080 — **WEB:** www.cheburechnaya1.com
Lunch Sun - Fri Dinner Sat - Thu

PRICE:

CASA ENRIQUE ✿

Mexican • Contemporary décor

MAP: B3

Chiapas. Puebla. San Luis Potosí. One can literally taste the regions and cities that Chef Cosme Aguilar's amazingly complex menu explores—including his own childhood recipes to honor his mother's memory. A steady stream of hungry diners seek out this rather small, tasteful dining room for friendly yet professional service and soul-warming fare. Aim for the large, fantastic communal table.

Start your meal with hearty rajas con crema, combining none-too-spicy poblanos with sweet, fresh corn, Mexican sour cream and cheese served alongside a stack of fresh and slightly toasty tortillas. This kitchen's tender chicken enchiladas with mole de Piaxtla may induce swooning, thanks to a sauce that is unexpectedly sweet yet heady with bitter chocolate, raisins, almonds, cloves, cinnamon, chilies, garlic and sesame. The results? Incomparable. It's the kind of food that thrills palates (and tempts wanton thoughts). Expect the chamorros de borrego al huaxamole to arrive falling off the bone and redolent of epazote, allspice and pulla chilies. Its fruity-spicy broth is drinkable.

Every bit of every spongy and buttery layer of the cow and goat's milk pastel tres leches is absolutely worth the indulgence.

5-48 49th Ave. (bet. 5th St. & Vernon Blvd.)

Vernon Blvd - Jackson Av

(347) 448-6040 — **WEB:** www.henrinyc.com

Lunch Sat - Sun Dinner nightly

PRICE: $$

CHRISTOS 🍴

Steakhouse • Elegant

MAP: F1

This beloved Astoria steakhouse has a lot going for it, but its cause for celebration is that authentic Greek accent that imbues everything here. Excellent quality beef, as in the signature prime "wedge" for two, is dry-aged in-house, charbroiled to exact specification and finished with sea salt and dried oregano. Vibrant starters and sides underscore the Aegean spirit at play with pan-fried vlahotyri cheese, charred octopus with roasted peppers and a red wine dressing, as well as smoked feta-mashed potatoes.

Christos has a commanding presence on a quiet tree-shaded corner just off bustling Ditmars Blvd. Mixing shades of brown, the cozy and elegant dining room has a separate bar area and is lined with fish tanks stocked with live lobsters.

41-08 23rd Ave. (at 41st St.)
Astoria - Ditmars Blvd
(718) 777-8400 — **WEB:** www.christossteakhouse.com
Dinner nightly **PRICE:** $$$

DA XI SICHUAN

Chinese • Elegant

MAP: A3

Unlike many other spicy retreats, Da Xi Sichuan doesn't go for the jugular with that tongue-numbing chili oil one-two punch. Instead, this elegantly designed spot on the second floor of the New World Mall shares a more nuanced approach to this regional Chinese cuisine. In fact, dishes such as the pig ear and wild mushroom or the crispy cucumber roll showcase a clear finesse and regard for restraint, while the Tibet-style pork ribs dusted with peppercorns are deliciously juicy, fatty and rich in the best possible way. Even the straightforward house special, featuring a mix of fluffy rice, pork bits and potatoes in a stone bowl, has been known to satisfy many an appetite.

Warm, attentive service makes this large space feel especially warm and welcoming.

136-20 Roosevelt Ave., Ste. 2R (at Roosevelt Ave.)
Flushing - Main St
(718) 621-9999 — **WEB:** N/A
Lunch & dinner daily **PRICE:** $$

DE MOLE

Mexican • Neighborhood

MAP: A2

If the words sweet, competent, clean and authentic come to mind, you're most likely thinking of this heartwarming haunt for delightful Mexican. Albeit a tad small, with a second dining room in the back, rest assured that De Mole's flavors are mighty, both in their staples (burritos and tacos) and unique specials—seitan fajitas anyone?

This delightful pearl rests on a corner of low-rise buildings where Woodside meets Sunnyside, yet far from the disharmony of Queens Boulevard. Fans gather here for hearty enchiladas verdes con pollo, corn tortillas smeared with tomatillo sauce and queso blanco. Crispy chicken taquitos are topped with sour cream; steamed corn tamales are surprisingly light but filled with flavor; and the namesake mole is a must.

45-02 48th Ave. (at 45th St.)
46 St - Bliss St
(718) 392-2161 — **WEB:** www.demolenyc.com
Lunch & dinner daily **PRICE:**

DUMPLING GALAXY

Chinese • Family

MAP: A3

Neon bounces off all the shiny surfaces at Dumpling Galaxy inside the Arcadia Mall. Navigate beyond the phone retailers and stalls to find this modern arena donning red booths and hanging lights. Spiffy and inviting, this «galaxy» is lauded for crafting scores of these little parcels, as well as comforting mains that shouldn't be ignored.

Fill your table with a dumpling feast, chock-full of duck and mushroom, spicy-sour squash or lamb and celery redolent of lemongrass. Soup dumplings, too, are worth your time. Larger dishes are equally memorable; those cold, thick, slurp-inducing green bean noodles soaked in tart black vinegar with raw white sesame seeds, cilantro, cucumbers and wood-ear mushrooms will have you coming back for more...and then some more.

42-35 Main St. (in Arcadia Mall)
Flushing - Main St
(718) 461-0808 — **WEB:** www.dumplinggalaxy.com
Lunch & dinner daily **PRICE:**

GAIJIN

Japanese • Neighborhood

MAP: F2

Chef Mark Garcia isn't your typical chef. This Chicago-born itamae definitely has his own ideas about sushi; thus the name, which translates to "outsider." Alas, Queens needs Garcia and his eats, so he's definitely «in.» Displaying a deft hand with garnishes like sweet Fuji apples, smoky, spicy roasted banana peppers and mushrooms brushed with chive butter, the chef's approach is definitely inventive. Yet, the food never feels contrived and his respect for fish (flown in four times a week from Japan's Tsukiji market) is unwavering.

Reservations are a must, as there are just nine counter seats and a sprinkle of tables in the back. Typically packed with locals, expect commuters from other boroughs to snag in-demand seats as this kitchen's reputation grows.

37-12 31st Ave. (bet. Broadway & 31st Sts.)
Broadway
(929) 328-2890 — **WEB:** www.gaijinny.com
Dinner nightly

PRICE: $$$$

GRAIN HOUSE

Chinese • Simple

MAP: D1

It may be situated at the eastern edge of Queens, but a meal at Grain House is worth the trek to Little Neck. The room is amiably attended to and minimally adorned, with blue-and-white ceramics lending a distinct Chinese tone to the otherwise staid but comfortable room.

Grain House brings joy to enthusiasts of Chinese cookery with a menu representing the many regions of the country's culinary map. There is a clear penchant for Sichuan cooking, though don't expect that familiar tongue-numbing heat since the owners aren't from the region. Yibing burning noodles may not deliver the namesake singe, but this tangle of garlic oil-dressed thin noodles piled high with minced pork, scallions, peppercorns and chili ash is decidedly delicious.

249-11 Northern Blvd. (bet. 249th St. & Marathon Pkwy.)
(718) 229-8788 — **WEB:** N/A
Lunch & dinner daily

PRICE: $$

GREGORY'S 26 CORNER TAVERNA

Greek • Simple

MAP: F1

Judge a book by its cover and miss the rustic pleasures found within this old-time Greek retreat. The room is tiny and the tables are bare, topped with butcher paper, but of all the many tavernas that line these Astoria streets, Gregory's is one of the more serious and charming, turning out refreshingly honest and intensely flavorful cooking.

Begin with tirokafteri, a satisfying spread of feta blended with pickled red chili peppers and served with hot pita points. Lightly fried eggplant and zucchini plated with a garlicky potato spread demonstrate an epic study in crunchy textures and creamy flavors. Then gently cooked sole seasoned with sweet red pepper powder and served with asparagus as well as cauliflower depicts the best in cuisine, Greek style!

26-02 23rd Ave. (at 26th St.)
Astoria - Ditmars Blvd
(718) 777-5511 – **WEB:** N/A
Lunch & dinner daily **PRICE:** $$

GUAN FU SICHUAN

Chinese • Elegant

MAP: A3

Ornate wood-carved screens, heavy Imperial furniture and enormous serving utensils make this the most stylized and grand Sichuan restaurant in town.

The menu's photos simplify ordering from a range of familiar favorites, like the best bean jelly salad around, intensely savory with a good dose of black vinegar and garlicky chili oil. Other inventive (read: unfamiliar) dishes are just as worthwhile, especially that massive platter of gan ma-style stewed pork leg, surrounded by vibrant Chinese greens. While the cuisine strives to showcase subtlety and dimension rather than decimate the palate with spice, rest assured as some items still boast that tongue-numbing tang from Sichuan's beloved peppercorns.

Portions are large so bring a gang.

39-16 Prince St. (bet. 39th & Roosevelt Aves.)
Flushing - Main St
(347) 610-6999 – **WEB:** www.guanfuny.com
Lunch & dinner daily **PRICE:** $$$

HAHM JI BACH

Korean • Simple

MAP: C1

This beloved Queens institution enjoys fine digs where they serve popular and praiseworthy Korean food. The contemporary dining room is spacious and airy, with the warm, always informative staff buzzing from table to table. It's not uncommon for the manager to roll up her own sleeves when the pace elevates—and elevate it does, for this is not your average Korean barbecue.

It's hard to go wrong on Hahm Ji Bach's delightful menu, but don't miss the samgyeopsal, tender slabs of well-marinated pork belly sizzled to crispy perfection tableside for you to swaddle in crisp lettuce with paper-thin daikon radish, spicy kimchi and bright scallions; or the mit bachan, a hot clay pot with soft steamed eggs, kimchi, tofu, pickled cucumbers and spicy mackerel.

40-11 149th Pl. (bet. Barclay & 41st Aves.)
Flushing - Main St
(718) 460-9289 — **WEB:** www.hahmjibach.nyc
Lunch & dinner daily

PRICE: $$

HIMALAYAN YAK

Tibetan • Family

MAP: F3

Broadly appealing yet truly unique, Himalayan Yak transports diners from Jackson Heights to Central Asia for a hybrid of Nepalese, Tibetan and Indian cuisines. The room is a bit worn—a testament to its long-standing popularity—but orange walls invoke mountain sunsets. Carved dark wood and colorful fabrics create a far-flung ambience.

Start with an order of momo: these steamed minced meat-filled dumplings are seasoned with scallions, cilantro and ginger. Then sample yak in the form of sausage, stew, or cheese. Labsha is a beef and daikon curry served with tingmo, a multi-layered steamed bun for sopping up the mildly spiced sauce, which simply must not be missed. And finally the lassi, a traditional yogurt-based drink, is the perfect complement to every meal.

72-20 Roosevelt Ave. (bet. 72nd & 73rd Sts.)
74 St - Broadway
(718) 779-1119 — **WEB:** www.himalayanyak.net
Lunch & dinner daily

PRICE: $$

HINOMARU RAMEN

Japanese • Simple

MAP: F1

What this simple spot lacks in décor, it makes up for in charming details (think: friendly service, an energetic open kitchen, and a chalkboard menu). Order a Sapporo on tap and a small plate like shrimp nikuman, shrimp tempura wrapped in a steamed bun, and prepare for the main event: truly remarkable ramen. The menu lists several slurp-worthy varieties, including a Hakata-style tonkatsu. This pork bone distillation is vigorously simmered to produce a creamy broth infused with bone marrow and stocked with noodles, char siu, nori and fish cake. Equally delicious is the vegetarian variety, highlighting a soy milk base teeming with carrots, ginger and broccoli.

For Manhattan residents, Lucky Cat, an offshoot, sits on busy East 53rd Street.

33-18 Ditmars Blvd. (bet. 33rd & 34th Sts.)
Astoria - Ditmars Blvd
(718) 777-0228 – **WEB:** www.hinomaruramen.com
Lunch & dinner daily

PRICE: $$

HOUDINI KITCHEN LABORATORY

Pizza • Rustic

MAP: B2

Located in an industrial stretch of Ridgewood, this inventive pizzeria pulls off a number of tricks with carefully curated ingredients. Taking residence in a repurposed brewery built in the late 1800s, the red brick structure sits near the borough's massive cemeteries where this establishment's namesake has been laid to rest. While the "lab» isn't large, it feels cavernous nonetheless, thanks to high ceilings, sparse digs that include a sprinkling of tables with views of the cement dome oven and an ample covered terrace.

Tuck in to salads, homemade pastas and burrata, as well as wood-fired pies that include the Guido BK which celebrates the bitter beauty of broccoli rabe and shares its charred crust with red wine-cured sausage and mozzarella.

15-63 Decatur St. (at Wyckoff Ave.)
Halsey St
(718) 456-3770 – **WEB:** N/A
Dinner Tue - Sun

PRICE:

HUNAN CAFÉ

Chinese • Elegant

MAP: A3

Located along quiet Northern Boulevard in Flushing, Hunan House offers a delicious reprieve from the street. The interior is crisp and sophisticated, with dark, ornately carved wood and thick linen tablecloths. But, the real draw here is the wonderfully authentic Hunanese fare, with its myriad fresh river fish; flavorful preserved meats; complex profiles; and mouth-puckering spice.

Hunan House's menu is filled with exotic delights, but don't miss the wonderful starter of sautéed sour string beans featuring minced pork, chilies, ginger and garlic; smoky dried bean curd with the same preserved meat; or spicy sliced fish-Hunan style, perfectly cooked, served in a delicious pool of fiery red sauce and plated with tender bulbs of bok choy.

137-40 Northern Blvd. (bet. Main & Union Sts.)
Flushing - Main St
(718) 353-1808 — **WEB:** www.hunancafeflushing.com
Lunch & dinner daily **PRICE:**

HUNAN KITCHEN

Chinese • Family

MAP: A3

The look is simple, but this small space has its own charms and the comfort level is a few notches higher than the typical Main Street digs. Not so small is the menu though, which is an encyclopedia of all things Hunanese, and of course, there are plenty of specialties boasting that trademark heat, smoke and sour notes.

You'll smell the chili wafting off the tender and intoxicating cumin lamb as it is seared to perfection and spiced to the hilt with red and green chilies as well as bell peppers. Braised smoked bamboo with sliced pork won't take home top prize for its looks, but with intense barbecue-like smoke and a meaty crunch, it's a total winner. Do keep an eye out for those sneaky red and green chili seeds lurking in this dish.

42-47 Main St. (bet. Blossom & Franklin Aves.)
Flushing - Main St
(718) 888-0553 — **WEB:** N/A
Lunch & dinner daily **PRICE:**

HYDERABADI BIRYANI & CHAT

Indian • Simple

MAP: C1

In an area known for Chinese eats, this mom-and-pop spot stands tall and is best known for its goat biryani. Composed with morsels of succulent goat meat that is mingled with ground spices and fluffy rice, this eponymous dish is a signature for good reason.

Inside, the room is small and minimally adorned with a buffet station full of freshly made curries, as well as a TV playing Bollywood hits. They do a thriving takeout business; and classics like samosas, palak paneer and aloo gobi are also popular. But, that is not why you're here—also delve into such regional specialties as Kerala pepper chicken cooked in a savory sauce of black peppercorns and minced chives. Sop this up with a soft naan, slicked with ghee and dotted with flecks of jalapeño.

44-27 Kissena Blvd. (bet. Cherry & 45th Aves.)
Flushing - Main St
(718) 353-5577 — **WEB:** www.biryaniandchat.com
Lunch & dinner daily **PRICE:** ⊜

IKI

Japanese • Elegant

MAP: A3

While One Fulton Square hasn't quite caught on, this upscale gem tucked into the Hyatt Place Hotel is a worthy anchor and addition to the local scene. Duck behind the modern glass façade and you're greeted with curving leather booths and beautiful blonde floors. You've seen this before, you think to yourself, but this is a curious outlier—think Queens in high heels.

Diners can opt for omakase or à la carte. While the former might begin with a chilled bowl of soft tofu topped with creamy uni; the latter showcases cool kanpachi, shima aji, tai and kinmedai nigiri. Then, tender-cooked rice, cooked in an earthenware pot, is tinted with the addition of dashi, topped with maitakes and folded with flakes of salmon for a bright assortment.

133-42 39th Ave. (bet. College Point Blvd. & Prince St.)
Flushing - Main St
(718) 939-3388 — **WEB:** www.ikicuisine.com
Lunch & dinner daily **PRICE:** $$$

IL POETA

Italian • Trattoria

MAP: B2

Queens is teeming with family-owned Italian restaurants dishing up the red sauce, and yet Il Poeta manages to carve out a unique place among its competitors by cooking real classics that locals can't help but enjoy. Perched on a quaint corner of Forest Hills, the fresh décor is simple but elegant, with a suited staff and vibrant pieces of art lining the walls.

Chef Mario di Chiara knows a thing—or ten—about Italian fare: you can't miss with items like cannelloni gratinati al profumo di tartufo, a homemade pasta plump with veal and carrot, baked in buttery béchamel and kissed with truffle oil; or pollo spezzatino alla pizzaiola con salsiccia, a rustic chicken stewed in a light-as-air tomato sauce pocked with sweet porky sausage and roasted peppers.

98-04 Metropolitan Ave. (at 69th Rd.)
(718) 544-4223 — **WEB:** www.ilpoetarestaurant.com
Lunch & dinner Tue - Sun **PRICE:** $$

JOE'S SHANGHAI

Chinese • Family

MAP: A3

Diners at this venerable Flushing institution are greeted with menus and a dish of black vinegar dipping sauce, as it's practically a given that you'll be ordering their famous xiao long bao here. Despite stiff competition, these soup dumplings—soft and delicate with spiraled shoulders and a mouthful of lip-smacking golden broth wrapped inside—still stand a head above most. In fact, these chefs have made it their mission to ensure biting into them is a sensual experience.

But there are other pleasures to be had here, too, such as the nourishing steamed cabbage in light broth scattered with dried shrimp, or the popular Shanghainese lion's head meatballs. Made from ground pork, the latter are incredibly light and lacquered with a dark, savory glaze.

136-21 37th Ave. (bet. Main & Union Sts.)
Flushing - Main St
(718) 539-3838 — **WEB:** www.joeshanghairestaurants.com
Lunch & dinner daily **PRICE:** $$

JORA

Peruvian • Cozy

MAP: B3

Peruvian pottery and tapestries set a casually elegant scene at this neighborhood gem, which is quickly earning a loyal following for its frothy pisco sours and dishes full of spice and flavor. Beyond the limestone façade, the deep, narrow dining room is filled with sunlight from arched windows. It also boasts a wall covered in river stones and a relaxed bar with striking artwork.

The diversity of Peruvian cuisine is on tasty display here, from classic items like ceviche mixto with crunchy red onion, oversized kernels of corn and sweet potato, to chupe de camarones—a thick, restorative soup of rice, seafood and gently poached eggs. A juicy skirt steak with sautéed onions, peppers, cilantro and sweet plantains on the side will satisfy carnivores.

47-46 11th St. (at 48th Ave.)
Vernon Blvd - Jackson Av
(718) 392-2033 — **WEB:** www.jorany.com
Lunch Fri - Sun Dinner nightly **PRICE:** $$

KANG HO DONG BAEKJEONG

Korean • Family

MAP: C1

The Korean barbecue of the moment is a short LIRR trip away, and well worth the ride. This was the first East Coast branch of (Korean wrestler and TV personality) Kang Ho Dong's growing empire—and it is among the best in the city. A younger sib now resides in midtown.

The menu is focused, the space is enormous, the air is clean and the service is friendly. Start your grill off with steamed egg, corn, cheese and more to cook along the sides, while marbled pork belly or deeply flavorful marinated skirt steak strips sizzle at the center. Bibimbap is a classic rendition, mixing beef seasoned with gochujang, vegetables, sesame, nori and crisp sprouts in a hot stone bowl—so hot that it sears the bottom rice to golden while cooking the raw egg on top.

152-12 Northern Blvd. (bet. 153rd & Murray Sts.)
Flushing - Main St (& Bus Q13)
(718) 886-8645 — **WEB:** N/A
Lunch & dinner daily **PRICE:** $$

KATSUNO

Japanese • Cozy

MAP: B2

To find Katsuno, look for the white lantern and those traditional noren curtains. Featuring less than ten tables, what this jewel lacks in size it makes up for in flavor and attitude. The owner's wife greets each guest at the door, while Chef Katsuyuki Seo dances around the miniscule kitchen crafting precise Japanese dishes from top-quality ingredients.

His elegant plating of sashimi may reveal the likes of amberjack topped with a chiffonade of shiso, luxurious sea urchin, translucent squid crested with needle-thin yuzu zest, as well as luscious fluke, tuna and mackerel. Meanwhile, carb fans will enjoy a bowl of warm soba in duck broth with tender breast meat; or the fantastically brothy inaniwa udon, served only on special nights.

103-01 Metropolitan Ave. (at 71st Rd.)
Forest Hills - 71 Av
(718) 575-4033 — **WEB:** www.katsunorestaurant.com
Dinner Wed - Sun **PRICE:** $$

KITCHEN 79

Thai • Bistro

MAP: F3

Shiny black subway tiles and glowing fixtures set a dateworthy tone at this Thai standout. Patient, helpful servers assist in exploring the menu, focused mainly on dishes of Southern Thailand. Patrons can choose to be as adventurous as the sometimes familiar yet authentic and funky menu allows.

Thick green curry (gaeng kiew warn) is packed with tender shrimp, bamboo shoots, eggplant, Chinese long beans and holy basil simmered in coconut milk with pleasantly restrained spicing. A whole flounder (pla neung ma nao) is brilliant, distinct and steamed to perfection with sour and spicy notes from garlic, minced ginger and a Thai hot sauce. Flat noodles (ka nom jeen gang tai pla) with pumpkin, mackerel and curry paste is a powerful, spicy dish.

37-70 79th St. (bet. Roosevelt & 37th Aves.)
82 St - Jackson Hts
(718) 803-6227 — **WEB:** www.kitchen79nyc.com
Lunch & dinner daily **PRICE:**

KURRY QULTURE

Indian • Contemporary décor

MAP: F2

Noted Chef Hemant Mathur and owner Sonny Solomon bring their considerable talents to this contemporary collaboration set on a busy stretch of Astoria. Inside, the vibe is friendly and casual, in an attractive room that extends from a front bar to brick-lined dining room and open back patio.

The regional (and sub-regional) Indian cooking is both tasty and high achieving, beginning with mirchi ka salan featuring a complex peanut- coconut- and sesame seed-base spiced with fresh-ground tamarind, curry leaf and fenugreek. More notable is the fact that this may be a mere accompaniment to a very interesting South Indian riff on vegetarian biryani, made wonderfully fragrant with fluffy rice and jackfruit. The slow-cooked bhuna gosht is silky, gamey excellence.

36-05 30th Ave. (bet. 36th & 37th Sts.)
30 Av
(718) 674-1212 — **WEB:** www.kurryqulture.com
Lunch Sat - Sun Dinner nightly **PRICE:** $$

LEGEND OF TASTE

Chinese • Contemporary décor

MAP: C1

This corner gem proves that New York City is ablaze with Sichuan spots. Discover you're in for a treat from the moment peanuts—coated with extra sweet and spicy chili powder—arrive at your paper-covered table.

The uninitiated come for the crab Rangoon and General Tso's chicken, but those in the know are here for the likes of Sichuan-style crispy eggplant, which are not the least bit greasy and particularly unique, thanks to their creamy center and glass-like crust. Thin shavings of intensely smoked pork with garlic leaf is even better than what tea-smoked duck would taste like if made with bacon. The "tears in eyes" bean jelly salad may not induce actual tears, but it's stocked with chillies, seeds, peanuts and is absolutely worth ordering.

2002 Utopia Pkwy. (at 20th Ave.)
Flushing - Main St (& Bus Q16)
(718) 423-4888 — **WEB:** www.legendoftasteny.com
Lunch & dinner daily **PRICE:**

MAR'S

Seafood • Brasserie

MAP: E2

If it were in the middle of Manhattan, the line would be out the door, but oh how lucky Astoria is to have Mar's. This charming oyster bar seems plucked out of another century with its weathered seaside tavern décor, whitewashed walls and curving bar. You'll feel dropped into a sun-bleached, turn-of-the-century photo.

Most of the menu is given over to raw seafood and New England classics; part to Mediterranean tavern small plates like sweetbreads and steak tartare. Seafood stew, pork belly skewers and steak frites are also on offer, and striped bass shows off a fine sense of technique, but that mussel toast with its griddled sourdough brushed with butter and tucked in a bowl brimming with fresh mussels bathed in a cream sauce is love letter worthy.

34-21 34th Ave. (at 35th St.)
Steinway St
(718) 685-2480 — **WEB:** www.lifeatmars.com
Lunch Sat - Sun Dinner nightly

PRICE: $$

MU RAMEN

Japanese • Minimalist

MAP: B3

What began as a pop-up found an insanely popular home behind an unmarked door in this industrial yet residential nook of Long Island City. Lines never cease; arrive early if possible. A thick wood block serves as a communal table in the dining room, where slurpers can witness the focus and dedication of chefs working within an open kitchen in the back.

The kitchen's methodical devotion results in a superior bowl of ramen. In the spicy miso ramen, springy noodles (from Sun Noodle) are nested in a red miso- and pork-based soup of rich bone broth that slowly simmers for over 24 hours. Topped with scallion, ground pork, sesame and chili oil, it is one of many rewarding bowls. Okonomiyaki are ethereally light, with smoked trout and shaved bonito.

12-09 Jackson Ave. (bet. 47th Rd. & 48th Ave.)
Vernon Blvd - Jackson Av
(718) 707-0098 — **WEB:** N/A
Dinner nightly

PRICE: $$

M. WELLS STEAKHOUSE

Gastropub • Rustic

MAP: B3

First impressions can be deceiving at this hip Queens gastropub. From the outside, M. Wells Steakhouse looks like the old auto body garage it's housed in, but step inside and the interior is all gloss and swagger. The dining room is a dark, sultry space—from its gold-and-black wallpapered ceiling and crystal chandeliers, to its sexy red walls, stunning bar area and open, wood-burning kitchen. Of course, the service is just as polished as the design.

Though the kitchen bills itself as a steakhouse, you can't go wrong with the excellent raw bar, creative fish entrées (maybe the "trout no trout" composed with potatoes and cabbage?) and unique appetizers. Of course desserts, like pouding chômeur topped with maple syrup, remain as outstanding as ever.

43-15 Crescent St. (bet. 43rd Ave. & 44th Rd.)
Court Sq - 23 St
(718) 786-9060 — **WEB:** www.magasinwells.com
Dinner Wed - Sat

PRICE: $$$$

MYTHOS

Greek • Mediterranean décor

MAP: C1

A gathering place for Greeks and non-Greeks alike, this family-run and friendly restaurant tempts with impeccably fresh fish, cooked over charcoal and basted simply with olive oil, lemon juice and herbs. Beyond the whitewashed exterior and dark blue awning is a large dining room with rows of neat tables for indulging in Hellenic pleasures—from zesty appetizers to boisterous conversations.

Settle into an array of pikilia; cold appetizers such as melitzansalata, eggplant whipped with herbs and olive oil. Chargrilled fish, priced by the pound, has a delightfully smoky essence and moist flesh. Whole smelts are a rare and traditional treat, simply pan-fried with a lemony-herb dressing. Finish with a choice of authentic, nutty and syrup-soaked pastries.

196-29 Northern Blvd. (bet. 196th St. & Francis Lewis Blvd.)
(718) 357-6596 — **WEB:** www.mythosnyc.com
Lunch & dinner daily

PRICE: $$

NATURAL TOFU

Korean • Simple

MAP: A2

This is the sort of place you've walked by a hundred times and never noticed, but look up, because the house-made tofu here is unrivaled. The space may be more functional than cozy, but this staff knows how to treat their customers—from welcoming each table with a succulent assortment of banchan to happily adjusting a dish's spice level.

They also clearly know the many secrets of tofu: the kitchen makes its own, on view at the front of the restaurant, then deploys it in a series of silken soondubu (soft bean curd stews). Served scalding hot in a ddukbaegi or glazed earthenware cauldron, this bubbling piquant broth contains your choice of pork, seafood or even beef intestine. But kimchi, the funky favorite, is the hands-down winner.

40-06 Queens Blvd. (bet. 40th & 41st Sts.)
40 St
(718) 706-0899 – **WEB:** N/A
Lunch & dinner daily **PRICE:** $$

PAET RIO

Thai • Cozy

MAP: F3

With so many Thai places around, it's easy to get lost in this exceptional concentration; just be sure to find yourself at Paet Rio. The design of this long and inviting room may elevate the experience, but it is their spicy and unusual cooking that makes everything shine.

The menu here is a dance of sensations—tart, spicy, sour, fresh—as seen in Chinese broccoli leaves (miang kha-na) with pork, chilies, peanuts, garlic and lime. Delicate, fluffy catfish offset by the funk of fish sauce takes center stage in the yum pla duk fu, while the beautiful tangle of fried egg noodles steals the spotlight in the curry broth-based khao soi. Khua kling is peppered-up pork belly cooked to a slight crisp and bathed in a curry paste that brings on the heat. Ka-pow!

81-10 Broadway (bet. 81st & 82nd Sts.)
Elmhurst Av
(917) 832-6672 – **WEB:** N/A
Lunch & dinner daily **PRICE:**

PATA CAFE 

Thai • Simple

MAP: B2

Just off the main drag on a residential block in Elmhurst, Pata Cafe is a tidy and convivial haunt run by a mother-daughter team. Planks and beams of unfinished wood along with light fixtures crafted from old soup cans lend to this space a treehouse-cum-workshop vibe. No matter—as all of it simply adds to the overall warmth.

Skip the bodega items for sale and scan the short, sweet menu. There is a keen eye for textures, acidity and electric heat here. Order a bowl of tom yum goong with its clear broth and sinus-clearing spice, before slurping up minced chicken-topped glass noodles dressed with a lime-fish sauce. Ga prao kai dow (beef with chili) certainly isn't anything novel, but fans of this familiar dish will relish the classic rendition on offer here.

56-14 Van Horn St. (bet. 56th & 57th Sts.)
Woodhaven Blvd
(347) 469-7142 – **WEB:** N/A
Lunch & dinner daily **PRICE:**

PICCOLA VENEZIA

Italian • Vintage

MAP: F2

This old-time idol deserves its landmark status as it has been going strong since opening in 1973. With Italian-American cooking so rampant in the city, it's wholly refreshing to happen upon a classic of such welcoming comfort. The décor is outdated, but white tablecloths are clean and crisp, and glasses gleam at the prospect of great wine varietals.

With a trio of pasta, you needn't choose between fusi swirled in a grappa- mushroom- and Grana-sauce; squid ink taglierini; or maltagliati in a roasted tomato and basil sauce with a touch of cream. Branzino in bianco is delightfully flaky and smothered in a delicious lemon, butter, white wine and caper sauce.

The wine list, with vintage Italian legends and California cults, is incredible.

42-01 28th Ave. (at 42nd St.)
30 Av
(718) 721-8470 – **WEB:** www.piccola-venezia.com
Lunch Mon – Fri Dinner nightly **PRICE:** $$$

SABRY'S

Seafood • Simple

MAP: F1

There are no distractions at this authentic Egyptian café. The look is simple and alcohol isn't offered since this is a strictly Muslim establishment, but friendly service provides the small space with just enough ambience.

Seafood is without a doubt the star attraction here. Whole fish are pulled from their icy display and thrown onto a sizzling flattop to be barbecued Egyptian-style (blackened and sprinkled with spices and chopped herbs); and the fried shrimp are also a very popular option. But regardless of what main you decide on, a platter of cool and creamy spreads is the only accompaniment you'll need—especially since it's served with pillows of wonderfully chewy pita that arrives so hot you might burn your fingers ripping into it.

24-25 Steinway St. (bet. Astoria Blvd. & 25th Ave.)
Astoria Blvd
(718) 721-9010 – **WEB:** N/A
Lunch & dinner daily

PRICE: $$

SALT & BONE SMOKEHOUSE

Barbecue • Tavern

MAP: F2

You can thank the oak-burning smoker for the glistening slabs of meat at this Texas-style barbecue spot. Provenance is a big deal here, and the menu is littered with references to farms from which the various cuts hail. Unsurprisingly, the space has a casual flair with white wooden chairs and thick wooden beams.

From the kitchen, meals arrive on metal trays and may reveal mouthwatering pulled pork with a thick tomato-based Memphis-style sauce, as well as beef ribs with a charred salt-and-pepper bark that belies the tender meat within. Meat takes center stage here no doubt, but the sides aren't an afterthought. Mac and cheese with a mornay sauce; potato salad with dried sage, caramelized onions and chives; and even smoked beets demand your attention.

32-07 30th Ave. (at 32nd St.)
30 Av
(917) 832-7819 – **WEB:** www.saltandbone.com
Lunch & dinner daily

PRICE:

SUSHI DAIZEN

Japanese • Minimalist

MAP: B3

The staff is upbeat, and the room is attractively minimal in design, but what really stands out here is the adoration of this little sushi-ya's devoted clientele. Sushi Daizen is one of the only places in the area that offers omakase and the mood is light and engaging as everyone digs in, with options to add sashimi or a small list of à la carte pieces.

Start your meal with a cool appetizer of enoki mushrooms in soy and dashi broth, or crisp green beans over creamy tofu. The sushi course presents a progression of neatly trimmed, hand-formed morsels of fish. Highlights include excellent poached tiger shrimp, Santa Barbara sea urchin and kawa kawa from Japan. The fatty tuna hand roll, tucked with scallions for a delicious pop, is a perfect finale.

47-38 Vernon Blvd. (bet. 47th Rd. & 48th Ave.)
Vernon Blvd - Jackson Av
(718) 729-1297 — **WEB:** N/A
Dinner Tues - Sun

PRICE: $$$$

SWEET YUMMY HOUSE

Chinese • Simple

MAP: F3

This tiny, impeccably clean dining room is drawing diners left and right to Elmhurst these days. But wait, you argue—isn't this just another Chinese joint along a stretch of Broadway? Not quite. In fact, Sweet Yummy House is a diamond in the rough for those hunting down authentic spice levels, as well as Taiwanese specialties they've never heard of.

A meal here might kick off with a duo of sautéed cabbages, one cooked in a delicate Taiwanese style, the other in the Shanghai tradition, sporting fiery oil. You could also order by temperature from this menu, starting with cold chicken dunked in a red-hot chili sauce, before moving on to sweet, sour, and bitter jelly noodles. Finally, tuck in to lamb home style for a spicy Sichuan take on pomodoro sauce.

83-13 Broadway (bet. Cornish & Dongan Aves.)
Elmhurst Av
(718) 699-2888 — **WEB:** N/A
Lunch & dinner daily

PRICE:

TAIWANESE GOURMET

Chinese • Neighborhood

MAP: F3

A truly local spot, Taiwanese Gourmet puts diners in the mood with its semi-open kitchen (a rarity for Chinese restaurants) and tasty food. Natural light floods the walls, which showcase an impressive collection of ancient warrior gear, all beautifully framed as if museum-ready. Menu descriptions are minimal but the staff is happy to elaborate.

Excellent technique shines through the Taiwanese specialties. The classic aromatic broth of the beef with chili pepper noodle soup staves off a head cold with its serious firepower and satisfying slurpy noodles. Sautéed A vegetables earn high marks for their garlicky crunch and sweet green leaves, but it's the fried pork chop over rice and sour mustard greens that tastes of home to Taiwanese far from Mom.

84-02 Broadway (at St. James Ave.)
Elmhurst Av
(718) 429-4818 – **WEB:** N/A
Lunch & dinner daily **PRICE:**

TANG

Korean • Neighborhood

MAP: C1

When craving authentic Korean specialties, Tang is an absolute must-visit. The restaurant's impeccably cool style extends from its angled exterior ablaze in beams of yellow light to its sleek interior with exposed brick walls and bare wood tables. Flat-screens loom large, creating a high-end cafeteria vibe.

Don't let the 24/7 hours fool you; this is one of the stronger Korean kitchens around. Meals begin with an unending supply of wonderfully crisp kimchi. Also try the hearty bibimbap of marinated beef strips, root vegetables and mushrooms alongside a bowl of ox-bone broth. The main attraction is the sensational jeon, traditional Korean pancakes grilled to order (weekend dinners only). Boyang tang, a tropical-hued stew, is not to be skipped if you love goat.

196-50 Northern Blvd. (at Francis Lewis Blvd.)
(718) 279-7080 – **WEB:** N/A
Lunch & dinner daily **PRICE:** $$

TAVERNA KYCLADES

Greek • Mediterranean décor

MAP: F1

You will only find happy people here, and the Aegean-blue awning feels as essential to the neighborhood as traffic lights. This beloved Greek spot (with a second location in the East Village) is a lively one where the bustling kitchen is in view. Quick, straightforward servers may address you in Greek if you look the part—that's just how local it gets here.

Grab a seat on the enclosed patio for some serenity and get things going with garlicky and bubbling-hot crab-stuffed clams; or the cold, classic trio of powerful skordalia, cooling tzatziki and briny taramosalata served with toasted pita triangles. Order a side of horta (steamed escarole and dandelion) to accompany a plate of sweet and delicate mullets, served with a side of lemon potatoes.

33-07 Ditmars Blvd. (bet. 33rd & 35th Sts.)
Astoria - Ditmars Blvd
(718) 545-8666 — **WEB:** www.tavernakyclades.com
Lunch & dinner daily **PRICE:** $$

THAI ROCK

Thai • Family

MAP: C3

The "rock" in Thai Rock is not just a reference to the restaurant's location in the beachside Rockaways, but a nod to the live music that takes over after the sun dips down. Inside, you'll find tightly packed wooden tables and comfortable high-backed chairs, but the large uncovered patio overlooking the bay is certainly the place to be come summer.

The menu covers the usual standards—think pad Thai, curries and stir-fries—as well as a few Northern specialties, with aplomb. Don't miss the plump and tender dumplings stuffed with crunchy turnips, peanuts and fragrant garlic; or the refreshing chicken larb gai laced with a bright and zesty sauce enriched with mint and scallions. Delicious and savory, the Issan sausage is a staple for suitable reason.

375 Beach 92nd St. (at Beach Channel Dr.)
Beach 90 St
(718) 945-5111 — **WEB:** www.thairock.us
Lunch & dinner daily **PRICE:** $$

TITO RAD'S GRILL

Filipino • Family

MAP: E3

This eclectic grill seduces with its perfectly encapsulated fusion of the Malay, Spanish, Chinese and Japanese flavors that typify the wholly unique cuisine of the Philippines. Cozy touches accent the décor and a mix of light stone with dark wood strikes just the right balance between contemporary and familiar.

Bold and generously portioned, the authentic specialties here have amassed a devout following. Highlights from the extensive pork- and seafood-dominated menu might include binagoongang baboy, tender chunks of pork cooked in a shrimp paste-sparked sauce made rich with melted fat; and adobo fried rice studded with crunchy and delicious bits of pork belly skin. If it's on offer, be sure to opt for the inihaw na panga or grilled tuna jaw.

49-10 Queens Blvd. (bet. 49th & 50th Sts.)
46 St - Bliss St
(718) 205-7299 — **WEB:** www.titorads.com
Lunch & dinner daily **PRICE:**

TONG SAM GYUP GOO YI

Korean • Simple

MAP: C1

Murray Hill is no stranger to Korean food, but this prized, pig-loving barbecue destination is always packed. Inside, the bright room's décor forgoes all frills to focus on regional specialties. Smiling servers are earnest and hospitable.

Begin with the usual but very exquisite banchan-like pickled turnips, fermented bean paste soup and specially aged house kimchi—funky, garlicky and a total pleasure. The kimchi pancake has a delightfully delicious crust and sear that recalls a slice of pizza. Yet what makes this place unique is that barbecue grill on each table, used for sizzling slices of flavorful duck with miso, garlic cloves and bean sprouts; spicy, tender bits of octopus; and sweet, fatty pork with soy sauce, red chili paste and scallions.

162-23 Depot Rd. (bet. Northern Blvd. & 164th St.)
Flushing - Main St (& Bus Q13)
(718) 359-4583 — **WEB:** N/A
Lunch & dinner daily **PRICE:** $$

TRATTORIA L'INCONTRO

Italian • Family

MAP: F1

A neighborhood restaurant in its true sense, everything and everyone seems comfortable at this Italian-American institution. Delightful dishes set the stage for a festive evening, while frescoes of tranquil scenes adorn the coral walls of this unfussy dining room. Servers are affable, adept and even theatrical in their recitation of specials.

Flavors are classic and robust, from eggplant rollatini stuffed with ricotta to the ravioli golosi filled with ground filet and veal, then topped with a sauce of mushrooms and sausage. Dentice rosso reveals red snapper set in a pool of brown butter and tarragon, but wait, there's a twist. Sliced peaches and lemon are then added to said sauce for a bit of sweet and sour. Tiramisu is easy to eat...and complete.

21-76 31st St. (at Ditmars Blvd.)
Astoria - Ditmars Blvd
(718) 721-3532 — **WEB:** www.trattorialincontro.com
Lunch & dinner Tue - Sun **PRICE:** $$

UMA'S

Central Asian • Neighborhood

MAP: C3

Thanks to a warm and natural vibe, ukulele tunes and the talented husband-and-wife team at its helm, this Far Rockaway haven of central Asian cuisine is as easy and breezy as its surf town environs.

This kitchen's unique interplay of flavors guarantees a delightful meal that's as hearty and fragrant as it is unpretentious: shredded Korean-style carrot salad is dressed with chili flakes and aromatic herbs; and the signature butternut squash manti—here topped with caramelized onions—are an utterly satisfying vegetarian take on the typically meat-stuffed dumplings. Daily specials are always a treat, and may reveal the likes of succulent braised lamb seasoned with cumin and rosemary, plated with sundried apricots, as well as a fluffy mound of kasha.

92-07 Rockaway Beach Blvd. (bet. Beach 92nd & 94th Sts.)
Beach 90 St
(718) 318-9100 — **WEB:** N/A
Lunch & dinner daily **PRICE:** $$

URUBAMBA

Peruvian • Neighborhood

MAP: F3

Named for Peru's intensely beautiful river, the Rio Urubamba, this hacienda-inspired space features indigenous paintings and artifacts that echo the rustic fare pouring out of the kitchen.

On weekends, the eatery serves traditional desayuno, a gut-busting feast of chanfainita beef stew and other hearty favorites. Here, tamales are a broad and flat banana leaf wrapped and stuffed with chicken and olives—a tasty contrast to the familiar Meso-American counterpart. For ultimate comfort, go for the seco de cabrito, a fantastically tender lamb and aji panca stew served with chunks of cassava and extra sauce in a tiny clay kettle. The dense alfajor cookie sandwich filled with dulce de leche and crema volteada flan is a perfectly decadent ending.

86-20 37th Ave. (at 86th St.)
82 St - Jackson Hts
(718) 672-2224 — **WEB:** N/A
Lunch & dinner daily

PRICE: $$

VESTA TRATTORIA

Italian • Trattoria

MAP: E1

Ever-changing daily specials and a respectable wine list—celebrated with a weekday happy hour—have fostered the favorable reputation of Astoria's favorite trattoria. Local foodies fill the wee room, a moderately dressed space with sage-green banquettes and a wall-mounted blackboard displaying the names of farms and producers sourced for the menu's array of contemporary Italian food.

To that end, tender meatballs are braised in a serrano chili-sparked tomato sauce; and free-range chicken Milanese is plated with a swipe of roasted lemon purée. For dessert, la torta del piccolo bambino Gesu Cristo reveals a block of excellent sticky toffee pudding cake that arrives warm, caramel-soaked, and capped with a refreshing scoop of crème fraîche sorbet.

21-02 30th Ave. (at 21st St.)
30 Av
(718) 545-5550 — **WEB:** www.vestavino.com
Lunch Sat - Sun Dinner nightly

PRICE: $$

VIA VAI

Italian • Trattoria

MAP: F1

Via Vai may be understated in décor—think white walls, grey wooden tables and a brick oven surrounded by subway tiles. But rest assured, as its food doesn't mince words.

From their wine list to the menu, it's all about Italy here. The kitchen spends every morning making fresh pastas and with the likes of gnocchi orecchiette and pappardelle among the choices, you can't go wrong. Bucatini tossed with guanciale and peppery tomato sauce is straightforward but very satisfying; and if the vast menu of 12-inch pizzas has you in a tizzy, just ask one of the servers well-versed in all the details. Otherwise, go for the Montanara white pizza, featuring a cracker-crisp crust topped with fior di latte, mascarpone, porcini purée and a sprinkle of prosciutto.

31-09 23rd Ave. (bet. 31st & 32nd Sts.)
Astoria - Ditmars Blvd
(347) 612-4334 — **WEB:** www.viavai-ny.com
Lunch & dinner daily **PRICE:** $$

ZUM STAMMTISCH

German • Vintage

MAP: B2

Family owned and operated since 1972, this unrelenting success story has expanded over the years and welcomed Stammtisch Pork Store & Imports next door.

Zum Stammtisch hosts a crowded house in a Bavarian country inn setting where old-world flavor is relished with whole-hearted enthusiasm. The goulash is thick and hearty, stocked with potatoes and beans, but that's just for starters. Save room for sauerbraten, jägerschnitzel or a platter of succulent grilled sausages that includes bratwurst, knockwurst and hickory-smoked krainerwurst served with sauerkraut and potato salad. The Schwarzwälder Kirschtorte (classic Black Forest cake) layers dense chocolate sponge with Kirsch-soaked cherries and cream, and is absolutely worth the indulgence.

69-46 Myrtle Ave. (bet. 69th Pl. & 70th St.)
(718) 386-3014 — **WEB:** www.zumstammtisch.com
Lunch & dinner daily **PRICE:** $$

STATEN ISLAND

d Ferry
CITY OF NEW

STATEN ISLAND

Staten Island may be the least populated borough of New York City, but the building of the Verrazano-Narrows Bridge ended its once bucolic existence. This fact is especially fitting because one of the strongest, most accurate simplifications is that this "island" is home to a large Italian-American population, and no self-respecting pizza lover visits here without picking up a calamari pizza from **Joe & Pat's**, a calzone from **Nunzio** or a thin-crust pie from **Denino's Pizzeria & Tavern**. Hankering for a clam pie? **Reggiano's** has the best. Locals make a beeline to **Lee's Tavern** for food, drink and neighborhood news.

CULINARY CORNUCOPIA

While it is revered as an Italian-American hub, Staten Island's shores, marinas and waterfronts continue to surprise visitors and tourists alike with its ethnically diverse enclaves. During your time here, take a culinary tour of the Mediterranean by way of the island's numerous Italian establishments proffering such Old Country classics as pizzas, pastas, calzones and so much more. Alternatively, stop by those popular old-time Polish delis that seem to comfortably thrive on their takeout business and homemade jams alone.

Spice heads will rejoice at the fantastic Sri Lankan food finds

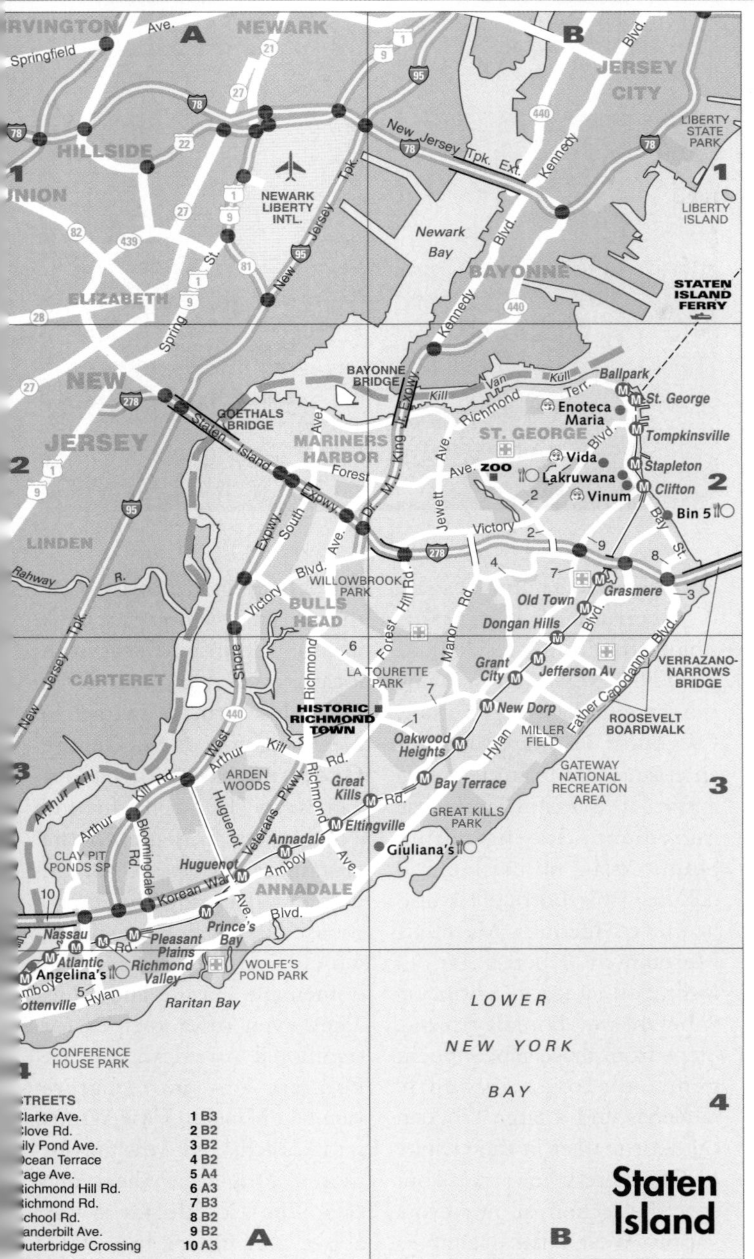
Staten
Island
STATEN
ISLAND
FERRY
NEWARK
JERSEY
CITY
LIBERTY
STATE
PARK
LIBERTY
ISLAND
HILLSIDE
NIION
ELIZABETH
NEW
JERSEY
LINDEN
CARTERET
BAYONNE
NEWARK
LIBERTY
INTL.
Newark
Bay
New Jersey Tpk. Ext.
New Jersey Tpk.
Kennedy Blvd.
Springfield Ave.
Spring St.
Rahway R.
BAYONNE
BRIDGE
GOETHALS
BRIDGE
Kill Van Kull
Richmond Terr.
Staten Island Expwy.
Dr. M. L. King Jr. Expwy.
MARINERS
HARBOR
Forest Ave.
Jewett Ave.
Victory Blvd.
ST. GEORGE
ZOO
Ballpark
St. George
Tompkinsville
Stapleton
Clifton
Enoteca
Maria
Vida
Lakruwana
Vinum
Bin 5
Bay St.
Grasmere
Old Town
Dongan Hills
Grant
City
Jefferson Av
New Dorp
Oakwood
Heights
Bay Terrace
Great
Kills
Eltingville
Annadale
Huguenot
Prince's
Bay
Pleasant
Plains
Richmond
Valley
Atlantic
Nassau
Angelina's
Giuliana's
VERRAZANO-
NARROWS
BRIDGE
ROOSEVELT
BOARDWALK
Father Capodanno Blvd.
MILLER
FIELD
Hylan Blvd.
GATEWAY
NATIONAL
RECREATION
AREA
GREAT KILLS
PARK
WILLOWBROOK
PARK
BULLS
HEAD
South Ave.
Forest Hill Rd.
Manor Rd.
LA TOURETTE
PARK
HISTORIC
RICHMOND
TOWN
Richmond Rd.
West Shore Expwy.
Arthur Kill Rd.
ARDEN
WOODS
Richmond Pkwy.
Veterans
Huguenot Ave.
Bloomingdale Rd.
CLAY PIT
PONDS SP
Korean War
Amboy Rd.
ANNADALE
WOLFE'S
POND PARK
Raritan Bay
Arthur Kill
CONFERENCE
HOUSE PARK
ottenville
LOWER
NEW YORK
BAY
STREETS
larke Ave. 1 B3
love Rd. 2 B2
ily Pond Ave. 3 B2
cean Terrace 4 B2
age Ave. 5 A4
ichmond Hill Rd. 6 A3
ichmond Rd. 7 B3
chool Rd. 8 B2
anderbilt Ave. 9 B2
uterbridge Crossing 10 A3

in and around Thompkinsville. A spectrum of restaurants (think storefronts) reside here, including **New Asha** serving the same nation's fiery cuisine. Of course, **Lanka Grocery** is an epicurean's dream featuring a riot of colorful, authentic ingredients Staying within South Asia—its cuisine and culture—this borough is also home to Jacques Marchais Museum of Tibetan Art, an institution aimed at advancing Tibetan and Himalayan art. Steps from these subcontinent gems, discover authentic taquerias and a large Liberian outdoor market in the vicinity of Grasmere, where a small but special selection of purveyors supply West African staples and other regional treats. Take these to enjoy at home; or cook up a globally inspired feast with locally farmed produce from **Gerardi's** farmer's market in New Brighton or **St. George Greenmarket**, open on Saturdays. Historic Richmond Town pays homage to the sustainable food movement here by organizing the family-focused festival **Uncorked!**, which features the best in homemade cuisine and wine. They even offer recipes for traditional American classics. For rare and more mature varietals, **Mission Fine Wines** is top-notch, but if yearning for more calorie-heavy (heavenly) eats, **The Cookie Jar** is way above par. Opened in 2007, this youngest sibling of **Cake Chef**, a beloved bakeshop up the road and **Piece A Cake** further south on New Dorp Lane, not only incites its audience with a range of sweets but savory focaccias and soups galore.

FOOD, FUN & FROLIC

Given its booming culinary scene and cultural merging, it should come as no surprise that the Staten Island of the future includes plans for a floating farmer's market, aquarium and revamped waterfronts, giving residents and tourists another reason to sit back and savor a drink at one of the bars along Bay Street. Couple these sips with abundant small plates at **Adobe Blues**, a cantina preparing sumptuous Southwestern food and prettified with a fireplace, clay walls and collectibles depicting the island's... yee-haw...rodeo days! Residents and locals of course adore this neighborhood hangout for its modest demeanor and gratifying grub, and will probably continue to flock to it until the end of time. After dawdling on Lafayette Avenue, drive through some of the city's wealthiest zip codes, featuring mansions with magnificent views of Manhattan and beyond. Whether here to glimpse the world's only complete collection of rattlesnakes at the zoo, or seek out the birthplaces of such divas as Christina Aguilera and Joan Baez, a visit to Staten Island is nothing if not interesting.

ANGELINA'S

Italian • Elegant

MAP: A4

Angelina's has become a beloved institution thanks in large part to this borough's love for Italian-American food. The restaurant takes full advantage of its unique location, inside a Victorian home and decorated with original woodwork as well as sculpted windows. A loyal clientele appreciates the grandiosity of it all, as well as the knowledgeable and engaging service.

The cooking is elegant, careful and revolves around faithfully rendered classics made with top-notch ingredients. Some dishes are more innovative, as in their version of spaghetti "pomodoro," which adds seafood and crunchy panko breadcrumbs. But the tender veal scaloppini, simply and quickly sautéed with a wine reduction and bit of lemon, has been and always will remain perfect.

399 Ellis St.
(718) 227-2900 — **WEB:** www.angelinasristorante.com
Lunch & dinner daily

PRICE: $$$

BIN 5

Contemporary • Bistro

MAP: B2

At this intimate bistro in Rosebank, dinner comes with a view of the Manhattan skyline. Complete with teardrop chandeliers and exposed brick, Bin 5's romantic setting has long drawn locals seeking good food and quiet conversation (plus that fantastic panorama!).

The playful menu—complete with solid daily specials—may reveal a perfect pan-seared and golden-brown pork loin, set atop slices of pickled red and green peppers and surrounded by a generous amount of pan sauce made from prosecco and vinegar. Then, cauliflower florets are pulsed to form couscous-like beads and cooked in the style of fried rice, studded with veggies and seasoned by soy. A tall wedge of pistachio-walnut cake dusted with powdered sugar is a light, fluffy and fitting finale.

1233 Bay St. (bet. Maryland & Scarboro Aves.)
Bus S51, S81
(718) 448-7275 — **WEB:** www.bin5nyc.com
Dinner Tue - Sun

PRICE: $$

ENOTECA MARIA

Italian • Family

MAP: B2

No need to venture far on Staten Island for excellent Italian. Enoteca Maria is just blocks from St. George Terminal and brought to you by Joe Scaravella, whose cookbook Nonna's House has been earning him (and this tiny gem) much applause. With its Carrara marble and lively vibe, most foodies flock here for a certain authenticity that is rarely sacrificed.

Each night, the menu changes depending on which nonna is presiding over the kitchen, as in Nina from Belarus, who might serve a salat Odessa mingling grilled eggplant, red onion, tomato and parsley. Lasagna di Adelina arrives as an inspired layering of zucchini, basil pesto and creamy cheese, all topped with parmesan. And for a bit of sweet, try the torta di vaniglia di Melissa served with whipped cream.

27 Hyatt St. (bet. Central Ave. & St. Marks Pl.)
(718) 447-2777 — **WEB:** www.enotecamaria.com
Lunch Wed - Fri Dinner Wed - Sun **PRICE:** $$

GIULIANA'S

Italian • Trattoria

MAP: B3

Staten Island may swarm with Italian-American eateries, but this festive classic does a masterful job in keeping its kitchen distinct and the patrons loyal. Guiliana's is the queen bee amid shops, catering halls, and ample competition. The interior is modest and charming, with framed pictures of smiling patrons and a fully stocked bar.

Hearty stracciatella is loaded with spinach and a comforting sauce of eggy parmesan, finished with a generous shower of black pepper. Seek out the perciatelle con sarde, a Sicilian-style pasta tossed in a powerful blend of fennel, saffron, raisins, sardines, anchovy paste, and a crunch of toasted breadcrumbs. A trio of gelatos—pistachio, chocolate and bitter almond, served with biscotti—is a divine ending.

4105 Hylan Blvd. (at Osborn Ave.)
Bus S54, S78, S79
(718) 317-8507 — **WEB:** www.giulianassi.com
Lunch & dinner Tue - Sun **PRICE:** $$

LAKRUWANA

Sri Lankan • Rustic

MAP: B2

Prepare for a sensory overload the moment you set foot into Lakruwana—the Sri Lankan hot spot is covered from floor-to-ceiling in murals, sculptures, flags, and more. The kaleidoscope of textures and colors is a welcome sight in an otherwise downtrodden part of the borough, as is the energetic owner who drifts from table to table.

Those familiar with Indian food will love Lakruwana's abundance of curries, green chili-spiked kothu roti, as well as refreshingly salty-and-sour lassi. But their flavorful fare is considerably spicier, packing heat into everything from fiery red chili lunu miris chutney to deviled chicken. Loaded with ginger and garlic, this stellar tomato-based chicken specialty comes with cooling raita and tangy vegetable curry.

668 Bay St. (at Broad St.)
Bus S51, S76
(347) 857-6619 — **WEB:** www.lakruwana.com
Lunch Fri - Wed Dinner Tue - Sun **PRICE:** $$

VIDA

American • Colorful

MAP: B2

All the locals love Vida, where popular Chef/owner Silva Popaz has created a cozy little restaurant with a firm commitment to simple, but well-executed, dishes. Inside the café-like atmosphere, you'll find unique artwork lining brightly painted walls, and a smattering of tables surrounding a long communal wood table in the center.

The charming Popaz travels quite often, and the flavors she picks up along her journeys tend to make their way back into her menu at Vida. The "Mexican Duo"—her most popular dish—features pulled pork- and chicken-stuffed tortillas, topped with a vibrant Chimayo chile and tangy cheese sauce, and paired with tender stewed beans sporting bright green onion; while a delicate bread pudding arrives puddled in creamy vanilla ice cream.

381 Van Duzer St. (bet. Beach & Wright Sts.)
Bus S78
(718) 720-1501 — **WEB:** www.vidany.com
Dinner Tue - Sat **PRICE:** $$

VINUM

Italian • Osteria

MAP: B2

As its name would suggest, this bijou on Bay Street is centered around wines, with many offered by the glass. Inside, find an unexpected décor that looks and feels like an osteria out of Italy.

The menu is designed for sharing, making the salumi and cheese platters a prevalent choice. "The Meatball Bar" is another treat, with unlikely twists on tired offerings—think truffled veal or lamb. Chef Massimo Felici's passion for baking and pastries is clear in the house-made breads, and carries through to desserts that are worth getting excited over. Find sweethearts diving into the Napoleon, layering puff pastry with vanilla Chantilly custard and blueberries. Nightly specials augment the bill of fare, though every item is made with equal care and authenticity.

704 Bay St. (bet. Broad St. & Vanderbilt Ave.)
Bus S51, S76
(718) 448-8466 – **WEB:** www.vinumnyc.com
Lunch & dinner daily **PRICE:** $$

Avoid the search for parking. Look for valet.

INDEXES

ALPHABETICAL LIST OF RESTAURANTS

A

B

C

D

E

F

G

H

L

M

N

O – P

Q – R

S

U

V – W

X – Y – Z

RESTAURANTS BY CUISINE

AMERICAN

ASIAN

AUSTRIAN

BARBECUE

BRAZILIAN

CAMBODIAN

CARIBBEAN

CENTRAL ASIAN

CHINESE

CONTEMPORARY

DELI

EASTERN EUROPEAN

ETHIOPIAN

EUROPEAN

FILIPINO

FRENCH

FUSION

GASTROPUB

GERMAN

GREEK

INDIAN

ITALIAN

JAMAICAN

JAPANESE

KOREAN

LAO

LATIN AMERICAN

LEBANESE

MALAYSIAN

MEDITERRANEAN

PERUVIAN

PIZZA

POLISH

PUERTO RICAN

RUSSIAN

SCANDINAVIAN

SEAFOOD

SENEGALESE

SOUTHERN

SPANISH

SRI LANKAN

STEAKHOUSE

THAI

CUISINES BY NEIGHBORHOOD

BROOKLYN

DOWNTOWN

MANHATTAN

CHELSEA

CHINATOWN & LITTLE ITALY

EAST VILLAGE

GRAMERCY, FLATIRON & UNION SQUARE

GREENWICH & WEST VILLAGE

HARLEM, MORNINGSIDE & WASHINGTON HEIGHTS

STATEN ISLAND

THE BRONX

STARRED RESTAURANTS ✿

✿✿✿

✿✿

✿

BIB GOURMAND

I – J – K

L – M – N

O – P

R – S

T – U

V – X – Z

UNDER $25

CREDITS

MICHELIN TRAVEL PARTNER
Société par actions simplifiées au capital de 15 044 940 EUR
27 Cours de l'Ile Seguin - 92100 Boulogne Billancourt (France)
R.C.S. Nanterre 433 677 721

Dépôt légal august 2018
Printed in Canada - august 2018
Printed on paper from sustainably managed forests

Impression et Finition : Transcontinental (Canada)

Tell us what you think about our products.

Give us your opinion

satisfaction.michelin.com

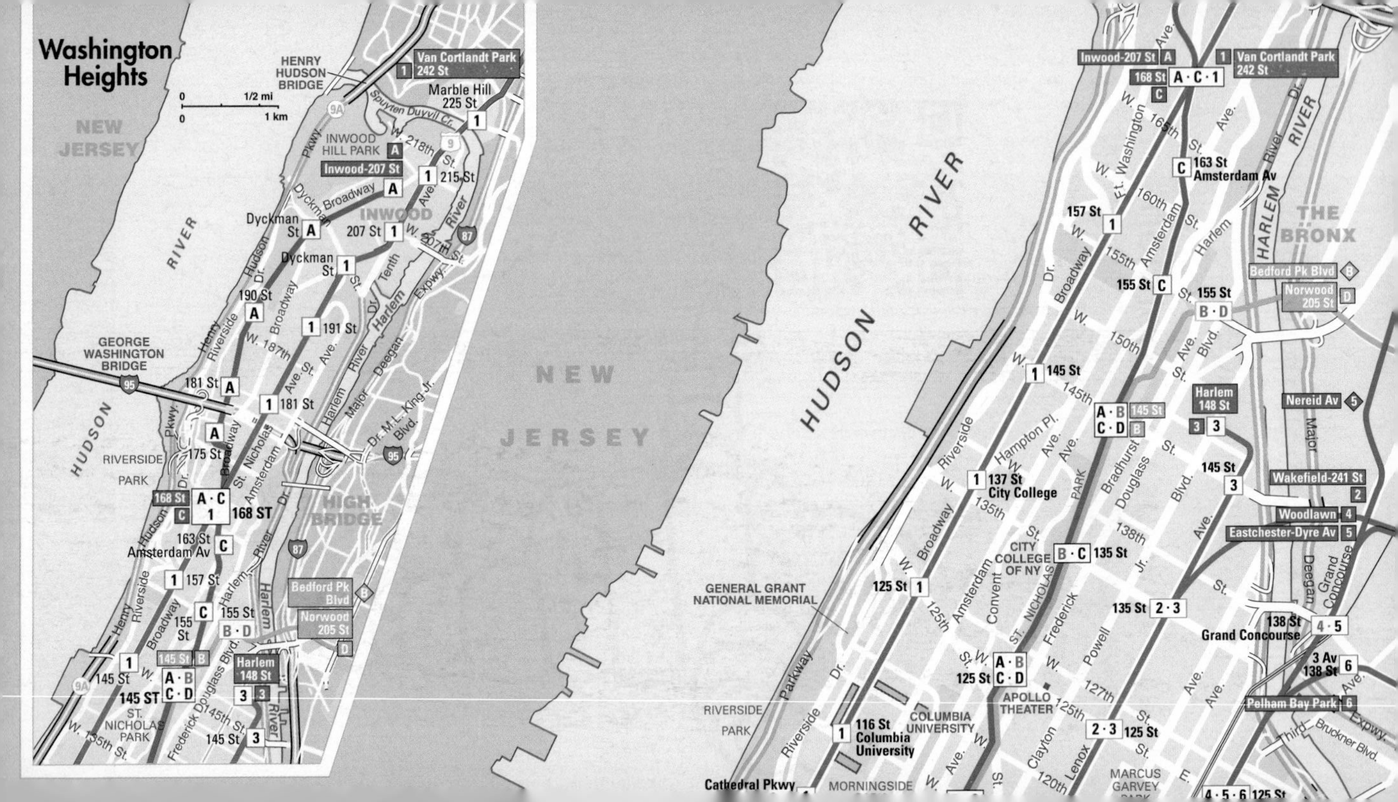
Washington Heights
0 1/2 mi
0 1 km
NEW JERSEY
HUDSON RIVER
HENRY HUDSON BRIDGE
Van Cortlandt Park 242 St
Marble Hill 225 St
Spuyten Duyvil Cr.
INWOOD HILL PARK
Inwood-207 St
215 St
INWOOD
Dyckman St
207 St
190 St
191 St
GEORGE WASHINGTON BRIDGE
181 St
175 St
RIVERSIDE PARK
168 St
168 ST
HIGH BRIDGE
163 St Amsterdam Av
157 St
155 St
Bedford Pk Blvd
Norwood 205 St
Harlem 148 St
145 St
145 ST
ST. NICHOLAS PARK
145 St
THE BRONX
HARLEM RIVER
Nereid Av
Wakefield-241 St
Woodlawn
Eastchester-Dyre Av
137 St City College
CITY COLLEGE OF NY
135 St
GENERAL GRANT NATIONAL MEMORIAL
125 St
138 St Grand Concourse
3 Av 138 St
Pelham Bay Park
APOLLO THEATER
COLUMBIA UNIVERSITY
116 St Columbia University
RIVERSIDE PARK
Cathedral Pkwy
MORNINGSIDE
MARCUS GARVEY
125 St